MEMORY AND THE MEDIEVAL TOMB

Memory and the Medieval Tomb

Edited by Elizabeth Valdez del Alamo
with Carol Stamatis Pendergast

ASHGATE

Published by
Ashgate Publishing Limited
Gower House
Croft Road
Aldershot
Hants GU11 3HR
England

Ashgate Publishing Company
Old Post Road
Brookfield
Vermont 05036–9704
USA

British Library Cataloguing-in-Publication data

Memory and the Medieval Tomb
    1. Sepulchral monuments, Medieval – Social aspects
    2. Sepulchral monuments, Medieval – Psychological aspects
    3. Sculpture, Medieval – Religious aspects   4. Christian art
    and symbolism
    I. Valdez del Alamo, Elizabeth   II. Pendergast, Carol Stamatis
    736.5′0902

Library of Congress Cataloging-in-Publication data

Memory and the medieval tomb / edited by Elizabeth Valdez del Alamo, with Carol
Stamatis Pendergast.
    p. cm.
  Includes bibliographical references and index.
  ISBN 0–7546–0076–9 (alk. paper)
    1. Sepulchral monuments. 2. Recollection (Psychology) 3. Christian art and
symbolism. 4. Civilization, Medieval. I. Valdez del Alamo, Elizabeth. II. Pendergast,
Carol Stamatis.

GT3320 .M45   2000
393′.1—dc21

00–025504

ISBN 0 7546 0076 9

Printed on acid-free paper
Copy-edited and typeset in Palatino by
The Running Head Limited, www.therunninghead.com
Printed at the University Press, Cambridge

Contents

The editors

ELIZABETH VALDEZ DEL ALAMO is Associate Professor of Art History in the Department of Fine Arts at Montclair State University in New Jersey. Site-specific artworks and the relationship between word and image are the focus of her studies on Romanesque art. In addition to the article reprinted in this volume, her publications relevant to the topics of memory and the medieval tomb include: 'Ortodoxia y heterodoxia en el estudio de la escultura románica española: estado de la cuestión,' *Anuario del Departamento de Historia y Teoría del Arte*, Universidad Autónoma de Madrid, vols 9/10, 1997–8, pp.9–33; 'Triumphal Visions and Monastic Devotion: The Annunciation Relief of Santo Domingo de Silos,' *Gesta*, vol. 29, no. 2, 1990, pp.167–88; 'Visiones y profecía: el Arbol de Jesé en el claustro de Silos,' in the Acts of *El románico en Silos: 9° centenario de la consagración de la iglesia y claustro, 1088–1988*. Burgos, 25–29 September, 1988, Santo Domingo de Silos: Abadía de Silos, 1990, pp.173–202. She is presently preparing a book about the cloister of Silos.

CAROL STAMATIS PENDERGAST is Executive Director of the Carmel Public Library Foundation in California. A specialist in Burgundian Romanesque art, her recent work is on the juridical implications of the Peace of God for architectural sculpture: 'Outside the Walls: Jurisdiction and Justice on a Gateway at Anzy-le-Duc,' in *Peace, Negotiation and Reciprocity: Strategies of Co-Existence in the Middle Ages and Renaissance*, Arizona Studies in the Middle Ages and the Renaissance, vol. 4, Turnhout: Brepols, 2000, pp.93–124. Other publications include: 'The Cluny Capital of the Three-Headed Bird,' *Gesta: Current Studies on Cluny*, vol. 27, nos. 1/2, 1988, pp.31–9; 'The Lintel of the West Portal of Anzy-le-Duc,' *Gesta: Essays in Honor of Sumner McK. Crosby*, vol. 15, nos. 1/2, 1976, pp.136–42. She has held teaching and administrative positions at several institutions in the United States and Europe. While in Prague as Director of Faculty Development and member of the founding academic team at the Czechoslovak Management Center, she co-authored a cross-cultural study on introducing western case-teaching into the Czech Republic.

List of contributors

CAROLYN M. CARTY is Professor of Literature, Humanities, Rhetoric and Art History at Oakland Community College, Michigan. She has written on the role of dreams and dream images in medieval art, and on their function in interpreting medieval building campaigns. Publications include: 'The Role of Medieval Dream Images in Authenticating Ecclesiastical Construction,' *Zeitschrift für Kunstgeschichte*, vol. 62, 1999, pp.45–90; 'The Role of Gunzo's Dream in the Building of Cluny III,' *Gesta*, vol. 27, 1988, pp.113–23; and 'Albrecht Dürer's *Adoration of the Trinity*: A Reinterpretation,' *The Art Bulletin*, vol. 67, 1985, pp.146–53.

KYLE R. CROCKER is Associate Professor of Art History in the Department of Visual Arts, Bemidji State University, Minnesota. A specialist in the medieval art of Scandinavia, his works include: 'The Lame Smith: Parallel Features in the Myths of the Greek Hephaestos and Teutonic Wayland,' *Archaeological News*, vol. 6, 1977, pp.67–71; and '"Fotr risti" – a runographer's style in the context of eleventh-century Upplandic memorial art,' unpublished PhD thesis, Department of Art History, University of Minnesota, 1982.

THOMAS E. A. DALE is Assistant Professor of Art History at the University of Wisconsin, Madison. He has explored the cult of relics and the commemoration of the saints in two previous studies: *Relics, Prayer and Politics in Medieval Venetia: Romanesque Painting in the Crypt of Aquileia Cathedral*, Princeton, NJ: Princeton University Press, 1997; and 'Inventing a Sacred Past: Pictorial Narratives of Saint Mark the Evangelist at Aquileia and Venice, c.1000–1300,' *Dumbarton Oaks Papers*, vol. 48, 1994, pp.53–104.

GERALDINE A. JOHNSON is a Lecturer in the Department of the History of Art at Oxford University. For Cambridge University Press she co-edited a prize-winning volume titled *Picturing Women in Renaissance and Baroque Italy*, 1997, and edited *Sculpture and Photography: Envisioning the Third Dimension*, 1998. Her publications on Italian Renaissance sculpture, on Peter Paul Rubens, on the patronage of Maria de' Medici, and on the photography of contemporary public sculpture have appeared in essay collections and journals such as *The Art Bulletin, Burlington Magazine, Art History* and *Renaissance Quarterly*. At present, she is completing a book on the production and reception of sculpture in Early Modern Italy.

STEPHEN LAMIA is Chair of the Department of Visual Arts at Dowling College, Oakdale, New York. His studies of medieval tomb sculpture began with '*Sepulcrum Domini*: the iconography of the holed tomb of Christ in Romanesque and Gothic art,' his unpublished PhD thesis defended at the University of Toronto in 1982. He published three articles 'Funerals / Burials,' 'Labor, Trades and Occupations,' and 'Themes of Night' in the *Encyclopedia of Comparative Iconography*, edited by H. Roberts, Chicago and London: Fitzroy Dearborn, 1998. In addition, he has authored texts on medieval art and architecture for the visually impaired, to be published under the auspices of Art Education for the Blind. He is now preparing an article, 'The Cross, the Crown and the Tombs: The Lost Shrines of Thomas Becket at Canterbury and Edward the Confessor at Westminster,' to be included in the volume of papers about saints' tombs that he is editing with Elizabeth Valdez del Alamo, *Decorations for the Holy Dead*.

PATRICK LENAGHAN is Curator of Prints and Photographs in the Iconography Department at The Hispanic Society of America, New York. His work on Spanish and Italian art of the sixteenth and seventeenth centuries includes: 'Reinterpreting the Italian Renaissance in Spain: Attribution and Connoisseurship,' *The Sculpture Journal*, vol. 2, 1998, pp.13–23; *Images for the Spanish Monarchy: Art and the State, 1516–1700*, New York: The Hispanic Society, 1998; entries for Spanish sculptors and painters for the *Oxford Companion to Western Art*, Oxford University Press, forthcoming; and 'The arrival of the Italian Renaissance in Spain: the tombs by Domenico Fancelli and Bartolomé Ordóñez in Spain, 1500–1525,' unpublished PhD thesis, 1993, Institute of Fine Arts, New York University.

ANNE MCGEE MORGANSTERN is Associate Professor in the Department of History of Art at The Ohio State University, Columbus, Ohio. She has published extensively on French Gothic tomb sculpture. Her book, *Gothic Tombs of Kinship in France, the Low Countries, and England*, University Park, PA: Pennsylvania State University Press, 2000, has just been published. Recent articles include: 'Le tombeau de Philippe le Hardi et ses antécédents,' *Actes des journées internationales Claus Sluter*, Dijon, 1992, pp.175–91; 'The Bishop, the Lion and the Two-Headed Dragon: The Burghersh Memorial in Lincoln Cathedral,' in *Memory and Oblivion*, Proceedings of the XXIXth International Congress of the History of Art, Amsterdam, 1–7 September 1996, Dordrecht: Kluwer Academic Publishers, 1999, pp.515–26.

KATHLEEN NOLAN is Associate Professor of Art History at Hollins University, Roanoke, Virginia. Her publications on Early Gothic sculpture include: ' "*Ploratus et Ululatus*": The Mothers in the Massacre of the Innocents at Chartres Cathedral,' *Studies in Iconography*, vol. 17, 1996, pp.95–141; 'Ritual and Visual Experience in the Capital Frieze of the Cathedral of Chartres,' *Gazette des Beaux-Arts*, vol. 123, 1994, pp.53–72; 'Narrative in the Capital Frieze of Notre-Dame in Etampes,' *The Art Bulletin*, vol. 71, 1989, pp.166–84. She is currently studying the relationship between royal women in twelfth- and thirteenth-century France and the visual commemoration of death.

ROCÍO SÁNCHEZ AMEIJEIRAS is *Profesor Titular* in the Department of Art History at the Universidad de Santiago de Compostela, Spain. Medieval imagery in León, Castile, and Galicia is the object of her research. Her many publications include: 'El "çementerio real" de Alfonso VIII en Las Huelgas de Burgos,' *Semata, Ciencias Sociales y Humanidades,* no. 10, 1998, pp.77–109; 'Una empresa olvidada del primer gótico hispano: el programa escultórica de la sala capitular de la catedral de León,' *Archivo Español de Arte,* no. 276, 1996, pp.389–406; and 'Espiritualidad mendicante e iconografía gótica gallega,' *Semata, Ciencias Sociales y Humanidades*, no. 6, 1994, pp.141–57. She is presently preparing a book on funerary sculpture in medieval Iberia.

DOROTHY HOOGLAND VERKERK is Assistant Professor of Art History, and Faculty Fellow, Institute for the Arts and Humanities, at the University of North Carolina, Chapel Hill. She has published articles on Early Christian funerary art, the Ashburnham Pentateuch, and Irish High Crosses. Relevant publications include: 'Exodus and Easter Vigil in the Ashburnham Pentateuch,' *The Art Bulletin*, vol. 77, 1995, pp.94–105; 'Job and Sitis: Curious Figures in Early Christian Funerary Art,' *Mitteilungen zur Christlichen Archäologie*, vol. 3, 1997, pp.20–29; 'Roman Book Illumination 400–700 AD and the Ashburnham Pentateuch,' in *Imaging the Early Medieval Bible*, edited by J. Williams, University Park, PA: Pennsylvania State University Press, 1999. Currently, she is preparing a book on the Ashburnham Pentateuch.

List of figures

List of abbreviations

Acknowledgments

The following articles first appeared in *The Art Bulletin* and are reprinted here with the kind permission of the editors: 'Lament for a Lost Queen: The Sarcophagus of Doña Blanca in Nájera' by Elizabeth Valdez del Alamo, vol. 78, no. 2, June 1996, pp.311–33; and 'Activating the Effigy: Donatello's Pecci Tomb in Siena Cathedral' by Geraldine A. Johnson, vol. 77, no. 3, September 1995, pp.445–59.

'The tomb as prompter for the chantry' by Anne M. Morganstern includes excerpts from the introduction and chapter 6 from her book, *Gothic Tombs of Kingship*, University Park, PA: Pennsylvania State University Press, 2000, reproduced by permission of the publisher; and from 'The Bishop, the Lion and the Two-Headed Dragon: The Burghersh Memorial in Lincoln Cathedral,' in *Memory and Oblivion*, Proceedings of the XXIXth International Congress of the History of Art, Amsterdam, 1–7 September 1996, Dordrecht: Kluwer Academic Publishers, 1999, with kind permission from Kluwer Academic Publishers.

We would like to thank the following for their generous support:

The Samuel H. Kress Foundation;

Montclair State University, especially Dean Geoffrey W. Newman of the School of the Arts; Daryl Moore, Chair, Department of Fine Arts; Susan Nanney, Director of Research and Sponsored Programs; and Doris Ackerman, former Director of the Office of Major Gifts;

Kyle Crocker and Bemidji State University;

Stephen Lamia, Dean James E. Caraway, and the Long-Range Planning and Development Committee of Dowling College;

Dorothy H. Verkerk and the University of North Carolina, Chapel Hill;

And special thanks to Elizabeth's parents Elizabeth Valdez and Norbert R. Wirsching.

Gratitude is also owed to Stephen Lamia and Constancio del Alamo for their assistance in the crucial final stages of preparation.

Introduction

Elizabeth Valdez del Alamo and Carol Stamatis Pendergast

In honor of, and in memory of, our mothers

Reverent memorial for the dead was the inspiration for the production of a significant category of artworks during the Middle Ages, artworks aimed as much at the laity as at the clergy, and intended to maintain, symbolically, the presence of the dead. This volume explores the ways in which medieval Christians sought to memorialize the deceased: with tombs, cenotaphs, altars and other furnishings connected to a real or symbolic burial site. Our interest is to analyze strategies for commemoration from the fourth to the fifteenth century: the means by which human memory could be activated or manipulated through the interaction between monuments, their setting, and the visitor.[1]

As the papers presented here demonstrate, commemoration was far from a static recollection of the defunct, a mere reminiscence of things past. Memory is *praxis*, an active, even interactive, process.[2] Monuments designed for the purpose of commemoration utilize many devices to trigger memory: vivid images that are both marvelous and active; strategically placed figurations or inscriptions which contextualize the site; and a kinetic relationship between the funerary monument and its visitors, often manifested in ritual acts involving movement around or in the monument. These memorial strategies established a dialogue between the living and the dead and articulated mutual benefits for both parties. Dependent on a dynamic interplay between burial site, visual cues, and liturgical ritual, memory was the guarantor of eternity for the deceased and for the community of believers. It was the bridge across the permeable membrane separating the living and the dead.

The essays represent an investigation that builds upon, but is different from, the growing body of literature on memory in the Middle Ages. In the past several years, the exploration of the role and operation of 'memory' has become a benchmark for historians within the larger field of cultural history.[3] For the study of the Middle Ages, the investigations of Karl Schmid, Joachim Wollasch, Otto Gerhard Oexle, and others of the Münster-Freiburg School provide a base with their research into memorial practices.[4] Philippe Ariès and Peter Brown added a poetic dimension to the exploration of the relationship between the dead and the living.[5] The explicit inquiry into techniques for remembering in the medieval period was the focus of Frances Yates's *The Art of Memory*, which appeared in 1966. Mary Carruthers, in the 1990s, expanded our understanding of mnemonics as a technique for rhetorical invention.[6] In the past decade, investigations of memory in the Middle Ages have proliferated. Among the most important sources for the essays collected in this volume are the studies of Carruthers, James Fentress and Chris Wickham, Patrick Geary, Karl Morrison, Megan McLaughlin, Amy Remensnyder, Paul Binski, as well as the Schmid–Wollasch group mentioned above.[7] The emphasis of most of these studies has been on literature, history, and monasticism.

While indebted to these inquiries, our own work focuses on the tomb monument and its context as a complex of strategies to define what is to be remembered, to fix memory, and to facilitate recollection in order to commemorate the deceased. Few scholars have applied medieval memory theory to artworks intended to memorialize the dead.[8] Yet the intersection of theory with art is frequently manifest in the design of memorial monuments and their settings. This should not be surprising since, as has often been noted, medieval culture was memorial in nature.[9] 'Do this in memory of me,' Christ's words spoken at the Last Supper, established the commemorative character of Christian ritual, dedicated to the remembrance of the deceased by the living. *Memoria*, the term that describes the formal, liturgical memory of the dead, may also refer to artworks intended to house and honor the deceased.[10] Additionally, the term applies to a variety of technical practices for the transmission of knowledge. In the Middle Ages, ritual, tomb, artistic and physical setting orchestrated the construction of memory through image, design, and affective context. In commemoration of the deceased, the heightened emotional and sacral overtones of the occasion conferred, and still confers, added power to acts of remembering. For the purpose of examining the relationship of memory and the medieval tomb, we employ the concept of memory broadly to include the faculty for recollection, trained or untrained, by an individual or group as stimulated by image, object, ritual, space, and action.

According to recent studies of neuropsychology, the processes that store and recall data, and that reconfigure elements of experience into memory depend on a gamut of physiological, affective and intellectual constructs, both external and internal.[11] Mnemonic devices, however elaborate, do not build or activate memory in a vacuum. The entire contextual surround of sensate, psychological and perceptual phenomena, as well as the interpersonal dynamics of solitary or collective participation in memory processes aid in configuring the pathways of recollection. Moreover, recall is constructed from both present and stored information. Implicit memory – the residue of collected experiences, perceptions, as well as culturally determined cognitive paradigms – colors the way in which we decipher memory cues.[12] Information or experience may be encoded into memory through cognitive, psychological and physiological routes, and then decoded through stimuli, or cues that combine with a memory trace to produce a new entity: the recollective experience. This experience of remembering differs in a fundamental way from the generating event: it has often been found to have a more profound impact on an individual or community than the original impetus.[13]

These findings are in accord with the understanding of the multiple stimuli and strategies required to foster memory development in ancient and medieval memory treatises. In these early texts, three elements emerge as fundamental to stimuli acting as memory triggers:

- they should be schematically ordered and placed within specific, clear locations in the mind;
- they should be derived from sense impressions; and
- they should be emotionally charged.[14]

The link between what is to be remembered and the means to remember it is through signs or signals, which may include images arranged in deliberate places; the process of memory is comparable to reading imprinted signs.[15] The concepts of 'visual' and 'image' in ancient and medieval memory treatises are not always intended to refer to physical images, but may imply instead a series of mental constructs. According to the *Rhetorica ad Herennium*: 'The art of memory is like an inner writing ... For the places are very much like wax tablets or papyrus, the images like the letters, the arrangement and disposition of the images like the script, and the delivery is like the reading.'[16] The phrase *imagines verborum* (images of words, or a type of writing) that occurs in this passage to describe memory and cognitive systems could perhaps have served as a justification for the use of figures in art in the Middle Ages.[17] Images were not always viewed as subservient to verbal knowledge. As Aquinas put it: 'Man cannot understand without images (*phantasmata*); the image is a similitude of a corporeal thing, but understanding is of universals which are to be abstracted from particulars.'[18]

Medieval memory technique was 'locational,' that is, dependent on a cognitive schema that generated structured patterns from discrete units through relational stratagems.[19] In order for an idea or event to become memorable, it had to be placed within these physical and mental constructs, mediated through 'images' designed with mnemotechnical markers.[20] 'Artificial' memory, created via mnemonic technique, is established from internalized mental 'places' and 'images,' ordered according to specified rules (*Constat igitur artificiosa memoria ex locis et imaginibus*).[21] A 'place' might be a house or an intercolumnar space; 'images' could be forms, marks, or *simulacra* of what we wish to remember.

These locational mnemonic devices often bear a striking resemblance to the design of medieval artworks.[22] When applied to the funerary arts, whose purpose is to give form to the memory of an individual, mnemonic systems have special resonance. For example, the design of the sarcophagus or reliquary as a house, often with intercolumnar space, filled with shapes or *simulacra* is intended to recall whatever was considered most significant. This could be the individual, the theological framework for death, or the socio-historical significance of the deceased for the community, now 'framed' by the commemorative construct. The continuous tradition for placing figures, such as the Apostles, under an architectural arcade may have been the product of this mnemonic device.[23] The term '*simulacrum*' also illustrates how enmeshed the concept of remembering is with the experience of the dead by the living: the word means both 'image,' in mnemonics, and 'spectre' of the dead.[24]

Medieval memory treatises describe the potential of images to trigger memory, particularly if they incorporate affective and sensate elements. Techniques for prayer and contemplation also embrace an understanding of the importance of 'imaging' and sensory impact for the formation and recollection of memory.[25] Medieval artists and patrons were well aware that an experience or a monument had to be distinctive in order to be remembered, and that their task was to make a sensory imprint on the mind – hence sight, placement, touch, taste, smell, and sound were all important components in the manipulation of human response, and for the maintenance of memory. These components needed to be incorporated, therefore, into the design of a monument.

These precepts are critical both in a figurative and in a literal, physical manner in the commemorative contexts examined in our studies. The sense of 'place,' either of funerary chapel, ancestral turf, or perspectival matrix governs the parameters of the memory experience. The specific ordering of images into concrete *loci* in relationship to each other or to elements of the site documents the systematic nature of artworks as memory stimuli. As the papers in this volume illustrate, the interactive system of cross-referencing through structured cues embedded in sepulchral monuments – a combination of object, site, and ritual – was designed to assist the living to remember the dead. At the same time, sense impressions and emotional aura played a significant role in construction of the memory experience of the defunct, and frequently in the definition of the 'image' or 'sign' utilized for the commemoration. Whether in the tactile experience of the reliquary tomb of Christ or the locus created by placement of an effigy, specific sensate or affective elements could transfigure the emotionally charged contexts of funerary rituals and sites for the participant in the commemorative rite, however removed in time.

Imaginative synaesthesia produced by ritual and the senses accounted for the significant role of artworks in the medieval religious experience. Karl Morrison's lyrical analysis of the cognitive pathway complements Carruthers' exploration of the construction of memory as image, a visual context for what was to be remembered.[26] The intellectual and affective processes they describe find restatements in the case studies assembled here. For instance, the wall paintings in Cubiculum C of the Via Latina Catacombs in Rome link the rituals of baptism and death for the tomb's visitors by means of visual cues in an environment fraught with emotion. In another example, human feeling is palpably rendered in the reliefs on the sarcophagus of Queen Blanca of Nájera, where a full range of grieving is illustrated – from the ritual but heartfelt lament of her husband to the anguish of biblical mothers whose children are murdered. The carvings are captivating, memorable images, and this quality derives from the affect of their representation.

The power of the affective response, recognized intuitively by artists and articulated in treatises on memory, is also borne out by scientific research. Emotional arousal can have a decided impact on the attention paid to an event or artwork. That, in turn, affects the process of retention. As William James described it, 'An experience may be so exciting emotionally as almost to leave a scar on the cerebral tissues.'[27] Recent studies of neuromodulatory systems and memory have demonstrated the physiological foundations of the encoding process used in medieval memory theory.[28] Experiments confirm that subjects will remember a story that affects their emotions, and that memory may be enhanced by epinephrine, a hormone released under stress.[29] Not only is 'emotional arousal induced by an experience . . . an important determinant of the strength of memory for the event . . . ,' but it also affects the consolidation process in the brain, varying the strength of the memory according to its significance for the individual.[30] Stimulation which releases stress-related hormones can affect memory retention for a period of time after the event, as can repetition.[31]

Although memory enhancement is most efficacious when close in time to the original event, 'each act of remembering creates new memories of old experiences.'[32] Cues provided in a present context map related information from past and present to form wholly new constructs. In addition, memory for personally experienced events can merge with reported or imagined events.[33] Medieval memorial strategies capitalized on the potent combination of visual, liturgical, and physical elements in a sacred space; these could produce a heightened aesthetic, or synaesthetic, experience which directed memory paths. Through repeated experiences, the affective elements of the commemorative environment could cement recall of an individual or event – or even supplant an undesirable history with a new interpretation. Thus the physiological process of memory formation, already noted by Aristotle and understood during the Middle Ages, has been validated.[34]

The memorial process accesses and, inevitably, transforms the past. Ritual remembrance of the dead is a form of intergenerational storytelling: it links us to the past while constructing a new reality that supports present needs. It provides a forum for shared social interactions and plays a role in 'social cognition.'[35] Commemoration consolidates ties among the living through communal participation in defining and mourning the past. Sepulchral environments permit the time frame of the dead, the day of death, to intersect with the collective time of the living, thereby perpetuating their relationship to the dead. Remembrance of the dead was also a mechanism for taming and socializing fear of the dead, a construction of pathways for their benign connection to the living, in dreams, through images, and stories.[36]

Patrick Geary documents 'the structures by which memories of all sorts are transmitted and created.'[37] His focus on collective memory and the means of transaction between the deceased and their living heirs informs several of our essays about sepulchral monuments, which literally are 'the structures in which the past is preserved.'[38] Upplandic memorial stones, for instance, are structures that marked inherited property as they commemorated the feats of their deceased owners. The tombs designed for the bishops of León represent the charity and virtue of their occupants and, at the same time, document episcopal authority. The tomb of Queen Adelaide of Maurienne at Saint-Pierre-de-Montmartre in Paris commemorates her patronage of the convent, a transaction that took place both in life and in death. Giftgiving was an effective memorial strategy for the wealthy: their names and images would be maintained, and their souls would benefit from the prayers of those who benefitted from their bequests.[39]

Through commemorative practices, certain sepulchral environments become repositories of public memory and can assume political or institutional functions. The visual devices by which a story may be institutionalized are thematic strands woven throughout the papers included in the present volume. The designers of monuments were certainly aware of the power of images and how, in time, their story would gain authority, even if altering the historical record. The Venetian version of the events that brought the relics of St Mark to the Cathedral, depicted in its mosaics, is one example of a conscious attempt to fix that version of a story in the public mind. Morrison's discussion of history writing as an art of the imagination finds its complement in these mosaics at S. Marco, true representations of Venetian power.[40] A similar manipulation of history by means of art is demonstrated in Toledo Cathedral, in the design of the funerary chapel of Alvaro de Luna, who was executed as a traitor to the King. Thanks to the efforts of his heirs, the expurgated version of the Constable's character, as represented in his chapel, was soon accepted in many official histories. On a smaller scale, the story of St Heribert depicted on his shrine served to establish the authoritative narrative of his life in a medium accessible to the clergy as well as to the general public. In all three cases, at Venice, at Toledo, and at Deutz, visual representations of the deceased served to authenticate and maintain official, verbal versions of history.

Whether for individual devotion, moral reflection on the deceased, or as an instrument of communal myth-making, the potent, active involvement of the participants in the process of commemoration provided pathways for reconfiguring the past to adapt to present concerns. That understanding of the modalities of memory formation and implementation went beyond the literate few to many among the Church faithful finds support in several contributions to this volume.[41] The sepulchral arts render, in tangible form, a symbiosis between ritual and personal expression.[42] Early Christian authors were well aware of this. A passage attributed to Augustine maintained that honors due the dead were intended primarily to console the living. He says: 'For the dead, in so far as they are commended to God, can pray and intercede for the salvation of the living. For everyone should believe it to be true that the souls of the dead have the same efficiency for the salvation of the living as those of the living have for the peaceful rest of the dead.'[43] Effective mediators between the living and the dead, medieval funerary rituals and artworks were the product of both private and communal concerns, the medium of gift and countergift between the living and the dead.[44] They lend themselves, therefore, to an analysis that seeks to understand the multiple avenues created to activate this 'dialogue' between the present and the past in visual language.

The cognitive processes that facilitate and maintain links between present and past, the living and the dead, have been described thoroughly in the studies of medieval monastic mentality by Jean Leclercq and Marie-Dominique Chenu.[45] The sanctified imagination of a monk could blend sacred history with present or personal history. The blending occurs through a process by which images, or combinations of images and text trigger associations conditioned by the monk's immersion in religious life. Art historians have applied these principles very fruitfully to monastic art.[46] While the sanctified imagination may have greater breadth in a trained religious, the vocabulary of the Christian Church articulated the hopes and desires of most of medieval Europe. As the examples in this volume demonstrate, the language of tombs and relics was understood by priest and public alike.

Carruthers commented in the conclusion of *The Book of Memory* that 'the term memorial, . . . to modern readers . . . has connotations only of death.'[47]

Just as she wished to open out the meaning of the term to 'a more medieval idea,' we want to call attention to the fact that what was to be remembered was not always a text, but sometimes an image, an object, or even an individual. The funerary arts provide a doubly rich lode to mine, for their *raison d'être* is to recall the deceased. They provide an arena to unify all the discussions about memory, cognition, cult, and death to which we have referred above.

*   *   *

The authors in this volume describe processes designed to access memory and to control its path. Strategies include images or design elements whose affective or organizational features contextualized the site and the audience. The first group of papers concentrates on individual tombs and the ways in which memorial strategies define the dialogue between the living and the dead. For example, the stimulation of the imagination, memory, and faith not only by sight, but also by touch and movement is made possible through a special type of pierced tomb enclosure for saints. Such a tomb had been designed for Christ in Jerusalem, and Stephen Lamia documents the intensely physical expression of the pilgrim's desire for direct experience of relics. In order to emphasize the tangibility of Christ's relics, the pierced *sepulcrum Domini* was represented in the sculpture of several twelfth-century pilgrimage sites. These images of the tomb simulated the sensation of experiencing the sacred burial place. The immediacy of the synaesthetic experience has a parallel in the overt expression of personal grief, and the response it calls forth from the viewer, in the sarcophagus of Doña Blanca in Nájera, analyzed by Elizabeth Valdez del Alamo. In one case, empathy is mediated by tomb design, in the other, by the modelling of mourning behaviors. The affect of the tomb reliefs reminds visitors and the monastic community to recall the Queen in prayer. Through their prayers, the living recall the deceased and ensure their salvation. The dead in heaven intercede on behalf of the living. The salvational exchange between living and dead is fully illustrated here.

The liturgical remembrance for the dead and for the living is the motivation for the design and positioning of many later medieval tombs. In her study on how a tomb may be used as a prompter for the chantry, Anne Morganstern demonstrates the conscious application of architectural organization as mnemonic device in the decoration of a sepulchral monument. In addition to placing the figures of living and deceased members of Lady Montacute's family under an arcade on the sides of her tomb, coats of arms provided the priests charged with commemorating them, visual prompts with which to remember their names. The Montacute and Burghersh tombs in Oxford and Lincoln may have drawn inspiration from the treatise on memory attributed to Thomas Bradwardine, who was connected to both sites.[48] The strategic placement of an effigy may be used to guarantee perpetual commemoration, as Geraldine Johnson points out. Donatello's tomb for Giovanni di Bartolomeo Pecci, Bishop of Grosseto, skillfully employed new artistic techniques to activate medieval conventions for liturgical commemoration efficiently and economically. The bronze relief was originally located in front of the high altar in the center of the old canons' choir in Siena Cathedral. The tomb's position and the use of mathematical perspective in its design enabled every celebrant of the mass to trigger the transcendent power of the liturgy and to recapitulate the original burial rite without intervening visual prompts. In this way, Pecci's commemoration was incorporated into the daily performance of mass. The illusion that funeral ceremonies are forever in progress is created by different devices in the fifteenth-century funerary chapel of Alvaro de Luna in Toledo Cathedral, analyzed by Patrick Lenaghan. There, life-sized figures of knights and friars kneel in perpetual prayer at the effigy of a man presented as an ideal Christian knight. The reverent postures model appropriate behaviors for contemporary visitors as part of the recreation of an ideal history, via his monument, for this individual who was executed for treason.

Our second section addresses the idea that funerary art shapes communal memory. In traditional Christian art, pictorial systems establish visual prompts for recalling the defunct in conjunction with liturgy to celebrate or to ensure eternal life. For example, in the Via Latina catacomb, pictorial hieroglyphs such as the candle determine the 'reading' of the Old Testament images by cross-referencing baptismal rituals, according to Dorothy Hoogland Verkerk. Communal psalm singing, surrounded by those visual references, transform funerary rites into a celebration of rebirth and resurrection, as promised by Christian baptism. Thus, the images access and reinterpret past events. Stones are the dynamic structures of memory in Kyle Crocker's study of eleventh-century Upplandic commemorative practice. The conversion to Christianity disrupted traditional Scandinavian practices for burial on family property. Their inventive response to communal burials in the churchyard was to use cenotaphs, strategically placed stones to mark property and to record the exploits of their predecessors, without the presence of the body of the deceased. Maintaining native custom, they continued to make property and commemoration the media of exchange between the living and the dead.

The transformation from individual memorial to institutional statement, a means to transfer power from the dead to the living, is analyzed in the last papers. Whereas the Chapel of Alvaro de Luna created an idealized memory of a traitor, the Venetians had to rewrite history in a similar manner to justify their theft of the relics of St Mark. In S. Marco in Venice, the mosaic and sculptural programs contextualize the reliquary pier to confer legitimacy to

Venetian institutions. Thomas Dale deconstructs the image systems that orchestrate a collective commemoration of supra-historical events in communal rites; they tap the talismanic power of St Mark's relics to convey a perpetual present to the reconstituted past. The transmission of saintly power through an architectural environment is often recreated in the design of reliquaries. The saint's dual role as leader in the spiritual and political spheres is mediated in the Heribert Shrine by the intangible: dreams. As Carolyn Carty demonstrates, images of dream sequences on the shrine authorize and commemorate St Heribert's actions, while the reliquary is also a casket for his physical remains. The shrine embodies a metaphor for memory, *arca*. The compartmentalization of figures and images localizes them within a symbolic memorial architecture, clarifying the link between human and divine. That link may also be constructed through the choice of burial place. The burial of the Capetian Queen, Adelaide of Maurienne, at Saint-Pierre-de-Montmartre served to confirm the convent as one of the *loca sancta* of the cult of St Denis in the environs of Paris: it was the site of Saint Denis's martyrdom. The mosaic tomb of the Queen, descended from Carolingian royalty, forms part of a program to glorify the convent's history through the evocation of its past. Kathleen Nolan demonstrates how the presence of the Queen's body, and the historicizing elements of her tomb and the church's architecture, link the convent, the royal family, the saint and the city of Paris. The interface between civic and churchly concerns is also visible in the thirteenth-century episcopal pantheon of León Cathedral. Rocío Sánchez Ameijeiras traces the programmatic alteration of individual bishop's tombs into a visually unified ensemble that articulates episcopal authority. The monuments appropriate traditional imagery of heroes' and saints' tombs to remind the public of the bishops' acts of charity and their role as civic and spiritual leaders. In the environment of the chevet, within their 'shrines,' the bishops are presented as the building blocks from which the Church itself was constructed.

All the papers demonstrate how these funerary monuments make what is remote in time or space present for the visitor. Memorial strategies in the Middle Ages were designed to establish an active dialogue between the living and the dead. They channeled power and reframed the past. Operating through visual cues, whether of actual representations, or of intersecting design systems and liturgical choreography, memory held time. The activation of memory by the interplay of tomb, image, and visitor triggered reciprocal benefits to the communities of the deceased and the living. Whether of a layperson, cleric, or saint, the medieval tomb depended on a matrix of mnemonic devices designed to assure the deceased's successful passage from death into a new life by means of eternal commemoration. That commemoration also empowered the living, the custodians of memory, when their sensory experiences of the art and rite concentrated the past, present, and future into one moment in time.

Selected bibliography

Ariès, P., *The Hour of Our Death*, translated by H. Weaver, New York: Alfred A. Knopf, 1981 (originally published in French as *L'homme devant la mort*, Paris: Editions du Seuil, 1977).

Binski, P., *Medieval Death: Ritual and Representation*, Ithaca, NY: Cornell University Press, 1996.

Blum, H., *Die Antike Mnemotechnik*, Spudasmata, vol. XV, Hildesheim: Georg Olms, 1969.

Boase, T. S. R., *Death in the Middle Ages: Mortality, Judgment and Remembrance*, New York: McGraw-Hill, 1972.

Bransford, J., *Human Cognition: Learning, Understanding and Remembering*, Belmont, CA: Wadsworth, 1979.

Brown, P., *The Cult of the Saints: Its Rise and Function in Latin Christianity*, Chicago: The University of Chicago Press, 1981.

Burgin, V., 'Brecciated Time,' in idem, *In/Different Spaces: Places and Memory in Visual Culture*, Berkeley: University of California Press, 1996, pp.179–275.

Cahill, L., R. J. Haier, J. Fallon, M. T. Alkire, C. Tang, D. Keator, J. Wu, and J. L. McGaugh, 'Amygdala Activity at Encoding Correlated with Long-Term, Free Recall of Emotional Information,' *Proceedings of the National Academy of Science. USA*, vol. 93: *Neurobiology*, July 1996, pp.8016–21.

— B. Prins, M. Weber, and J. L. McGaugh, 'ß-Adrenergic Activation and Memory for Emotional Events,' *Nature*, vol. 371, 20 October 1994, pp.702–4.

Camille, M., *Master of Death: The Lifeless Art of Pierre Remiet, Illuminator*, New Haven, CT: Yale University Press, 1996.

Carruthers, M. J., *The Book of Memory: A Study of Memory in Medieval Culture*, Cambridge: Cambridge University Press, 1990.

— *The Craft of Thought: Meditation, Rhetoric, and the Making of Images, 400–1200*, Cambridge: Cambridge University Press, 1998.

Chenu, M.-D., *Nature, Man, and Society in the Twelfth Century*, translated by J. Taylor and L. K. Little, Chicago: University of Chicago Press, 1968.

Confino, A., 'Collective Memory and Cultural History: Problems of Method,' *American Historical Review*, vol. 102, no. 4–5, 1997, pp.1386–403.

Crane, S. A., 'Writing the Individual back into Collective Memory,' *American Historical Review*, vol. 102, no. 4–5, 1997, pp.1372–85.

Fentress, J., and C. Wickham, *Social Memory*, Oxford: Oxford University Press, 1992.

Freedberg, D., *The Power of Images: Studies in the History and Theory of Response*, Chicago: University of Chicago Press, 1989.

Geary, P. J., *Living with the Dead in the Middle Ages*, Ithaca, NY/London: Cornell University Press, 1994.

— *Phantoms of Remembrance: Memory and Oblivion at the End of the First Millennium*, Princeton, NJ: Princeton University Press, 1994.

Gennep, A. van, *The Rites of Passage*, translated by M. B. Vizedom and G. L. Caffee, Chicago: University of Chicago Press, 1975.

Harrah, B. K. and D. F., *Funeral Service: A Bibliography*, Metuchen, NJ: Scarecrow Press, 1976.

Lamia, S., 'Funeral/Burial,' *Encyclopedia of Comparative Iconography*, vol. 1, Chicago and London: Fitzroy Dearborn, 1998, pp.347–55.

Lauwers, M., *La mémoire des ancêtres, le souci des morts: Morts, rites et société au moyen âge (diocèse de Liège, Xie–XIIIe siècles)*, Théologie Historique, vol. 103, Paris: Beauchesne, 1997.

Leclercq, J., *Love of Learning and the Desire for God: A Study of Monastic Culture*, 3rd edition, translated by C. Misrahi, New York: Fordham University Press, 1982.

Le Goff, J., *Histoire et Mémoire*, Paris: Gallimard, 1988. In English as: *History and Memory*, translated by S. Rendall and E. Claman, New York: Columbia University Press, 1992.

McGaugh, J. L., 'Emotional Activation, Neuromodulatory Systems, and Memory,' in D. L. Schacter, ed., *Memory Distortion: How Minds, Brains, and Societies Reconstruct the Past*, Cambridge, MA: Harvard University Press, 1995, pp.255–73.

— and L. Cahill, 'Interaction of Neuromodulatory Systems in Modulating Memory Storage,' *Behavioural Brain Research*, vol. 83, 1997, pp.31–8.

McLaughlin, M. M., *Consorting with Saints: Prayer for the Dead in Early Medieval France*, Ithaca, NY/London: Cornell University Press, 1994.

Morrison, K. F., *History as a Visual Art in the Twelfth-Century Renaissance*, Princeton, NJ: Princeton University Press, 1990.

Nora, P., 'Between Memory and History: les Lieux de Mémoire,' *Memory and Counter-Memory*, in *Representations*, vol. 26, 1989, pp.7–25.

Oexle, O. G., 'Memoria und Memorialbild,' in K. Schmid and J. Wollasch, eds, *Memoria: Der geschichtliche Zeugniswert des liturgische Gedenkens im Mittelalter*, Münstersche Mittelalter-Schriften, vol. XLVIII, Munich: Wilhelm Fink Verlag, 1984, pp.384–440.
— 'Die Gegenwart der Lebenden und der Toten. Gedanken über Memoria,' *Gedachtnis, das Gemeinschaft Stiftet*, K. Schmid, ed., Munich and Zürich: Verlag Schnell und Steiner, 1985.
— ed., *Memoria als Kultur*, Veröffentlichungen des Max-Planck-Instituts für Geschichte, vol. 121, Göttingen: Vandenhoeck & Ruprecht, 1995.
Panofsky, E., *Tomb Sculpture: Four Lectures on Its Changing Aspects*, New York: Abrams (1964), 1992.
Remensnyder, A. J., 'Legendary Treasure at Conques: Reliquaries and Imaginative Memory,' *Speculum*, vol. 71, no. 4, 1996, pp.884–906.
Schacter, D. L., *Searching for Memory: The Brain, the Mind, and the Past*, New York: Basic Books, 1996.
— ed., *Memory Distortion: How Minds, Brains, and Societies Reconstruct the Past*, Cambridge, MA: Harvard University Press, 1995.
Schmitt, J.-C., *Ghosts in the Middle Ages: The Living and the Dead in Medieval Society*, translated by T. L. Fagan, Chicago: University of Chicago Press, 1998 (originally published as *Les revenants: les vivants et les morts dans la société médiévale*, Paris: Gallimard 1994).
Small, J. P., *Wax Tablets of the Mind: Cognitive Studies of Memory and Literacy in Classical Antiquity*, London and New York: Routledge, 1997.
Solomon, P. R., G. R. Goethals, C. M. Kelley, and B. R. Stephens, eds, *Memory: Interdisciplinary Approaches*, New York: Springer Verlag, 1989.
Yates, F. A., *The Art of Memory*, London: Routledge and Kegan Paul, 1966.
Zemon Davis, N. and R. Starn, eds, *Memory and Counter-Memory*, in *Representations*, vol. 26, Spring 1989.

Notes

1. The essays were selected from the sessions we organized for several conferences: 'Memory and the Medieval Tomb' for the 1994 meetings of the College Art Association; 'Between the Living and the Dead: Commemoration and the Funerary Arts in the Middle Ages' for the International Congresses of Medieval Studies at Western Michigan University, Kalamazoo, and the University of Leeds, England, in 1995.

2. Carruthers, *The Book of Memory*, p.13.

3. See, for example, the two essays by A. Confino and S. A. Crane in *American Historical Review*, vol. 102, 1997, in which the relationship of current studies on memory to the field of cultural history is discussed. They provide an extensive bibliography for the field of cultural studies. Additionally, see the volume dedicated to historical forms of memory, *Memory and Counter-Memory*, edited by N. Zemon Davis and R. Starn, in *Representations*, vol. 26, Spring 1989, which includes their very useful essay, pp.1–7, and a translation of the introduction to Pierre Nora's *Les lieux de mémoire* (Paris: Gallimard, 1984–) as 'Between Memory and History: les Lieux de Mémoire.' Also valuable is V. Burgin, 'Brecciated Time.' For medievalists, the studies of J. Le Goff, including his *Histoire et mémoire*, 1988 (in English as *History and Memory*, 1992) are fundamental.

4. W. Jorden, *Das cluniazensische Totengedächtniswesen vornehmlich unter den drei ersten Äbten Berno, Odo und Aymard (910–954). Zugleich ein Beiträge zu den cluniazensischen Traditions-Urkunden*, Münstersche Beitrage zur Theologie 15, Münster, 1930; O. G. Oexle, 'Memoria und Memorialbild'; idem, 'Die Gegenwart der Lebenden und der Toten. Gedanken über Memoria'; idem, ed., *Memoria als Kultur*, which includes a very valuable survey of the subject of memory in cultural history. For thorough bibliographic references on this material, see the review by M. McLaughlin, *Consorting with Saints*, pp.5–20; and D. Iogna-Prat, 'The Dead in the Celestial Bookkeeping of the Cluniac Monks around the Year 1000,' *Debating the Middle Ages: Issues and Readings*, edited by L. K. Little and B. H. Rosenwein, Malden, MA: Blackwell, 1998, nn.6–7 pp.341–2.

5. Ariès, *The Hour of Our Death*, 1981 (originally published in French, 1977); Brown, *The Cult of the Saints*, 1981.

6. Carruthers, *The Book of Memory* and *The Craft of Thought*. Carruthers draws a distinction between her approach and that of Yates. Carruthers states that for Yates, the goal of medieval mnemonics was to repeat previously learned material, whereas for herself it is a point of departure for invention, imagination, and creativity; *Craft of Thought*, pp.9, 35.

7. Please refer to the bibliography at the end of this Introduction for full citations.

8. Oexle laid the groundwork for medieval art when he discussed the placement of names and figures in architectural forms, but he did not point out a specific parallel between manners of composition in the visual arts and mnemonics, 'Memorialbild,' pp.395–407. See below, n.22.

9. Le Goff, *Histoire et mémoire*, pp.130–48, cited by Geary, *Phantoms of Remembrance*, p.15; Geary, *Living with the Dead in the Middle Ages*, pp.2–3; Brown, *Cult of the Saints*, p.1; Carruthers, *Book of Memory*, pp.8, 260; Oexle, *Memoria als Kultur*.

10. Geary, *Phantoms of Remembrance*, p.18. For *memoria* as used in psychological research, U. Neisser, 'Domains of Memory,' in Solomon et al., eds, *Memory: Interdisciplinary Approaches*, p.68.

11. It has been demonstrated that memory is not a single faculty, but rather a variety of distinct processes acting in concert: Schacter, *Searching for Memory*, pp.5–6. This was understood by Aristotle, *De anima* and *Parva naturalia*, discussed by Carruthers, *Book of Memory*, pp.47–54.

12. ibid., pp.8–9, 29, 189–91.

13. ibid., p.93.

14. Carruthers, 'Descriptions of the Neuropsychology of Memory,' chapter 2 of *The Book of Memory*, pp.46–79; [Cicero], *Rhetorica ad Herennium (Ad C. Herennium libri IV De ratione dicendi)* III, xvi–xxiv, edited and translated by H. Caplan, Loeb Classical Library, Cambridge, MA: Harvard University Press, 1954, p.206 and passim, and as cited in Yates, *Art of Memory*, especially pp.6–10; Thomas Aquinas, *In Aristotelis libros De sensu et sensato, De memoria et reminiscentia commentarium*, edited by R. M. Spiazzi, Turin–Rome, 1949, p.107, as cited by Yates, *Art of Memory*, pp.70–73; Albertus Magnus, *De Bono*, in *Opera omnia*, edited by H. Kuhle, C. Feckes, B. Geyer, W. Kubel, *Monasterii Westfalorum in aedibus Aschendorff*, XXVIII, 1951, p.247, cited by Yates, *Art of Memory*, p.63; Thomas Bradwardine, *De Memoria Artificiai*, translated by Carruthers from Fitzwilliam Museum, Cambridge, MS McClean 169, in Carruthers, *Book of Memory*, pp.281–6.

15. Yates, *Art of Memory*, pp.6–7. Carruthers describes the construction of memory as the crafting of images in the mind; through those images, memories were carried and so had a symbiotic relationship to actual pictures and words: Carruthers, *Craft of Thought*, pp.10, 118–22; *Book of Memory*, pp.28–9, 60, 224–8.

16. *Rhetorica ad Herennium*, III, xvi–xxiv, in Yates, *Art of Memory*, pp.6–7; also in Carruthers, *Book of Memory*, p.72. See additional discussion in Small, *Wax Tablets*, pp.95–116.

17. Carruthers, *Book of Memory*, p.222, discusses several medieval authors' views on images as equivalent to writing. In *Craft of Thought*, she amplifies her discussion of the relationship between rhetoric, mnemonics, and the visual arts. See also Morrison, 'Visualizing *Istorie*,' in *History as a Visual Art*, pp.36–47.

18. Aquinas, *De memoria et reminiscentia commentarium* (as in n.14), p.91, cited by Yates, *Art of Memory*, p.70. See also the discussions of Carruthers, *Book of Memory*, pp.52, 54–5, 253–5; and Morrison, *History as a Visual Art*, pp.37, 65.

19. Carruthers, *Craft of Thought*, p.10. Neisser, 'Domains of Memory,' pp.76–8.

20. Carruthers notes that the medieval cognitive pattern-making facility 'locates' knowledge, but within and in relation to other things, *Book of Memory*, pp.34–5, 124, 144; Carruthers, *Craft of Thought*, p.39. Coherent 'relational organization' and 'imageability' are fundamental to recollection: J. T. E. Richardson, *Mental Imagery and Human Memory*, New York: St Martin's Press, 1980, p.99, cited by Carruthers, p.292 n.17.

21. *Rhetorica ad Herennium*, III, xvi–xxiv, in Yates, *Art of Memory*, p.6; described by Carruthers, *Book of Memory*, pp.148–50.

22. The correspondence has been noted but not fully appreciated by many. See Small, *Wax Tablets*, pp.235–9. H. Blum linked ancient decoration to mnemonics: *Die Antike Mnemotechnik*, especially pp.1–17, cited by Carruthers, *Book of Memory*, pp.221 n.1, 340. Yates suggests that the inner memory images might have found their way into outer expression: *Art of Memory*, pp.79–81. In *Book of Memory*, Carruthers provides an extensive study of book design: pp.224–8, 257. In *Craft of Thought*, she develops the parallel between rhetoric and the design of artworks. This last work was published as we were in the final stages of preparation of this volume, and we have added references where appropriate.

23. Oexle discusses figures and names placed under arcades and other architectural devices as a manner of commemoration: see above, n.8. In the monumental arts, see the sarcophagus of Junius Bassus, *c*.359; the lintel at Saint-Génis-des-Fontaines; the *Apostolados* of Spanish Romanesque façades, and the galleries of kings on French Gothic cathedrals. A good example of the combination of texts to be remembered with figures under arcades is the Beatitudes Casket

of San Isidoro in León, illustrated in *The Art of Medieval Spain, ad 500–1200*, New York: Metropolitan Museum of Art, 1993, no. 117, p.253. For a reliquary, see the article by C. Carty in this volume.

24.   Whereas *simulacra* may be images of what one wishes to remember, as discussed above, a *simulacrum* could also be an immaterial double of a deceased individual that a living person had the experience of ' "seeing and hearing face to face" as if the dead person were still alive': Schmitt, quoting Lucretius, in *Ghosts in the Middle Ages*, p.12; for further discussion, see pp.21–8. Similarly, an *eidolon* is the image of a recently deceased person: p.12.

25.   Leclercq, *Love of Learning*, pp.73–9; Carruthers, *Book of Memory*, p.46; Morrison, 'Cognition and Cult,' in *History as a Visual Art*, especially pp.48–67.

26.   Morrison, *History as a Visual Art*, pp.61, 64, and passim; Carruthers, *Book of Memory*, on synaesthesia, pp.78–9, 95, 229–30; on image in memory, p.257.

27.   W. James, *The Principles of Psychology*, New York: Henry Holt, 1890, cited by McGaugh, 'Emotional Activation, Neuromodulatory Systems, and Memory,' p.256.

28.   McGaugh, 'Emotional Activation,' pp.256–9. For elaborative encoding, memory-improvement techniques, and engrams, see Schacter, *Searching for Memory*, pp.46–8, 58–9.

29.   McGaugh, 'Emotional Activation,' p.256. See also idem, 'Modulation of Memory Storage Processes,' in Solomon et al., eds, *Memory: Interdisciplinary Approaches*, pp.33–64; L. Cahill et al., 'ß-Adrenergic Activation and Memory for Emotional Events'; L. Cahill et al., 'Amygdala Activity at Encoding Correlated with Long-Term, Free Recall of Emotional Information'; J. L. McGaugh and L. Cahill, 'Interaction of Neuromodulatory Systems in Modulating Memory Storage.'

30.   Schacter tested this idea with the staff of the Museum of Modern Art: *Searching for Memory*, pp.50–52; McGaugh, 'Emotional Activation,' p.256; F. Heuer and D. Reisberg, 'Vivid Memories of Emotional Events: The Accuracy of Remembered Minutiae,' *Memory and Cognition*, vol. 18, 1990, pp.496–506; G. Goethals and P. Solomon, 'Interdisciplinary Perspectives on the Study of Memory,' in Solomon et al., eds, *Memory: Interdisciplinary Approaches*, p.9.

31.   For stimulation, see McGaugh, 'Emotional Activation,' pp.257–8; McGaugh and Cahill, 'Interaction of Neuromodulatory Systems,' pp.32, 35. For repetition, H. Ebbinghaus, *Über das Gedächtnis*, Leipzig: Duncker and Humbolt, 1885, cited by McGaugh, 'Emotional Activation,' p.255. There is, therefore, some somatic basis for mnemonic systems, which suggests that the distinction between human capability and training is one of degree, a formalization of a natural process. This fact may, perhaps, qualify Carruthers' assertion that, 'Cognition, in cultures that value *memoria*, is presupposed to require various sorts of mental maps and organizing structures . . . But we do not just "have" these, by virtue of brain physiology or Nature: we must be able *to make* such patterns': *Craft of Thought*, p.83. On the other hand, it is certainly true that experiences are not 'recorded somewhere in our brains, only awaiting the appropriate retrieval cue,' as Schacter warns: *Searching for Memory*, p.64.

32.   McGaugh, 'Emotional Activation,' pp.265–6; Schacter, *Searching for Memory*, pp.8–9, 28, 63–4, 70–71.

33.   McGaugh, 'Emotional Activation,' p.266. For a discussion of the permeability of memories of facts and of borrowed images, particularly with respect to modern visual culture, see V. Burgin, 'Brecciated Time,' especially pp.212–64, 272–3.

34.   See above, nn.25, 28.

35.   Collective memory and social cognition are discussed by T. M. Ostrom, 'Three Catechisms for Social Memory,' and D. L. Hamilton, 'Understanding Impression Formation: What Has Memory Research Contributed?' both in Solomon et al., eds, *Memory: Interdisciplinary Approaches*, pp.201–20, especially pp.212–16, and pp.221–42, especially pp.222–3. Oexle characterizes liturgical *memoria* as the tie that binds the living and the dead: 'Memorialbild,' p.394. Similarly, Schmitt considers how stories establish the solidarity between the living and dead, and shaped the listener's, or reader's, views of the world: *Ghosts in the Middle Ages*, pp.171, 224. Schacter discusses storytelling and intergenerational links in the creation of cultural memory: *Searching for Memory*, p.301. Carruthers notes that memorials like the Vietnam Memorial in Washington, DC, trigger each individual's associational networks and also provide a forum for a shared activity: *Craft of Thought*, pp.36–7. The artist Maya Lin understood this, as is clear in her description of the design process in the documentary *Maya Lin: A Strong Clear Vision*, directed by F. Lee Mock, Sanders & Mock Productions/American Film Foundation, 1994; video tape, 1995.

36.   The contractual ties that bind individuals in life remain in effect after death through the recollections about the dead, and the prayers offered for them: Schmitt, *Ghosts in the Middle Ages*, p.173. According to Schmitt, '*memoria*, as a form of collective memory, was a social technique

of forgetting . . . to "cool off" the memory of the deceased . . . to recall the names of the dead . . . without fear or emotion.' Liturgical remembrance served 'to help the living separate from the dead, and to shorten the latter's stay' in Purgatory: *Ghosts in the Middle Ages*, pp.5–6. For the return of the dead in different guises, including dreams, see pp.10–11.

37.   Geary, *Phantoms of Remembrance*, p.10.

38.   ibid.

39.   Oexle describes the social exchange of maintaining names and images of the deceased by those who benefit from their gifts: 'Memorialbild,' pp.410–12; almsgiving as a device for salvation is described by M. Mollat, *The Poor in the Middle Ages: An Essay in Social History*, translated by A. Goldhammer, New Haven, CT: Yale University Press, 1986, pp.71–2 (originally published in French as *Les pauvres au moyen âge*, Paris: Hachette, 1978); Schmitt, *Ghosts in the Middle Ages*, pp.33–4, 66, 224.

40.   'History as an Art of the Imagination,' in *History as a Visual Art*, especially pp.26 n.17, 28, 36–8.

41.   For a discussion of the cultural role of trained memory, see Carruthers, *Book of Memory*, pp.10–13.

42.   Ariès develops this idea as the body of his book, *The Hour of Our Death*: see especially 'The Death of the Self,' pp.95–293; Brown, *The Cult of the Saints*, pp.24–7.

43.   London, Brit. Lib., Add. MS 11695, fol. 271v, cited by O. K. Werckmeister, 'The First Romanesque Beatus Manuscripts and the Liturgy of Death,' *Actas, Simposio para el estudio de los códices del 'Comentario al Apocalipsis' de Beato de Liébana*, Madrid: Joyas Bibliográficas, 1980, pp.167–92, especially p.191 n.99; and by E. Valdez del Alamo, 'Lament for a Lost Queen: The Sarcophagus of Doña Blanca in Nájera,' *The Art Bulletin*, vol. 78, no. 2, June 1996, pp.311–33, reprinted in this volume, n.85; Ariès, *The Hour of Our Death*, p.41, provided no citation. These ideas are found in a twelfth-century treatise, *Liber de spiritu et anima*, attributed to Augustine but likely written by a Cistercian, Alcher of Clairvaux; Schmitt, *Ghosts in the Middle Ages*, p.28.

44.   Geary, 'Exchange and Interaction between the Living and the Dead in Early Medieval Society,' in *Living with the Dead*, pp.77–92.

45.   Leclercq, *Love of Learning*; Chenu, *Nature, Man, and Society*, passim.

46.   Only a sample may be given here: Werckmeister, 'The First Romanesque Beatus Manuscripts'; idem, 'Art of the Frontier,' in *The Art of Early Medieval Spain*, New York: Metropolitan Museum of Art, 1993, pp.121–32, especially p.124; T. G. Verdon, ed., *Monasticism and the Arts*, Syracuse, NY: Syracuse University Press, 1984; I. Forsyth, 'The *"Vita Apostolica"* and Romanesque Sculpture: Some Preliminary Observations,' *Gesta*, vol. 25, no. 1, 1986, pp.75–82; L. Seidel, 'Medieval Cloister Carving and Monastic *mentalité*,' Medieval Studies at Minnesota, no. 2, *The Medieval Monastery*, Saint Cloud, MN: North Star Press of Saint Cloud, 1988, pp.1–16; L. Rutchick, 'Sculpture programs in the Moissac cloister: Benedictine culture, memory systems, and liturgical performance,' unpublished PhD thesis, University of Chicago, 1991; E. Valdez del Alamo, 'Triumphal Visions and Monastic Devotion: The Annunciation Relief of Santo Domingo de Silos,' *Gesta*, vol. 29, no. 2, 1990, pp.167–88.

47.   Carruthers, *Book of Memory*, p.260.

48.   Bradwardine's recommendation to use architectural frames to demarcate elements manifests the application of the architectural mnemonic in the thirteenth century. Carruthers notes that the architectural mnemonic was out of favor between the first and twelfth centuries, then was revived in the thirteenth: *Book of Memory*, p.122. Yates suggests that the organizational features of thirteenth-century art may reflect the structuring rubrics of the images of artificial memory in contemporary texts: *Art of Memory*, pp.60–81. See discussion above and in n.22.

I

The tomb: between the living and the dead

1

Souvenir, synaesthesia, and the *sepulcrum Domini*: sensory stimuli as memory stratagems[1]

Stephen Lamia

I dedicate this article to the memory of my thesis advisor, G. S. Vickers.

The tomb of Christ was indisputably central to the faith and popular imagination of Western medieval culture. Its site bore witness to an article of dogma – the mystery of the Resurrection. By nature of this very fact, it was one of the most important relics of Christianity and, hence, of paramount interest to pilgrims who kept alive its memory through visitation and souvenir – one an action, the other a memento. Both embraced sensory dimensions – the first through direct visual and physical experience, the second through mental recollection triggered by holding or gazing at the keepsake. The associative encounter between souvenir and beholder itself engendered a vicarious, symbolic visitation to the holy site. Undoubtedly, an even more vivid reminiscence would be evoked if the image on the souvenir was based on the actual appearance of the shrine in Jerusalem. Thus, imagery designed to recall a past experience compounded with synaesthetic activities that occurred at the site of the *sepulcrum Domini* – emotional, visual, aural, olfactory, and tactile – might very well have imprinted the pilgrim with potent mnemonic codes that were retained for a long time.[2]

Already in the fourth century the first descriptions of the Lord's sepulchre appeared in the chronicles of pious travelers. For example, the experiences of a wealthy Roman matron named Paula, who undertook a pilgrimage to the Holy Land *c*.384–92, were recorded by St Jerome in vivid, sensory-rich prose:

Upon entering the sepulchre of the Resurrection, she kissed the stone which the angel moved from the door of the tomb, and with faithful mouth kissed the very place on which the body of the Lord has lain as one who thirsts drinks long-desired waters.[3]

Coeval with the pilgrimage of the Holy Paula, Egeria, a Galician nun, kept a diary of her journey to Jerusalem. It is one of the most comprehensive of all

Early Christian accounts describing not only the numerous building sites she visited, but also the liturgies she attended while there.[4] In one instance, Egeria observed the rituals of Easter Sunday, the Feast of the Resurrection, in the rotunda of the Anastasis itself:

> At four o'clock they have . . . Lucernare.
> All the people congregate . . . in the Anastasis,
> and lamps and candles are all lit . . .
> The fire is brought not from outside, but
> from the cave – inside the screen –
> where a lamp is always burning.[5]

In each of these excerpts the recorded pilgrimage is associated respectively with emotional or temporal experiences – mnemonic elements which induce recollection. For Paula, her action is tactile, which prompts the mental image of the dead Christ outstretched on the tomb slab. For Egeria, the processing of information is largely visual. Her account describes meticulously the architectural setting for the Easter liturgy, thereby reinforcing the memory of her visit through detailed visualization.[6] In fact, Egeria's writings conform, in some measure, to the image displayed on a number of small leaden flasks manufactured in Jerusalem for pilgrims – the lattice-work screen which designated the entrance to the cave of the Holy Sepulchre in the rotunda of the Anastasis. Souvenirs such as this are most certainly memory stratagems since they function as associative keepsakes of the site visited. These vials, dated to the second half of the sixth century, contained holy oil siphoned from the lamps which burned in the Church of the Holy Sepulchre.[7] They were considered *brandea* – relics sanctified by contact with a holy site or with the remains of a saint – and worn around the neck for prophylactic purposes. Pilgrims like Egeria might recall their own experience of the dramatic Lucernare ritual complete with its flickering lamps and candles in the Church of the Holy Sepulchre in Jerusalem through holding and looking at these objects. Moreover, most of these ampullae incorporate other visual devices that are also mnemonic in nature, namely, the depiction on the same circular field of the Crucifixion and Resurrection – the latter metaphorically represented by the Visit of the Holy Women to the Tomb of Christ. In this way, they evoke two fundamental events in Christian history and two principal *loca sancta* situated near each other in the Holy Land. That an active market for mementos of the *sepulcrum Domini* was in existence during the Middle Ages is proven not only by the many ampullae preserved at Monza and Bobbio, but also by *quinquets*, small lamps shaped like miniature aediculae or rotundas which actually burned the oil brought back from the lamps in the Holy Sepulchre.[8]

Despite the existence of a graphic, accurate representation of the tomb of Christ, western European images dating from the Early Christian period followed a radically different archetype, which responded to a different psychological need, that of familiarity. The artists of the early Middle Ages in the Latin West disregarded the literary evidence of both pilgrims' chronicles and biblical descriptions of the tomb of Christ, preferring to rely, instead, on sepulchral evidence with which they were most familiar – indigenous funerary structures and conventional burial containers.[9] They visualized Christ's tomb as a two-storied edifice whose origins lay in the funerary monuments of Late Antiquity; an ivory plaque of *c*.400 (now in Munich), carved with scenes of the Visit of the Holy Women and the Ascension, demonstrates this alternative.[10] The image prevailed with minor modification well into the twelfth century. This tendency to invest the *sepulcrum Domini* with a predictable, identifiable form fulfilled for the viewer a tangible impression of verisimilitude, though in reality, the appearance was fundamentally different from what we know of the tomb's actual form.

Around the ninth and tenth centuries, the image of a coffin for Christ's sepulchre began to emerge. The miniature of the Deposition and Entombment from the *Codex Egberti* of the late tenth century is perhaps the most celebrated of these Early Medieval examples.[11] Once the sarcophagus as paradigmatic image of the *sepulcrum Domini* appeared with a pronounced degree of regularity in the visual arts of the eleventh and twelfth centuries, it began to receive embellishment of a decorative sort: lozenges, strigils, arcuations, floral patterns, and other motifs.[12]

The dynamic of memory is manifested in yet a different way in a third type of image for Christ's tomb, one which parallels certain practices of the Christian cult of saints. Although it, too, is a sarcophagus, its long side, visible to the spectator, contains three circular forms aligned on an even horizontal axis. In order to explain this rather curious alteration in the iconography of the tomb of Christ – and one which appeared quite spontaneously in western Europe toward the middle of the twelfth century – it will first be necessary to return to Jerusalem, to the *locus sanctus* of the Entombment and Resurrection, and to information found in contemporary pilgrims' chronicles.

During the years 1106–7, an abbot from the fringes of Eastern Orthodoxy journeyed to the Holy Land and conscientiously documented a great deal of useful and interesting items concerning the Church of the Holy Sepulchre and its famous tomb.[13] This pilgrim, known simply as Daniel, came from an undetermined monastery in present-day Russia and, among other data, recorded this detail:

When one has entered the grotto (of the Holy Sepulchre) . . . one sees on the right a sort of bench, cut in the rock of the cavern, upon which the body of Our Lord, Jesus Christ, was laid; it is now covered by marble slabs. This sacred rock, which all Christians kiss, can be seen through three round openings on one side.[14]

Later in the century, *c.*1172, a German priest by the name of Theoderich, visited the same site and left this description:

No one can enter the mouth of the sepulchre itself except by crawling upon one's knees, and (then) . . . one finds that most wished-for treasure – I mean the sepulchre in which our most gracious Lord Jesus Christ lay for three days – which is wondrously adorned with white marble, gold, and precious stones. In the side it has three holes, through which pilgrims give their long-wished-for kisses to the very stone on which their Lord lay.[15]

Based on the information found in these two twelfth-century accounts, the innovative image for the *sepulcrum Domini* may now be understood as an exact reflection of the shrine's disposition in the Church of the Holy Sepulchre during that time. A marble revetment, or outer casing, covered the tomb slab almost entirely except for three apertures large enough for thrusting a head or hand in order to gain visible and tactile access to the relic inside. Thus, upon arriving at the *locus sanctus*, the pilgrims knelt down to enter the grotto which contained the cenotaph; and to fulfill their ardent desire for proximity, they poked their heads or their hands through one of the three openings enclosing it to kiss or touch the sacred slab. This arrangement and motion thereby afforded them visual and tangible proof of the existence of the *sepulcrum* and provided them with an outlet for emotional expression through the act of kissing or touching the relic. Both of these sensory activities must have stamped the pilgrims' memory with an unforgettable moment of spiritual ecstasy attained through synaesthetic experience.

The visual documentation which corresponds identically with these descriptions is manifested in sculpted form in several regions of western Europe. From the Ile-de-France the new image may be seen on two capitals which run along the frieze on the west façade of Chartres Cathedral (Fig. 1.1).[16] These carvings, dated 1145–55, display on the one hand, the conflated episodes of the Anointing and Entombment of Christ and, on the other, the Visit of the Holy Women to the Sepulchre. This latter biblical narrative is the one more frequently associated with representations of the tomb of Christ; and at the church of Notre-Dame, Etampes, we find in a sculpted capital on the south portal the identical scene including the identical pierced sepulchre (Fig. 1.2).[17] What is significant is that this new imagery is shared by at least two artists working almost simultaneously in the Ile-de-France around the middle of the twelfth century.

Provence also yields versions of the *sepulcrum Domini* which conform to the precise arrangement found in Jerusalem. One of the earliest instances, at the abbey church of St-Gilles-du-Gard, is prominently located on the lintel of the south portal of the west façade (Fig. 1.3).[18] Again, the scene depicts the Visit of the Holy Women and the three apertures appear quite noticeably on the sarcophagus. Slightly later, and with a certain degree of variation, the pierced *sepulcrum Domini*, inscribed as such, was carved on the northwest pier in the cloister of St-Trophime, Arles (begun *c.*1150–60).[19] Here the tomb shows two small openings: the one on the right is a circle, that on the left a quatrefoil (Fig. 1.4). The third hole at center is covered by the shroud which is draped over the side of the coffin.

In addition to the French examples, two areas of Italy, notably Tuscany and Apulia, likewise produced twelfth-century works of art that included this novelty. One securely dated object, which displays the type in the pre-dictable scene of the Visit of the Holy Women, is a carved pulpit originally intended for the Cathedral at Pisa but subsequently transported to the Cathedral at Cagliari, Sardinia where it still stands (Fig. 1.5).[20] Executed between 1158–62, its authorship has been ascribed to a certain Guglielmo active in Pisa around the fifth and sixth decades of the twelfth century.[21] The three-holed tomb of Christ recurs in the oeuvre of yet another Pisan master, Bonano, also active in the second half of the twelfth century. This artist was responsible for the execution of two sets of bronze doors, one of which was installed in the south transept at Pisa Cathedral, the so-called Porta di S. Ranieri, and the other sent to adorn the main portal of the Cathedral at Monreale in Sicily.[22] In both works, Bonano consistently employed the motif of the triple-apertured sepulchre in the scene of the Marys at the Tomb (Figs 1.6, 1.7). Finally, in Apulia, two sculpted reliefs of the Holy Women at the Sepulchre – one on an architrave formerly at the Cathedral of Monopoli now removed to the sacristy, the other on the lintel of the so-called Tumba di Rotari at Monte Sant' Angelo – demonstrably delineate the innovative image (Figs 1.8, 1.9).[23]

Regardless of the complex means by which the three-holed version of the tomb of Christ was transmitted to western Europe, the formula suggests that firsthand knowledge and vivid synaesthetic stimuli factored strongly in de-veloping this type – a methodology which Mary Carruthers herself observes with respect to medieval memory stratagems.[24] The veristic visualization conflates souvenir with physical activity to produce a sensorial commem-oration. Ultimately, this accurate rendition implies proof, devotion, and remembrance: declaratory proof of direct visitation, the reinforcement of the experience by a devout, yet sensory, encounter with the holy relic through movement, sight, osculation, and touch, and the imprint of that intimacy in a precise representation – the image of the tomb complete with its pierced openings for access.

The compelling visibility of images of the real *sepulcrum Domini* displayed on such strategic areas of ecclesiastic architecture as façades, doors, piers, and pulpits compounded with the richness of dynamic, unusual, and syn-aesthetic activities at the sacred place more than amply suggests a tendency to document and memorialize the exact arrangement of the site of the burial and resurrection of Christ, thus maintaining perpetually not only the geo-graphically distant city but also the historically remote event. In other words, the images literally must have assumed the important but familiar function of souvenirs or mementos – albeit monumental in scale – of the place visited and, as such, reminded the viewers in a most immediate way, even those who were not fortunate enough to have undertaken the pilgrim-age, of the precise appearance of the sepulchre in Jerusalem.

To be sure, the examples of the *sepulcrum Domini* discussed are the excep-tion rather than the rule in standard twelfth-century iconography of the tomb of Christ, and the analysis of these rarities is by no means inclusive. How-ever, they point to specific, but not isolated phenomena, for the arrangement of a pierced tomb is not the exclusive domain of the sepulchre of the Lord. Instead, it is part of a more widespread western European practice whose origins may be traced to an Early Christian form, the *fenestella confessionis*, literally, the 'window of witness' found in a number of saints' shrines in medieval Europe.

As is commonly known, medieval Christians held in high esteem the bodily remains of saints, and these were venerated both for their sanctity and for the healing properties associated with them. In a late-fourth-century treatise entitled *De laude sanctorum*, written by Victricius, Bishop of Rouen, an important aspect, later to become a central issue, of the medieval cult of relics is articulated. Victricius contended that the close relationship between body and soul, the latter so filled with holiness, invested with sacramental grace the physical remains of saints and objects that came into contact with them.[25] This belief gave further strength to the practice of cherishing the relics of the heroes and heroines of the Early Church. One means of commu-nicating with the earthly remains of saints was through the small window or hole known as the *fenestella confessionis*. This aperture allowed the devout to thrust their heads inside to kiss the sarcophagus which contained relics or to touch it with their hands. If, for some reason, the tomb was not easily within reach, the *fenestella* would provide the optimum means for indirect contact at least by visual means.

There are several examples of this type of structure documented from the earliest Christian shrines. One pilgrimage site that remained popular through-out the Middle Ages was St Peter's in Rome. An aedicula built in the late second century over his tomb maintained its *fenestella confessionis* during successive building campaigns. Its setting and function are best detailed in the sixth-century account by Gregory of Tours:

This tomb is placed below the altar . . . But whoso wishes to pray, for him the doors that give access are unbolted, and he enters the precinct over the tomb, and a small window is opened, and placing his head within he asks for whatever he requires . . .

And if he wishes to carry away a holy token, a piece of cloth weighed in a scale is hung within . . . And if his faith prevails, when the cloth is raised from the tomb . . . it is so imbued with holy virtue that it weighs far more than it did before; and then he knows that he has received, along with the sign of grace, a favorable answer to his prayer.[26]

From this description we learn that a *fenestella* situated under the altar in the martyrium of Old St Peter's in Rome was the means by which the faithful were able to view, to venerate, and to communicate with the remains of the Apostle buried below. The pilgrim would either poke his/her head through this opening, lower a cloth to touch the sarcophagus, or perhaps both. The *fenestella* was also a control mechanism to safeguard the tomb from the over-zealous crowds that frequently flocked to this holy site.

Similar situations are recorded in tombs and altars of other Early Christian saints. For example, St Augustine of Hippo's *De Stephani martyris, detectione, translatione, et miraculis* in the appendix to his *De civitate Dei* recounts the healing of a mute at the shrine of St Stephen, the cure being effected by a cloth sent through the *fenestella* of the tomb and subsequently applied to the mouth of the afflicted.[27] For Merovingian Gaul, Gregory of Tours informs us of this special provision. In the *Liber de gloria confessorum*, for example, he describes the tomb of St Venerandus at Clermont-Ferrand:

And here is the sepulchre of the bishop saint Venerandus into which whoever desires puts his head through the little window, asking to bring about what is necessary, and obtains the effect soon if he will ask it in a just manner.[28]

Although the tomb of St Venerandus no longer survives, that of St Didier, an Alsatian bishop of the late seventh century, gives us insight into the type of pierced tomb which Gregory of Tours encountered (Fig. 1.10). This structure, which has the shape of a saddle-roofed sarcophagus, is in fact a richly decor-ated cenotaph. The actual coffin is located under the floor. According to local legend, those suffering from weak powers of reasoning placed their heads inside one of two round-headed arches to receive the benefits from the holy bishop's remains.[29] These openings are located on either side of the monu-ment but are not aligned.

In addition, the Venerable Bede in his *History of the English Church and People* provides us with a description of the now lost shrine of St Chad, Bishop of Mercia, who died in 672, attesting to the existence of a pierced tomb in the British Isles contemporary with Continental examples:

Chad's burial place is covered by a wooden tomb made in the form of a little house with an aperture in the wall through which those who visit it out of devotion may insert their hand and take out some of the dust. They mix this in water and give it to sick men and beasts to drink, by which means their ailment is quickly relieved and they are restored to health.[30]

Here is a case where the *fenestella confessionis* functioned not only as a means to gain proximity to relics, but also, as seen elsewhere, as a means of access to take a souvenir from a saint's shrine. It is not clear whether the 'dust' mentioned in the chronicle refers to the remains of St Chad or the dirt flooring over which, presumably, the simple tomb chamber was erected.

As a later example, we cite the tomb of St Urlou located in the crypt below the altar of the Church of Ste.-Croix, Quimperlé. Urlou, first abbot of the monastery of the Holy Cross in this Breton town, died in 1057 and in 1083 his body was translated to the crypt. The low-relief *gisant*, a Gothic addition, rests upon a block-like base into which an arch for passage has been provided.[31] A smaller hole is located on the short side below the head of Urlou's effigy. Pilgrims pass through the larger opening to pray for cures against gout, rheumatism, and headaches. The smaller opening would be reserved for the insertion of diseased limbs.[32]

The employment of apertures in tombs of saints continued throughout the Middle Ages in the West; and the physical action of crawling, touching, kissing, or thrusting on the part of the pilgrim involved both an ordeal of sorts and an unforgettable proximity to the holy dead.[33] Thus, motion in concert with visualization and tactility bring to bear a number of sensory stimuli which effectively imprint themselves on memory. Moreover, by attaining such extreme closeness to the relics of saints one not only would absorb the healing virtues which emanated from them, but also would share in the benefit of their eternal glory – a destiny which awaited the faithful at the end of their mortal existence.

With the addition of a *fenestella*, or more precisely three *fenestellae*, the tomb of Christ was now accorded a characteristic which conjoined it to relic cults and tombs of local saints in the Latin West: all rewarded the journey to a sacred burial place with a spiritual as well as a synaesthetic experience. Additionally, the pilgrimage to Jerusalem encompassed a dimension of imitating the Passion of Christ. Pilgrims symbolically took up Christ's Cross, endured hardships along the road, and sometimes met death; hence their travels and travails were equated with Christ's own suffering and death.[34] This commemorative affirmation of the *imitatio Christi* raised the level of interest in relics associated with Christ's Passion and his ultimate triumph over death which was realized in the tomb itself; and the reward of a special papal indulgence – liberation from the punishment of sin – had an even further appeal if a pilgrim ran the risk of dying for the cause.[35] Given, then, this concept of *imitatio Christi*, what more powerful means for pilgrims to identify themselves with the Passion than to possess a relic connected with it or to retain the personal, intimate memory of direct access through sensory actions such as seeing, kissing and touching the sacred bier?

The biblical narrative which most closely parallels the tactile actions at tomb shrines and the resulting proof which these motions afford is The Doubting of St Thomas. In the Gospel of St John, 20.27, Christ beckons the apostle to thrust his hand into the wound on Christ's side as reinforcement of his faith. Medieval art is rife with examples of this event: the dynamic Ottonian ivory carving at the National Museum in Berlin and the more regimented Romanesque relief on the northwest pier in the cloister of Santo Domingo de Silos are two of a legion of examples which come to mind.[36]

A somewhat different, but perhaps more cogent, biblical analogy may be offered in the symbolic relationship that existed between the Visit of the Holy Women to the Tomb of Christ and the medieval pilgrims who traveled to the Holy Sepulchre.[37] All approached the sacred place in an act of devotion – the holy Marys to anoint the body of Christ and the pilgrims to fulfill their desire to venerate the most prestigious burial site of their faith. A parallel iconographic phenomenon to these western European pilgrims is the visual juxtaposition of the Holy Women with the pierced *sepulcrum Domini* discussed above in the French and Italian twelfth-century sculpted and cast reliefs. In addition, we have identified specific passages in pilgrims' chronicles that vividly describe the physical rituals that such an arrangement prompted. That the Church itself recognized the need for these types of sensory stimuli is manifested in *fenestellae* outfitted at many saints' shrines from the Early Christian era onward where synaesthetic experiences similar to those which took place at Christ's tomb also occurred.

The French and Italian monuments that employed the veristic image of the *sepulcrum Domini* did not merely inform their medieval audience of the actual conditions at Jerusalem, but perhaps also recalled practices at local shrines with which the observers must have been familiar in order to create an artificial memory. The mechanics of this associative method as a mnemonic aid are not singular to this situation; Hugh of St Victor likewise stressed this as a learning concept in the twelfth century.[38]

The theoretical construct of memory formed by the accurate representation of the tomb of Christ is created by the perpetual and very visible souvenir of visitation, itself triggered by the synaesthetic occurrences at the holy site. Indeed, the potency of visual imagery as memory stratagems in the Middle Ages cannot be overstated. Freedberg declares that the belief in the ability of images to aid memory is found from the earliest days of Christianity. Carruthers argues strongly for the temporal significance of pictures. According to Fentress and Wickham, images were signposts specifically designed to guide the mind to higher truths. As Remensnyder notes, the memorial potency of images is activated when the object – in this case, the *sepulcrum Domini* – is physically integrated within a narrative context, here the biblical

episode of the Visit of the Holy Women to the Sepulchre.[39] Thus, both physical site and historical event factor dynamically with respect to memorial
strategies. The representations of the tomb were designed to imprint the
memory with the sensory experiences which occurred there, the reinforcement of which was embedded in the biblical narrative, The Visit of the Holy
Women to the Sepulchre. Geary stresses that memory, together with those
objects and actions by which it was preserved, was a key organizing principle of medieval life.[40] While he mentions tombs and ritual commemoration
of the dead, we may also include souvenirs and synaesthetic activities.

Commemorating the 'special dead,' that is to say, the saints and, above all,
Christ, was an essential component of medieval faith. The various devices
both active and passive, mental and physical that were employed in those
commemorative rituals – prayers, meditation, relic veneration, pilgrimages,
souvenirs, and site-specific sensory experiences – engaged the believer in a
most immediate way by serving to reinforce the memory of past events
through present practices.[41]

Generally speaking, motives and goals for pilgrimage to holy tombs in the
Middle Ages were either penitential, thaumaturgical, or devotional; and all
three are relevant to a pierced tomb's arrangement. The openings afforded
proof and protection of the relic, witness and ordeal for pilgrims, attention
and decoration to the tomb itself, and intimate, synaesthetic, and spiritual
communication between the living and the dead. In the specific case of the
tomb of Christ, the representation of the empty tomb with its triple *fenestella*
imbued the holy object with a sense of vivid presence in the temporal context of biblical narrative, namely, the Visit of the Marys to the Tomb, and, by
extension, made it feasible for the viewers to identify vicariously with those
Holy Women. Finally, the image also commemorated, actualized, and reinforced that article of Christian faith, the mystery of the Resurrection, the
center of whose cult was considered to be the holiest tomb on earth.

Frequently cited sources

Carruthers, M., *The Book of Memory: A Study of Memory in Medieval Culture,* Cambridge: Cambridge
    University Press, 1990.
— *The Craft of Thought: Meditation, Rhetoric, and the Making of Images, 400–1200,* Cambridge: Cambridge
    University Press, 1998.
Lamia, S. ' *"Sepulcrum Domini"*: the iconography of the holed tomb of Christ in Romanesque and
    Gothic art,' unpublished PhD thesis, University of Toronto, 1982.

Notes

I would like to express my sincerest gratitude to Elizabeth Valdez del Alamo and Carol Pendergast
for their many valuable editorial comments and suggestions. In addition, Francie Davis, Kathy Levine,
and Lynn Lotz, my colleagues at Dowling College, and Diana Reeve of Art Resource likewise ought
to be acknowledged for their assistance. This article is derived from my unpublished PhD thesis,
' *"Sepulcrum Domini"*: the iconography of the holed tomb of Christ in Romanesque and Gothic art,'

University of Toronto, 1982. I am indebted to my thesis advisor, the late G. S. Vickers, for so generously sharing with me his ideas, speculations, and criticisms.

1. The common dictionary definition of 'synaesthesia' states that it is a sensation or feeling produced in one part of the body by a stimulus applied at another part; or, a concomitant sensation, especially a subjective sensation or image of another sense than the one being stimulated. Synaesthesia involves one or more of the human senses that serves as a strategy for *memoria*. For additional discussion on this phenomenon, see M. Carruthers, *Craft of Thought*, pp.148, 207; K. Morrison, *History as a Visual Art in the Twelfth-Century Renaissance*, Princeton, NJ: Princeton University Press, 1990, pp.38, 55, 62, 102, 249.

2. See: Carruthers, *Book of Memory*; eadem, *Craft of Thought*; J. Fentress and C. Wickham, *Social Memory*, Oxford: Basil Blackwell, 1992; P. J. Geary, *Phantoms of Remembrance: Memory and Oblivion at the End of the First Millennium*, Princeton, NJ: Princeton University Press, 1994; J. Le Goff, *History and Memory*, translated by S. Rendall and E. Claman, New York: Columbia University Press, 1992; and A. J. Remensnyder, 'Legendary Treasure at Conques: Reliquaries and Imaginative Memory,' *Speculum*, vol. 71, 1996, pp.884–906.

3. St Jerome, *The Pilgrimage of the Holy Paula*, translated by A. Stewart, The Library of the Palestine Pilgrims' Text Society, 1, London: The Palestine Pilgrims' Text Society, 1896, p.5.

4. J. J. Wilkinson, *Egeria's Travels to the Holy Land*, rev. ed. Warminster: Aris and Phillips, 1981.

5. ibid., p.123.

6. Carruthers argues strongly for the retention and retrieval of information not only through written documents but also by visual means, a concept that actually pre-dates medieval thought and which can be found in the writings of Cicero. See Carruthers, *Book of Memory*, especially pp.17, 60, 73, 221ff. More recently, Carruthers explicitly refers to text passages in journals written by Early Christian pilgrims to Jerusalem who experienced the *loca sancta* themselves as places for conjuring memory images and relating them to appropriate biblical narratives: *Craft of Thought*, pp.42–3. See also D. Freedberg, *The Power of Images: Studies in the History and Theory of Response*, Chicago: University of Chicago Press, 1989, pp.162–3, on memory and images. Even in the field of cognitive psychology, researchers have demonstrated the important role of visualization and other sensory experiences in formulating the recollection of past events and distant places. See U. Neisser, 'Domains of Memory,' in P. Solomon et al., eds, *Memory: Interdisciplinary Approaches*, New York: Springer-Verlag, 1989, pp.67–83; and D. Schacter, *Searching for Memory*, New York: Basic Books, 1996, passim, especially pp.4, 11, 17, 18, 23, 27, 45–7.

7. André Grabar, *Ampoules de Terre Sainte*, Paris: C. Klincksieck, 1958, pp.63–7. Also Freedberg (as in n.6), pp.130–31. Several examples of these ampullae may be found in Grabar. See plates V, IX, XI–XIV, XVI, XVIII, XXII, XXIV, XXVI, XXVIII for those retained in the cathedral treasury at Monza, and plates XXXIV–XL, XLV, XLVII, XLVIII for others at the Monastery of St Columba at Bobbio. Freedberg corroborates the idea that pilgrimage souvenirs are tangible stratagems for recalling the memory of the journey to holy sites: Freedberg (as in n.6), p.124.

8. I. Q. van Regtern-Altena, 'Hidden Records of the Holy Sepulchre,' in *Essays in the History of Architecture Presented to Rudolf Wittkower*, London: Phaidon, 1967, pp.17–21.

9. Lamia, '*Sepulcrum Domini*,' p.86.

10. For the Munich ivory, see D. Gaborit-Chopin, *Ivoires du moyen âge*, Fribourg: Office du Livre, 1978, no. 15. For examples of late antique two-storied tombs, see A. Boëthius and J. Ward Perkins, *Etruscan and Roman Architecture*, Harmondsworth: Penguin, 1970, pp.299–301, 356; and A. de Franciscis and R. Pane, *Mausolei romani in Campania*, Naples: Editore Scientifiche Italiane, 1957, passim.

11. See Schiller, *Iconography of Christian Art*, translated by J. Seligman, Greenwich, CT: New York Graphic Society, vol. II, 1972, fig. 544.

12. Lamia, '*Sepulcrum Domini*,' pp.164–7.

13. Daniel the Abbot, *The Pilgrimage of the Russian Abbot Daniel in the Holy Land*, edited by C. W. Wilson, *The Library of the Palestine Pilgrims' Text Society*, III, London: The Palestine Pilgrims' Text Society, 1895, pp.iii–82; also A. de Noroff's *Pélerinage en Terre Sainte de l'igoumène russe Daniel au commencement du XII siècle*, St Pétersbourg: Académie impériale des sciences, 1864, a French translation accompanying the original text.

14. Daniel the Abbot (as in n.13), p.12.

15. Theoderich of Würzburg, *Guide to the Holy Land*, translated by A. Stewart; 2nd edition, with a new introduction by R. G. Musto, New York: Italica Press, 1986, p.9. The concordance between Daniel the Abbot's description and that of Theoderich: 'Tria in latere rotunda habet foramina,

per quae ipsi lapidi, in quo Dominus jacuit, optata peregrini porriguntur oscula,' is also mentioned in V. Corbo, *Il Santo Sepolcro di Gerusalemme: aspetti archeologici dalle origini al periodo crociato*, Jerusalem: Franciscan Printing Press, 1981, pp.198–9. The tomb shrine, rebuilt in the early nineteenth century, no longer possesses this arrangement. See D. Kroyanker, *Jerusalem Architecture*, London: Tauris Parks, 1994, p.38.

16. R. Crozet, 'A propos des chapiteaux de la façade occidentale de Chartres,' *Cahiers de la civilisation médiévale*, vol. 14, 1971, pp.159–65; A. Heimann, 'The Capital Frieze and Pilasters of the Portail Royal, Chartres,' *Journal of the Warburg and Courtauld Institutes*, vol. 31, 1968, pp.73–102; R. Dressler, 'Medieval narrative: the narrative frieze in the royal portal, Chartres Cathedral,' unpublished PhD thesis, Columbia University, 1992.

17. See K. Nolan, 'Narrative in the Capital Frieze of Notre Dame at Etampes,' *The Art Bulletin*, vol. 71, 1989, pp.166–84.

18. See especially, R. Hamann, *Die Abteikirche von St Gilles und ihre künstlerische Nachfolge*, Berlin: Akademie Verlag, 1956; M. Colish, 'Peter of Bruys, Henry of Lausanne, and the Façade of St Gilles,' *Traditio*, vol. 28, 1972, pp.451–60; W. S. Stoddard, *The Façade of St-Gilles-du-Gard*, Middletown: Wesleyan University Press, 1973; C. Ferguson O'Meara, *The Iconography of the Façade of Saint-Gilles-du-Gard*, New York: Garland, 1977.

19. Stoddard (as in n.18), pp.199ff.; also see E. Dyggve, 'Sepulcrum domini – Form und Einrichtung,' *Festschrift Friedrich Gerke*, Baden-Baden: Holle-Verlag, 1962, pp.11–20.

20. R. Zech, *Meister Wilhelm von Innsbruck und die Pisaner Kanzel im Dome zu Cagliari*, Bottrop: Wilhelm Postberg, 1935; G. H. Crichton, *Romanesque Sculpture in Italy*, London: Routledge and Paul, 1954, pp.97–101; C. D. Sheppard, 'Romanesque Sculpture in Tuscany: A Problem in Methodology,' *Gazette des Beaux-Arts*, vol. 54, 1959, pp.97–108. A new ambo was constructed for the Cathedral in 1302–10 by Giovanni Pisano and Guglielmo's was then removed to Cagliari where it was later divided into two pulpits.

21. Crichton (as in n.20), p.98. This may bear a relationship to works by Bonano of Pisa discussed presently. The theory that Guglielmo originally came from Innsbruck is based on flimsy evidence: ibid., p.99.

22. Albert Boeckler, *Die Bronzetüren des Bonanus von Pisa und des Barisanus von Trani*, Berlin: Deutscher Verein für Kunstwissenschaft, 1953, pp.9–44. For the doors on the Porta di San Ranieri see also Dyggve (as in n.19), pp.12–14; for the Monreale doors see R. Salvini, *Il chiostro di Monreale e la scultura romanica in Sicilia*, Palermo: S. F. Flaccovia, 1962, pp.235ff.

23. For the Monopoli architrave see E. Bertaux, *L'art dans l'Italie méridionale*, vol. I, Paris: A. Fontemoing, 1903, pp.465–78; for the Monte Sant'Angelo tympanum, ibid., vol. II, pp.679–82. More comprehensive bibliographies for each of these monuments will be found in D. F. Glass, *Italian Romanesque Sculpture: An Annotated Bibliography*, Boston: G. K. Hall, 1983, pp.168, 174–5.

24. Carruthers, *Book of Memory*, pp.48ff., especially p.78. For a discussion of the military, political, ecclesiastical, and mercantile connections which the Ile-de-France, Provence, Tuscany, and Apulia maintained with the Holy Land during the eleventh and twelfth centuries, and thus speculation on modes of transmission of the image of the pierced *sepulcrum Domini* see Lamia, 'Sepulcrum Domini,' pp.189–97, 204–10, 248–9, 256.

25. See Victricius of Rouen, *De laude sanctorum*, in PL, vol. XX, cols 443–58; also see R. Herval, *Origines chrétiennes de la IIe Lyonnaise gallo-romaine à la Normandie ducale*, Rouen: H. Mayard, 1966, a French translation of the Bishop's sermon. The basic ideas in this sermon, which Victricius wrote on the occasion of the acquisition of relics for his new cathedral, are summarized in E. Kemp, *Canonization and Authority in the Western Church*, Westport, CT: Hyperion, 1948, pp.3–5.

26. J. Toynbee and J. W. Perkins, *The Shrine of St Peter and the Vatican Excavations*, London: Longmans Green, 1956, pp.212–13. In addition, see the definition of *fenestella* in F. Cabrol and H. Leclercq, DACL, vol. V, part 1, cols 1355–7. Indeed, several archeologists and cultural anthropologists have pointed to the existence and possible cultic significance of holed stones and have traced them as far back as the Neolithic Period. For an illustration of the reconstruction of the *memoria* to St Peter, complete with its *fenestella*, see R. Krautheimer, *Early Christian and Byzantine Architecture*, Harmondsworth: Penguin, 1965, fig. 2.

27. Augustine of Hippo, *De Stephani martyris, detectione, translatione, et miraculis*, in Migne, PL, vol. XLI, cols 805–54, especially 840: 'Proinde exuens sibi manicam tunicae suae . . . per fenestellam Memoriae ad interiora loca sanctuarum reliquiarum manu injecta mittebat, atque inde rursum deteram reducens ori suo admovebat, et linguam contigendo paulatim modos loquendi gratia fidei resolvebat.'

28. Gregory of Tours, *Liber der gloria confessorum*, in PL, vol. LXXI, col. 857: 'Est ibi et sepulcrum ipsius sancti Venerandi episcopi . . . super quod caput per fenestellam quicunque vult, imittit, praecans quae necessitas cogit, obtinetque mox effectum, si juste petierit.' See also M. Vieillard-Troiekouroff, *Les monuments religieux de la Gaule d'après les oeuvres de Grégoire de Tours*, Paris: H. Champion, 1976, p.100; and L. Maître, 'Remarques sur les tombeaux percés d'une fenêtre, *Revue archéologique*, 5e série, IV, 1916, pp.265–85, especially p.280.

29. J. Hubert, 'Les monuments funéraires de l'église de Saint-Dizier en Alsace,' *Bulletin monumental*, vol. 94, 1935, pp.215–35; A. de Barthélemy, 'Tombeau de Saint Dizier, eveque et martyr,' *Annales archéologiques*, vol. 18, 1858, pp.49–56; H. Gaidoz, *Un vieux rite médical*, Paris: Rolland, 1892, p.38; P. Sébillot, *Le folk-lore de France*, Paris: Maisonneuve et Larose, vol. IV, 1968, p.158.

30. Bede, *A History of the English Church and People*, edited by B. Colgrave and R. A. B. Mynors, Oxford: Oxford University Press, 1968, book IV, chapter 3, p.212. See also J. C. Wall, *Shrines of British Saints*, London: Methuen, 1905, p.97.

31. Kemp (as in n.25), pp.66–7. Also see G. Le Scouëzec, *Guide de la Bretagne mystérieuse*, Paris: Tchuou, 1966 pp.577–8; Gaidoz, *Un vieux rite médical*, p.45; Maître (as in n.28), pp.271–3. For an illustration of the tomb of St Urlou, see Le Scouëzec, *Guide de la Bretagne mystérieuse*, p.578.

32. Le Scouëzec (as in n.31), p.578; Maître (as in n.28), p.272.

33. See Lamia, '*Sepulcrum Domini*,' pp.344–421, for additional examples of saints' shrines outfitted with openings for accessibility.

34. See A. Dupront, 'La spiritualité des croisés et des pèlerins d'après les sources de la première croisade,' *Pellegrinaggi e culto dei santi in Europa fino alla Ia crociata*, Todi: Presso L'Accademia tudertina, 1963, pp.449–83. Also see Musto's introductory comments to Theoderich (as in n.15), pp.xxiv–xxv.

35. This is corroborated in E. O. Blake, 'The Formation of the Crusade Idea,' *Journal of Ecclesiastical History*, vol. 21, 1970, pp.11–31; and P. Alphandéry, *La chrétienté et l'idée de croisade*, Paris: A. Michel, 1954, part I, passim. Pope Eugenius III reissued the indulgence granted by his forerunner, Urban II, to whomever would undertake arms for the Second Crusade. See K. M. Setton, ed., *A History of the Crusades*, Madison, WI: University of Wisconsin Press, vol. I, 1969, p.467; G. Constable, 'The Second Crusade as Seen by Contemporaries,' *Traditio*, vol. 9, 1953, pp.213–79, especially pp.248–9; L. Rothkrug, 'Popular Religion and Holy Shrines: Their Influence on the Origins of the German Reformation and Their Role in German Cultural Development,' in J. Obelkevich, ed., *Religion and the People, 800–1700*, Chapel Hill: University of North Carolina Press, 1979, pp.20–86, especially pp.22, 50; and D. Sox, *Relics and Shrines*, London: G. Allen and Unwin, 1985, p.24.

36. I am indebted to E. Valdez del Alamo for making me aware of this reference. For the Ottonian ivory carving depicting the scene of Doubting Thomas, see J. Snyder, *Medieval Art: Painting, Sculpture, Architecture, 4th–14th Century*, Englewood Cliffs, NJ: Prentice-Hall, 1989, ill. 297; ill. 315, for the limestone relief at Silos.

37. Pope Gregory the Great, for instance, equated the Holy Women who visited Christ's tomb with the Christian congregation considering all as searching for God. See O. B. Hardison, *Christian Rite and Christian Drama in the Middle Ages*, Baltimore, MD: Johns Hopkins Press, 1965, p.229. The pivotal role of the iconography of the Visit of the Holy Women and its relationship to the liturgical drama, *Officium sepulcri*, is outside the scope of this article, but a summary may be found in Lamia, *Sepulcrum Domini*, pp.140–61. For an additional discussion of this topic, see P. K. Sheingorn, 'The Easter sepulchre: a study in the relationship between art and liturgy,' unpublished PhD thesis, University of Wisconsin, 1974.

38. For Hugh of St Victor, see Carruthers, *Book of Memory*, pp.60, 245.

39. Carruthers, *Book of Memory*, pp.221–3; Fentress and Wickham (as in n.2), p.50; Freedberg (as in n.6), p.90; Remensnyder (as in n.2), p.904. In her more recent study, Carruthers also comments upon the association between physical place and biblical narrative: *Craft of Thought*, pp.42–4.

40. Geary (as in n.2), p.18.

41. ibid., p.7, and Le Goff (as in n.2), p.13; both acknowledge medieval society's tendency to frame past events in the context of the present.

1.1   Anointing and Entombment of Christ, Visit of the Holy Women to the
Sepulchre, Chartres Cathedral, west façade, 1145–55

1.2   Visit of the Holy Women to the Sepulchre, Etampes, Notre-Dame, south portal,
1145–55

1.3   Holy Women at the Tomb, St-Gilles-du-Gard, west façade, mid-twelfth century

1.4 *Sepulcrum Domini*, Arles, St-Trophime, northwest pier of cloister, begun
c.1150–60

1.5   Guglielmo, Holy Women at the Tomb, detail of pulpit, Cagliari Cathedral, 1158–62

1.6   Bonano, Holy Women at the Tomb, Porta di S. Ranieri, Pisa Cathedral, *c.*1180

1.7   Bonano, Holy Women at the Tomb, Porta Maggiore, Monreale Cathedral, 1186

1.8   Holy Women at the Tomb, architrave, Monopoli Cathedral, early twelfth century

1.9   Holy Women at the Tomb, Tumba di Rotari, lintel, Monte Sant' Angelo, twelfth century

1.10   Tomb of St Didier, St-Dizier, late seventh century

2

Lament for a lost Queen: the sarcophagus of Doña Blanca in Nájera

Elizabeth Valdez del Alamo

The death of a Queen in childbirth and the grief of her bereaved husband are represented on one of the most memorable tombs produced in Spain during the twelfth century: that of Doña Blanca of Navarre (†1156), wife of Sancho III, King of Castile (Figs 2.1–2.3).[1] In addition to Blanca's deathbed, a scene that includes her husband swooning, biblical stories concerning mothers and their children – dramas of sacrifice and salvation – are represented. The simplicity with which the figures are rendered makes their powerful emotions seem all the stronger; these images impress themselves indelibly onto the mind of the spectator. The tomb reliefs achieve thereby the central purpose of a funerary monument: to perpetuate the memory of the deceased by recalling her to the living. Such a reminder had to be specific, and rendered in vivid visual terms, in order to be efficacious.[2] The designer of the tomb utilized a number of inventive devices to individualize the memory of this Queen and her death. Conventional compositions for deathbed and lamentation scenes were altered, and biblical imagery was employed to describe her salvation in terms specific to her sex. This is distinct from other historiated sarcophagi of the period.[3]

The choice of such individualized imagery must have been affected by the fact that this young royal couple were truly devoted to one another, with great expectations for themselves and their progeny. The King, Sancho, could well have played an active role in the design of the sarcophagus, for he mentions in several donations his concern with his wife's burial. It is even possible that Blanca herself had a hand in the choice of subject, since, as documents suggest, her death was slow rather than sudden. My discussion will center upon the ways in which subject matter and gestural language communicate those qualities of his wife that Sancho wished to commemorate, and how the memory of her was molded by contemporary religious and social institutions. As the historical context for the highly personal yet theologically rich imagery unfolds, it becomes clear that Blanca's sarcophagus is a significant example of the exploration of human emotion in the visual and literary arts of the twelfth century.

Blanca's original burial was in a cave that formed the royal pantheon of the Navarrese kings adjoining the church of Santa María la Real, in Nájera. Only the gabled lid of her sarcophagus has survived. Its ends were apparently cut off when the tomb was later installed in a niche to create an arcosolium. The sarcophagus basin used in the arcosolium, possibly the original, does not appear to have been carved. Today, the lid is displayed as a free-standing monument in the church, outside the pantheon proper.[4] Originally, the tomb may have been positioned so that the visitor could walk around it, since the images are oriented in different directions and most easily legible from their respective sides.[5] The esteem in which Blanca and her memorial were held is attested to by the fact that this lid survived a sixteenth-century reconstruction of the pantheon; as part of that project Blanca and other members of the Navarrese royal family were provided with new tombs and effigies.[6] The lid of Blanca's sarcophagus is the only original element with figural sculpture known to have survived this reconstruction, making it a valuable witness to the quality of the royal tombs of the twelfth century.

The story of Doña Blanca

Doña Blanca Garcés was an infanta, or princess, of the kingdom of Navarre, a crucial link in the power structure of Christian Spain in the eleventh and twelfth centuries. Nájera was an early capital of that state, and the residence of the Navarrese kings. In 1151, Blanca became the wife of Sancho III el Deseado (the Beloved).[7] The two reigned briefly as King and Queen of Castile, so designated by Sancho's father, Alfonso VII, Emperor of Castile and León. With her husband, Blanca confirmed royal documents, a traditional role for Spanish queens, and therefore the movements of the couple can be traced during the years 1151–5.[8] An unknown number of infants were born to Blanca and Sancho, but they died and were buried in the church of San Pedro in Soria. Their only surviving child, a son named Alfonso, was born on 11 November 1155.[9] After the last day of December 1155, Blanca ceased to confirm documents; she is not even mentioned in a document of 29 July 1156. Her death date is recorded as 12 August 1156, in the *Anales Compostelanos*.[10] At the end of the month, Sancho made a donation to the monastery of Santa María la Real in Nájera, where he had his wife buried.[11] Apparently, as her disappearance from the royal documents suggests, she died as a result of complications after Alfonso's birth. Because of the long period of illness that the Queen suffered, it has been suggested that she died of a subsequent miscarriage; documents, however, do not support this.[12] Her death was recorded in a lost epitaph once inscribed on her tomb; the verses praise Blanca, stricken down in childbirth when she brought forth a noble son.[13] The text of the epitaph suggests that the child survived, pointing to the birth of Alfonso as the crucial event. Sadly, Alfonso was left an orphan before reaching the age of three; his father died of unspecified causes in 1158.[14]

The preservation of Blanca's memory and of her tomb is probably due to the fact that her son, who went on to become Alfonso VIII el Noble (the Noble) of Castile, was one of the great kings of medieval Spain; he decisively weakened the Muslim hold on the Peninsula. Among his progeny, Blanca's grandchildren, can be counted not only Spanish kings, but Blanche of Castile, mother of the Capetian King and saint, Louis VII. As the seventeenth-century historian Yepes stated, Blanca 'was so fortunate in her [single] offspring . . . that from her descend a number of kings whom we see today in Europe.'[15] Other historians of the sixteenth and early seventeenth centuries swore devotion to the young Queen in their writings, probably because she was viewed as a significant maternal figure in Spanish history. In part, they seem inspired by her husband's expression of grief in documents and on her tomb.[16] The affective quality of the tomb's carving is such that the scenes of Blanca's death and Sancho's grief were reproduced in Julio González's 1960 history of the reign of Alfonso VIII.[17] Blanca stands, therefore, as a romantic figure to the historians of the past, while the expressive quality of her tomb remains a source of fascination to the viewer of today.

Sepulchral imagery for women from the tenth to the twelfth centuries

The designer of the sarcophagus interwove an evocative combination of images of maternity, martyrdom and salvation to commemorate the royal mother. On one side, in the lower register, is the scene of Blanca's death surrounded by mourning members of the royal court (Fig. 2.1). Angels lift the Queen's soul, in the form of a newborn child, over her body. In the upper register is Christ in Majesty flanked by the symbols of the four Evangelists and the Apostles in a row; the last Apostle on the right is now missing. On the other side, in the lower register, are three scenes: from left to right, the Adoration of the Magi (damaged); the Judgment of Solomon; and the Massacre of the Innocents (Fig. 2.2). Above, the Wise and Foolish Virgins process toward the Bridegroom between two doors; again, a figure is missing, that of the fifth Wise Virgin. To the right of the five Foolish Virgins, two women embrace before an arched doorway, possibly Mary and Elizabeth at the Visitation. On the short end between the Massacre of the Innocents and the mourning women of the court, are the fragmentary remains of a Descent from the Cross (Fig. 2.3).[18] The relief at the other end has been completely cut off, as evidenced by the missing figures; the lost scene was possibly either an Annunciation or a Coronation of the Virgin, such as appear on later tombs.[19] The lid, with its gabled roof, friezelike arrangement, and flattened figures with projecting heads not only utilizes the traditional house-sarcophagus form, but also resembles reliquary caskets – for example, an ivory casket now in the Pitcairn Collection, or the reliquary of Saint Emilian, now divided among several collections.[20] It is particularly close to the twelfth-century altar frontal of Santo Domingo de Silos. The utilization of a form associated with saints may have been intentional, since, by dying in childbirth, Blanca achieved a type of martyrdom.[21] Her sarcophagus, a striking evocation of a shrine, serves to sanctify her memory.

The extent to which Blanca's sarcophagus developed a specifically feminine imagery for its occupant may be best appreciated by comparison with tombs designed for other aristocratic women in the Iberian Peninsula between the tenth and twelfth centuries. In the Peninsula, as elsewhere, aristocrats frequently used sarcophagi of Late Antiquity for their tombs, and the custom often appears intended to lend an aura of antiquity, continuity, and legitimacy to the political position of the tombs' new occupants.[22] One example is the tomb of Doña Sancha, wife of the tenth-century founder of the County of Castile, Fernán González. Now in the collegiate church of Covarrubias, the third-century sarcophagus is decorated with pastoral scenes flanking a clipeus with portraits of the tomb's original occupants – a couple – over a personification of the world. This particular sarcophagus might have been selected to express the dominion of Sancha and Fernán González over the newly formed political entity of Castile. A contemporary lid decorated with rich ornamental foliage was placed on top of the sarcophagus, suggesting that its reuse was purposeful and not necessarily due to lack of skill on the part of contemporary artists. Although the tomb is that of Sancha alone, it is interesting to note that the antique sarcophagus selected for her depicts a couple; her identity is that of spouse.

One of the best-known Spanish tombs of the early twelfth century is identified with another Doña Sancha (†1096), daughter of King Ramiro I of Aragón (Fig. 2.4).[23] Sancha was originally buried in the convent of Santa Cruz de la Serós, together with her sisters, Urraca and Teresa. In the seventeenth century, the sarcophagus was transferred to the nuns' new convent in Jaca, where it remains today. The sarcophagus of Doña Sancha in Jaca is an example of developing Spanish traditions in tomb decoration, some of which come into play in the sarcophagus of Blanca of Navarre. First, Sancha's soul, at the center of the relief, is depicted as a nude child (eidolon), standing in a mandorla, which is supported by angels in her ascent to heaven. Second, the rituals of her funeral are depicted at the left: a bishop with a crozier gives a blessing with his right hand; he is flanked by two clerics, one with a censer and incense boat, the other with an open book. Third, the deceased and her family are identified at the right, where three women are represented – a central figure flanked by two smaller ones. While some have described the three as mourners, they are not in attitudes of lament.[24] This is most likely the trio of sisters who were eventually buried in the chapel that they built at Santa Cruz de la Serós. On the face of the sarcophagus, therefore, the aristocratic status of the tomb's occupant and the female line of her family are commemorated. The images leave little doubt about her rank in earthly society and the expectation of her salvation. On the reverse and ends, however, the imagery is not gender specific. There are scenes of combat on the reverse: two knights on horseback and a man wrestling with a lion – either Samson or David.[25] These battles are usually read as a combat between virtue and vice, possibly alluding to the wars of the Reconquest. At the ends, griffins and a chrismon reiterate the theme of everlasting life and Christian salvation. Thus, the Jaca sarcophagus, while specifying the female identity of its occupant, does not develop a particularly feminized approach to its religious imagery. Nor, apparently, did the imagery of another aristocratic woman's sarcophagus, that of Elvira (†1135), daughter of Alfonso VI. Her tomb is known to us only through historians such as Sandoval, who described it as 'magnificent' and decorated with reliefs of Christ and his Apostles holding books.[26] These figures may have provided an important precedent for the same group that was carved on Blanca's tomb, but the subject matter was by no means specific to a woman.

What remains of Blanca's tomb in Nájera, however, is gender specific, and has a visual unity that ties the various scenes and levels of the lid into a cohesive entity. The surviving reliefs express the grief of the court and the expectation of Blanca's entry into heaven. On the reverse of the lid, the representation of biblical episodes concerning women leaves no doubt about the gender of the tomb's occupant and the role she played on earth. As with the sarcophagus of Sancha in Jaca, Blanca's identity and family ties are made clear. She and Sancho, as well perhaps as other members of the court, were identified by inscriptions on the band below their feet; hers, still legible, reads REGINA DONA BLANCA (Fig. 2.5).[27] Blanca's tomb also represents events following her death, but rather than the funeral, the reliefs depict members of her family and court mourning her loss (Fig. 2.6). So far as can be determined from surviving monuments, the theme of lamentation was not yet as widespread as it would eventually become in Spanish tomb sculpture. Its appearance on the Queen's tomb, however, is indicative of a trend toward greater specificity in the representation of individual grief in the funerary arts.

Sancho's lament and the rebirth of his Queen

There are a few earlier representations of obsequies and mourning on Hispanic tombs, one being that of Sancha in Jaca, as we have already seen, and
another, that of Blanca's uncle Ramón Berenguer III (†1131), Count of Barcelona, buried in Ripoll.[28] Among the surviving fragments of his biographical
sarcophagus are framed scenes of his soul being transported to heaven and
of his funeral – with priests and coffin – all treated with visual balance,
dignity, and emotional restraint. A different modality is employed for Blanca's
monument. Sancho's grief, carved so vividly on his wife's tomb, is an illustration of an ancient Spanish custom: *faciendo el llanto*, or 'making lament.'
Although few earlier representations survive, it is clear that Sancho was
following established tradition in life, if not also in art, when he had himself
depicted swooning with grief; the practice of open and vocal lament on the
death of a loved one was by 1156 a centuries-old custom. For example, a
chronicler described how, at the funeral of Alfonso VI in 1109, men tore their
hair and ripped their clothes, while women scratched their faces and shrieked
to the high heavens.[29] As far back as 589, in the Third Council of Toledo, and
again in the seventh-century writings of Isidore of Seville, Spanish church-
men had expressed their doubts about the dignity of such dramatic mourning.[30] In the context of Mediterranean culture, the practice is not surprising.
Both mourners and funerary rituals appear in Greek, Roman, and Byzantine
art, so that the practice and its expression in the arts of the Iberian Peninsula
are examples of cultural continuity.[31] In medieval Spain, authors such as
Isidore of Seville were fully aware of the ancient origins of their contemporary practices: Isidore traces Spanish funerary lamentation back to the biblical
lament of Jeremiah and to the Greek lyric poet Simonedes.[32]

One indicator that the lament was already part of the vocabulary of tomb
sculpture in the Iberian Peninsula is the sarcophagus of Count Egas Moniz
(†1144; Fig. 2.7).[33] His tomb, in Paço de Sousa, Portugal, depicts the funeral
ceremony and ritual lamentation by women. As his bloated body is placed
on a funeral bier, a bishop says prayers over him, and weeping women beat
their breasts and tear their hair. Their gestures correspond to those in lamentations of Late Antiquity, such as those of the mourners in the miniature
representing the Death of Dido in the Vatican Virgil, and to those of the
female mourners on Blanca's sarcophagus.[34] In a review of mourning scenes
on Greek vases, Christine Mitchell Havelock noted gender distinctions in
their representation: it is women who openly express their grief, for it is they
who traditionally perform the ritual *threnos*, or lamentation; men are more
contained, albeit intense, as they bid their friends farewell.[35] Plato, in describing the death of Socrates, distinguishes between female weeping and more
restrained behavior; but as pointed out by Havelock (and as evidenced by

Alfonso VI's funeral), his was not the popular attitude. That attitude, how-ever, is only occasionally made available to us in the visual arts, particularly in the early Middle Ages.[36] One example from Antiquity is the Roman tomb of the Haterii, on which both male and female mourners beat their breasts to express their grief.[37] On Spanish Gothic tombs, men are sometimes shown being supported by their companions at the funeral, and extravagant dis-plays of emotion by both sexes are frequent on thirteenth- and fourteenth-century sarcophagi such as that of Doña Leonor Ruiz de Castro in Villalcázar de Sirga.[38] Rarely is a man shown fainting, however, as is the case with Sancho.[39]

It is clear that the sculptor of Blanca's sarcophagus drew upon a number of sources, some predictable, others innovative and certainly congruent with the societal ideals of the time. The image of Sancho as he faints appears within the context of what would be a traditional gathering of mourners around the Queen's deathbed. The process of dying was fairly public during the Middle Ages, and included such gatherings of family, members of the court, and mourners in the death chamber.[40] Sancho's grief goes beyond the ritual lamentation expected of him; his pose easily distinguishes him from the other members of the court. Among the mourning men, to the far right of the sarcophagus, the fragmentary figure of a courtier can still be seen to be raising his hand to his luxuriant beard, a traditional gesture of strong emo-tion and defeat.[41] He is being restrained from tearing his beard by another courtier. More dramatically, the King is shown fainting: eyes closed, arms extended, cape flung back, supported by his courtiers. His figure and the group surrounding him are paralleled by the group of mourning women to the left, but the female figure that functions as Sancho's double only weeps; she does not faint. It may be that the designer of the relief devised the striking scene of the King fainting from grief to distinguish his spontaneous behavior from the formulaic laments of professional mourners. Philippe Ariès pointed out that, despite the customary obligation of lamentation, in litera-ture these scenes are not presented as rites but as the spontaneous, personal expression of grief.[42] This principle may apply as well to the relief, for tradi-tional societies often utilize ritual as a means to channel individual emotion.

Sancho's pose is reminiscent of that of a suffering or dying hero in both Christian and classical art. An easily available prototype could be found on many Early Christian sarcophagi visible during the twelfth century: the Arrest of Peter.[43] On these sarcophagi, in which a single row of figures fills the field from top to bottom, Peter often appears with arms extended down-ward, held on either side by soldiers. One such example, formerly in Astorga Cathedral, could even have been considered an appropriate model for a royal tomb; according to tradition, it may have been used briefly as the tomb of Alfonso III.[44] The scene of Peter's arrest forms part of the story of his martyrdom. Interestingly, the same pose appears in the early twelfth-century Byzantine fresco of the Forty Martyrs in Asinou, Cyprus, and in some representations of dying classical heroes.[45] Thus, a pictorial type for a hero about to die was secularized to represent the grieving King. The implication for Sancho is that his life seemed to end with the loss of his beloved.

In fact, Sancho's lament represents continuity with tradition as much as does the female *threnos*, but more examples of this type of behavior can be found in literature than in the visual arts, in the ancient traditions for lamentation indicated by Isidore of Seville.[46] Free, open weeping, groaning, and wailing accompany the prophet Jeremiah's lamentation for his people, for example. Beyond the sources cited by Isidore, many examples of lamentation by heroes abound in biblical and classical literature. In Homer's *Iliad*, the warrior Achilles fell to the earth and tore his hair as he mourned the death of Patroklos.[47] Similar expressions of deep, almost uncontrollable grief occur in many Greek and Roman tragedies.

Although this emotional model for masculine behavior is frequently encountered in the chivalric literature of the twelfth century, at the time of Blanca's death it occurs most often in the lamentation of one hero for another.[48] Heroic lament forms a central part of the *Chanson de Roland*, for example, in which Charlemagne and his men faint with grief on learning of Roland's death.[49] The image on the tomb elevates Sancho and his loss to the level of legendary warriors and kings such as Charlemagne. In courtly literature examples of a man's lament for a beloved woman can be found, but the texts do not necessarily constitute precedents for the tomb imagery. One such example is Chrétien de Troyes's romance *Cligès*, written around 1176 and therefore slightly later than Blanca's tomb.[50] In *Cligès*, the Emperor Alis falls unconscious to the floor when the court doctors predict that his wife, Fénice, will die before the day is out. After her feigned death, her lover, Cligès, unsure of whether she is dead or alive, 'suffers and laments more than all the others do, and it is strange he does not kill himself.'[51] The exaltation of the grief of separation is an essential element in the expression of romantic love, a concept celebrated in courtly literature.[52] The relief depicting Sancho's lament vividly represents the grief of a bereaved husband in much the same terms as in *Cligès*; it is an early expression in the visual arts of the passionate grief that may be felt by the characters in epic and courtly literature.

Sancho's lamentation, therefore, is at once profoundly traditional and contemporary in its expression. Both Chrétien de Troyes and the Spanish sculptor of the sarcophagus must have relied on a shared well of experience that included oral narrative and cultural conventions in the creation of their mourning scenes.[53] Castilian royalty was in direct contact with court poets from the north, which would have enabled the sharing of such new forms as they developed. William X, son of the Aquitainian poet, died while visiting his cousin Alfonso VII in 1137, and at least one French troubadour, Marcabrú, passed through Alfonso's court.[54] When the tomb was designed, Sancho, his theological adviser, and the artist appear to have been aware not only of the heroic lament in secular and religious literature, but also of mourning scenes in the visual arts, and poses appropriate for a mourning or dying hero.

In addition, the tomb image may share some of the more subtle commemorative functions of *chansons de geste*. Eugene Vance suggested that the *Song of Roland* may be understood as a drama of memory, in which there is a cognitive congruence between the actors of the drama and those who will celebrate them in song later.[55] Roland and Charlemagne exhibit a consciousness that their feats will be sung by future poets; mindful that they will be remembered in this way, they measure their actions accordingly. An analogous function might be posited for the image of Sancho's lament on Blanca's tomb. Sancho chose to represent himself and his court in the throes of their epic grief. This lamentation is reenacted in perpetuity on the sarcophagus, thus preserving the history and memory of this Queen and King. The sculptor's acknowledgment of the future audience for the drama of Blanca and Sancho is clearly stated in the deathbed scene, where angels hold Blanca's soul, the eidolon. One angel and the eidolon look directly out at the spectator, confident in their ability to catch the future viewer's attention. Thus, these figures gesture toward posterity in the same way that Roland exhorts his men to become celebrated heroes through their actions.

The tomb's imagery is richly suggestive of the circumstances of Blanca's death and the care of her soul in its afterlife. The lamentation, as we shall see, plays an important part in this concern with her life after death. On one side of the lid, in the center of the lower register, the Queen is shown, eyes closed, on her deathbed. The bed is flanked by two angels who lift a small, nude, wide-awake eidolon over her body. Within the traditions of tomb sculpture, this eidolon conforms to the established image – the soul as a newborn child. However, the sculptor utilized the circumstances of Blanca's demise to manipulate the image so as to make transparent the complex relationship between birth, death, and rebirth. The way in which the angels tenderly support the eidolon's back and legs, holding its undraped figure over Blanca's body, easily suggests a birth scene and the act of lifting the newborn over its mother.[56]

A viewer need not know Blanca's story in order to understand the events being played out on this relief; my own response upon seeing the lid for the first time was that it was surely the tomb of a woman who had died in childbirth. The newborn is being displayed for approval to the spectator: the angel on the right and the eidolon look directly at us, engaging us in the memory of that earthly drama of childbirth and death. Furthermore, the newborn is also being displayed by the angel-midwives to Christ in Majesty in the register above.[57] The double role of the figure of the infant, both as the human newborn and as the eidolon of its mother, is clearly articulated by glance, gesture, and compositional grouping. The blurring of distinction between the process of life on earth and the progression of the soul's ascent to heaven is manifestly intended, because the pose of Blanca's eidolon is not completely traditional. As we have already seen in the sarcophagus of Doña Sancha in Jaca, the eidolon may be depicted standing in a mandorla, rising into Heaven, or as a head, half-figure, or even full body in a cloth lifted up by angels.[58] Another alternative was to show the soul being exhaled by the body, as in the sarcophagus of Egas Moniz. In all these examples, the presentation of the eidolon as the essence exclusively of the deceased is unambiguous, unlike its treatment in Blanca's sarcophagus. Here, composition and gesture charge the episode with multiple meanings. The scene simultaneously signifies the birth of her son, her death, and the rebirth of her soul as it goes to Heaven.

The angels lifting Blanca's soul up to the enthroned Christ provide a link between the dramatic lamentation scene in which the earthly actors mourn in groups, and the orderly, celestial college of Apostles above. In fact, the closely linked scenes were perhaps meant to stem possible criticisms of the lamentation. Patristic authors often pointed out that excessive grief on the death of a loved one suggested doubt concerning the resurrection.[59] On the other hand, grief as a means to express the pain of separation was deemed natural by Church Fathers. John Chrysostom, in a homily, counseled, 'Weep, but gently, but with decorum . . . If you were to weep thus, you would not weep as one who distrusts the Resurrection, but as one who cannot bear being separated.'[60] The composition of Blanca's deathbed scene closely parallels that of the Dormition of the Virgin, traditional in Byzantine art and known in the West, and a scene in which men openly and dramatically grieve the death of a woman. Because of the visual analogy to the Virgin's Dormition, a female triumph over death, the representation of Blanca's demise and Sancho's lamentation appears to affirm the King's belief in the Christian doctrine of resurrection. In fact, lamentation was encouraged by authors such as Ambrose, who believed that lamentation and prayer were efficacious in achieving salvation: 'If the tears of a few widows could obtain for Tabitha the return to life, the tears of an entire city could certainly touch the heart of Christ for the salvation of our departed loved one and acquire for him the patronage of the Apostles.'[61] The juxtaposition of Blanca's deathbed, the lament of her husband and court, and Christ in Majesty flanked by his Apostles, seems to illustrate Ambrose's words.

Furthermore, the assumption of Blanca's soul in the sight of Christ in Majesty and the Apostles may reflect the words of the liturgical response said at the moment of death, when the soul leaves the body, and with which a burial service traditionally begins, the 'Subvenite': 'Come to her aid, O saints of God, hasten to meet her, angels of the Lord: raising up her soul, offering it within sight of the Most High.'[62] The richly suggestive visual imagery of the relief may even have been inspired by this response. The verb *suscipere*, used to describe the angels' receiving the soul to offer it to God, is also used to describe the action of taking a newborn from the ground and so acknowledging it, or even simply to have a child.[63] Surely the designer of Blanca's sarcophagus was aware of these layers of meaning in the word, and they have been effectively rendered in the image. Thus, the memory of the circumstances of Blanca's death, the birth of her son, the ritual of her burial, and her soul's triumphant ascent to Heaven were all given one locus in this scene on the front of the sarcophagus lid.

The image also sets the stage for the soul's judgment, as described in the New Testament and in the rites for the dead. Traditional Christian belief held that the soul ascended to Heaven at the moment of death, and would be judged upon the resurrection of the body on the Last Day, after which the elect will reside with God in eternity, ideas expressed in the 'Subvenite.'[64] The sarcophagus artist conflated these two moments by linking the deathbed scene with that of the soul, in bodily form, ascending to Christ in Majesty above. Christ enthroned, surrounded by the symbols of his Evangelists, was a familiar evocation of the vision of John as he described the judge on the Last Day (Apoc. 4.2–8, 5.1, 20.12).[65] On the lid, the Apocalyptic Christ holds open a book, the Book of Life that plays an important role in the Last Judgment. Paul also described the Book of Life in his Epistle to the Philippians, 4.3: 'And I entreat thee also . . . help those women who have laboured with me in the gospel . . . and with the rest of my fellow labourers, whose names are in the book of life.'

A Christian's longing for salvation may be articulated in the hope that his or her name will be written in the Book of Life, as Paul and the Apocalypse make clear (Apoc. 3.5, 13.8, 17.8). For those with means, this was not an abstract wish: Early Christians had their names inscribed on ivory diptychs, which resemble books, to be read by the clergy at memorial services after their deaths.[66] Since 1063, Cluniacs had been similarly ministering to the souls of the kings buried in Nájera, a relationship evoked by the image of Christ and his Apostles receiving Blanca's eidolon.[67] Those individuals, living or dead, who were privileged with membership in Cluniac confraternities (as were the royalty of Navarre and Castile) had their names inscribed in memorial books, called *libri vitae* or *libri memoriales*, so that they would be remembered during liturgical services at Cluny. As the heavenly clergy, the Apostles holding books and scrolls appear to enact this Cluniac practice.[68] The relief's *libri vitae* seem to express the hope that Blanca's name would be among those written in the heavenly Book of Life, as, indeed, her name is inscribed below her figure.

The Cluniac dimension of this image is substantiated by the location of Blanca's burial at Santa María la Real in Nájera, for which the tomb was designed. Blanca was a member of two royal families with long-standing ties to Cluny; she was buried in a Cluniac monastery, and some of the donations for the care of her soul and tomb were recorded both in Nájera and in Cluny.

To understand the historical context of Blanca's burial place requires a brief exploration of the tangled relationships between the Hispanic kings and the monastery of Cluny. The Queen's burial in Nájera served, in part, to confirm Castilian claims to Navarre, and Cluniac rights over the monastery itself.

Blanca was a direct descendant of Sancho el Mayor (the Great), who brought Cluniac monasticism to Navarre, Aragón and Castile around 1025, and who was rewarded with the status of *socius* of Cluny, thus sharing in the monks' prayers for their benefactors.[69] Blanca's husband, Sancho III of Castile, also a descendant of Sancho el Mayor, was the heir of a family that received privileged liturgical intercession at Cluny, thanks to the munificence of Fernando I of Castile and León (1038–65) and his son, Alfonso VI (1066–1109).[70] In his 1077 donation charter to Cluny, Alfonso VI had specified that the spiritual benefits he sought were to be extended to all kinsmen who might come after him to the throne, the 'reges Hispaniorum.'[71] In addition, there was a collect to be recited 'pro regina Hispaniorum et pro sororibus et aliis feminis familiaribus' (for the Queen of the Spains, and her sisters and all her female relatives).[72]

The monastery of Nájera embodied the various relationships of the Navarrese and Castilian monarchs with the Burgundian abbey. Santa María la Real and its royal pantheon were founded in 1052 by Blanca's great-grandfather, King García III, after he had a vision on the site; García's own close relationship to Cluny is known from his surviving correspondence with abbot Odilo (†1048).[73] In 1063, at the King's request, Abbot Hugh the Great (1049–1109) sent a prior and other monks to administer Santa María; the rest of the community were from local monasteries.[74] At that time, García made Santa María an episcopal seat: as was the case with many foundations housing royal pantheons, the monastery was subject to Rome.[75] The situation changed under the Castilian Alfonso VI, whose dominion, after 1076, extended through parts of Navarre, including Nájera.[76] On the urging of his wife, Constance of Burgundy, Abbot Hugh's niece, Alfonso VI gave Santa María to Cluny in 1079.[77] Yepes suggests that not only was Alfonso's devotion to Cluny involved, but also his assertion of power over the region of La Rioja. What better way than submitting the defeated kings' pantheon to his ally, Cluny? In the donation he specified that the monastery of Nájera belonged to him; thus, it was his to give. From then on, the priors of Santa María were selected and sent by the abbots of Cluny, and eventually a relic of Hugh the Great – his arm – went to Nájera.[78]

It was Blanca's father-in-law, Alfonso VII, who negotiated a reduction of Alfonso VI's annual contribution to Cluny, but he recalled his family obligations to the Cluniacs in a donation to the monks of Nájera in 1149. There, he asked that special mention be made of himself and his parents in the monks' daily prayers.[79] Thus, the souls of the Castilian as well as the Navarrese kings were remembered by the monks of Nájera. To consolidate the relationship, in 1155, two weeks after Blanca gave birth, Alfonso VII, his wife Rica, and his sons Sancho and Fernando, confirmed for the prior and monastery that everything originally bestowed on them by the founder, King García, was theirs.[80] When Blanca died and Sancho had her buried in Nájera, he made a gift of the church of Santa María in Santoño which was described as a donation 'to God, blessed Mary of Nájera, Saint Peter the Apostle of the Monastery of Cluny, and to you Raymond, Prior of this church [of Nájera] and to all your successors, and to the monks who there serve God, blessed Mary, and Saint Peter . . . for the remedy of my soul and that of my wife, the venerable Queen Blanca, whom I had buried in the church of Nájera.'[81] A copy of this donation was filed in Cluny itself.[82]

Blanca's burial in her family pantheon in Nájera, therefore, fulfilled many functions. The institutional interests of Cluny and Nájera were clearly being served by the emphatic repetition of the names of Saint Peter and Cluny in the donation. The dynastic interests of the kings of Navarre were served, as well as those of the Castilians, who thereby consolidated their claims to Navarre. Sancho even named the Navarrese King García as his ancestor in the donation, something he could legitimately do. Finally, the memorial to his wife is arranged by a bereaved husband. Immediately after his signature, he charges the prior with the responsibility of keeping her tomb perpetually illuminated. Sancho's sincere sense of loss can be seen in that charge, and in another donation he made in 1158 to the house of Nájera, 'where I had my wife buried, so that the memory of our anniversary when we were forever joined in one would be perpetually celebrated.' During the seventeenth century, this anniversary was still being celebrated.[83]

In many ways, the sarcophagus image functions like the texts of Sancho's donations: by presenting her eidolon before Christ and his Apostles, the image represents a prayer for Blanca's soul through the intercession of the monastic community, suggested by the Apostles on the relief, and through the prayers of visitors to the royal pantheon. Honorius Augustodunensis commented on just this function of tombs: '[the dead] benefit from the prayers said by their relatives when they come to these places and when the tombs call to their minds the memory of the deceased.'[84] Sancho's concern was as much for his own soul as for hers. In return for his prayers, Blanca, once in heaven, could play a role in assuring her husband's salvation. A text attributed to Augustine the priest, found in the Silos *Beatus*, reads: 'For the dead, in so far as they are commended to God, can pray and intercede for the living. For everyone should believe it to be true that the souls of the dead have the same efficacy for the salvation of the living, as those of the living have for the peaceful rest of the dead.'[85]

Feminized imagery on the sarcophagus of Blanca

While the front of the sarcophagus identifies the deceased, the circumstances of her death, and the hope for her salvation, the balance of the sarcophagus is carved with a sequence of biblical scenes referring to judgment and salvation. The personal tone developed for the deathbed scene was maintained for the selection of these scenes, for they are all episodes in which women play a major role. Most of the imagery on the lower register of the reverse is given over to events narrated in the gospel of Matthew: below, the Adoration of the Magi and the Massacre of the Innocents are represented, with the interpolation of the Judgment of Solomon at the center, a point to which I shall return. The stories involving mothers and children articulate an appreciation of the sacrifice involved in maternity and the protective role that a mother should assume.[86]

At the left, Mary and the Child receive homage from the Three Kings. The image, appropriate to the regal status of the tomb's occupant, could have served as an affirmation of the faith and social status of the royal family, while the divine Child as a personification of wisdom offered them a model for the good ruler. In addition, one can speculate that, had Blanca participated in court rituals involving the presentation of her son, the ceremonies might have resembled these Epiphany scenes.

At the right of the lid, the Massacre of the Innocents is depicted, but without the evil King Herod. As one soldier seizes a newborn in its swaddling clothes, another decapitates an older boy; they are positioned over a jumble of body parts, the remains of at least two other children. Three mourning mothers appear to the right. The one closest to the soldiers, eyes wide with horror, wrings her hands helplessly. The other two turn toward each other, incline their heads, and raise their covered hands toward their faces. The three mothers provide a visual counterpoint for the Three Kings, who walk away from the center and toward the Virgin and Child at the left end of the lid. The mothers' grief may be contrasted with the kings' joy at finding the Messiah. And the loss of their children presages the martyrdom of Christ.

That theological link is made visible by the sequence of scenes on the sarcophagus. The mourning mothers appear to have formed a continuous group that once melded with the scene of the Descent from the Cross, carved on the short end of the lid. The fragmentary remains of this image resemble the Depositions in the cloisters of Silos and Pamplona Cathedral, as well as the tympanum of the Puerta del Perdón of the royal church of San Isidoro in León. In all these examples, angels hover over the Cross as they mourn the death of Christ. Below, Nicodemus removes the nail from Jesus' hand, and Joseph of Arimathea supports the weight of his body as he is removed from the Cross. To the left, Mary takes her dead son's hand and tenderly holds it to her cheek. On the sarcophagus, fragments of an angel, the arms of the Cross, Christ's head, and parts of the heads of Mary and Joseph of Arimathea can still be made out. When the scene was intact, the mourning mothers of the Innocents would have joined Mary as she mourns the dead Christ, all of them accepting the martyrdom of their sons. The frieze progresses from the mourning mothers on one side of the sarcophagus lid to the female mourners at Blanca's deathbed (Fig. 2.3). Thus, the union of individual with biblical history was achieved in the sculpture. The association between a person's own history and the biblical past was an essential element in the minds of the Christian faithful, and this tomb provides a clearly articulated example of how that cognitive process worked.[87] The relief makes apparent the likeness between mourners at the deathbed of a Queen and mourning mothers of the Bible, rendering both with equal immediacy. The perceptive viewer's imagination is thereby directed toward the congruence between these acts of mourning, and perhaps also to the gradations of pain and sacrifice in motherhood.

That congruence extends as well to the theological links between scenes on the lower register of the lid's reverse. According to Gertrud Schiller, the pairing of the Adoration of the Magi with the Massacre of the Innocents was a device intended to contrast the true Christian King with the false pagan.[88] The combination of the Adoration of the Magi with the Massacre of the Innocents has a foundation that is not only ideological, as Schiller suggests, but also liturgical and temporal. The celebration of the two events forms part of the observances of the Christmas season, the events surrounding Christ's birth and infancy. In the Roman liturgy, followed by the Cluniacs, the Innocents were celebrated on December 28 and Epiphany on January 6. In the old Hispanic liturgy these two events were commemorated only two days apart, the Epiphany on January 6 and the Innocents on January 8.[89] The close relationship between the two events – the fact that the Massacre was triggered by the Magi's search for the Child – is also manifested in the pairing of the Epiphany and the Massacre of the Innocents on some Early Christian sarcophagi, as on Blanca's tomb.[90] In a series of sermons written for the feast day of the Innocents, Augustine comments that they were born to be sacrificed for Christ, that in being so sacrificed they died innocent, and were 'born happily into life; they went straight from infants' cradles to [martyrs'] crowns.'[91] As he develops the theme of martyrdom in the three sermons, Augustine describes Herod as foolish, and foretells how he will suffer on Judgment Day; how the just will be separated from the wicked; and how they will be rewarded, like the Innocents.[92]

On the sarcophagus, the representation of the Massacre without Herod shifts the emphasis of the episode away from the evil that he would represent and toward the concept of salvation. While Herod's presence is implicit, and the result of his behavior explicit, the visual focus is on the death of the Innocents and on mourning. As pointed out by Henry Maguire, the episode of the Massacre of the Innocents was one place in which violent gestures of grief were considered appropriate, even by the Church Fathers.[93] Augustine and others provide lurid descriptions of the mothers' struggle for their children, and their lamentation over their loss, making of these mothers models of behavior imitable by the average person. The scene of the mothers grieving for their dead children alludes to the grief of the court on the other side, and suggests that Blanca's death was also a sacrifice. In Blanca's case, the mother and martyr are one and the same. As we have seen, the linkage between the scenes, biblical and contemporary, is not merely allusive, but rendered visually by the mourning women who unify the Massacre with the Deposition and ultimately Blanca's deathbed. The implication for her soul is that, like the martyred innocents, she too will be redeemed through Christ's sacrifice on the Cross.[94]

Between the Adoration of the Magi and the Massacre of the Innocents, the discourse on wisdom, judgment, and salvation is brought together in the person of King Solomon. He is shown making the judgment between the two mothers who claimed the same child after the infant of one of them had died. The identification of this scene as the Judgment of Solomon is not immediately obvious because there has been an intentional blurring of lines with the Massacre of the Innocents; where one would expect to see Herod directing his soldiers in the massacre, there are an enthroned king, a pleading woman, a man holding a sword over two infants, and another woman looking on.[95] The figures' gestures and actions, however, correspond to Solomon's story as narrated, with variants, in the Bible, in Josephus' *History of the Jews*, and in Patristic texts by authors such as Augustine and Isidore of Seville.[96] Although visual representations of this scene vary, a related composition is used on a ninth-century Visigothic ivory now in the Pitcairn collection.[97] At the center of the sarcophagus, Solomon is enthroned and holds a sceptre in his left hand while he places his right hand on the head of a kneeling woman; she takes the hem of his robe into her hands and appears to be pleading with him. His gesture suggests approval. It is, in fact, a gesture loaded with multiple meanings. The placing of hands on someone's head may be a gesture of blessing, but it also has judicial significance. It is the gesture with which a judge declares a defendant innocent, or, in the case of the two women, indicates which person has spoken the truth.[98] It is even used in scenes representing the judgment of the dead. Although the Judgment of Solomon is not often included in funerary sculpture, the scene is appropriate here, for it serves as an Old Testament type for the Last Judgment, when the good are separated from the wicked.[99] To the right of the kneeling woman, Solomon appears a second time, identified by his distinctive costume, turban, and beard. As in Isidore of Seville's account, the King himself raises a sword over the bodies of two infants, which he holds by the ankles in order to slice both of them in half.[100] The lying mother has a distinctly nasty expression on her face – her brows are furrowed and she seems to encourage dividing the living child. Augustine and Isidore interpreted the two women as an allegory for Ecclesia, a true mother, and Synagoga, a false and destructive one.[101]

Several compositional devices clarify the relationship of Solomon's judgment with the other episodes depicted on the sarcophagus lid. Parallel groupings are utilized to mark contrasts as well as similarities between the figures. First, the standing Solomon, sword raised, does not kill the child, whereas Herod's soldier next to him brings his sword down to decapitate one of the Innocents. The dishonest mother actively encourages killing the other woman's child, while the Innocent's mother helplessly mourns her own loss. The reversal of the outcome is graphically illustrated by the reversal of poses and facial expression, and the contrast of order with disorder in the composition. Second, the enthroned Solomon is seated in profile, in a pose that echoes the pose of the Christ Child in the damaged Epiphany to the left of the lid. His wisdom in judgment, therefore, parallels that of the Child, who is wisdom incarnate. Finally, the artist has created a sophisticated interlace of ideas by placing the figure of Solomon just under another variant on the theme of judgment, the parable of the Wise and Foolish Virgins.

The parable, which contrasts foresight with foolishness, is a story in which women metaphorically act out the Last Judgment in the form of a wedding ritual. On the sarcophagus, the episode of acceptance or rejection is placed above the sequence of biblical images concerning wisdom, judgment, and salvation, concepts fundamental to the Virgins' story. Christ's parable, recorded in Matt. 25.1–13, uses the simile of ten maidens for the kingdom of heaven, where prudence is rewarded, and imprudence punished. It forms part of a larger description of the Last Judgment. The narrative is based on the ancient custom of a nocturnal procession in which the bridegroom is escorted to the house of his bride by young women carrying torches.[102] The Foolish Virgins, in preparation for the event, bring their lamps but no oil; the Wise ones are more provident. While waiting for the groom, the maidens sleep. When called at midnight to meet the groom, the Foolish Virgins ask the Wise to share their oil, but, as there might not be enough for all, are told to go out and buy their own. The imprudent, unprepared Virgins then return too late, and so are excluded from the ceremony. The parable ends with a warning to be vigilant, 'because you know not the day nor the hour,' of either death or of the Last Judgment. Patristic commentaries describe the oil in the maidens' lamps as the good works done over the course of a lifetime, the means by which the soul gains entry into Heaven; that is why the oil cannot be shared.[103]

Because of the eschatological context of the parable in Matthew's gospel, it was frequently associated with the Last Judgment in art. On church portals and cloister capitals, the parable of the Virgins was often used in the visual discourse on the rewards of virtue and the punishment for imprudence.[104] As early as the fourth century it is found in a funereal context, in the catacombs.[105] Throughout the Early Christian and Early Medieval periods, images and inscriptions referring to the parable appeared on many women's tombs, although scant note has been made of its appropriateness as such. For example, in the fourth-century catacomb of S. Ciriaca, Rome, a female orant accompanied by two men who open the curtains to Paradise appears as part of an ensemble in which Christ accepts the Wise Virgins with their lit lamps and rejects the Foolish ones without their lamps. In the abbey of St-Pierre, Vienne, an inscription compares a deceased sister, Celsa, to the Wise Virgins, coming to the Bridegroom Christ, like them, with her lamp lit.[106] In Jouarre, a Benedictine abbey in northern France, the seventh-century sarcophagus of the founding abbess, Theodechilde, is ornamented with foliage and an inscription, which, summarized, declares: 'Mother of this convent, she invites her daughters, consecrated to God, to hasten to meet the bridegroom, [like] the Prudent Virgins with oil in their lamps.'[107] As Beat Brenk and Joseph Wilpert have noted, the images and inscriptions articulate the hope of the deceased woman to join the Wise Virgins and be admitted to the banquet of everlasting bliss.[108] The use of this subject on Blanca's tomb reflects Early Medieval tradition for women's burials.

Several aspects of the parable conjoin well with the rest of the imagery on Blanca's tomb. As a feminized image of the Last Judgment, the representation of the Virgins flanking the Bridegroom Christ provides an effective counterpoint to the Apocalyptic Christ on the other side. The visual association of the parable with the Judgment on the opposite face is made by means of the resemblance of the orderly row of processing Virgins with that of the Apostles; and also with the centralized, framed, figures of Christ and the Bridegroom, whose features, poses, and gestures parallel one another. The interface between the bridal ritual and the suggestion of death enhances this parallel. The sleep of the Virgins as they await the Bridegroom was commonly understood as a metaphor for death; their awakening, resurrection on the Last

Day.[109] The Virgins' lamps are an essential feature of a wedding procession, but also of a funeral cortège.[110] On the sarcophagus, furthermore, the Wise Virgins, processing with their glowing lamps, figuratively perform the function of keeping the tomb perpetually lit, as Sancho specified to the prior of Nájera in his donation.[111] And although the image of the Virgins was often utilized for nuns, the prudent maidens were not exclusively a metaphor for the celibate women of the convent; they stood, too, for the souls of all Christians, and for conjugal fidelity.[112] The image of female prudence as a fueled lamp occurs in Prov. 31.18, in praise of a good wife. In that respect, Blanca, as wife, could be counted among the Wise Virgins, and the reliefs of her tomb suggest the high value of a good wife and mother.[113] The reference to matrimony and motherhood in this scene is reinforced if one reads the last two figures at the right as Mary and Elizabeth at the Visitation, a reading suggested by the embrace of the two women in front of an arched doorway.[114] Their gesture resembles that in the Visitation on the façade of the monastic church at Leyre (Navarre), not far away. On the sarcophagus lid, a complementary scene might have formed part of the relief cut off to the left of the Wise Virgins. Mary and Elizabeth's state of pregnancy would accord with the rest of the sarcophagus imagery about maternity, and their miraculous conceptions locate them within the theme of selection and judgment articulated by the Virgins with whom they appear. Furthermore, their location above the two mourning mothers of the Innocents and adjacent to the Deposition from the Cross emphasizes the fact that their sons escaped the Massacre but were later martyred.[115]

Just under the Bridegroom, in the register below, is Solomon, who, as the author of the Song of Songs, is also identified as a bridegroom. The two types for Christ the Judge are linked not only by proximity but also by the fruited tree growing behind Solomon's throne, up to the open doorway of the Bridegroom's palace. When Isidore of Seville described Solomon as a prototype for Christ, he noted that Solomon built his palace of wood, while Christ built the house of God in the celestial Jerusalem, a comparison suggested visually by Solomon's tree reaching to the Bridegroom's palace gates.[116] The tree might also suggest the parable of the fig tree (Matt. 24.32–3): just as 'summer is nigh' when the tree puts forth leaves, great signs and wonders will be harbingers of the Last Judgment. As we have seen, the Last Judgment is the central theme of the sarcophagus imagery. Solomon's tree also recalls the two trees that frame Blanca's deathbed; there, the suggestion is of Paradise, salvation, and perhaps the fruitful tree of good (Matt. 7.17–20), an allusion to the Queen's maternity.[117]

The sculptor interwove bridal imagery with images of the Last Judgment both horizontally and vertically on this face of the sarcophagus lid, and in the mind's eye – depending upon the viewer's memory. While the visitor to

the Queen's tomb walks around it, as the orientation of the images suggests
was intended, he sees his own motion reflected in the processions of the
Virgins and of the mourning mothers as they move toward the lamentation
of the court; the viewer is engaged by the angels offering the eidolon for
approval, and is made to comprehend the similarities between the Virgins'
Bridegroom and Christ the Judge. A Visitation situated above the mourning
mothers of the Massacre of the Innocents and the Descent from the Cross
around the corner is a potent reminder of the progress of life into death, and
the role that women play in it. The inclusion of both Solomon and the Parable of the Virgins seems to have been unusual among contemporary tombs;
yet the sarcophagus, by the creative combination of images, provides an
integrated, sensitive invocation of hope for the Queen's salvation.

The twelfth-century *Elucidarium*, attributed to Honorius Augustodunensis,
discusses matrimony and death in ways which illuminate the tomb imagery
for us. First, the author develops an image of death as a celestial wedding
that seems to resonate in the imagery of Blanca's tomb: 'As the bridegroom
comes in procession to find his bride, when the just person dies, her guardian angel comes with a flock of angels and lifts up her soul, the bride of
Christ, away from the prison of the body to lead it with sweet songs to the
immense light and perfumes of the celestial palace in the paradise of the
spirit.'[118] In these phrases, marriage, death, angels as escorts for the soul, and
love for the deceased all form a constellation of images similar to those on
both sides of Blanca's sarcophagus. In addition, when discussing which souls
go directly to heaven, the writer explains: 'Only the souls of the perfect are
taken there . . . The perfect are . . . martyrs, monks, and virgins . . . There is
one category of the just who are imperfect, and who, nevertheless, are inscribed into the book of God: these are married people.'[119] While a direct link
between this text and the reliefs is not demonstrable, what is clear is the
mentality of the age that is manifested in both text and image. Like the
Elucidarium, Blanca's sarcophagus articulates the expectation that a married
woman was valued just as much as the celibate, that she might be among the
saved. The reliefs praise the good works that such a woman might perform
during her life, and they are defined by mother love – a love often compared
to the love that God has for the human race, his children.[120] The reliefs,
therefore, exemplify the Queen's maternal devotion and at the same time
they suggest that her soul is in the care of a yet greater parent or spouse.

We can never know Blanca as a personality, but Sancho's donations and
the individuality of the sculptural program of her tomb suggest that more
than ritual lamentation and commemoration were performed for her. With
their vivid and moving figures, the reliefs demonstrate the ways in which a
tomb can function as mediator between the living and the dead. The creative
imagery of her memorial allows us a glimpse into the relationship between

that twelfth-century husband and wife, the devotion that must have existed between them, and the expectations that he had of her – articulated in contemporary terms. Accordingly, Sancho made of the sarcophagus an epitaph that visually constructs the memory of his beloved Queen as virtuous, prudent, a devoted mother who sacrificed herself for her child. It is of interest to note that, while there are specific models for a king in the wise and regal figures of Solomon, Christ, and the Magi, the models provided for a queen are not defined by their royalty. The models for Blanca and for women receptive to the message of the tomb, are the queenly Virgin Mary, Mother of God and mourner of her son; her virtuous cousin Elizabeth, mother of the martyr John the Baptist; the Wise Virgins, whose lamps are the manifestation of their good works; the honest mother of Solomon's judgment, who is prepared to give up her child so that he might live; and the mourning mothers of the Innocents, who lose their sons unexpectedly and by force. Except for Mary and Elizabeth, the women represented in the reliefs, though noble in their behavior, do not have the status of sainthood.

The imagery of this tomb suggests that twelfth-century attitudes toward women were not as purely misogynistic as is frequently maintained. Contemporary scholarship often posits that a woman, in order to achieve sainthood, must give up her sex or escape her female body, and then extends this concept to exclude all noncelibate women from the approbation of society and church.[121] In this respect the reliefs lauding maternal devotion are a harbinger of the openly expressed appreciation of motherhood that is generally credited to the thirteenth century.[122] However, Jean Leclercq has demonstrated that despite its ideological admiration for virginity, the Church – for practical reasons – has always had to recognize the necessity for marriage and maternity.[123] This very sentiment was expressed by Paul (1 Tim. 2.15): 'Yet she shall be saved through childbearing; if she continue in faith, and love, and sanctification, with sobriety.' Approbation of marriage and motherhood, therefore, has a much longer history in Christian culture than is often recognized. The imagery of the sarcophagus provides, for the twelfth century, the kind of information that is difficult to find: models, not for saintly virgins and cloistered women, but for women in the world.[124] The reliefs suggest the high value of a good wife and mother: she is prudent, honest, and self-sacrificing; her maternal love is like God's love for humankind; she intercedes for her children. The women depicted on the lid of Blanca's sarcophagus do not deny their sex. They perform wisely and as good women, and that is their salvation.

By association with the good and prudent women on her tomb, Blanca was transformed into an ideal.[125] The selection of biblical women who embody a wide range of female experience – from triumph to grief – manifests a clear intent to create a feminized Christian imagery, an imagery appropriate for the virtuous mother who lost her life giving birth to a future king. In addition, the perpetual reenactment of the King's lamentation and the evocation of funerary rites in the sarcophagus reliefs recall the Queen and King to the spectator, and renew the charge to pray for their souls. The effectiveness of the tomb's design ultimately derives from the commemorative culture of the Middle Ages, founded on the Christian theology of memory and memorial rituals. So numinous are the images, particularly of the Queen's death and the King's lament, that they embed themselves in the spectator's mind. For this reason, Spanish historians from the seventeenth century to the present day inevitably pause over the story of Doña Blanca, and even profess a special devotion to her. In that, the carved tomb achieved its objective, and truly represents the victory of memory over oblivion.

Postscript

In order to facilitate references for the reader, in this postscript I include significant additions to the version of this article published in *The Art Bulletin*. That version has additional illustrations: details of the sarcophagus and related monuments.

Karl Werckmeister pointed out to me the resemblance between Sancho's pose and that of Saint Benedict as he dies, his arms supported by his monks. That a Benedictine image provides a close match for the innovative imagery of a sarcophagus made for a Cluniac monastery supports several suggestions I put forth. First, that the Cluniac context may well be a significant factor in the design of the relief. Second, that a classical image for a dying hero was Christianized during the Middle Ages (see n.45). Finally, that secular expressions of grief so strong as to seem that the mourner would die, often described in epic and courtly literature, can be traced, to a large degree, to the representation of saints' lives. A broad selection of deathbed and burial scenes including the eidolon may be found in B. Abou-El-Haj, *The Medieval Cult of Saints: Formations and Transformations*, Cambridge: Cambridge University Press, 1994, pp.347–66, figs 73–106; that of St Benedict is on p.358, fig. 93. The imagery on Blanca's sarcophagus has utilized effectively the ritual language of death and grief to express emotion nonetheless heartfelt. Margarita Ruiz Maldonado has suggested that the sarcophagus of Egas Moniz might be later than 1146, the time of the hero's death (see n.33). Whether or not it is the first, the 1158 sarcophagus of Blanca in Nájera remains one of the earliest surviving examples of *faciendo el llanto* in tomb sculpture.

For the ranking of the married within a moral hierarchy, see D. Iogna-Pratt, 'The Dead in the Celestial Bookkeeping of the Cluniac Monks Around the Year 1000,' in *Debating the Middle Ages*, L. K. Little and B. H. Rosenwein, eds, Oxford: Blackwell Publishers, 1998, p.345. For resurrection imagined as a fruitful tree (as on p.61), see C. W. Bynum, *The Resurrection of the Body in Western Christianity, 200–1336*, New York: Columbia University Press, 1995, pp.24–5.

To produce the hypothetical reconstruction of the Deposition from the Cross, I combined figures from extant examples with others from the sarcophagus. In the Deposition on the capital from the cloister of Pamplona (Navarre), Mary is supported by another figure below the Cross: see P. de Palol, *Early Medieval Art in Spain*, translated by A. Jaffa, London: Thames and Hudson, 1967, plate 141. I have suggested something similar for the fragmentary sarcophagus reliefs because the field available for figures suggests three figures on either side of Christ.

Frequently cited sources

Alvarez-Coca, M. J., *Escultura románica en piedra en La Rioja Alta*, Logroño: Diputación Cultural, 1978.

Arco, R. del, *Sepulcros de la Casa Real de Castilla*, Madrid: CSIC, 1954.

Ariès, P., *The Hour of Our Death*, translated by H. Weaver, New York: Alfred A. Knopf, 1981.

Bishko, C. J., 'Liturgical Intercession at Cluny for the King-Emperors of Leon' (1960), revised in *Spanish and Portuguese Monastic History, 600–1300*, London: Variorum Reprints, 1984, pp.53–82A.

Bynum, C. W., *Jesus as Mother: Studies in the Spirituality of the High Middle Ages*, Berkeley: University of California Press, 1982.

Carderera y Solano, V., *Iconografía española: colección de retratos, estatuas, mausoleos y demás monumentos inéditos de reyes, reinas, grandes capitanes, escritores, etc. desde el siglo XI hasta el XCVII copiados de los originales*, 2 vols, Madrid: R. Campuzano, 1855–64.

Castillo, B., J. C. Elorza, and M. Negro, *El Panteón Real de las Huelgas de Burgos: los enterramientos de los reyes de León y de Castilla*, León: Editorial Evergráficas, 1988.

Dillard, H., *Daughters of the Reconquest*, Cambridge: Cambridge University Press, 1984.

Férotin, M., *Le Liber Ordinum en usage dans l'Eglise wisigothique et mozarabe du cinquième au onzième siècle, Monumenta Ecclesiae Liturgica 5*, Paris: Firmin-Didot, 1904.

Fita, F., 'El Concilio de Lérida en 1193,' *Boletín de la Real Academia de la Historia*, vol. 26, 1895, pp.332–83.

Gómez Bárcena, M. J., 'La liturgia de los funerales y su repercusión en la escultura gótica funeraria en Castilla,' in M. N. Rodríguez and E. Portela Silva, eds, *La idea y el sentimiento de la muerte en la historia y en el arte de la Edad Media*, Santiago de Compostela: Universidad de Santiago de Compostela, 1988, pp.31–50.

González, J., *El reino de Castilla en la época de Alfonso VIII*, 3 vols, Madrid: CSIC, 1960.

Hassig, D., ' "He Will Make Alive Your Mortal Bodies": Cluniac Spirituality and the Tomb of Alfonso Ansúrez,' *Gesta*, vol. 30, no. 2, 1991, pp.140–53.

Honorius Augustodunensis, 'Elucidarium,' in Y. Lefèvre, ed., *L'Elucidarium et les Lucidaires*, Mélanges d'archéologie et d'histoire des écoles françaises d'Athènes et de Rome, fasc. 180, Paris: E. de Boccard, 1954.

Iñiguez Almech, F., 'Sobre tallas románicas del siglo XII' *Príncipe de Viana*, vol. 29, nos 112–13, 1968, pp.181–235.

Kirschbaum, E., G. Bandmann, W. Braunfels, J. Kollwitz, W. Mrazek, A. A. Schmid, and H. Schnell, eds, *Lexikon der christlichen Ikonographie*, 8 vols, Rome: Herder, 1968–76.

Maguire, H., 'The Depiction of Sorrow in Middle Byzantine Art,' *Dumbarton Oaks Papers*, vol. 31, 1977, pp.123–74.

Metropolitan Museum of Art, *The Art of Medieval Spain, A.D. 500–1200*, exhibition catalogue, New York: Abrams, 1993.

Moralejo, S., 'The Tomb of Alfonso Ansúrez (†1093): Its Place and the Role of Sahagún in the Beginnings of Spanish Romanesque Sculpture,' in B. F. Reilly, ed., *Santiago, Saint-Denis, and Saint Peter: The Reception of the Roman Liturgy in León-Castile in 1080*, New York: Fordham University Press, 1985, pp.63–100.

Ntedika, J., *La évocation de l'au-delà dans la prière pour les morts: étude de patristique et de liturgie latines (IVe–VIIe s.)*, Louvain: Editions Nauwelaerts, 1971.

O'Callaghan, J. F., *A History of Medieval Spain*, Ithaca, NY: Cornell University Press, 1975.

Panofsky, E., *Tomb Sculpture* (1964), reprinted, New York: Abrams, 1992.

Porter, A. K., *Spanish Romanesque Sculpture* (1928), reprinted (2 vols in 1), New York: Hacker Art Books, 1969.

Réau, L., *Iconographie de l'art chrétien*, 6 vols, Paris: Presses Universitaires, 1955–9.

Sánchez Ameijeiras, R., 'Ecos de la *Chanson de Roland* en la iconografía del sepulcro de Doña Blanca (†1158) en Santa María la Real de Nájera,' *Ephialte*, vol. 2, 1990, pp.206–14.

Sandoval, P. de, *Historia de los Reyes de Castilla y de León: Don Fernando el Magno . . . y Don Alonso séptimo, emperador de las Españas . . . sacadas de los privilegios, libros antiguos, memorias . . .* [etc.] (1615); reprinted (1 vol. in 2): vol. I, *Don Fernando el Magno . . . Don Alonso, sexto de este nombre . . .* ; vol. II, *Doña Urraca . . . y Don Alonso séptimo, emperador de las Españas*; vols XI, XII of F. de Ocampo and A. de Morales, *Corónica general de España*, Madrid: D. Benito, 1791–2.

Yepes, A. de, *Corónica general de la orden de San Benito*, vol. VI, Valladolid: F. Fernández de Cordova, 1617.

Notes

I would like to express my gratitude to Montclair State University for its support of my research in the form of Career Development grants. I also want to thank the many friends and colleagues who contributed to the development of this article, particularly Father Juan Manuel Núñez, father superior of the Franciscan community at Santa María la Real in Nájera. Special thanks go to Stephen Lamia, Constancio del Alamo and my parents.

Preliminary observations about the tomb were presented at the 1992 conference 'The Roles of Women in the Middle Ages: A Reassessment,' at SUNY, Binghamton, in the session 'Innovation and Commemoration: Aristocratic Women and the Arts of Eleventh- and Twelfth-Century Spain,' organized by myself and sponsored by the Medieval Feminist Art History Project; Bailey Young's session, 'The Grave,' at the meeting of the Medieval Academy of America in Tucson, 1993; the Robert Branner Forum for Medieval Art, Columbia University, 1994; and at the Second International Medieval Congress, University of Leeds, 1995, in the session 'Women, Childbirth, Babies and Nurses: Depictions in Medieval Art,' organized by Paula Gerson and Pamela Sheingorn and sponsored by the Medieval Feminist Art History Project. Bible references are to the Douay Rheims version, unless otherwise indicated. Translations, unless otherwise attributed, are mine.

1.   For a brief discussion of the style of the sarcophagus and its bibliography, see Valdez del Alamo, 'The Sarcophagus Lid of Doña Blanca,' in Metropolitan Museum of Art, *The Art of Medieval Spain*, no. 106, pp.232–4. Sánchez Ameijeiras, 'Ecos de la *Chanson de Roland*,' pp.206–14, also deals with this subject, and although we concur on many points, we develop them differently. The recent doctoral dissertation on Sangüesa by B. Müller at the University of Hamburg, which I have not seen, surveys stylistic issues for this group of Navarrese monuments: 'Santa María la Real, Sangüesa (Navarra). Die Bauplastik Santa Marias und die Skulptur Navarras und Aragóns im 12. Jahrhundert. Rezeptor, Katalysator, Innovator?,' 3 vols, unpublished PhD thesis, Berlin, 1997.

2.   A discussion of the links between affect, empathy, and the visual component of memory may be found in the introduction to the present volume; it stands as an extension of the ideas I first began to explore in this article on Blanca's sarcophagus. The link between visual and emotional elements is described thus by Nelson Goodman: 'in aesthetic experience the emotions function cognitively. The work of art is apprehended through the feelings as well as through the senses,' cited by D. Freedberg, *The Power of Images: Studies in the History and Theory of Response*, Chicago: University of Chicago Press, 1989, p.25 n.27. See also M. Carruthers, *The Book of Memory: A Study of Memory in Medieval Culture*, Cambridge: Cambridge University Press, 1990, pp.16–24.

3.   Although one might assume it natural that the imagery on a woman's sarcophagus would reflect her gender, this was not usually the case, as the following discussion will demonstrate. Bynum, *Jesus as Mother*, p.141 n.109, observes that in the twelfth century there is 'no general pattern of using female imagery especially when addressing women.'

4.   The piece is the lid for a sarcophagus basin, since it is hollowed out on the interior. Iñiguez, an architect who played a major role in restorations of Spanish monuments during this century, removed the tomb from the arcosolium at an unspecified date. Convinced that the lid was a cenotaph, he installed it as such in the church: Iñiguez, 'Sobre tallas románicas,' p.200. Father Marino Martínez, former superior of Santa María la Real, recalls hearing from the convent historians that the tomb was removed between 1931 and 1934. I would like to thank Father Marino for sharing this information with me. Del Arco published a photograph of the sarcophagus in the arcosolium, *Sepulcros de la Casa Real*, plate X. For types of Spanish tombs and their decoration, see del Arco, pp.15–17; and for more recent illustrations, Castillo et al., *El Panteón Real de las Huelgas de Burgos*.

5.   An example of a sarcophagus lid meant to be read from a single side is that of Alfonso Ansúrez now in the Museo Arqueológico Nacional of Madrid. According to Sandoval, it was installed against a pillar in the choir of the church of San Benito in Sahagún. See Sandoval, *Fundaciones*

de los monasterios del Padre Benito, vol. I, Madrid: Luis Sánchez, 1601, part 3, fol. 54, cited by Porter, *Spanish Romanesque Sculpture*, vol. I, p.59; Moralejo, 'The Tomb of Alfonso Ansúrez,' p.80 n.1; and Hassig, 'He Will Make Alive Your Mortal Bodies,' p.147.

6. Yepes, *Corónica general*, fol. 153, credits the abbot Rodrigo de Gadea with 'putting the tombs of the kings in order . . . in their Royal Chapel' in 1556. In 1664, the remains of Blanca's sister Doña Sancha Garcés, wife of Gastón, viscount of Béarn, were added to the arcosolium: Carderera, *Iconografía española*, vol. I, plate III, p.1; and del Arco, *Sepulcros de la Casa Real de Castilla*, p.125.

7. Blanca's birth date is unknown; Sancho was born between 1131 and 1133, making him between 18 and 20 years old when they were wed. The marriage was arranged in 1140 to consolidate Castilian claims to the region of La Rioja, already an issue when in 1135 the King of Navarre, García IV Ramírez, Blanca's father, became the vassal of Alfonso VII of Castile: O'Callaghan, *History of Medieval Spain*, p.223; González, *Alfonso VIII*, vol. I, pp.137–41; L. Serrano, *El Obispado de Burgos y Castilla primitiva desde el siglo V al XIII*, vol. II, Madrid: Instituto de San Juan de Valencia, 1935, pp.20, 43 n.4, 59; and Sandoval, *Reyes de Castilla y de León*, vol. II, p.302. Sancho was already referred to as King (*rex*) by 1151, although the official coronation did not take place until 1157: O'Callaghan, p.235, and González, vol. I, p.139. This has occasionally led to confusion about the correct titles of Sancho and Blanca. For example, Alvarez-Coca, *Escultura románica*, p.27, stated that Blanca never became Queen despite the title 'Regina' used on the sarcophagus lid.

8. Among those published by González, she is mentioned in the only surviving document of this period which she did not confirm. One other published document from the period of her marriage which she neither signed nor in which she is mentioned is a confirmation of the possessions of the monastery of Nájera by Alfonso VII, made two weeks after her son's birth; see below, n.80. For the documents, see González, *Alfonso VIII*, vol. II, pp.15–50. For the active partnership that Spanish women had in marriage, see Dillard, *Daughters of the Reconquest*, p.10, and chapter 3, especially p.71. While on the subject of documents and donations, I would like to take the opportunity of making a correction concerning a golden altar in Santa María la Real, sometimes attributed to the Sancho and Blanca under discussion: Porter, *Spanish Romanesque Sculpture*, vol. II, p.20, nn.803–4; M.-M. Gauthier, *Emaux meridionaux: Catalogue international de l'oeuvre de Limoges*, vol. I, *L'époque romane*, Paris: Centre nationale de la recherche scientifique, 1987, cat. 317, pp.243–4; and Sánchez, 'Ecos de la *Chanson de Roland*,' p.210 n.33. Yepes, 1610, vol. VI, fols 124v–125, published the inscription on this altar, which reads in part: 'Nos Sancius Rex Garsiae Regis filius, una cum Blanca coniuge dilectissima, hoc aureum altaris frontispitium . . . oferimus [sic]' (We, Sancho, son of García the King, and Blanca his beloved wife, offer this golden altarpiece). Thus, it is clear that this is not the same couple.

9. 'Nació el Rey D. Alfonso noche de San Martín, e fue día de viernes, Era M.CXCIII,' *Anales Toledanos*, vol. I, cited by González, *Alfonso VIII*, vol. I, p.144 n.31; by Sandoval, *Reyes de Castilla y de León*, vol. II, p.334; and published by F. de Berganza, *Antigüedades de España*, vol. II, Madrid: Francisco de Hierro, 1721, p.567. González pointed out that Alfonso must have had siblings who died young: vol. I, p.145 n.37; vol. II, pp.137–9, no. 81. In a donation to San Pedro de Soria in 1166, Alfonso wanted the tomb of his siblings to be adorned ('quoniam eam sacrorum relquiis atque sepultura regum fratrum meorum ilustrissimi imperatoris nepotum . . . adornari').

10. 'Era MCLXXXIII. II Idus Aug. Regina Branca mater istius Ald. Regis Castelle. Haec fuit filia Garsiae Reg. Nav.'; ibid., p.564. The *Anales Compostelanos* might more accurately be called the *Chronicon Burgense*, but this chronicle has been published under the first title because the best known copy was in Santiago de Compostela: P. David, *Etudes historiques sur la Galice et le Portugal du VIe au XIIe siècle*, Paris: Société d'Edition 'Les Belles Lettres,' 1947, p.400. It is cited by Sandoval, *Reyes de Castilla y de León*, vol. II, 333–5, (and others) as the 'tumbo negro' (black volume). As Sandoval states, the interpretation of the various documents to confirm the Queen's death date is difficult, and so I have presented above as much information as possible. Insofar as the tomb itself is concerned, the years 1156–8, before Sancho's death, seem secure.

11. [Madrid], Archivo Histórico Nacional, vol. I of documents from the monastery of Nájera, fols 182–3, cited by Fita, 'El Concilio de Lérida,' pp.341–2.

12. González, *Alfonso VIII*, vol. I, p.145, follows the suggestion of Sandoval, *Reyes de Castilla y de León*, vol. II, p.335.

13. Since the epitaph does not mention the death of Sancho III, it is possible that it was composed for the original tomb. The seventeenth-century historians Sandoval and Yepes recorded the inscription, which has been published with slight variations: 'Nobilis hic regina jacet, quae Blanca vocari / Promeruit, pulcherrima specie, candior nive / Candoris pretium festinans, gratia morum / Faeminei sexus hanc dabat, esse decus. / Imperatoris natus Rex Sancius illi vir fuit / Et tanto laus erat ipso viro, partu pressa ruit / Et pignus nobile fudit, ventris Virginei

filius assit ei. / Era millena centena, nonagesima quarta / Reginam constat obisse piam.'
Loosely translated, this reads: 'Here lies a noble queen, who deserved her name, Blanca [Pure
White], most beautiful vision, whiter than snow, hastening to the reward of her candor,
gracious by custom, she gave honor to the female sex. King Sancho, born of the emperor, was
her husband, and in so many ways she was a glory for that man. Stricken down in childbirth,
she brought forth a noble son, pledge of love; the Son born of the Virgin's womb assisted her.
Let it be known that in era 1194 [A.D. 1156] the pious queen died.' See Yepes, *Corónica general*,
vol. VI, fol. 131v; and Sandoval, *Reyes de Castilla y de León*, vol. II, pp.333–4. Sandoval notes that
these verses 'are' inscribed on the edge of her tomb; Yepes describes them as 'once having been'
inscribed on the tomb; Carderera, *Iconografía española*, vol. I, plate III, says that they were on
'the circumference of a narrow band . . . of which only a few letters can be read today.' Fita,
'El Concilio de Lérida,' p.343 n.1, states that the original text was lost. Most likely Sandoval,
Yepes, and Fita had access to a document recording the inscription that disappeared in the
reconstruction of the royal pantheon. The letters that Carderera actually saw and drew were
those inscriptions directly under the figures (Fig. 2.5).

14.   The month of August during the years 1156–8 hit the royal house of Castile very hard. A year
      after Blanca's death on August 12 in 1156, Alfonso VII fell ill and died on August 21, 1157. The
      following year, on August 31, Sancho III died, leaving the future Alfonso VIII an infant orphan
      in the hands of rival factions of Castilian nobles: O'Callahan, 1975, pp.232, 235; and González,
      Alfonso VIII, vol. I, pp.146–7. As the Castilian kings were establishing their hegemony in the
      Peninsula, these early rulers had no unified pantheon, and each generation sought to
      establish one. Both Emperor Alfonso VII and King Sancho III were buried in the Cathedral of
      Toledo. Alfonso VIII was buried with his wife Leonor Plantagenet, daughter of Henry II of
      England, in the new pantheon of Las Huelgas in Burgos: del Arco, *Sepulcros de la casa real de
      Castilla*, pp.240–41, plates V, VI, VIII, IX; Castillo et al., *El Panteón Real*, pp.9–10, 56, 58–9.

15.   Yepes, *Corónica general*, vol. VI, fol. 131v.

16.   Sandoval, *Reyes de Castilla y de León*, vol. II, pp.333, 335, openly professes a special devotion to
      Blanca, and provides an empathetic description of the King's grief; see
      also Carderera, *Iconografía española*, vol. I, plate III, p.1. The texts of Sancho's donations are
      recorded in Fita, 'El Concilio de Lérida,' pp.341–2; Yepes, *Corónica general*, vol. VI, fol. 131v;
      Sandoval, *Reyes de Castilla y de León*, vol. II, pp.335–6; and A. Bernard, ed., *Recueil des chartes
      de l'abbaye de Cluny*, vol. VII, part 5, of *Collection de documents inédits sur l'histoire de France*,
      A. Bruel, ed., 1st series, Paris: Imp. National, 1894, no. 4190, pp.536–8. They are discussed in
      greater detail below.

17.   González, *Alfonso VIII*, vol. I, pp.143, 146.

18.   Although Iñiguez, 'Sobre tallas románicas,' p.201, had mentioned seeing a cross-nimb and
      fragments of figures, this was overlooked in subsequent research because of the difficulty of
      seeing them. Constancio del Alamo and I found them by chance because of the photographer's
      lamp we employed; Father Juan Manuel had been unaware that the fragments were there.
      Sánchez, 'Ecos de la *Chanson de Roland*,' n.23, mentions but does not illustrate these fragments,
      nor does she integrate the information into her analysis; Alvarez-Coca makes no mention of
      them.

19.   The sarcophagus closest in imagery to Blanca's is the thirteenth-century tomb of Doña
      Berenguela in the royal convent of Las Huelgas in Burgos. There, a Coronation of the Virgin
      is carved at the head of the sarcophagus, the eidolon at the foot. On the lid is a cycle of the
      Infancy of Christ, from the Annunciation to the Flight into Egypt, with the Adoration of the
      Magi and the Massacre of the Innocents on the basin. See M. J. Gómez Bárcena, *Escultura gótica
      funeraria en Burgos*, Monografías Burgalesas, Burgos: Excelentísima Diputación Provincial de
      Burgos, 1988, pp.196–7, figs 152–5. On another thirteenth-century sarcophagus now in the
      Worcester Art Museum, the Annunciation and Crucifixion occupy the short ends of a basin
      which represents the funeral and mourners on the front. See D. Gillerman, ed., *Gothic Sculpture
      in America*, vol. I, New York and London: Garland, 1989, no. 217, pp.282–3.

20.   Several examples are provided in Metropolitan Museum of Art, *Art of Medieval Spain*, cat. nos.
      69–71, 117, 122–3, 125a–g, 132–4.

21.   There is a parallel between a loving mother and the sacrifice of the pelican (also a symbol of
      Christ) which opens her breast to feed her young with her own blood. See T. H. White, *The
      Bestiary* (1954), New York: G. P. Putnam's Sons, 1960, 132–3; and Bynum, *Jesus as Mother*,
      pp.132–3, 143.

22.   S. Moralejo, 'La reutilización e influencia de los sarcófagos antiguos en la España medieval,'
      in *Colloquio sul reimpiego dei sarcofagi romani nel medievo*, Marburg-an-der-Lahn: Verlag des
      Kunstgeschichtlichen Seminars, 1984, pp.189–90.

23. This sarcophagus forms part of a group of monuments whose dates are hotly debated. See D. L. Simon (who proposes a date in the first quarter of the twelfth century): 'Le sarcophage de Doña Sancha à Jaca,' *Les cahiers de Saint-Michel de Cuxa*, vol. 10, 1979, pp.107–24; and Metropolitan Museum of Art, *Art of Medieval Spain*, pp.229–32; See also *Signos: arte y cultura en el Alto Aragón medieval*, exhibition catalogue, M. C. Lacarra and C. Morte, eds, Huesca: Gobierno de Aragón, Dip. de Huesca, 1993, pp.107, 272; M. Ruiz Maldonado, 'La contraposición Superbia-Humilitas: el sepulcro de Doña Sancha y otras obras,' *Goya*, vol. 146, 1978, pp.75–81; and A. K. Porter, 'The Tomb of Doña Sancha and the Romanesque Art of Aragón,' *Burlington Magazine*, vol. 45, 1924, pp.165–79.

24. Ariès, *Hour of Our Death*, p.250.

25. Ruiz Maldonado (as in n.23), pp.75–81.

26. Sandoval, *Reyes de Castilla y de León*, vol. I, p.343; J. Pérez, *Historia de la Real Monasterio de Sahagún*, edited by R. Escalona, Madrid: J. Ibarra, 1782, pp.233, 236; and del Arco, *Sepulcros de la Casa Real de Castilla*, p.91. It was Moralejo, 'The Tomb of Alfonso Ansúrez,' p.83 n.12, who called attention to the possibility that this sarcophagus may have served as a precedent for the Nájera sarcophagus lid.

27. According to the drawing by Carderera, *Iconografía española*, vol. I, plate III, the letters RE were still visible on the ground line under the figure of the King, but they have since disappeared. Carderera believes that the figure that most closely corresponds to that of Sancho, a mourning woman supported by two ladies-in-waiting to the left of the deathbed, was intended to represent Blanca's sister Sancha Garcés (see above, n.6), but no document supports this logical conclusion.

28. The fragments of his tomb, dispersed after a fire in 1835, have been reassembled and installed in the church of Santa María in Ripoll. See Porter, *Spanish Romanesque Sculpture*, vol. II, p.23, plate 77; and X. Barral i Altet, 'La sculpture à Ripoll au XII siècle,' *Bulletin Monumental*, vol. 131, no. 4, 1973, pp.332–4, fig. 22.

29. The *Chronicón de D. Pelayo*, in E. Flórez, ed., *España sagrada*, vol. XIV, 2nd edition, Madrid: Pedro Marín, 1786, p.475, cited by J. Filgueira Valverde, 'El "planto" en la historia y en la literatura gallega,' *Cuadernos de Estudios Gallegos*, vol. IV, 1945, p.518.

30. For many of the Early Christian Fathers, the lamentation and other burial rituals seemed too similar to pagan practices: Ntedika, *La évocation de l'au-delà*, pp.8–9, 235–6, 256.

31. Maguire, 'The Depiction of Sorrow,' pp.126–7, 173; M. Barasch, *Gestures of Despair in Medieval and Early Renaissance Art*, New York: New York University Press, 1976, pp.22–3; Panofsky, *Tomb Sculpture*, p.16; and Ariès, *Hour of Our Death*, p.326. For Spanish customs, see Dillard, *Daughters of the Reconquest*, pp.96–7; Filgueira Valverde (as in n.29), pp.512–17; and Gómez Bárcena, 'La liturgia de los funerales,' pp.31–50.

32. Isidore of Seville, *Etymologies*, 1:39, 19, in *Etimologías*, vol. I, edited by J. Oroz Reta, BAC, vol. CDXXXIII, Madrid: La Editorial Católica, 1982, pp.354–5.

33. For the sarcophagus of Egas Moniz, see M. Ruiz Maldonado, 'Algunas sugerencias en torno al sepulcro de Egas Moniz,' *Sessiones artísticas entre Portugal y España*, Junta de Castilla y León, 1986, pp.235–45; J. Monteiro d'Aguilar, 'The Tombs at Paço de Sousa,' *Art Studies*, vol. 4, 1926, p.90; and Porter, *Spanish Romanesque Sculpture*, vol. I, p.94 n.107; vol. II, pp.24, 30.

34. For The Death of Dido, see Panofsky, *Tomb Sculpture*, fig. 99. For additional examples, see Barasch (as in n.31), pp.24–31; Maguire, 'The Depiction of Sorrow,' passim.

35. C. M. Havelock, 'Mourners on Greek Vases: Remarks on the Social History of Women,' *Feminism and Art History: Questioning the Litany*, edited by N. Broude and M. S. Garrard, New York: Harper & Row, 1982, pp.51–2.

36. Maguire points out that the visual arts are more conservative in depicting extreme emotion and grief during the early Middle Ages, a situation that changed later on, 'The Depiction of Sorrow,' p.132.

37. The status and identity of these mourners is discussed by W. M. Jensen, 'The sculptures from the tomb of the Haterii,' unpublished PhD thesis, University of Michigan, 1978, pp.43–9.

38. Gómez Bárcena, 'La liturgia de los funerales,' pp.46–8. For Villalcázar de Sirga, see S. A. Ordax, J. M. Martínez Frías, and M. Moreno, *Castilla y León*, vol. I, Madrid: Editorial Encuentro, 1989, pp.278–9.

39. The tomb of an earlier Castilian Queen may have served as a precedent for the lamentation scene on Blanca's sarcophagus, that of Constance of Burgundy (†1093), second wife of Alfonso VI, Sancho III's great-grandfather. Alfonso VI was buried in the Benedictine monastery in

Sahagún with four of his several wives and other family members, such as Elvira (see above and n.26). A. de Morales (†1535) and Sandoval, c.1600, described the royal tombs. Constance's was at that time set into the wall on the south side of the main apse (the side of the Epistle). Sandoval states that on her sarcophagus there were figures in medium relief depicting some events of the Queen's death and the emotion of her family, as was typical for royal tombs of the time: 'estan figuras labradas de media talla con algunos passos de la muerte desta Reyna, y sentimiento de los suyos: que tales obras se usaban en aquellos tiempos en las sepulturas de los Principes'; Sandoval (as in n.5), fols 73–73v. Sandoval – who was so touched by the representation of Sancho's grief on Blanca's tomb – made no mention of such a scene on Constance's sarcophagus. According to Morales, Constance had a tall stone tomb with relief, 'una tumba alta de piedra con vulto': *Viage de Ambrosio de Morales*, edited by E. Flórez, Madrid: A. Marín, 1765, pp.36–7. Flórez, in a marginal note, stated that the tomb was no longer extant when he edited Morales's text in 1765. Moralejo, 'The Tomb of Alfonso Ansúrez,' pp.64–5 and nn.11–12, called attention to the possible relationship to Blanca's tomb, and suggested that the 'vulto' could have been a effigy added in the thirteenth century, as the term is often used in that sense. I agree with Moralejo that the tomb may have been altered, as its setting into a wall also suggests. In support of that is information provided by Sandoval, who tells us that he copied Constance's epitaph from a very old book. As in the case of Blanca's tomb in Nájera, the text of the epitaph may have been recorded when the original tomb was altered or replaced. It is difficult to ascertain, therefore, whether Constance's 1093 sarcophagus is the one described. Oddly, Alfonso VI's sarcophagus, which has survived, was undecorated except for its lion supports and a covering of textiles; the tombs and tomb markers of his other wives were also undecorated, according to Morales and Sandoval. The question arises as to why Constance's tomb would have been selected for ornamentation as opposed to Alfonso's or another of his wives.

40.   Ariès, *Hour of Our Death*, pp.141, 144; and Gómez Bárcena, 'La liturgia de los funerales,' p.37.

41.   Barasch (as in n.31), pp.18, 24–33.

42.   Ariès, *Hour of Our Death*, p.144.

43.   M. Sotomayor, *Sarcófagos romano-cristianos de España: estudio iconográfico*, Granada: Fac. de Teología, 1975, pp.23–4, 47–8, 233.

44.   ibid., pp.47–8; and *Datos históricos sobre los sarcófagos romano-cristianos de España*, Granada: Fac. de Teología, 1973, pp.25–30.

45.   Refer to the postscript at the end of this article for an additional example, the death of St Benedict, and to D. Verkerk's remarks about the desire to associate oneself with the heroic dead in her introduction to, 'The Font is a Kind of Grave' in this volume. See, for the Forty Martyrs in Asinou, Maguire, 'The Depiction of Sorrow,' fig. 56; for Achilles struck by Paris on the Achilles sarcophagus in Madrid, see S. Reinach, *Répertoire de reliefs grecs et romains*, vol. II, Paris: Leroux, 1909, p.193; and for the dying Talos supported by Kastor and Polydeukos on an Attic krater in the Jatta Collection, see R. Brillant, *Arts of the Ancient Greeks*, New York: McGraw Hill, 1974, figs 7–19.

46.   See above, n.32.

47.   *Iliad*, book 18, lines 22–31; translated by R. Lattimore, *The Iliad of Homer*, Chicago: University of Chicago Press, 1951, pp.375–6.

48.   D. L. Sayers, ed. and trans., *The Song of Roland*, New York: Penguin, 1957, p.30; and Ariès, *Hour of Our Death*, pp.142–5. I would like to thank Bradford Blaine and Eugene Vance for their suggestions regarding this material.

49.   *La Chanson de Roland*, verses 205–10, edited by J. Bédier, Paris: L'édition d'art, 1966, pp.239–45. Sánchez, 'Ecos de la *Chanson de Roland*,' pp.208–9, also noticed the correspondence between Sancho's grief and Charlemagne's mourning.

50.   D. D. R. Owen, introduction to Chrétien de Troyes, *Arthurian Romances*, translated by W. W. Comfort, London: Everyman's Library, 1975, p.viii.

51.   *Cligès*, verses 5719–814, 6051–162, translated by Comfort, *Arthurian Romances*, pp.165–6, 170–71.

52.   In the twelfth century, conjugal love, even passion, was a sought-for ideal and a reality for some couples, despite the practice of arranged marriages for the upper classes. R. H. Bloch, *Medieval Misogyny and the Invention of Western Romantic Love*, Chicago: University of Chicago Press, 1991, pp.8, 10, 156–60, proposes that the concept of romantic love was 'invented' in the eleventh and twelfth centuries. Others, however, recognize that courtly literature, saints' lives, and theological writings may express the ideal of a loving marriage at this time and even earlier. See J. Leclercq, *Le mariage vu par les moines au XIIe siècle*, Paris: Les Editions du Cerf,

1983, pp.11–23, 74–80 (in English as *Monks on Marriage: A Twelfth-Century View*, New York, 1981); and D. Herlihy, *Medieval Households*, Cambridge, MA: Harvard University Press, 1985, p.120.

53. It is to be expected that the art of Castile and Navarre should share intellectual and literary trends with those in the courts of western France at this time, since there were many marriages between royal houses of the Iberian Peninsula and the ducal house of Aquitaine. For example, daughters of Duke William VIII of Aquitaine were married to Pedro of Aragón and Alfonso VI of León and Castile. Their brother was William IX, duke of Aquitaine (1071–1127), whose poems mark the literary development of concepts of courtly love: Bloch (as in n.52), p.160. His daughter married Ramiro el Monje of Aragón (brother of the King of Navarre, and Blanca's great-uncle) in 1135. See P. Boissonnade, 'Les relations des ducs d'Aquitaine, comtes de Poitiers, avec les états chrétiennes d'Aragon et de Navarre (1014–1327),' *Bulletin de la Société des Antiquaires de l'ouest*, 1934, pp.264–316; I thank Virginia Stotz for this reference. Sancho III's sister, Costanza, married Louis VII of France after his divorce from Eleanor of Aquitaine. Blanca and Sancho's son, Alfonso VIII of Castile, married Leonor, daughter of Eleanor of Aquitaine and Henry II Plantagenet. See Sandoval, *Reyes de Castilla y de León*, vol. II, pp.313–15; and González, *Alfonso VIII*, vol. II, p.137.

54. C. Flores Varela, 'El Camino de Santiago en la encrucijada de la lírica medieval,' in *Santiago: Camino de Europa*, exhibition catalogue, Santiago de Compostela: Xunta de Galicia, 1993, pp.214–16.

55. E. Vance, 'Roland and Charlemagne: The Remembering Voices and the Crypt,' *Mervelous Signals: Poetics and Sign Theory in the Middle Ages*, Lincoln: University of Nebraska Press, 1986, pp.51–85. A similar pattern of cognition stimulated by 'elaborate cross-references between verbal and visual signs' is described by K. F. Morrison, *History as a Visual Art in the Twelfth-Century Renaissance*, Princeton, NJ: Princeton University Press, 1990, pp.36–7.

56. For later but similar scenes of childbirth, see examples in the *Cantigas of Santa María* made for Alfonso X during the second half of the thirteenth century: Cantiga VII, a miraculous birth by Caesarean section, which both mother and child survive; and Cantiga LXXX, a Christological narration with no identifying inscriptions; Cantiga CVIII, the birth of a Jewish child; Cantiga CXV, the birth of a Christian child; Cantiga CXVIII, births of stillborn children: J. Guerrero Lovillo, *Las Cantigas*, Madrid: CSIC, 1949, plates 10, 89, 120, 127, 131.

57. For a similar treatment of an infant soul carried to heaven by a winged figure, or *psychopompos*, see the reliefs from the Tomb of the Harpies in the British Museum: Panofsky, *Tomb Sculpture*, fig. 25. For the reception of the soul by angels, see Gómez Bárcena, 'La liturgia de los funerales,' pp.38–40.

58. For the sarcophagus of 'Santa Froila,' in which the soul takes the form of a nude, very attenuated figure, see Porter, *Spanish Romanesque Sculpture*, vol. II, plate 148; and M. Chamoso Lamas, *Escultura funeraria en Galicia*, Orense: Instituto de Estudios Orensanos 'Padre Feijó,' 1979, p.236.

59. The idea is already present in Paul, 1 Thess. 4.12–18. See Ntedika, *La évocation de l'au-delà*, pp.233–5; Maguire, 'The Depiction of Sorrow,' p.128; Gómez Bárcena, 'La liturgia de los funerales,' p.46.

60. John Chrysostom, *In Joannem homilia* LXII, PG, vol. LIX, col. 346, cited by Maguire, 'The Depiction of Sorrow,' p.128.

61. Ambrose uses Acts 9.36–41 as an example: *De excessu fratris sui Satyri*, book 1, line 29, PL, vol. XVI, cols 1299–1300, discussed by Ntedika, *La évocation de l'au-delà*, pp.52–3.

62. Response: 'Subvenite Sancti Dei, occurrite Angeli Domini: Suscipientes animam ejus: Offerentes eam in conspectu Altissimi.' Verse: 'Suscipiat te Christus, qui vocavit te, et in sinum Abrahae Angeli, deducant te.' R: 'Suscipientes . . .' V: 'Requiem aeternam dona ei, Domine, et lux perpetua luceat ei.' The Response is spoken with the verses cited above as the body of the deceased is carried into the church for the burial mass. For the history of its use in the liturgy, see DACL, vol. XII, s.v. 'Mort,' cols 31, 34; D. Sicard, *La liturgie de la mort dans l'église latine des origines à la reforme*, Liturgiewissenschaftliche Quellen und Forschungen, 63, Münster Westfalen: Aschendorff, 1978, pp.66, 75–6, 172; Ntedika, *La évocation de l'au-delà*, p.222; and Ariès, *Hour of Our Death*, p.248. For the text, see a Roman Catholic Missal, e.g. the Latin and English *New Marian Missal for Daily Mass*, by S. P. Juergens, SM, Turnhout: Henri Proost, 1959, p.1376. Blanche of Castile is said to have died speaking the 'Subvenite': 'La déposition de Charles d'Anjou pour le procès de canonisation de Saint Louis,' *Notices et documents publiés pour la Société de l'Histoire de France*, 1884, p.169, cited by F. and J. Gies, *Women in the Middle Ages* (1978), New York: Barnes and Noble, 1980, p.119.

63. R. de Miguel, *Nuevo Diccionario Latino-Español*; and *Cassell's New Latin Dictionary*, s.v. 'suscipio.'

64. Ntedika, *La évocation de l'au-delà*, p.222. Ariès, *Hour of Our Death*, pp.146–54, traces the development of the concept that the souls of the just went to the bosom of Abraham to await resurrection at the end of the world; thus, the intercession of the living could modify the condition of the dead.

65. As pointed out by Hassig, 'He Will Make Alive Your Mortal Bodies,' p.148, on many Spanish tombs the eagle of John is emphasized. On the Jaca sarcophagus, animated eagles perch on the capitals that flank Sancha's mandorla. At Nájera, the eagle is made more prominent by scale and by the large, open scroll that it holds in its claws. Panofsky, *Tomb Sculpture*, p.59, observed that eagles are traditionally associated with apotheosis.

66. This practice by the Cluniacs was an appropriation from earlier liturgies; in their case, the direct source must have been the Gallican liturgy, but elaborate recitations of the names of the community of the living and the dead were also performed in the Hispanic liturgy; hence, the Cluniacs did not introduce the custom into the Iberian Peninsula. See Ariès, *Hour of Our Death*, pp.103, 148–51; Ntedika, *La évocation de l'au-delà*, p.224; and Férotin, *Liber Ordinum*, pp.429–30.

67. Hassig, 'He Will Make Alive Your Mortal Bodies,' p.146; and Bishko, 'Liturgical Intercession,' pp.53–4.

68. Hassig, 'He Will Make Alive Your Mortal Bodies,' pp.146–8, demonstrated the important role that Cluniac liturgy played in the imagery of the sarcophagus of Alfonso Ansúrez, formerly at Sahagún (see n.5). She explained the books held by the Evangelists on this lid as their gospels, which is certainly correct, but some angels there also hold books. At Sahagún and Nájera, the numerous and prominent books in the hands of the angels, Evangelists, and Apostles also may refer to the Last Judgment and *libri vitae*, as discussed above. For the Apostles at the Last Judgment, see P. L. Gerson, 'Suger as Iconographer: The Central Portal of the West Façade of Saint-Denis,' *Abbot Suger and Saint-Denis*, ed. eadem, New York: Metropolitan Museum of Art, 1986, p.189.

69. Bishko, 'Liturgical Intercession,' pp.54–5. In his study of the relationship between Cluny and the Hispanic kings, Bishko originally minimized the importance of the Navarrese once the Leonese became important benefactors of Cluny: pp.58–9. He later revised this view somewhat, recognizing that, while less privileged than the Leonese, the Navarro-Aragonese did continue to have a significant relationship with Cluny: pp.78A–82A. I would like to add that, with the complexly intermingled genealogies of the Hispanic rulers, figures like Blanca brought many of the royal families together.

70. ibid., pp.54ff.

71. ibid., pp.63–4, 68, 71.

72. ibid., pp.68–70.

73. ibid., p.55.

74. Yepes, *Corónica general*, vol. VI, fol. 121–121v.

75. ibid., fol. 122v.

76. O'Callaghan, *History of Medieval Spain*, p.200.

77. Bishko, 'Liturgical Intercession,' pp.62–3, 69, 71; Yepes, *Corónica general*, vol. VI, fol. 123 (misprinted as 213); and Fita, 'El Concilio de Lérida,' pp.336–7. This move was unacceptable to the Archbishop of Nájera, who was forced to transfer his seat to Calahorra. An account of the dispute about the dependency of Nájera on Cluny, raised by the Archbishop of Calahorra, is given by Fita; the dispute lasted until finally settled by Rome in 1193. See above, n.39, for a discussion of Constance's tomb in Sahagún.

78. Yepes, *Corónica general*, vol. VI, fols 148v, 136v.

79. Bishko, 'Liturgical Intercession,' pp.75, 68 n.52.

80. Fita, 'El Concilio de Lérida,' pp.338–40, cites [Madrid], Archivo histórico nacional (as in n.11), fols 180–181v.

81. See above, n.11.

82. Paris, Bib. Nat. MS or. 254, cop. 283–154, edited by Bernard (as in n.16).

83. The donation was made on 30 August 1156; Yepes, *Corónica general*, vol. VI, fol. 131v. According to Yepes, in 1165, when he was nine years old, Blanca's son, Alfonso VIII, made donations to, and conferred benefits on, the monastery of Nájera 'for the soul of my mother whose body rests

in the Church of Blessed Mary in Nájera, and for the good service which you have rendered and are rendering to me.'

84. Honorius Augustodunensis, *Elucidarium*, book 2, line 104, edited by Lefèvre, 1954, pp.164, 442.

85. London, Brit. Lib. Add. MS 11695, fol. 271v, cited by O. K. Werckmeister, 'The First Romanesque Beatus Manuscripts and the Liturgy of Death,' *Actas del simposio para el estudio de los códices del 'Comentario al Apocalipsis' de Beato de Liébana*, Madrid: Joyas Bibliográficas, 1980, vol. I, p.191 n.99.

86. C. W. Atkinson, *The Oldest Vocation: Christian Motherhood in the Middle Ages*, Ithaca, NY/London: Cornell University Press, 1991, pp.125–7, 134–7, 143, 193; and Herlihy (as in n.52), pp.121–2.

87. For a description of the sanctified imagination and the facility to link sacred history with the present, see J. Leclercq, *Love of Learning and the Desire for God: A Study of Monastic Culture*, translated by C. Misrahi, 3rd edition, New York: Fordham University Press, 1982, pp.75, 158; and M.-D. Chenu, 'La mentalité symbolique,' in *La théologie au douzième siècle*, Etudes de philosophie médiévale, 45, Paris, J. Vrin, 1957, especially pp.160–61, 166.

88. G. Schiller, *Iconography of Christian Art*, translated by J. Seligman, Greenwich, CT: New York Graphic Society, 1971, vol. I, p.97.

89. Férotin, *Liber Ordinum*, pp.450–51, especially n.8; P. Guéranger, *El año litúrgico*, translated by the monks of Silos, Burgos: Editorial Aldecoa, 1954, vol. I, pp.401–3.

90. DACL, vol. VII, part 1, cols 608–13, figs 5856–7.

91. Augustine, *Sermo* CCXCVIII, in PL, vol. XXXIX, cols 2149–50.

92. idem, *Sermones* CCXCVIII, CCXIX, CCXX, in PL, vol. XXXIX, cols 2149–54.

93. Maguire, 'The Depiction of Sorrow,' pp.130–31. See also K. Nolan, ' "Ploratus et ululatus": The Mothers in the Massacre of the Innocents at Chartres Cathedral,' *Studies in Iconography*, vol. 17, 1996, pp.95–141; the chapters on local cults and the Massacre in the Chartres capitals in R. Dressler, 'Medieval narrative: the capital frieze on the royal portal, Chartres Cathedral,' unpublished PhD thesis, Columbia University, 1992; and L. Spitzer, 'The Cult of the Virgin and Gothic Sculpture: Evaluating Opposition in the Chartres West Façade Capital Frieze,' *Gesta*, vol. 33, no. 2, 1994, pp.132–50.

94. Although not directly applicable to Blanca, it is of interest to note that the Hispanic liturgy expresses the hope that a child who dies will join the Holy Innocents of Bethlehem: Ntedika, *La évocation de l'au-delà*, p.225; and Férotin, *Liber Ordinum*, p.136.

95. Iñiguez, 'Sobre tallas románicas,' p.201, and Alvarez-Coca, *Escultura románica*, p.32, interpret the enthroned king and kneeling figure as Abraham receiving souls into his bosom. Sánchez, 'Ecos de la *Chanson de Roland*,' pp.209, 213 n.24, also rejects their interpretation.

96. 3 Kings 3.16–28; Josephus, *History of the Jews*, book 8, lines 26–34, translated by H. St J. Thackeray and R. Marcus, Loeb Classical Library, Cambridge, MA: Harvard University Press, 1976, vol. V, pp.587–9; Augustine, *Sermo X*, in PL, vol. XXXVIII, cols 91–7; Isidore of Seville, *Quaestiones in Vet. Testam.* book IV, 1–2, in PL, vol. LXXXIII, cols 416–17.

97. I would like to thank Charles T. Little of the Metropolitan Museum of Art for generously sharing his knowledge about the ivory with me.

98. L. de Bruyne, 'L'imposition des mains dans l'art chrétien ancien,' *Rivisita di archeologia cristiana*, vol. 20, 1943, pp.113–278, 248–9, 251–60.

99. See Réau, *Iconographie*, vol. II, part 1, p.289; Kirschbaum, *Lexikon*, vol. IV, p.22. Augustine praises Solomon's wisdom and his capacity to judge as a prefiguration for the Last Judgment; *De civitate Dei*, book XX, chapter 3, in PL, vol. XLI, col. 661, and in BAC, vol. CLXXI–CLXXII, pp.1443–4. The scene of the Judgment of Solomon is explicitly associated with the Last Judgment on some French Gothic portals: C. Schaeffer, 'Le relief du Jugement de Salomon à la façade de la cathédrale d'Auxerre,' *Gazette des Beaux Arts*, vol. 26, 1944, pp.183–94. In reference to the Judgment of Solomon, Josephus (as in n.96) describes the King's wisdom as godlike.

100. The creative blend of a variety of literary sources is particularly evident in this representation of Solomon with a sword held over the two infants. In the Bible, 3 Kings 3.25, only the living child was ordered to be cut in half in order to give a piece to each mother. The sarcophagus shows both the living and dead child about to be divided, corresponding to Josephus' account (as in n.96, book 8, lines 30–32). Furthermore, a soldier is usually represented with sword drawn to carry out Solomon's orders, but on the sarcophagus Solomon himself prepares to perform the act – as described by Isidore of Seville (as in n.96).

101. Augustine (as in n.96); and Isidore (as in n.96).

102. See Réau, *Iconographie*, vol. II, part 2, p.353.

103. Augustine, *De verbis Evangelii Matthaei*, book XXV, *Sermo XCIII*, in PL, vol. XXXVIII, cols 573–80, and *Sermo LXXVI* in PL, vol. XXXIX, cols 1892–3; Isidore of Seville, *Allegoriae quaedem scripturae sacrae*, 197–8, in PL, vol. LXXXIII, cols 123–4.

104. Surprisingly little has been written on the subject of the Wise and Foolish Virgins. Réau, *Iconographie*, vol. II, part 2, pp.354–5, characterizes the motif as 'an accessory' in French art of the twelfth century, one which appears in small scale as a supplement to a major subject. See E. Mâle, *Religious Art in France: The Twelfth Century* (1922), Princeton, NJ: Princeton University Press, 1978, pp.151–3; A. Katzenellenbogen, *Allegories of the Virtues and Vices in Medieval Art* (1939), Toronto: University of Toronto Press, 1989, pp.17–18, 58, 75; L. Seidel, *Songs of Glory*, Chicago: University of Chicago Press, 1981, pp.51–2; eadem, 'Medieval Cloister Carving and Monastic Mentalité,' in A. MacLeish, ed., *The Medieval Monastery*, Saint Cloud, MN: North Star Press of Saint Cloud, vol. I, 1988, pp.8–11; Gerson (as in n.68), pp.187–9; and the material cited below, nn.105–9.

105. Kirschbaum, *Lexikon*, vol. II, cols 458–9; B. Brenk, *Tradition und Neuerung in der Christlichen Kunst des ersten Jahrtausends: Studien zur Geschichte des Weltgerichtsbildes*, Wiener Byzantinische Studien III, Vienna: Böhlaus, 1966, pp.51–4; and DACL, vol. XV, part 2, s.v. 'Vierge, virginité,' cols 3096–8.

106. DACL, vol. XV, part 2, s.v. 'Vienne en Dauphiné,' col. 3072.

107. There are variants in the transcription of the inscription, which has many abbreviations. For a reconstruction of the text, see Brenk (as in n.105), p.52 n.48, who cites E. le Blant, *Inscriptions chrétiennes de la Gaule antérieures au VIIIe siècle*, vol. I, Paris, 1856, p.266 n.199. See also DACL, vol. XV, part 2, col. 3097; and Ariès, *Hour of Our Death*, p.210. The sarcophagus is illustrated in J. Hubert, J. Porcher, and W. F. Volbach, *Europe of the Invasions*, translated by S. Gilbert and J. Emmons, New York: Braziller, 1969, p.66.

108. Brenk (as in n.105), pp.52–3, cites J. Wilpert, *Die Malereien der Katakomben Roms*, Freiburg im Breisgau, 1903, p.427. Similar wishes for a deceased virgin are expressed in the Hispanic liturgy: Férotin, *Liber Ordinum*, p.147; and Ntedika, *La évocation de l'au-delà*, p.225.

109. Augustine gives a thorough explication of every important image in *Sermo LXXVI*, in PL, vol. XXXIX, cols 1892–3. Other exegeses were written by John Chrysostom, *Homiliae LXXVIII, LXXIX* on Matt. 25, in PG, vol. LVIII, cols 711–18; Gregory the Great, *Homilia XII*, in PL, vol. LXXVI, cols 1118–23; and Isidore of Seville, *Allegoriae*, as in n.103.

110. *Cassell's New Latin Dictionary*, s.v. 'Fax, facies.' A torch turned upside down appears on many Roman sarcophagi. Since Antiquity, candles have been used for funerals as a way to honor the dead and to console the living, a custom maintained by the Christians: DACL, vol. II, s.v. 'cierges,' cols 1613–22. During a funeral mass, the deceased's body is surrounded with candles: see F. X. Lasance, *With God*, New York: Benziger Brothers, 1911, p.251. On the later tomb of Doña Urraca Díaz López de Haro, in the Monastery of Santa María la Real de Vileña (Burgos), dogs with candles strapped to their bodies are represented alongside the image of her coffin during the last rites: illustrated in Castillo et al., *El Panteón Real*, n.p.

111. See above, n.11.

112. Augustine, *Sermones XCIII*, chapter 2.2, chapter 3.4, in PL, vol. XXXVIII, cols 574–5.

113. Although, in the patristic literature, it is usually held that the most highly respected woman is a virgin and the least valued a matron, the exigencies of daily life created a different hierarchy in medieval Spain. The value placed on a married woman's honor is made clear in the body of law defending townswomen from offense; the highest fines for assault, molestation, and insults were for offenses committed against married women, the lowest for those against the unmarried. For the patristic view, see J. Ferrante, *Woman as Image in Medieval Literature from the Twelfth Century to Dante* (1975), Durham, NC, Labyrinth Press, 1985, p.20; for medieval Spanish law, see Dillard, *Daughters of the Reconquest*, pp.172–4.

114. The only other explanation of these figures that has been offered is that they represent one of the Foolish Virgins buying oil from a vendor, as in the liturgical drama performed in Limoges: Iñiguez, 'Tallas románicas,' p.203, and Alvarez-Coca, *Escultura románica*, p.32. Against this reading is, first, the absence of any indication of oil or lamps; the abrasion along the women's arms is not so profound as to erase their gestures or any objects that they might have been holding. Second, a vendor and customer would have no cause to embrace, as these women do. My suggestion is based upon the traditional use of the image of the Visitation in the twelfth century: Réau, *Iconographie*, vol. II, part 2, pp.195–210; Kirschbaum, *Lexikon*, vol. II, cols 229–35.

The Visitation rarely appears as an independent scene in the early Middle Ages, although it does occur as a pendant to the Annunciation on a fifth-century sarcophagus in Ravenna: DACL, vol. XV, part 2, s.v. 'Visitation,' cols 3130–33. Usually it forms part of a pictorial cycle about the life of the Virgin or the Infancy of Christ. Often it is given an architectural setting, as suggested by the biblical text (Luke 1.39–40).

115.   The Protoevangelium of Saint James, book 22, lines 1–4, *Los evangelios apócrifos*, 7th edition, edited by A. de Santos Otero, BAC, vol. CXLVIII, 1991, pp.166–7. Maguire, 'The Depiction of Sorrow,' pp.160–61, notes that the combination of lamentation with the Visitation clarifies the link between birth and death, making the embrace between the two women an embrace of both joy and grief.

116.   Isidore of Seville, *Allegoriae*, 91, in PL, vol. LXXXIII, col. 113. Augustine also refers to Solomon's building of the temple as a prefiguration for Christ: *In Psalmum CXXVI enarratio. Sermo ad plebem*, in PL, vol. XXXVII, col. 1668.

117.   'Even so every good tree bringeth forth good fruit . . . by their fruits you shall know them.'

118.   Honorius Augustodunensis, *Elucidarium*, book 3, chapter 1, in Lefèvre, pp.164, 443.

119.   ibid, 3.3–6, in Lefèvre, pp.165–6, 444.

120.   Bynum, *Jesus as Mother*, pp.131–3.

121.   A. J. Frantzen, 'When Women Aren't Enough,' *Speculum*, vol. 68, no. 2, 1993, pp.466–7. Bynum posits that it is the male biographer who views a woman as 'virile' when she makes spiritual progress, and that female biographers of women characterize their subjects as feminine and living an ordinary existence: C. W. Bynum, 'Women's Stories, Women's Symbols: A Critique of Victor Turner's Theory of Liminality,' in R. L. Moore and F. E. Reynolds, eds, *Anthropology and the Study of Religion*, Chicago: Center for the Scientific Study of Religion, 1984, pp.112–15.

122.   Atkinson (as in n.86), pp.145, 163–4, 180, 192–3.

123.   Leclercq (as in n.52).

124.   J. Tibbetts Schulenburg, 'Saints' Lives as a Source for the History of Women, 500–1100,' in J. T. Rosenthal, ed., *Medieval Women and the Sources of Medieval History*, Athens, GA: University of Georgia Press, 1990, p.309, pointed out that models for women in the world are harder to document than the female saint's life or the life of a cloistered woman.

125.   Bynum, *Jesus as Mother*, pp.82–109, discusses the importance of models in the definition of the self, and the contemporary focus on emotion as a source for the affective qualities of many works of art. The conclusion I reached above accords with Bynum's characterization, pp.131–3, of stereotypes of mothers in the twelfth century. While Bynum agrees, pp.142–3, that 'the increased use of marriage and motherhood as metaphors in the twelfth century reflects a more positive evaluation of these institutions,' she cautions that this may not reflect an increased respect for actual women by men at that time. For Spanish legislation concerning misconduct against women, see n.113. The social spectrum was extremely complex, and the surviving evidence is incomplete and selective. Therefore, we can discuss these issues only in tentative terms.

2.1 Sarcophagus lid of Doña Blanca, front, *c.*1156. Nájera, Santa María la Real

2.2 Sarcophagus of Doña Blanca, back

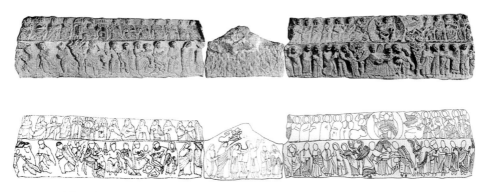

—— partially extant
—— hypothetical reconstruction

2.3 Sarcophagus of Doña Blanca, opened out, and hypothetical reconstruction

2.4   Sarcophagus of Doña Sancha, front and side: Funeral Service; Eidolon; Three Women; Chrismon, c.1100. Jaca, Benedictine Convent of Santa Cruz

2.5   Sarcophagus of Doña Blanca, detail of front: Deathbed and Eidolon

2.6   Sarcophagus of Doña Blanca, detail of front: Sancho's Lament

2.7   Sarcophagus of Egas Moniz, detail: Preparation of the Body; Mourners; Deathbed and Eidolon, c.1144, Paço de Sousa, former monastic church

3

The tomb as prompter for the chantry: four examples from Late Medieval England

Anne McGee Morganstern

In memory of my mother

'que une Tombe dalabastre soit fait . . . en remembrance de moy et que home puisse prier pour moi.'

The relationship between Late Gothic tombs and prayers for their occupants is attested in innumerable sepulchral inscriptions, and testaments like the one quoted above from the 1371 will of Sir Walter Manny, K. G.[1] But little or no connection has been made between the monumental tombs decorated with so-called 'weepers,' or family members, in England and elsewhere, and the accompanying foundations of prayers, or chantries, for the deceased and their families. Well before the monuments to be discussed here were erected, their eventual occupants had already established daily masses and prayers for themselves and their families in the institutions that they had chosen for burial and commemoration. These offices were expected to continue, and were even augmented, after they died. The masses and prayers were celebrated by special chaplains or priests for whom the foundation provided a living. This arrangement marks a fundamental difference between Late Medieval chantries and Early Medieval practice, in which religious communities had offered intercessory prayer for individuals and families in the conventual round of prayers as well as special masses.[2]

Establishing that prayer foundations are reflected in the design of tombs equipped with 'weepers' requires that the figures represented on them, or signified by their heraldry, be identified, and that the resulting program be compared with the commendations of individuals specified in the chantry ordinances. As we shall see, there is a relationship, but not an exact correspondence, between the long list of persons cited for commendation in the ordinances and the reduced assemblage represented on the tombs. The imagery on the tombs would have been sufficient for a chantry priest with a trained memory to be able to invoke by name all the prescribed family members, something made possible by the mnemonics known in England by the fourteenth century. As Otto Gerhard Oexle has explained in his work on liturgical *memoria* in the Middle Ages, invocation for the living and the dead by name was an important aspect of liturgical commemoration. Together with tomb effigies, the prayers evoked the continual presence of founders and benefactors in the religious communities that they had founded or endowed.[3] Recognizing the representation of family members on tombs as a reference to prescribed prayers extends Oexle's perception of the liturgical function of tombs in general, and of these tombs in particular. Moreover, it establishes tombs with 'weepers' as manifestations of covenants between the families of founders or benefactors and the institutions in which their relatives were buried, creating bonds that have been emphasized by Karl Schmid in his pioneering work on liturgical commemoration, as well as by Oexle.[4] As Schmid clarified as early as 1957, the resulting presence of the dead bound the living family together; often it also attached them to particular religious institutions for many generations.[5]

*   *   *

When on 16 February 1348, the prior and canons of St Frideswide in Oxford regulated the chantry recently established in their cloister by Elizabeth de Montfort, Lady Montacute, they approved a daily mass with an Office of the Dead to be celebrated in perpetuity for her and her family in the Chapel of the Virgin Mary. The beneficiaries of the Montacute chantry included the lady's parents, two husbands, ten children by the first husband, and the Bishop of the diocese, John Gynwell of Lincoln.[6] The prior and canons also agreed that after Lady Montacute died, her tomb in the same chapel would be the focus of the daily Office of the Dead, accompanied by a special prayer for her soul.[7]

To support these services, Lady Montacute had already deeded a meadow to the priory, Stockwell Mead, now part of Christ Church Meadow. The tomb of Lady Montacute remains in the church where it was erected, although it has been moved from the Lady Chapel to a confining space between two piers of the chapel's north arcade, as seen in a late nineteenth-century watercolor of the chapel (Fig. 3.1).[8] Although the priory was suppressed in the sixteenth century, its church was eventually promoted to Oxford Cathedral and the chapel of Christ Church College.[9] But, as a result of the Dissolution, the chantry has gone the way of all medieval chantries, except as petrified in the monument containing the lady's remains.

The tomb of Lady Montacute, like hundreds of comparable monuments created in the Late Middle Ages, consists of a rectangular tomb chest on which an effigy of the lady lies with her hands joined in prayer (Fig. 3.2). Angels support the pillows on which her head rests and a dog lies at her feet. The long sides of the chest are decorated with arcades framing figures carved in relief. These figures have been identified as the lady's ten children; their stations and gender correspond to the family record, and the shields in the spandrels above them, alternately Montfort for their mother, and Montacute for their father, seem appropriate for such a program.[10] The bishop in the central niche on the south side (Fig. 3.3) must represent Simon Montacute, Bishop of Ely at his death in 1345. He is flanked by two ladies in fashionable secular dress on his right and by two gentlemen in lay attire on his left, one of whom, a lord in a long robe and mantle who is holding gloves, must represent William Montacute, Earl of Salisbury. The Bishop of Ely's feminine counterpart occupies the central niche on the north side of the tomb, a lady in Benedictine habit, carrying the base of a crosier (Fig. 3.4). She must represent Matilda Montacute, Abbess of Barking until 1352. She is flanked on her right by her sister Isabel, who succeeded her as abbess, also dressed in a habit and carrying the base of a crosier against her left arm, and a brother in juvenile costume. On her left are two sisters, one a Benedictine, who must represent Elizabeth, Prioress of Holywell.

The short ends of the chest are virtually concealed from view today. Decorated with reliefs of the Virgin and Child with symbols of Matthew and John at the west, and a maiden saint with symbols of Luke and Mark at the east, they suggest that the tomb was originally free-standing.

The figures representing Lady Montacute's family are generally called weepers in the literature on this tomb, a term that is used rather indiscriminately to describe family members represented on English Gothic tombs.[11] I suggest, however, that this term as applied to Lady Montacute's tomb, and many others similar to it, is a misnomer. The figures represented on this tomb chest do not appear to weep, nor are they dressed in mourning robes for the funeral ceremony that the term usually implies. The bishop is not accompanied by the acolytes and subordinate clergy usual on a ceremonial tomb. Furthermore, three of the children predeceased their mother. Rather than depicting the family gathered for her funeral, I would suggest that the members of Lady Montacute's family represent those *for* whom prayers were to be offered, together with those for their mother, for they constitute an abbreviation of the chantry commendations.

The presence of two abbesses among the Montacute children proves that the tomb was completed after Isabel Montacute succeeded her sister Matilda as Abbess of Barking in 1352. But even if the tomb was commissioned only after Lady Montacute's death two years later, she must have planned it in relation to the prayers that she had established in 1348. The choice of those to be represented from a long list of loved ones suggests a mother's solicitude for the welfare of her children, in the midst of whom she wished to be immortalized. Besides containing her body, the tomb was a visual reminder of the chantry ordinance, and the focus of the prayers said daily for her and her loved ones.

Lady Montacute's tomb is one of the few known to me in which the family program can be compared with commendations in chantry ordinances. Three other examples may be cited here to reinforce my interpretation of the Mont-acute tomb program and to expand our understanding of some of the broader implications for medieval memory systems evident in these tombs.

*　　*　　*

Three tombs in the northeast corner of the Angel Choir of Lincoln Cathedral circumscribe a space formerly dedicated to St Katherine (Fig. 3.5) that was endowed with a lavish chantry by the Bishop of Lincoln, Henry Burghersh, in 1332, eight years before his death. Beyond supporting two chaplains and supplementing the maintenance of eleven poor cathedral clerks, Bishop Henry established a daily mass at the chapel altar for himself and his successor bishops of Lincoln, for King Edward III and Queen Philippa, for the Queen Mother, Isabella, and for the living members of his immediate family and his benefactors, some of whom were named. Moreover, prayers were prescribed for the souls of the deceased members of his immediate family.[12]

By the time that the chantry founded by Bishop Henry was amplified by his brother, Sir Bartholomew, in 1345, two tombs must have been erected on the south flank of the chapel (Fig. 3.6), one for the Bishop and one for their father, Sir Robert Burghersh (†1306). The ordinance of 1345 refers to the burial of both Burghershes in the chapel and specifically to the tomb of Sir Robert.[13] It expanded the number of chaplains to five, endorsed the benefici-aries of the prayers already established, with some exceptions, and made some additions.[14] This ordinance also established four solemn masses or anniversaries per year: one for King Edward III, one for Bishop Henry, one for Sir Robert and one for Sir Bartholomew himself after his death.

The Chapel of St Katherine apparently extended somewhat beyond the easternmost bay of the north aisle in order to link the tombs of Bishop Henry and Sir Robert to the base of the shrine of St Hugh's head. These three monuments stand in tandem, all part of one building campaign, to judge from their architectural and figurative detail, with the shrine base at the west, the tomb of Bishop Henry next, and finally that of Sir Robert, which abuts the eastern wall of the retrochoir.

On the side facing the chapel, the Bishop's tomb chest is decorated with an arcade housing five pairs of clerks seated at lecterns as if participating in the Divine Office, a likely reference to perpetual prayers. Above them, shields would remind the celebrant of those to be remembered besides the Bishop.[15] Reading from head to foot (west to east) are the arms of Edward III; those of his first four sons who survived; then those of Henry Plantagenet, Earl of Lancaster; a Burghersh relative; Laurence Hastings, Earl of Pembroke; Humphrey de Bohun, Earl of Hereford and Essex; and Gilbert de Clare, Earl of Gloucester. Six of these lords were mentioned in the chantry ordinances. The others could be covered in the blanket phrase of the ordinance of 1332 'the rest of our kinsmen and benefactors.'

The tomb of Bishop Henry's father, Robert Burghersh (Fig. 3.7), is also decorated on the side facing the chapel with an arcade of five niches housing figures, in this case, secular couples identified by the shields above them. They represent the surviving descendants of Sir Robert's sister and brother-in-law, Bartholomew Badlesmere, and their husbands, or, in one case, a son. Although none of them had been mentioned specifically in the chantry ordinances, their father and their brother, both deceased by the time the tomb was erected, were mentioned in the ordinance of 1332.

Finally, the program of Sir Bartholomew's tomb (Fig. 3.8) includes much of the heraldry found on that of Bishop Henry, originally illustrating some of it with figures. The tomb chest with its effigy is sheltered by a triple-arched canopy that displays a row of shields corresponding to those above the first three niches of Bishop Henry's tomb, reaffirming Sir Bartholomew's allegiance to Edward III and his family. Below on the tomb chest, surmounting six niches for figures, are eleven (originally twelve) shields that invoke his male kinsmen and brothers-in-arms. Only one of the blasons, for Badlesmere, refers to a kinsman mentioned in the chantry ordinances, but the blanket clause, 'the rest of our kinsmen and benefactors,' applies to all of them.

The Burghersh foundations raise some interesting questions regarding the relationship between the tombs and the chantries. Whereas clearly the most important persons are cited in the documents and represented on the tombs, sometimes named references in the ordinances seem to preclude representation on the tombs or vice versa. Moreover, protocol, family loyalty and pride, and affection must have conditioned the selection of those to be represented. But I wonder if there is not yet another factor that helps to explain the apparent discrepancies between the chantry ordinances and the tomb displays. The figures and shields represented on the tombs should have been sufficient to call to mind all of the relatives mentioned in the ordinances to a chaplain equipped with a trained memory. As discussed by Mary Carruthers, the architectural method for fixing mental images in the mind, which had been revived in the thirteenth century by such luminaries as Albert the Great and Thomas Aquinas, used the mental image of a series of orderly places, like a tomb chest arcade, as a setting for images to be remembered, along with associations attached to them.[16] As she points out, by adopting Cicero's linkage of memory to prudence, medieval writers made the conscious culti-vation of memory a moral obligation as well as a scholarly necessity.[17]

That the art of memory was cultivated in England in the first half of the fourteenth century is proven by a treatise on memory attributed to Thomas Bradwardine, theologian and mathematician, who was connected to both Oxford and Lincoln. Educated at Oxford, where he was a fellow at Merton College from 1325 and proctor in 1325 and 1326, he was summoned to Lon-don in 1335 by the Bishop of Durham and Chancellor of the realm, Richard de Bury.[18] He eventually became a chaplain to Edward III and, just before he died, Archbishop of Canterbury. Bradwardine had received a prebendary at Lincoln Cathedral in 1333, just a year after Bishop Henry founded the Burghersh chantry.[19] The text of his *Ars Memorativa* draws on the earlier writers on memory in postulating two things necessary for the trained memory: firm locations and images for the things to be remembered. He further recommends that each location should be of moderate size, as much as one's visual power can comprehend in a single glance. Among suitable locations, he cites both tombs and arcaded spaces. He recommends units of five. He says that the images in the locations should be wondrous and in-tense, most beautiful or ugly, joyous or sad, worthy of respect or ridiculous, in order to be memorable, and he gives some melodramatic examples.[20]

If we assume that the chaplains appointed to the Montacute and Burghersh chantries would have been expected to have well-trained memories in order to fulfill their duties adequately, and that they would have found the figures in the niches wondrous, most beautiful, or at least worthy of respect, the tombs at Oxford and Lincoln are amply provided with the cues needed to call forth the chain of commendations set forth in the ordinances. Whereas the statuettes on the tomb chest of Lady Montacute represented an abbrevi-ated version of the chantry commendations, those on the Burghersh tombs were designed both to reinforce the commendations specified in the ordi-nances and to expand the blanket clauses. A chaplain standing before the altar of the chapel would have had a view of each of the Burghersh tombs adequate to read the heraldry represented on the tomb chests. The shields of the King and his sons on the tombs of both Sir Bartholomew and Bishop Henry should have prompted him to mention not only these lords, but also the Queen Mother and Queen Philippa, both mentioned in the 1332 ordinance.

On Bishop Henry's tomb, the arms of Henry de Lancaster would have singled out this lord among the Bishop's benefactors, covered in the ordin-ance by the blanket clause 'the rest of our kinsmen and benefactors.' The arms of a Burghersh kinsman could have prompted a string of commendations specified in the 1332 ordinance: Bishop Henry's mother, his other brothers, and his sisters. The arms of Laurence Hastings would have invoked the Earl of Pembroke himself, and also his great aunt, Marie de Saint-Pol, mentioned by name in the ordinance of 1345. The next two shields refer to a distinguished ally of the Bishop, Humphrey de Bohun, and an illustrious kinsman, Gilbert de Clare, the latter mentioned in the ordinance of 1345.

Glancing at the tomb of Sir Robert in the adjacent space, the chaplain would have been able to read the arms of four Badlesmere daughters, one granddaughter, and their consorts. The sight of these ladies would certainly have invoked the memory of their father and brother, Bartholomew and Gilles Badlesmere, and their mother, Margaret de Clare.

Finally, a glance at the tomb of Sir Bartholomew against the opposite wall of the chapel would have evoked his presence, of course, but also the memory of his wife and children, who were mentioned in the ordinance of 1345, and of those barons whose arms appear on the tomb chest, again making specific the blanket clause 'the rest of our benefactors and kinsmen.'

By extending the ordinance commendations, the Burghersh tombs demonstrate very well how tombs of this type could be used over a long period of time to join the living with their dead. Not only does Bishop Henry's ordinance refer to the living members of his immediate family, but to his successors as Bishop of Lincoln, and the repeated clause in the chantry ordinances, 'the rest of our kinsmen,' could be extended indefinitely into the future, like much of the heraldry used on the tombs.

In short, the tombs of Lady Montacute at Oxford and of the Burghershes at Lincoln are not weepers' tombs, depicting the funerals of the deceased or even the perpetual mourning of their family and friends. Rather, their imagery seems to have prompted the chantry commendations, especially when viewed in relation to medieval memory systems. For as the focus of prayers in the chapels that sheltered them, the tombs called up the presence of Lady Montacute and the Burghershes in the religious communities that they had endowed as long as the chantry survived. Now, with a renewed consciousness of the original liturgical function of their tombs, they are linked again with their loved ones, benefactors and descendants, in history.

Frequently cited sources

Foster, C. W., and A. Hamilton Thompson, 'The Chantry Certificates for Lincoln and Lincolnshire returned in 1548 under the Act of Parliament of 1 Edward VI,' *Lincolnshire Architectural and Archeological Society Reports and Papers*, vol. 36, 1922, pp.207–17.

Notes

Much of the material in this article is extracted from my book, *Gothic Tombs of Kinship in France, the Low Countries, and England*, University Park, PA: Pennsylvania State University Press, 2000, which has appeared since this paper was presented at the meeting of the College Art Associaton in 1994. I discussed the Burghersh tombs in their political context in *Memory and Oblivion*, XXIXth International Congress of the History of Art, Amsterdam, 1996, Boston: Kluwer Academic Publishers, 1999. The heraldic research on the Burghersh tombs was conducted jointly with John A. Goodall, FSA, FRNS.

Dr. G. A. Knight, Principal Archivist of the Lincolnshire Archives, gave valuable advice on interpreting the Burghersh chantry documents. My field work in England was supported by grants from the College of the Arts of the Ohio State University. The illustrations were printed from my negatives by Ken Frick, except for Fig. 3.1.

1. Cited by W. H. St John Hope, 'On the Early Working of Alabaster in England,' *The Archaeological Journal*, vol. 61, 1904, p.227.

2. On the development of the chantry, especially in England, see K. L. Wood-Legh, *Perpetual Chantries in Britain*, Cambridge: Cambridge University Press, 1965, pp.1–5. Her study is the basic work on English chantries, but see also J. T. Rosenthal, *The Purchase of Paradise: Gift Giving and the Aristocracy, 1307–1485*, London: Routledge and Kegan Paul, and Toronto: University of Toronto Press, 1972, chapter 3. For a good explanation of all that a perpetual chantry endowment usually entailed, see G. H. Cook, *Medieval Chantries and Chantry Chapels*, London: Phoenix House Ltd., 1963, pp.12–13.

    For earlier intercessory prayer for the living and the dead, see A. Angenendt, 'Theologie und Liturgie der mittelalterliche Toten-Memoria,' in K. Schmid and J. Wollasch, eds, *Memoria: Der geschichtliche Zeugniswert des liturgische Gedenkens im Mittelalter*, Münstersche Mittelalter-Schriften, vol. XLVIII, Munich: Wilhelm Fink Verlag, 1984, pp.180–84, 189–90; and idem, 'Missa specialis: Zugleich ein Beitrag zur Entstehung der Privatmessen,' *Frühmittelalterliche Studien*, vol. 17, 1983, especially pp.169–75, 179–81, 189–215. For the important link between almsgiving and the celebration of mass in memory of the dead, see J. Wollasch, 'Gemeinschaftsbewusstsein und soziale Leistung im Mittelalter,' *Frühmittelalterliche Studien*, vol. IX, 1975, pp.268–86. For a brief discussion of liturgical commemoration from the early to the late Middle Ages, see the introduction to A. Morganstern, *Gothic Tombs*, pp.4–6.

3. O. G. Oexle, 'Memoria und Memorialbild,' in Schmid and Wollasch, eds, *Memoria*, pp.384–440, especially pp.386–8; and 'Die Gegenwart der Lebenden und der Toten. Gedanken über Memoria,' in K. Schmid, ed., *Gedächtnis, das Gemeinschaft stiftet*, Munich and Zürich: Verlag Schnell and Steiner, 1985, pp.74–107.

4. K. Schmid, 'Zur Problematik von Familie, Sippe und Geschlecht. Haus und Dynastie beim mittelalterlichen Adel,' *Zeitschrift für die Geschichte des Oberrheins*, vol. 105, NF 66, 1957, pp.46–7; reprinted in *Gebetsgedenken und adliges Selbstverständnis im Mittelalter*, Sigmaringen: J. Thorbecke, 1983, pp.228–9.

5. ibid. On the relation of families to burial churches in England, see S. Wood, *English Monasteries and their Patrons in the Thirteenth Century*, London: Oxford University Press, 1955, pp.3, 129–31; and Rosenthal, *The Purchase of Paradise* (as in n.2), chapters 4 and 5.

6. S. R. Wigram, ed., *The Cartulary of the Monastery of St Frideswide at Oxford*, Oxford: Historical Society, vol. XXXI, 1896, pp.8–9. In the fourteenth century, Oxford was within the diocese of Lincoln.

7. 'Dicent insuper dicti Sacerdotes . . . commendacionem . . . in dicta Capella, & . . . in eadem placebo & dirige pro animabus superius enumeratis specialiter, & pro omnibus alijs fidelium defunctorum, secundum vsum Sar', ad tumulum viz. dicte domine sic & cum eam ibidem contigerit sepeliri, captatis ad hoc horis congruis atque certis, prout eis videbitur commodius faciendum, in vna semper oracione animam dicte domine in specie nominando.' ibid., p.10. See also Wood-Legh, *Perpetual Chantries* (as in n.2), pp.139–40.

8. For the displacement of the tomb and the evidence for its original location, see J. Blair, ed., *Saint Frideswide's Monastery at Oxford: Archaeological and Architectural Studies*, Gloucester and Wolfeboro Falls, NH: Alan Sutton, 1990, pp.251–2.

9. For the vicissitudes of the institution after the suppression of the priory at the behest of Cardinal Wolsey in 1524, see S. A. Wagner, *Oxford Cathedral*, London: Society for Promoting Christian Knowledge, 1924, pp.221–43.

10. Matthew H. Bloxham, 'Sepulchral Monuments in Oxford Cathedral,' in *Memoirs Illustrative of the History and Antiquities of the County and City of Oxford* (Annual Meeting of the Royal Archaeological Institute of Great Britain and Ireland, 6, 1850), London: Office of the Institute, 1854, p.223; Wagner, *Oxford Cathedral*, pp.57–8, and E. G. W. Bill, 'Lady Montacute and St Frideswide's Priory,' *Friends of Christ Church Cathedral Report*, 1960, p.10. For a list of the Montacute children, see Wigram, ed., *Cartulary*, p.9, and G. E. Cokayne, *The Complete Peerage*, new edition revised by V. Gibbs et al., London: The St Catherine Press, 1910–59, vol. 11, pp.385–8.

11. Lawrence Stone's statement in *Sculpture in Britain: The Middle Ages*, Pelican History of Art, Harmondsworth: Penguin Books, 1955, p.181, that 'The *weepers* [emphasis mine] are lords and ladies and prelates of the church who can be identified with the relatives and friends of

Lady Elizabeth for whose souls she specifically ordered the two chantry priests to pray' is symptomatic of the general confusion over the function of the family members represented on the Montacute tomb.

12. Lincolnshire Arch., Bishop's Reg. IV, fols 39–40v; Foster and Thompson, 'Chantry Certificates,' pp.207–10.

13. *'domini Roberti de Burghersch patris dictorum dominorum Henri Bartholomique ad pedes dicti domini Henri in capella beate Katerine predicte tumulati . . . set missa in dicta capella sancte Katerine iuxcta funus suum cantabitur pro anima sua,'* Lincolnshire Arch., Bishop's Reg. VI, fols 147–147v; Foster and Thompson, 'Chantry Certificates,' p.213.

    Since the date of this document is instructive in dating the tombs, it is important to note that it is dated 28 April 1345, following the appearance of Sir Bartholomew before the cathedral chapter on the Feast of St George, 23 April (Lincolnshire Arch., Bishop's Reg. VI, fols 145 and 148), rather than on the Feast of St Gregory, as read by Foster and Thompson, 'Chantry Certificates,' p.210.

14. Lincolnshire Arch., Bishop's Reg. VI, fol. 145; Foster and Thompson, 'Chantry Certificates,' p.211.

15. Charges on the shields are fortunately in relief, since they have recently been repainted. The charges on all three tombs match those recorded by Dugdale in his Book of Monuments in 1641 (London, Brit. Lib., Add. MS 71474, fols 97v–98). With a few exceptions, our identifications of the coats-of-arms, which have been verified in coeval sources, agree with those proposed by R. Gough, *Sepulchral Monuments in Great Britain*, London: printed for the author, sold by T. Payne and Son, 1786–96, vol. I, pp.96–7, and 108–13.

16. M. J. Carruthers, *The Book of Memory: A Study of Memory in Medieval Culture*, Cambridge: Cambridge University Press, 1990, pp.62–3, 122–9, 271. For another example of the architectural mnemonic, see the article by C. Carty in this volume.

17. Carruthers, *Book of Memory*, p.70.

18. H. A. Oberman, *Archbishop Thomas Bradwardine: A Fourteenth-century Augustinian*, Utrecht: Kemink & Zoon, 1957, pp.12–17.

19. *Dictionary of National Biography from the earliest times to 1900*, London: Oxford University Press, 1950, vol. II, p.1097.

20. For a discussion of Bradwardine's treatise, see Carruthers, *Book of Memory*, pp.130–33; for a translation of the text, see pp.281–8.

3.1   *Lady Chapel, Oxford, Christ Church Cathedral*, watercolor, 1891

3.2   Tomb of Lady Elizabeth Montacute, after 1352, Oxford, Christ Church Cathedral (former Priory of St Frideswide)

3.3   Tomb of Lady Elizabeth Montacute, detail: Simon Montacute, Bishop of Ely

3.4   Tomb of Lady Elizabeth Montacute, detail: Matilda Montacute, Abbess of
Barking

3.5 Lincoln Cathedral, Angel Choir, former Chapel of St Katherine, begun 1256

3.6 Tombs of Bishop Henry Burghersh and Sir Robert Burghersh, *c.*1345, Lincoln Cathedral, former Chapel of St Katherine

3.7   Tomb of Sir Robert Burghersh, c.1345

3.8 Tomb of Sir Bartholomew Burghersh, after 1355, Lincoln Cathedral

Activating the effigy: Donatello's Pecci Tomb in Siena Cathedral

Geraldine A. Johnson

Most studies of tomb sculpture in Late Medieval and Early Modern Europe have focused on the attribution and dating of individual monuments, or have presented typological surveys that emphasize the formal development over time of genres such as wall monuments and floor tombs. Recently, some scholars have begun to turn their attention to the patronage of funerary monuments in terms of the concerns and characteristics of the social and economic groups commemorated in them.[1] The study of tomb sculpture, however, should not be limited to questions of authorship, style, and patronage. As I will demonstrate in this essay through my analysis of a single tomb designed by Donatello, the complex cultural and historical matrix in which tombs were commissioned, designed, and encountered in Late Medieval and Early Modern Europe can be understood more fully by considering two issues that have only occasionally been addressed in discussions of funerary art: the important role played by contemporary viewers, and the impact of ritual practices associated with death and postmortem commemoration on tomb design.[2]

Situating the Pecci Tomb

Sometime after 1427, Donatello cast and signed a bronze floor tomb for Giovanni di Bartolomeo Pecci of Siena, Bishop of Grosseto and apostolic protonotary, which depicts the dead prelate laid out in a concave bier in highly illusionistic low relief. (Figs 4.1, 4.2).[3] As I will discuss below, the tomb, currently in the northeastern transept of Siena Cathedral in the chapel of Saint Ansanus, was originally located in front of the high altar in the center of the old canons' choir over the site where the Bishop's body had been buried (Fig. 4.3).[4] The placement of the tomb in this choir was particularly appropriate because Pecci had himself been a canon in the Duomo.[5]

The tomb is first mentioned as being in the center of the choir in a cathedral inventory of 1458.[6] In a 1467 inventory, it is still clearly listed as being 'in mezo al coro,' where it most likely remained until the old choir was torn down in 1506 and the relief was moved to the nearby Saint Ansanus chapel patronized by the Pecci family.[7] In a document of 1452, members of the Pecci family discussed installing the relief over the Bishop's burial site, which suggests that it was first set up sometime between 1452 and 1458.[8] However, this document does not prove exactly when Donatello designed and cast the tomb, only that he must have done so in the years between Pecci's death in 1427 and the family's deliberations in 1452.[9] John Paoletti and John Pope-Hennessy have suggested that the tomb may at one time have been intended for a Pecci family chapel abutting the Cathedral's north flank, but the tomb's prominent placement in the choir over the Bishop's burial site suggests that this position was the one originally intended: it is unlikely that the tomb would have been moved from a private side chapel to a key location in front of the high altar more than a quarter of a century after Pecci's death.[10] Pecci's will stipulated that his tomb should be placed inside the Duomo – 'in Ecl[es]ia cathed[r]ali Senarum in loco honorato' – while the Pecci family chapel was connected to the main body of the church only in 1442, facts that lend further support to the conclusion that the relief was originally intended to be placed over the Bishop's remains in the center of the old canons' choir.[11]

The Pecci Tomb is designed so that the illusion of three-dimensionality, of a real body displayed in a fully concave bier, is best appreciated from one viewpoint in particular, namely, that of a beholder looking obliquely at the effigy while standing at the foot of the tomb (Fig. 4.2). This observation, mentioned briefly by H. W. Janson and somewhat elaborated in subsequent scholarship, has implications well beyond Donatello's interest in one-point perspective.[12] For here, as in several other projects by Donatello, the implied beholder is not simply any viewer standing in the correct position, but rather a historically specific viewer whose presence enhances, one could even say completes, the meaning of the tomb. The beholder most likely to stand in this position at the time the tomb was commissioned would, of course, have been a priest celebrating Mass at the Cathedral's high altar, which was dedicated to the Virgin, Siena's main patron saint, and was crowned in this period by Duccio's altarpiece, the *Maestà*.[13] As I will discuss below, I believe that the celebrant's position implied by Donatello's design would have re-called the Bishop's funeral, a service during which Pecci's body, like the bronze effigy, would probably have been placed before the priest on the high altar. Metaphorically, a beholder drawn thus into standing in this position by the tomb's perspective design would have reenacted Pecci's funeral Mass or, equally appropriately, would have evoked an intercessory Mass for the dead Bishop's soul.[14]

Bishop Pecci's funeral

At first glance, the realism of Donatello's relief would seem to suggest that this image accurately reflects the display of the dead Bishop on a bier during his funeral Mass. The face and body are carefully observed, with the ecclesiastical vestments wrapped around the Bishop in such a way that the corporeality of his upper legs is made visible beneath the drapery. Through a sophisticated and consistent use of perspectival illusionism organized for a viewer standing at the foot of the tomb, the bier in which Pecci lies seems to rise up from the floor with its long side poles, which serve as carrying handles, suggesting that it has just been set down before the altar.[15] This effect of three-dimensionality is achieved by depicting the flat frontal faces of the curved lower edge and forwardmost feet of the bier in such a way that the viewer seems to look into a concave trough. The illusion is further heightened by the fact that the soles of Pecci's shoes are visible, thus giving the beholder the sense of both looking down into the nichelike bier and up along the full length of the Bishop's body as if seen from just beyond the feet. Finally, the sense of viewing three-dimensional objects realistically positioned in space is reinforced by the fact that Donatello's signature – OPVS DONATELLI – barely visible under the scroll unfurled over it, is apparently inscribed on a pavement beneath the bier that seems to continue below the carrying poles on either side.

There is some evidence suggesting how Pecci's actual funeral service was performed, but it is unclear how reliable this information is. Sigismundus Titius's brief description of the Bishop's funeral in his Cinquecento history of Siena emphasizes how honorable the ceremony was and mentions that a wooden catafalque and many candles were set up for the rites.[16] A mid-seventeenth-century text on Sienese funerals by Isidoro Ugurgieri also mentions Pecci's burial in the Cathedral with more details than he provides for any other fourteenth- or fifteenth-century bishop's funeral, but the specifics are still quite sparse: 'He died in the year 1426 and great honor was paid to him at the burial, and a catafalque with twenty-four torches [was erected] in the Cathedral, and all the citizens honored him, and he is buried in Siena Cathedral in a very beautiful bronze tomb.'[17] In a marginal note, Ugurgieri cites an unspecified Sienese manuscript chronicle as his source, which makes it difficult to confirm the accuracy of his description, while Titius, writing a century after the event, provides no sources at all for his information. Examining Ugurgieri's text in general, one realizes that it was a great honor for a bishop of a town other than Siena itself to be buried in the Cathedral with such an elaborate ceremony. Indeed, only two other provincial bishops besides Pecci are said to have been buried in the Duomo in this period and, in both cases, Ugurgieri emphasizes that they were particularly venerated men.[18]

Roughly a century later, a collateral descendant of the Bishop, Giovanni Antonio Pecci, also described the funeral in his manuscript history of Siena: '[H]is corpse was displayed with . . . much magnificence in the main church, where he is still buried.'[19] Although Pecci seems to provide additional details of his illustrious ancestor's funeral, nevertheless, as he himself acknowledges, he has relied on Ugurgieri for much of his information. It is therefore unclear whether Pecci's specification that the Bishop's corpse was exposed in the Cathedral is simply his assumption that the catafalque mentioned by Ugurgieri must have been set up over the dead body (although such structures were often erected over closed coffins), or whether he is using other information unavailable to the earlier author. Thus, the known documents describing Bishop Pecci's funeral do not prove with any certainty that his corpse was actually displayed on a bier during the rites and, in any case, it is unlikely that Donatello himself would have attended this event.

Death rituals for high-ranking ecclesiastics

Given the sparse documentation on the Bishop's funeral, one must turn to ecclesiastical ceremonial books and diaries in order to determine whether the scene implied by the design of the Pecci Tomb accurately reflects the Late Medieval and Early Modern funerary rituals associated with high-ranking clergymen in general. Many of these types of texts include detailed descriptions of the robes and accessories put on the corpses of ecclesiastics such as popes, cardinals, and bishops. From the fourteenth to the sixteenth century, the funerary attire of important clerics remains remarkably consistent with certain texts specifying that the deceased should be vested as if to celebrate Mass, a convention to which Donatello conforms in his rendering of Pecci's garments.[20] Despite this correspondence, one should not assume that the Bishop's carefully attired body would necessarily have been open to public view during his funeral Mass, since corpses were generally kept hidden under shrouds or in coffins during such ceremonies in this period.[21] These customs, however, were often disregarded in funerals for members of the religious and secular elite, whose bodies (or sometimes wax face masks or full effigies) could be kept uncovered during both funeral masses and public processions.[22]

A wide range of visual evidence attests to the open display of the corpses of high-ranking clergymen, aristocrats, powerful *condottieri* and wealthy merchants and bankers. Italian sculpture, paintings, and frescoes from the late thirteenth century onward almost always show the deceased's face and body open to view. A particularly relevant example for Donatello is the cenotaph painted in 1422 in Florence Cathedral showing Pietro Corsini (†1405), Bishop of Florence, lying in his ecclesiastical robes exposed on a sarcophagus.[23]

The tomb sculpture produced for popes, kings, cardinals, and bishops from at least the early thirteenth century onward regularly portrayed such patrons as if laid out on their funeral biers or sarcophagi. Two Trecento examples of this genre that Donatello could well have known are Bishop Neri Corsini's tomb in S. Spirito, Florence, and Archbishop Simone Saltarelli's tomb in S. Caterina, Pisa.[24]

To corroborate the custom of openly displaying the bodies of high-ranking ecclesiastics in liturgical dress that is suggested by this wealth of visual material, one must turn to textual and archeological sources. Evidence from disinterred corpses, for instance, implies that the effigies on Gothic tombs correspond closely with how the bodies were laid out inside the grave; similarly, when the tombs of Boniface VIII, Sixtus IV, and Cardinal Baldassare Coscia were opened, all three corpses were dressed in liturgical robes much as depicted on their monuments.[25] Textual confirmation for the ritual display of the corpses of high-ranking clergymen in particular is provided by ecclesiastical ceremonial books and diaries. Pontifical texts from the fourteenth and fifteenth centuries, in specifying the protocols for the funeral ceremonies of high-ranking ecclesiastics, often speak of particular rites taking place around the body of the deceased, and describe the ritual display of corpses for public viewing.[26] Even more vivid are the accounts of funerals found in diaries. Johannes Burchard, for example, describing the burial of Cardinal Ferrari of Modena in 1502, speaks of the body being laid out on a bier in the middle of St Peter's basilica while various prayers were recited. Burchard goes on to describe the cardinal's body being taken from the bier and stuffed by a carpenter into the too-narrow coffin that had been ordered for it.[27] Burchard's diary includes many other descriptions of ecclesiastics' funerals that also specify that the bodies were laid out for public viewing during the funeral as, for instance, was the case at the Bishop of Pampeluna's funeral in 1491.[28]

Without going as far as the papal court in Rome, Donatello could have witnessed at first hand elite funerals in Florence itself, which may well have influenced even more directly his design of the Pecci Tomb. Fifteenth-century accounts of the public funerary rites for important Florentine citizens often mention the fact that the corpse was either fully or partially (i.e., just the face) uncovered. For example, during the funeral procession to S. Lorenzo in 1429, Giovanni di Bicci de' Medici's body was left open to view.[29] There are also cases of bishops' bodies in particular being left uncovered for public viewing in Florence; for instance, Archbishop Antoninus's corpse was displayed in the church of S. Marco for eight days in 1459.[30]

A particularly important precedent for Donatello's Pecci Tomb design was the funeral ceremony organized for Cardinal Baldassare Coscia, the former Pope John XXIII, who died in Florence in 1419. Quattrocento accounts speak of Coscia's uncovered corpse, dressed in ecclesiastical robes, being displayed first on the font of Florence's Baptistery for the funeral ceremony and then being moved to a position in front of the pulpit.[31] A contemporary diarist's description makes it clear that Coscia's corpse was openly displayed on its bier: '[F]u portato in San Giovanni in su la bara scoperto' ([H]e was carried into S. Giovanni uncovered on the bier).[32] Not only was this event the most elaborate ecclesiastical funeral in early Renaissance Florence, but a few years later Donatello would himself be involved in designing and executing the bronze effigy and bier for Coscia's tomb in the Baptistery.[33] Thus, the ceremonial display of Coscia's body dressed in liturgical garb might well have influenced Donatello's later attempts to evoke Pecci's funerary rites in his relief for the Bishop's tomb. Whether Pecci's corpse really was displayed uncovered on a bier and whether Donatello himself witnessed the Bishop's actual funeral are, in some ways, irrelevant: what matters is that Donatello's experiences in Florence, as well as the prevailing funerary customs for high-ranking clergymen in general, could well have led him to visualize the funeral of an ecclesiastic as one in which the corpse in liturgical robes was exposed on a bier during a public funeral Mass.

The specific ceremonies probably performed during Bishop Pecci's funeral are also important for understanding the full implications of Donatello's tomb design. Papal ceremonial books and diaries describe the various rites associated with ecclesiastical funerals and, as was the case for funerary dress, once again show much evidence of continuity in the pre-Tridentine period. Texts from the thirteenth through the sixteenth centuries on the funerary rituals for high-ranking ecclesiastics describe remarkably similar ceremonies being performed around the corpse, with particular attention being paid to rites of absolution using incense and holy water.[34] Several texts specify the ritual censing first of the altar before which the funeral ceremony is being performed and then of the body displayed on the bier. A Trecento ceremonial book, for instance, speaks of the four highest-ranking clerics to officiate at the funeral gathering at the shoulders and feet of the deceased to chant; one of the clerics then ascends and censes the altar before which the body is displayed, after which he returns to the body and in turn censes it as well.[35] A mid-Quattrocento text describes a similar ceremony using many of the same phrases found in the earlier text, and one finds numerous depictions of this ritual in fifteenth-century art as well.[36] It may well be the specific moment when the presiding cleric turns his back to the altar in order to cense the dead body lying on the bier that is being evoked in the Pecci Tomb. It is from such a position that the perspectival construction of Donatello's relief would be most effective, its illusionism most fully realized.[37]

Funeral ceremonies and tomb design

A number of earlier tombs also chose to highlight the funeral ceremony, often the moment of absolution in particular, within their compositions.[38] The late twelfth-century tomb of Saint Hilary in Poitiers, for example, illustrates the ritual censing of the corpse.[39] The early thirteenth-century marble relief tomb of Pope Lucius III (†1185) in the Cathedral of Verona, which, like the Pecci Tomb, was originally set before the high altar, depicts angels censing the dead Pope's body as they place the tiara on his head, while a priest kneels at his feet (Fig. 4.4).[40] By depicting heavenly rather than earthly censing figures, the designer of the Lucius III tomb changes the scene from the representation of a single, precise moment in the past (i.e., the Pope's funeral in 1185) to an eternal scene, endlessly reenacted in an indeterminate zone somewhere between this world and the next. As Henriette s'Jacob has noted with regard to the use of angels as acolytes in Late Medieval tombs in general, they 'rais[e] the concrete act to a metaphysical plane and eternally perpetuat[e] the brief scene enacted on earth.'[41]

Throughout the Duecento, such types of relief tombs continued to be produced; some, like the Lucius III tomb, mixed the earthly with the divine. Over the course of the century, the clerics and acolytes, depicted as either absolving the corpse or reading the funeral office from prayer books, evolved into independent friezelike groups lined up along one side of a three-dimensional effigy. An important example of such a group is associated with the later thirteenth-century tomb of a member of the Annibaldi family, its fragments now reassembled in S. Giovanni in Laterano in Rome (Fig. 4.5).[42] The high-relief frieze of clerics and acolytes includes a figure reading a prayer book, one about to sprinkle holy water, and another preparing to cense the body; it demonstrates a continued interest in representing in ecclesiastical tombs various parts of the funeral ceremonies, including the rites of absolution.

The same type of frieze is found in the first half of the Trecento in monuments produced for members of the French court of Anjou in Naples by Tino da Camaino and his workshop. Closer to home, Donatello could have seen the monumental tomb of Bishop Guido Tarlati (†1327) in the Cathedral of Arezzo, which includes a low-relief frieze of priests and an acolyte chanting while holding a censer, a prayer book, and candles.[43] Unlike the Annibaldi or Anjou tombs, however, the Tarlati monument frieze is not behind the effigy but rather is split into two halves at either end of the figure. This aspect of the design illustrates what seems to be a Tuscan tendency to concentrate depictions of funerary rituals at the heads and feet of effigies displayed parallel to the wall surface to which their tombs are attached.

This central Italian phenomenon is best illustrated by a group of late thirteenth- and fourteenth-century wall tombs found in Florence itself, a location that makes them important possible precursors of Donatello's Pecci relief. These monuments seem to echo older relief tombs such as Lucius III's in Verona. Like the Veronese tomb, the Florentine reliefs include the funerary rituals within the same frame that surrounds the effigy. Two of these tombs are still in the Florentine church of S. Jacopo in Campo Corbolini, formerly the seat of the order of the Knights of Saint John. The wall tomb of Prior Pietro da Imola (†1330), for example, shows him laid out in the habit of his order, his head on a pillow, with the smaller figure of a cleric reading a prayer book at his head, and another cleric swinging a censer at his feet (Fig. 4.6).[44] It is precisely this ritual censing of the body by a cleric standing at the foot of the bier before the altar during the funeral Mass that, I have suggested, is being evoked in Donatello's Pecci Tomb. Other examples of this type of tomb in Florence include a second tomb in S. Jacopo, two in S. Maria Novella, and one of an unidentified bishop in the Bardini Museum. A tomb in S. Domenico, Arezzo, for a bishop and another in Nice for a Florentine canon, who may have died while traveling through France, also seem to belong to this group of Tuscan wall tombs that include within their frames a representation of the funerary rituals.[45] It is worth noting that all of the surviving examples of this genre depict deceased ecclesiastics, another aspect that would have made them especially appropriate sources for Donatello's tomb for Bishop Pecci.

The links between the two reliefs in S. Jacopo and Donatello's tomb in Siena Cathedral may be even stronger than appears at first glance, since Pecci belonged to the order associated with S. Jacopo, the Knights of Saint John.[46] This affiliation is, in fact, one of the few details mentioned in nearly every text referring to Pecci.[47] Although Donatello does not list the Bishop's membership in this order in the inscription at the foot of the tomb, he may well have intended to make a visual reference to it by depicting a Greek-style cross on the maniple hanging from Pecci's left wrist, a cross that still has traces of reddish-orange enamel that would have originally made it stand out from the dark bronze surface. This type of cross was a sign of the Knights of Saint John, and both reliefs in S. Jacopo display it prominently on the shoulders of the effigies' habits. This relationship between Pecci and the Knights of Saint John may explain the particular relevance that Florentine tombs of the order could have had for Donatello when he began to design his relief for the Sienese Bishop's tomb.

Viewing the Pecci Tomb

There were, therefore, numerous precedents that could have influenced Donatello's bronze relief tomb in Siena Cathedral. Ecclesiastical funerary practices in general, some of the specific ceremonies that took place in Florence in the early Quattrocento, and the long history of depicting funerary rituals, especially the key moment of absolution, in tomb art may have inspired Donatello's conception for the Pecci Tomb. Such precedents and personal experiences, however, do not explain either Donatello's novel formal strategies or the multilayered symbolic and metaphorical associations that his solutions imply.

Like many earlier tombs, the Pecci Tomb seems to evoke the Bishop's funeral, possibly the moment of absolution performed by the officiating priest standing with his back to the altar. Unlike any previous tomb, however, the absolution rites are suggested neither by low-relief figures depicted in the same plane as a two-dimensional effigy, nor by higher-relief figures along one side or at either end of a three-dimensional effigy. Instead, the Pecci Tomb's evocation of the funeral ceremony is realized only by having a live person step into the specific position at the foot of the Bishop's bier that is suggested by the relief's perspectival construction and the orientation of the inscription. Only by responding to these visual clues and standing in the correct position could a viewer symbolically reenact the funeral's absolution rituals. When Donatello designed the tomb, he knew that the person most likely to stand in this particular position would have been a priest saying Mass at the high altar of the Cathedral. By choosing such a beholder to activate the composition, Donatello not only allowed Pecci's funeral Mass to be recalled, but also effectively transformed every Mass said at the high altar into an anniversary or commemorative Mass for the dead Bishop's soul. This interpretation of the function of Donatello's innovative design gains merit in light of contemporary interest in, one could even say obsession with, organizing memorial masses to be said after death for intercessory purposes.

The historical origins of intercessory masses for the dead in Western Christianity are unclear, but a key figure in the steady increase in the popularity of such ceremonies seems to have been Pope Gregory the Great (590–604).[48] Over the centuries, the practice of attempting to intercede for the dead through the medium of commemorative masses grew increasingly common. From the thirteenth century onward, masses for the dead spread beyond monastic institutions and were increasingly adopted by the secular elite.[49] By the later Trecento, these practices changed subtly to include a new emphasis, perhaps even a fixation, on accumulating masses for one's soul after death. No longer was a single anniversary Mass sufficient; instead, the idea of the perpetual Mass began to grow in popularity, and one now finds wills with requests for dozens, hundreds, sometimes even thousands of commemorative masses for a single testator. This new focus on accumulating masses seems to develop throughout Europe sometime between the last decades of the fourteenth century and the first two decades of the fifteenth.[50]

These pan-European trends become particularly relevant for the case of Bishop Pecci if one looks at Donatello's tomb design in light of specific Sienese data. Beginning in 1426, there was a marked increase in the value of commemorative masses as a percentage of pious bequests in Sienese wills.[51] In other words, at precisely the time that Bishop Pecci lay on his deathbed in the spring of 1427, his Sienese contemporaries were beginning to dedicate an ever larger portion of their estates to assuring that postmortem masses would be said for their souls. Donatello's ingenious solution in the Pecci Tomb was to create metaphorically a cost-free perpetual Mass for the Bishop's soul that was activated every time a priest stood at the altar. The damaged state of Pecci's will makes it impossible to determine whether he himself arranged for postmortem intercessory masses to be said on his behalf. Funds left by the Bishop, however, may have been used by some of his heirs when, in 1442, they endowed a chaplain to participate in perpetuity in the canons' Mass celebrated daily at the high altar of Siena Cathedral directly above Pecci's burial location.[52] These arrangements demonstrate the Pecci family's interest in assuring that perpetual prayers would be said for the family at the high altar and suggest, indirectly, that the position of the Bishop's tomb in front of the altar probably reflects the particular desires of the family members who would have supervised the project's execution after his death.[53]

Even if Pecci and his family did not specifically allocate funds for intercessory masses for the Bishop's soul, the placement of his tomb and corporeal remains directly before the Cathedral's high altar had important commemorative implications. Although Durandus's thirteenth-century text specifically prohibits the burial of non-saintly remains near altars, this and similar interdicts were routinely ignored in practice.[54] Indeed, burial as close as possible to an altar was a privilege avidly sought by both the ecclesiastical and secular elite. In one's parish or monastic church, one tried to be buried either near an altar in a private family chapel or, equally prestigious, near the high altar.[55] For example, the wealthy merchant of Prato, Francesco Datini (†1409), can still be seen in a relief effigy positioned in front of the high altar of the church of his patron saint, Saint Francis, and the non-figurative tomb of Cosimo de' Medici (†1464) spreads out in luxurious colored marbles before the main altar of S. Lorenzo in Florence while his body lies in the crypt directly below.[56] Several high-ranking medieval and Early Modern ecclesiastics also positioned their tombs in front of altars. For instance, Cardinal Hugues Aycelin's lost metal floor tomb was originally located in front of the high altar of S. Sabina in Rome, while Pope Martin V's raised bronze relief tomb was placed before the high altar of the Roman basilica of S. Giovanni in Laterano.[57]

Two bronze reliefs in Florentine churches provide even closer parallels to the Pecci Tomb's original position in the center of Siena Cathedral's choir.

One of these is Lorenzo Ghiberti's relief for Prior Leonardo Dati (†1423/4), a tomb that was originally in the center of the old choir before the high altar of S. Maria Novella.[58] The second example, a tomb for the Franciscan minister general Francesco Sansoni (†1499), is still *in situ* in the nave of S. Croce (Fig. 4.7). The Sansoni relief, oriented toward the high altar, was probably originally in the center of an enclosed choir as well.[59] There are also records of numerous high-ranking Sienese prelates being buried 'in front of' or 'near the high altar.'[60] In the case of Pecci's tomb, the screen and choir-stall complex that once closed off the central and eastern portions of Siena Cathedral would have served to emphasize its inclusion within the most sacred precincts of the church.[61]

Pecci's will makes very clear his preoccupation with the location of his tomb: '[O]ne should choose a tomb for his body in the Cathedral church of Siena in an honorable location so that it may seem good to and may please the heirs and trustees noted below who he is certain will make his tomb an honorable one.'[62] This will, written a few days before Pecci's death, bears closer scrutiny. The concerns it raises are similar to those that preoccupied many of his contemporaries, concerns that are also manifest in the formal solutions developed by Donatello in the Bishop's tomb. Pecci's request to be buried in Siena Cathedral is part of a much broader trend toward increased specificity in wills in this period in general.[63] In Siena in particular, from the last third of the Trecento onward, testators were increasingly specific in their wills about the burial sites for their corporeal remains, and they were ever more anxious to control the funeral services and postmortem masses to be said on their behalf.[64]

Pecci's desire to commission a tomb in an important and honorable location – 'in . . . cathed[r]ali . . . in loco honorato' – suggests that, like many of his contemporaries throughout Europe, he too wished to arrange for a permanent memorial that would remind passers-by to pray for his soul long after his death.[65] A later Trecento will by a fellow ecclesiastic, Cardinal Guillaume de Chanac (†1384), movingly articulates the implicit concerns of Pecci's testament:

I wish and order that an honorable alabaster tomb be built for my remains and . . . that my statue, my arms, and other necessary ornaments be placed upon it, so that my relatives and friends and those whom I shall have known, when passing by it, will remember me and will take care to implore the Most High on behalf of my soul.[66]

In the tomb he designed for Pecci, Donatello developed a unique solution to the problem of which Cardinal Chanac was so keenly aware: rather than relying on the off-hand prayers of chance passers-by, Donatello's relief guaranteed that the potent prayers associated with the Mass itself would regularly be said by an ecclesiastic standing on the altar overlooking the effigy of the dead Bishop.

The elusive connections between Pecci's body and the altar would have been made even clearer by the orientation of the effigy. Like the vast majority of representations of the deceased in sculpture and painting, the Bishop would probably have had his feet closest to the altar and his head facing up toward it.[67] The prevailing custom in Italian funerary art is, overwhelmingly, to orient the effigy either toward the high altar of a church or, if in a chapel or at a side altar, to the nearest secondary altar.[68] This convention may relate to an old tradition, mentioned by Durandus, of placing bodies in the grave so that they face the east, that is, oriented as Pecci's effigy probably was in Siena Cathedral.[69] The few exceptions to this general rule on the positioning of tomb effigies often can be explained by the later re-erection of a monument in a location different from the one originally intended. A case in point is Ghiberti's Dati tomb in S. Maria Novella in Florence: the tomb does not now face the nearest altar, but records indicate that it has been moved from its original location in the center of the old choir.[70]

The probable orientation of Bishop Pecci's tomb becomes particularly significant in light of the ceremonies that celebrants on the high altar of Siena Cathedral would have performed when facing toward the relief in the choir. In pre-Tridentine Europe, a priest celebrating Mass would have stood on the front (or west) side of the altar with his back to the choir and congregation during most of the service. When worshipers came to receive the Host, the celebrant and his acolytes would have turned away from the altar to face the approaching communicants. One of the only other moments when the priest would have faced west into the nave was when censing or asperging the choir and congregation.[71] As discussed above, these types of absolution rituals were key components of funeral masses and, from the twelfth century onward, were often reenacted during masses specifically dedicated to commemorating the dead.[72] Thus, it was while performing these rites or when distributing the Host that a celebrant would have seen the dead Bishop's illusionistic effigy most clearly and would have symbolically (if perhaps inadvertently) reenacted some of the most important ceremonies probably performed at Pecci's funeral. The incense, holy water, and Eucharistic wafers dispensed by the priest while overlooking Pecci's effigy thus metaphorically would have served to link the dead Bishop's mortal remains, buried beneath the bronze relief, to the eternal Body of Christ incarnate consecrated on the altar above.

One final comment on the orientation of Bishop Pecci's tomb relates to the significance of what it was that his effigy would have originally been facing, albeit with closed eyes, in the intervals between Eucharistic services when no Host or celebrant was on the altar. Until the tomb was moved in 1506, the high altar above it had as its altarpiece, as previously noted, Duccio's *Maestà*.

Although this altarpiece was executed more than a century before Donatello's relief, the saints and narratives depicted on it would only have enhanced the various symbolic and metaphorical resonances that, I have suggested, are implicit in the tomb. The *Maestà*'s most prominent figures, Siena's four 'Santi Avvocati' and the Virgin, supreme patron saint of the city and traditionally the principal intercessor on behalf of mortal sinners on the Day of Judgment, were particularly appropriate images for a recently deceased son of Siena to face for all eternity. In addition, the narrative panels in the pinnacles of the altarpiece all depicted scenes related to the death of the Virgin. The central crowning image of the pinnacles was probably the *Coronation of the Virgin* with either the *Assumption* or the *Dormition* directly below, again very appropriate subjects for Pecci's effigy to turn toward while awaiting the resurrection of the dead.[73] If one accepts that one of the goals of Donatello's relief was to transcend time and space metaphysically by mystically joining Bishop and priest and Host and altar in an eternal cycle of interaction between the earthly and the divine, then perhaps one can see in the *Maestà*'s theme of the mortal-born Virgin's eternal triumph over death a model for what the Pecci Tomb hoped to achieve, namely, to allow a mere mortal to be touched by the divine and thereby eventually achieve everlasting life.

Activating the effigy

It is, of course, impossible to prove whether such an understanding of the Bishop's tomb accurately reflects the original intentions of Donatello or the Pecci family. Much more likely, in light of the Late Medieval and Early Modern funerary and testamentary practices previously discussed, is the assumption that Donatello's depiction of the dead Bishop in an illusionistic bier before the altar was meant to evoke Pecci's funeral as well as to create metaphorically an eternally recurring Mass of the Dead for his soul. Such an interpretation of the relief is reinforced by examining a roughly contemporary funerary monument in S. Anastasia in Verona that has conceptual, rather than specific formal or stylistic, links to the Pecci Tomb.[74] This monument depicts its patron, Andrea Pellegrini, as an almost fully in-the-round effigy kneeling in prayer in a niche angled to face toward the altar of his family chapel (Fig. 4.8).[75] The effigy in its niche is set within an elaborate terra-cotta cycle, executed by Michele da Firenze in about 1435–6, which represents the Life of Christ in twenty-four reliefs positioned on all three walls of the chapel. It is Pellegrini's will commissioning this monument, however, that suggests that the project may have been consciously planned to ensure that intercessory prayers would be said on his behalf in perpetuity.

Pellegrini's testament first stipulates that he be buried in his family chapel. He then orders that a statue be made depicting him as a kneeling and praying effigy turned toward the altar, upon which he also arranges for intercessory masses of Saint Gregory to be celebrated:[76]

I order that my body be buried in the church of S. Anastasia . . . there where my father is buried . . . I order that after my death . . . for three years continuously the Mass of Saint Gregory shall be said for my soul . . . I want to be sculpted . . . in this chapel . . . kneeling [and] praying . . . I want this to be done and completed within three years of my death.[77]

The time sequence specified in the will implies what Pellegrini's intentions actually are. He requests masses of Saint Gregory to be said continuously for three years, exactly the same amount of time he allots for the making of his praying effigy. This suggests that, once the effigy is in place, the celebration of commemorative masses by clerics will no longer be necessary.

As with Donatello's Pecci Tomb design, Pellegrini in effect seems to have created a cost-free means of insuring that prayers would be said for his soul in perpetuity. However, unlike the Pecci Tomb, the Pellegrini monument, with its permanently praying effigy, does not require the presence of a priest at the altar in order for these intercessory prayers to be initiated. Although the formal means used in the Pecci Tomb and Pellegrini monument are quite different, these projects demonstrate a similar commitment to developing innovative strategies for trying to guarantee the salvation of their patrons' souls.[78] In the Pecci Tomb, Donatello's strategy for perpetual commemoration and intercession could be activated only by the presence of a historically specific beholder, a priest celebrating a Mass at the altar above the effigy, for only then would the tomb's design be complete and its meanings made manifest. Although the Pecci relief is in many ways an unusual monument, by placing it within the context of contemporary rituals related to death and commemoration, and by carefully defining its originally intended viewers, one gains new insights into the complex issues involved in producing tomb sculpture in Late Medieval and Early Modern Europe.

Frequently cited sources

Ariès, P., *The Hour of Our Death*, translated by H. Weaver, New York: Vintage Books, 1981.

Aronow, G., 'A Description of the Altars of Siena Cathedral in the 1420s' in H. van Os, ed., *Sienese Altarpieces, 1215–1460: Form, Content, Function*, Groningen: Egbert Forsten Publishing, 1990, vol. II, pp.225–42.

Bauch, K., *Das mittelalterliche Grabbild: Figürliche Grabmäler des 11. bis 15. Jahrhunderts in Europa*, New York: Walter de Gruyter, 1976.

Chiffoleau, J., 'Sur l'usage obsessionnel de la messe pour les morts à la fin du moyen âge' in *Faire Croire: Modalités de la diffusion et de la réception des messages religieux du XIIe au XVe siècle*, Collection de l'école française de Rome, vol. 51, 1981, pp.235–56.

Cohn, S. K., Jr., *Death and Property in Siena, 1205–1800: Strategies for the Afterlife*, Baltimore: Johns Hopkins University Press, 1988.

— *The Cult of Remembrance and the Black Death: Six Renaissance Cities in Central Italy*, Baltimore: Johns Hopkins University Press, 1992.

Gardner, J., *The Tomb and the Tiara: Curial Tomb Sculpture in Rome and Avignon in the Later Middle Ages*, Oxford: Clarendon Press, 1992.

Herklotz, I., 'Paris de Grassis "Tractatus de funeribus et exequiis" und die Bestattungsfeiern von Päpsten und Kardinälen in Spätmittelalter und Renaissance' in J. Garms and A. M. Romanini, eds, *Skulptur und Grabmal des Spätmittelalters in Rom und Italien*, Vienna: Verlag der Osterreichischen Akademie der Wissenschaft, 1990, pp.217–48.

Janson, H. W., *The Sculpture of Donatello*, Princeton, NJ: Princeton University Press, 1963.

Johnson, G. A., 'Activating the Effigy: Donatello's Pecci Tomb in Siena Cathedral,' *The Art Bulletin*, vol. 77, 1995, pp.445–59.

— 'In the eye of the beholder: Donatello's sculpture in the life of Renaissance Italy,' unpublished PhD thesis, Harvard University, 1994.

Lightbown, R. W., *Donatello and Michelozzo: An Artistic Partnership and Its Patrons in the Early Renaissance*, 2 vols, London: Harvey Miller, 1980.

Mollat, G., 'Contribution à l'histoire du Sacré Collège de Clément V à Eugène IV,' *Revue d'histoire ecclésiastique*, vol. 46, 1951, pp.566–94.

Munman, R., *Optical Corrections in the Sculpture of Donatello*, Transactions of the American Philosophical Society, vol. LXXV, part 2, 1985.

— *Sienese Renaissance Tomb Monuments*, Memoirs of the American Philosophical Society, vol. CCV, 1993.

Panofsky, E., *Tomb Sculpture: Its Changing Aspects from Ancient Egypt to Bernini*, London: Thames and Hudson, 1964.

Paoletti, J. T., 'La tomba Pecci di Donatello: nuovi documenti,' *Rivista d'arte*, series 4, year 43, vol. 7, 1991, pp.189–201.

Pines, D. S., 'The tomb slabs of Santa Croce: a new "Sepoltuario",' unpublished PhD thesis, Columbia University, 1985.

Pope-Hennessy, J., *Donatello Sculptor*, New York: Abbeville Press, 1993.

Rosenauer, A., *Studien zum frühen Donatello*, Vienna: Verlag Adolf Holzhausens, 1975.

— 'Donatellos römische Grabmäler' in J. Garms and A. M. Romanini, eds, *Skulptur und Grabmal des Spätmittelalters in Rom und Italien*, Vienna: Verlag der Osterreichischen Akademie der Wissenschaft, 1990.

Rowell, G., *The Liturgy of Christian Burial: An Introductory Survey of the Historical Development of Christian Burial Rites*, London: Alcuin Club, 1977.

s'Jacob, H., *Idealism and Realism: A Study of Sepulchral Symbolism*, Leiden: E. J. Brill, 1954.

Strehlke, C. B., 'Art and Culture in Renaissance Siena' in K. Christiansen, L. B. Kanter and C. B. Strehlke, eds, *Painting in Renaissance Siena, 1420–1500*, New York: Metropolitan Museum of Art, 1988, pp.33–60.

Strocchia, S. T., 'Burials in Renaissance Florence, 1350–1500,' unpublished PhD thesis, University of California, Berkeley, 1981.

— *Death and Ritual in Renaissance Florence*, Baltimore, MD: Johns Hopkins University Press, 1992.

Ugurgieri Azzolini, I., *Le Pompe Sanesi, o' vero relazione delli huomini, e donne illustri di Siena, e suo stato*, Pistoia, 1649.

Notes

This essay first appeared in *The Art Bulletin* (vol. 77, 1995, pp.445–59) with additional illustrations, to which I have added references in the notes below. I would like to thank *The Art Bulletin* for allowing me to republish this article in the present volume, and John Shearman and Joseph Koerner for their advice in preparing the original article. I am also grateful to Monika Butzek for showing me inventory transcriptions made for the Kunsthistorisches Institut in Florence, and to Samuel Cohn, Caroline Elam, Robert Munman, and John Paoletti for their comments on earlier versions of the text. In the Sienese archives, Stefano Moscadelli (Opera Metropolitana) and Dott. Petroni (Archivio Arcivescovile) were very helpful as well. The research and writing of the original article were funded by the Henry Moore Fellowship at University College London, the Fulbright Commission, the Harvard-Sheldon Traveling Fellowship, the Jacob Javits Fellowship, and the Mellon Fellowship in the Humanities. Minor revisions were made when preparing this essay for republication while I was a Fellow at the Harvard Society of Fellows and at the Harvard Center for Italian Renaissance Studies at Villa i Tatti in Florence. Please note that all English translations are my own. The following abbreviations appear in the notes: SAA (for Siena, Archivio Arcivescovile), SAOM (for Siena, Archivio Opera Metropolitana), and SBC (for Siena, Biblioteca Comunale).

1. Gardner's study of medieval ecclesiastical tombs, Paoli's examination of the social classes that commissioned fourth-century Pisan floor tombs, Butterfield's exploration of early Renaissance wall tombs for elite Florentines, and Etlin's analysis of eighteenth-century Parisian cemeteries are examples of a growing interest in the study of the social history of tombs in Europe. See M. Paoli, 'Un aspetto poco noto della scultura trecentesca pisana: la lapide sepolcrale con ritratto,' *Antichità Viva*, vol. 21, no. 5/6, 1982, pp.38–47; R. A. Etlin, *The Architecture of Death: The*

Transformation of the Cemetery in Eighteenth-Century Paris, Cambridge, MA: MIT Press, 1984; Gardner, *The Tomb and the Tiara*; and A. Butterfield, 'Social Structure and the Typology of Funerary Monuments in Early Renaissance Florence,' *Res*, vol. 26, 1994, pp.47–67.

2.   Many of the ideas proposed in this essay were first presented in a paper given at the College Art Association meeting in New York in February 1994 in a session organized by Elizabeth Valdez del Alamo and Carol Stamatis Pendergast. An expanded version of my study of Donatello's Pecci Tomb, as well as of other Late Medieval and Early Modern Italian funerary monuments, is found in Johnson, 'In the Eye of the Beholder,' chapter 2.

3.   The death date on the tomb is 1 March 1426, but, as noted by Paoletti, 'La tomba Pecci di Donatello,' pp.189–91 n.2, in new-style dating this would be 1427. It remains uncertain exactly when Donatello designed and cast the tomb. Janson, *The Sculpture of Donatello*, pp.75–6, reviews the earlier literature and suggests a date of *c.*1428–30. Since Janson, most scholars have dated the tomb between Pecci's death and *c.*1430. See E. Carli, *Donatello a Siena*, Rome: Editalia, 1967, p.13; C. Del Bravo, *Scultura senese del Quattrocento*, Florence: Editrice Edam, 1970, p.84; F. Hartt, *Donatello: Prophet of Modern Vision*, New York: Abrams, 1973, p.163; J. Poeschke, *Donatello: Figur und Quadro*, Munich: Wilhelm Fink Verlag, 1980, p.110 n.153; idem, *Die Skulptur der Renaissance in Italien: Donatello und siene Zeit*, Munich: Hirmer Verlag, 1990, vol. I, p.101; Munman, *Optical Corrections*, p.31 n.85; idem, *Sienese Renaissance Tomb Monuments*, pp.28–9; Pines, 'The Tomb Slabs of Santa Croce,' pp.40–41; J. Pope-Hennessy and G. Ragionieri, *Donatello*, Florence: Cantini Edizioni d'Arte, 1985, p.92; and J. Shearman, *Only Connect: Art and the Spectator in the Italian Renaissance*, Princeton, NJ: Princeton University Press, 1992, p.13. Paoletti, 'La tomba Pecci di Donatello,' p.194, has recently suggested a much later date of *c.*1449–52 based on documentary evidence that will be discussed below. Later dates have also been proposed by Strehlke, 'Art and Culture,' p.60 n.55; A. Bagnoli, 'Donatello e Siena,' in L. Bellosi, ed., *Francesco di Giorgio e il Rinascimento a Siena, 1450–1500*, Milan: Electa, 1993, p.166; and Pope-Hennessy, *Donatello Sculptor*, pp.90–91, 329 n.11.

4.   Despite extensive research, the exact appearance of the old choir is still unclear. The most convincing discussion of this topic is in the notes to A. Landi, *'Racconto' del Duomo di Siena*, edited by E. Carli, Florence: Casa Editrice Edam, 1992, pp.94–8 nn.10, 12. See also G. Milanesi, *Documenti per la storia dell'arte senese*, Siena: Onorato Porri, 1854, vol. I, pp.328–83; V. Lusini, *Il Duomo di Siena*, Siena: Editrice S. Bernardino, 1911–39, vols I–II; A. Middeldorf-Kosegarten, 'Zur Bedeutung der Sieneser Domkuppel,' *Münchner Jahrbuch der bildenden Kunst*, vol. 21, 1970, pp.73–98; Aronow, 'A Description of the Altars'; and K. van der Ploeg, *Art, Architecture and Liturgy: Siena Cathedral in the Middle Ages*, Groningen: privately published PhD thesis, 1993.

5.   V. Lusini, *Capitolo della Metropolitana di Siena: note storiche*, Siena: Tip. Editore S. Bernardino, 1893, p.65. In his will of 25 February 1426 (new style: 1427), Pecci's first bequests were to the Duomo and its canons: SAA, Dipl. VII, test. no. 7. The will is partially reproduced with some errors in V. L[usini?], 'Il testamento di M. Giovanni Pecci, e il monumento fatto dal Donatello,' *Miscellanea storica senese*, vol. 1, no. 2, 1893, pp.30–31, and reprinted in Paoletti, 'La tomba Pecci di Donatello' p.191 n.3. Pecci's active role as a canon is described in B. Sani, 'Artisti e committenti a Siena nella prima metà del Quattrocento,' in D. Rugiadini, ed., *I ceti dirigenti nella Toscana del Quattrocento*, Impruneta: Franc. Papafava Editore, 1987, p.501, and Strehlke, 'Art and Culture,' p.44.

6.   SAOM, 867, no. 7, fol. 28r.

7.   ibid., no. 8, fol. 15v. See also J. Labarte, *L'église cathédrale de Sienne et son trésor d'après un inventaire de 1467*, Paris, 1868, p.29. The date of the 1467 inventory is misprinted as 1463 in Paoletti, 'La tomba Pecci di Donatello,' pp.192, 201. Although 'in mezo al coro' should not be understood as an exact location, the fact that no other tombs are listed inside the choir in any Quattrocento inventories and that this site is still specified in Cinquecento texts (see n.10 below) does suggest that the Pecci relief was probably in a unique position somewhere near the center of the old choir.

8.   On the 1452 document, see Strehlke, 'Art and Culture,' p.45; Paoletti, 'La tomba Pecci di Donatello,' pp.191, 199–200; and E. Struchholz, 'Die Pecci-Grabplatte Donatellos: Dokumente zur Aufstellung im Dom von Siena,' *Zeitschrift für Kunstgeschichte*, vol. 54, 1991, p.580.

9.   Paoletti, 'La tomba Pecci di Donatello,' p.194, points out that the Pecci Tomb is not listed in the 1449 cathedral inventory, but this does not prove conclusively that Donatello did not design (or even cast) the relief before this date. Munman, *Sienese Renaissance Tomb Monuments*, pp.29 n.49, 34–8, suggests that the tomb was executed before the mid 1440s because of its influence on the tomb of Bishop Carlo Bartoli (†1444). However, the formal links between this tomb and the Pecci relief are minimal. M. G. Ciardi Dupré dal Poggetto, A. Chiti, and R. Jacopino, 'Un "Corpus" delle lastre tombali della Basilica di Santa Croce a Firenze' in J. Garms and A. M. Romanini, eds, *Skulptur und Grabmal des Spätmittelalters in Rom und Italien*, Vienna: Verlag der Österreichischen

Akademie der Wissenschaft, 1990, pp.334–5, point out that many floor tombs were executed long after the deceased's death. This suggests that, without further documentary evidence, it is difficult to date the Pecci Tomb more precisely than *c.*1427–52.

10. Paoletti, 'La tomba Pecci di Donatello,' pp.193–4, and Pope-Hennessy, *Donatello Sculptor*, pp.91, 329 n.11. On the Pecci family chapel, see also Strehlke, 'Art and Culture,' p.45. An eighteenth-century copy of a 1528 text by S. Titius, 'Historiarum Senensium,' confirms that Pecci was buried 'in Chori medio' with the relief placed directly above his remains. SBC, cod. B.III.6, vol. IV, p.206.

11. On Pecci's will, see n.5 above.

12. Janson, *The Sculpture of Donatello*, p.76. On the tomb's illusionism, see also Panofsky, *Tomb Sculpture*, p.72; Hartt (as in n.3), p.163; Rosenauer, *Studien*, pp.111–13; idem, 'Donatellos römische Grabmäler,' p.424; Poeschke, 1980 (as in n.3), p.63; idem, 1990 (as in n.3), p.101; Munman, *Optical Corrections*, pp.31–2; idem, *Sienese Renaissance Tomb Monuments*, pp.29–33; Pines, 'The Tomb Slabs of Santa Croce,' pp.41–2; Shearman (as in n.3), pp.13–15; and Pope-Hennessy, *Donatello Sculptor*, p.90. R. Krautheimer, *Lorenzo Ghiberti*, Princeton, NJ: Princeton University Press, 1970, vol. I, p.152, and B. A. Bennett and D. G. Wilkins, *Donatello*, Oxford: Phaidon, 1984, pp.105, 145 and 235 n.16, do not see the illusionism as completely successful.

13. On the *Maestà*'s placement on the high altar, see J. H. Stubblebine, *Duccio di Buoninsegna and His School*, Princeton, NJ: Princeton University Press, 1979, vol. I, pp.31ff.; and J. White, *Duccio: Tuscan Art and the Medieval Workshop*, London: Thames and Hudson, 1979, pp.80ff.

14. The terms 'funeral Mass' and 'office of the dead' are often mistakenly used interchangeably. The funeral (or requiem) Mass was celebrated at funerals and also, after the twelfth century, on other occasions to obtain blessings for the deceased. The office of the dead also served this latter purpose, but its psalms and antiphons do not, strictly speaking, constitute a mass, although this rite was often incorporated into funeral masses. This distinction is concisely explained in G. K. Fiero, 'Death Ritual in Fifteenth-Century Manuscript Illumination,' *Journal of Medieval History*, vol. 10, 1984, p.272.

15. See Shearman (as in n.3), fig. 6, and Rosenauer, 'Donatellos römische Grabmäler,' p.424.

16. Titius (as in n.10), vol. IV, p.206.

17. 'Morì l'anno 1426. ed alla sepoltura gli fù fatta grandissima honoranza, e un Castello in Duomo con 24. Doppieri, e fuui l'honoranza de' Cittadini, ed è sepolto nel Duomo di Siena in una bellissima sepoltura di bronzo.' Ugurgieri, *Le Pompe Sanesi*, vol. I, p.172.

18. ibid., chapters 6–7, specifies the burial sites of six bishops of Siena in the fourteenth and fifteenth centuries (out of nineteen mentioned in total). Of these six, five were buried in the Cathedral. In contrast, most Sienese ecclesiastics who were bishops of other provincial towns were buried either in their bishoprics or in Sienese churches other than the Duomo.

19. '[I]l di lui Cadavere fusse esposto con . . . molta magnificenza, nella chiesa maggiore, dove fi ancora seppolito.' G. A. Pecci, 'Lo Stato di Siena antico, e moderno,' SBC, cod. B.IV.8, vol. V, fols 80r–v. This undated manuscript was probably written before 1749.

20. The chasuble and maniples worn by Pecci are associated with the celebration of Mass. See *Lexicon für Theologie und Kirche*, Freiburg: Verlag Herder, 1932, vol. IV, cols 469–70, and P. Cunnington and C. Lucas, *Costume for Births, Marriages and Deaths*, London: Adam and Charles Black, 1972, pp.164–5. Ecclesiastical funerary dress is described in Mollat, 'Contribution,' p.588; M. Dykmans, *L'oeuvre de Patrizi Piccolomini, ou le cérémonial papal de la première Renaissance*, Vatican City: Biblioteca Apostolica Vaticana, 1980, vol. I, p.222; idem, *Le cérémonial papal de la fin du moyen âge à la Renaissance: le retour à Rome ou le cérémonial du Patriarche Pierre Ameil*, Brussels: Institut Historique Belge de Rome, 1985, vol. IV, p.247; and Herklotz, 'Paris de Grassis,' p.225.

21. P. Ariès, *Images of Man and Death*, translated by J. Lloyd, Cambridge, MA: Harvard University Press, 1985, p.124, and idem, *Hour of Our Death*, pp.127, 168, sees increased concern with concealing dead bodies from the thirteenth century onward. Strocchia, 'Burials in Renaissance Florence,' pp.171–2, 174–5, 181, and eadem, *Death and Ritual*, p.39, discusses Florentine regulations against displaying corpses during public funerary rites from the thirteenth to the fifteenth century.

22. On practices related to elite corpses and the use of effigies, see J. von Schlosser, 'Geschichte der Porträtbildnerei in Wachs,' *Jahrbuch der Kunsthistorischen Sammlungen des allerhöchsten Kaiserhauses*, vol. 29, 1911, pp.191ff.; E. H. Kantorowicz, *The King's Two Bodies: A Study in Mediaeval Political Theology*, Princeton, NJ: Princeton University Press, 1957, pp.419–37; W. Brückner, *Bildnis und Brauch: Studien zur Bildfunktion der Effigies*, Berlin: Erich Schmidt Verlag, 1966, passim; T. S. R. Boase, *Death in the Middle Ages: Mortality, Judgment and Remembrance*, London: Thames and Hudson, 1972, p.116; E. A. R. Brown, 'Death and the Human Body in the Late Middle Ages: The

Legislation of Boniface VIII on the Division of the Corpse,' *Viator*, vol. 12, 1981, pp.252–69; I. Herklotz, *'Sepulcra' e 'monumenta' del medioevo: Studi sull'arte sepolcrale in Italia*, Rome: Edizioni Rari Nantes, 1985, p.197; and Butterfield (as in n.1), p.60.

23.   This fresco is illustrated in Johnson, 'Activating the Effigy,' fig. 6. Corsini died in France and was not granted permission to be buried in the Duomo. The fresco may thus have served as a symbolic substitute for the funeral that never took place. On Corsini, see L. Gatti, 'The art of freedom: meaning, civic identity and devotion in early Renaissance Florence,' unpublished PhD thesis, University of London, 1992, pp.29–41. The fresco is often given to Bicci di Lorenzo, although this has been rejected by B. B. Walsh, 'The fresco paintings of Bicci di Lorenzo,' unpublished PhD thesis, Indiana University, 1979, p.198. It has been attributed to Giovanni dal Ponte by C. Frosinini, 'Proposte per Giovanni dal Ponte e Neri di Bicci: due affreschi funerari del Duomo di Firenze,' *Mitteilungen des Kunsthistorischen Institutes in Florenz*, vol. 34, 1990, pp.123–38.

24.   Both tombs are illustrated in Panofsky, *Tomb Sculpture*, figs 336–7.

25.   s'Jacob, *Idealism and Realism*, pp.19–20, 40; A. Schiavo, 'La Cappella Vaticana del Coro e vicende dei sepolcri di Sisto IV e Giulio II,' *Studi Romani*, vol. 6, 1958, p.300; Dykmans, 1980 (as in n.20), p.160 n.188; Lightbown, *Donatello and Michelozzo*, vol. I, pp.44–5; and Gardner, *The Tomb and the Tiara*, pp.13–14. See also Strocchia, *Death and Ritual*, p.42.

26.   See Mollat, 'Contribution,' pp.587–8; B. Schimmelpfennig, *Die Zeremonienbücher der römischen Kurie im Mittelalter*, Tübingen: Max Niemeyer Verlag, 1973, p.68; M. Dykmans, *Le cérémonial papal de la fin du moyen âge à la Renaissance: De Rome en Avignon ou le cérémonial de Jacques Stefaneschi*, Brussels: Institut Historique Belge de Rome, 1981, vol. II, p.504; idem, 1980 (as in n.20), pp.161, 235.

27.   J. Burchard, 'Johannis Burckardi: Liber Notarum,' edited by E. Celani, *Rerum italicarum scriptores*, vol. XXXII, part 1, 1907–13, section 2, p.333.

28.   See ibid., section 1, pp.121, 313–15, on this funeral and others in which ecclesiastics' corpses were left exposed. Paris de Grassis also mentions the use of uncovered biers at the funerals of elite clergymen: Herklotz, 'Paris de Grassis,' p.233.

29.   Strocchia, 'Burials in Renaissance Florence,' p.39. For other Florentine examples of corpses left uncovered on biers or in open coffins, see ibid., pp.19, 34, 37, 131; eadem, *Death and Ritual*, pp.2, 81 and 138–9; and Butterfield (as in n.1), p.60.

30.   Brückner (as in n.22), pp.34–5, and Strocchia, *Death and Ritual*, p.48. Antoninus's case may not be representative since he was highly venerated in his own lifetime and was later canonized.

31.   Lightbown, *Donatello and Michelozzo*, vol. I, pp.12–13; Strocchia, 'Burials in Renaissance Florence,' pp.130–34; eadem, *Death and Ritual*, pp.134–43; and S. B. McHam, 'Donatello's Tomb of Pope John XXIII' in M. Tetel, R. G. Witt, and R. Goffen, eds, *Life and Death in Fifteenth-Century Florence*, Durham, NC: Duke University Press, 1989, pp.154–5.

32.   G. O. Corazzini, 'Diario fiorentino di Bartolommeo di Michele Del Corazza anni 1405–1438,' *Archivio storico italiano*, series 5, vol. 14, 1894, pp.264–5.

33.   For an illustration of Donatello's bronze effigy and bier, see Johnson, 'Activating the Effigy,' fig. 7. On this project, see also: Janson, *The Sculpture of Donatello*, pp.61–3; Rosenauer, *Studien*, pp.53–70; McHam (as in n.31), pp.146, 157; Lightbown, *Donatello and Michelozzo*, vol. I, pp.22, 32–3; and Pope-Hennessy, *Donatello Sculptor*, pp.73–7, 328 n.5.

34.   Herklotz, 'Paris de Grassis,' p.235, sees absolution rites as the high points of funeral ceremonies. See also Ariès, *The Hour of Our Death*, pp.140–42, 146.

35.   '[A]scendunt ad altare et incensant illud . . . Deinde revertuntur ad corpus et incensant illud.' Dykmans, 1981 (as in n.26), p.504.

36.   Schimmelpfennig (as in n.26), p.368.

37.   I will discuss below the moments during normal masses when a priest would have turned his back to the altar to look down the nave, that is, toward the Pecci Tomb in the choir.

38.   s'Jacob emphasizes that absolution rituals are most often depicted on medieval tombs that include representations of the funeral: *Idealism and Realism*, p.73. See also Gardner, *The Tomb and the Tiara*, p.13.

39.   See Panofsky, *Tomb Sculpture*, pp.60–61 and fig. 243; Bauch, *Das mittelalterliche Grabbild*, pp.46, 159 and fig. 57.

40.   On this tomb, see: G. de Francovich, 'Contributi alla scultura romanica veronese,' *Rivista del R. Istituto d'Archeologia e Storia dell'Arte*, vol. 9, 1942, pp.106–8; Bauch, *Das mittelalterliche Grabbild*, pp.154, 335 n.327; Gardner, *The Tomb and the Tiara*, pp.29–30, 33.

41. s'Jacob, *Idealism and Realism*, p.29. See also ibid., pp.73, 232.

42. The tomb is usually attributed to Arnolfo di Cambio or Pietro Oderisi. Traditionally, the effigy has been thought to depict Cardinal Riccardo Annibaldi (†1275/6), and the tomb has been dated between this prelate's death and the 1280s. See J. Pope-Hennessy, *Italian Gothic Sculpture*, Oxford: Phaidon, 1985, pp.13–14, 181–2, and Bauch, *Das mittelalterliche Grabbild*, pp.147–8, 332–3 n.314. Several scholars have questioned the current reconstruction as well as the identity of the effigy, which may represent a nephew of the cardinal (also called Riccardo) who died in 1289. See J. Gardner, 'The Tomb of Cardinal Annibaldi by Arnolfo di Cambio,' *Burlington Magazine*, vol. 114, 1972, pp.136–41; idem, *The Tomb and the Tiara*, pp.104–6; Herklotz (as in n.22), pp.170–80; idem, 'Paris de Grassis,' p.236; F. Pomarici, 'Medioevo. Scultura' in C. Pietrangeli, ed., *San Giovanni in Laterano*, Florence: Nardini Editore, 1990, p.113; and A. M. Romanini, 'Ipotesi ricostruttive per i monumenti sepolcrali di Arnolfo di Cambio,' in J. Garms and A. M. Romanini, eds (as in n.9), pp.113–19.

43. For illustrations of this tomb, see Johnson, 'Activating the Effigy,' figs 10, 11. The tomb's Sienese sculptors, Agostino di Giovanni and Agnolo di Ventura, may have been influenced by Tino when he was in Siena. Payments for the tomb are recorded in 1329 and 1332. See s'Jacob, *Idealism and Realism*, p.76; Pope-Hennessy (as in n.42), pp.18, 187; C. F. Bullard, 'The development of pictorial space in Italian Gothic sculptural relief,' unpublished PhD thesis, Syracuse University, 1973, vol. I, pp.164–86; and H. A. Ronan, 'The Tuscan wall tomb 1250–1400,' unpublished PhD thesis, Indiana University, 1982, vol. II, pp.11–16. The Donatellesque reliefs on Arezzo Cathedral's font may indirectly suggest a trip by Donatello himself to Arezzo. See Rosenauer, *Studien*, pp.72–5, and Pope-Hennessy, *Donatello Sculptor*, pp.116, 331 n.4.

44. On this relief, see Ronan (as in n.43), pp.50–51; J. Garms, 'Ein Florentiner Trecento-Grabmal in Nizza,' *Römische historische Mitteilungen*, vol. 28, 1986, p.384; and S. Düll, 'Das Grabmal des Johanniters Pietro da Imola in S. Jacopo in Campo Corbolini in Florenz. Zur Renaissance-Kapitalis in erneuerten Inschriften des Trecento,' *Mitteilungen des Kunsthistorischen Institutes in Florenz*, vol. 34, 1990, pp.101–2. Düll believes that the 1320 date on the tomb is a mistake since Pietro da Imola died in 1330.

45. On these tombs, see s'Jacob, *Idealism and Realism*, p.81; Bauch, *Das mittelalterliche Grabbild*, pp.158–9, 336 n.340; Ronan (as in n.43), pp.2–4, 37–8, 48–51, 99–105; Garms (as in n.44), pp.379–85; E. N. Lusanna, ed., *Museo Bardini: Le sculture medievali e rinascimentali*, Florence: Centro Di, 1989, fig. 25; and Düll (as in n.44), pp.101–4.

46. On this order, see *Lexicon für Theologie*, Freiburg: Verlag Herder, 1933, vol. V, cols 544–7.

47. See F. Ughello, *Italia sacra sive de episcopis italiae et insularum adiacentium*, Rome, 1647, vol. III, col. 761; Ugurgieri, *Le Pompe Sanesi*, vol. I, p.171; B. Pecci, 'Relatio Status Ecclesiae Crassetanae,' 1717, SBC, cod. K.VII.64, fol. 1v; G. A. Pecci (as in n.19), fol. 80r; idem, *Ristretto delle cose piu' notabili della città di Siena*, Siena, 1761, p.11; F. Anichini, 'Cronologica da Vescovi della Città di Grosseto,' 1749, SBC, cod. A.III.5, fol. 55v; G. Cappelletti, *Le chiese d'Italia dalla loro origine sino ai nostri giorni*, Venice, 1862, vol. XVII, p.655; and a nineteenth-century Pecci family history manuscript, 'Memoria della famiglia Pecci,' SAA, 6549, 4, fol. 10r.

48. Different types of masses for the dead are discussed in n.14 above. On Pope Gregory and the origins of intercessory masses for the dead, see R. J. E. Boggis, *Praying for the Dead: An Historical Review of the Practice*, London: Longmans, Green, and Co., 1913, pp.88–90; J. A. Jungmann, *Missarum Sollemnia: Eine genetische Erklärung der römischen Messe*, Vienna: Herder, 1948, vol. I, pp.165–6, 275ff.; K. L. Wood-Legh, *Perpetual Chantries in Britain*, Cambridge: Cambridge University Press, 1965, pp.2–5; Ariès, *The Hour of Our Death*, p.158; and Chiffoleau, 'Sur l'usage obsessionnel,' pp.238–45.

49. See Ariès, *The Hour of Our Death*, p.161, and Chiffoleau, 'Sur l'usage obsessionnel,' pp.240–41.

50. See Rowell, *The Liturgy of Christian Burial*, pp.68–70; Ariès, *The Hour of Our Death*, pp.173–5; Chiffoleau, 'Sur l'usage obsessionnel,' pp.241–5; Cohn, *The Cult of Remembrance*, pp.160–61, 206–11.

51. After hovering at about one or two percent in the fifty previous years, the amount set aside by Sienese testators from 1426 to 1450 jumped to over ten percent, increasing to nearly a third from 1451 to 1475. From 1451 on, there was also an increase in the percentage of wills setting aside property or other funds to pay for postmortem masses: Cohn, *Death and Property in Siena*, pp.62–3.

52. On Pecci's will, see n.5 above. The 1442 document endows a 'capollano . . . [per] essere all'ore canoniche . . . in duomo et a la messa cantando . . . in perpetua.' SAOM, no. 21, 'Deliberazioni,' fol. 70v, 2 July 1442. The Pecci family members involved in this endowment included heirs listed in the Bishop's will.

53. The Pecci family was one of the richest clans in Siena in the fifteenth century. On the family's wealth, see D. L. Hicks, 'Sources of Wealth in Renaissance Siena: Businessmen and Landowners,' *Bulletino senese di storia patria*, vol. 93, 1986, p.17, and G. Catoni and G. Piccinni, 'Alliramento e ceto dirigente nella Siena del Quattrocento,' in D. Rugiadini, ed., *I ceti dirigenti nella Toscana del Quattrocento*, Impruneta: Franc. Papafava Editore, 1987, pp.456–60.

54. See Ariès, *The Hour of Our Death*, pp.46–8.

55. On the choice of burial location in churches, see Ariès, *The Hour of Our Death*, pp.178–81; Strocchia, 'Burials in Renaissance Florence,' pp.365–70; and Pines, 'The Tomb Slabs of Santa Croce,' pp.15–16. Cohn, *Death and Property in Siena*, p.108, quotes a Sienese will of 1500 in which the testator asks that his body be buried 'under the step and altar of the [family] chapel.'

56. On these tombs, see G. R. Goldner, 'Niccolò and Piero Lamberti,' unpublished PhD thesis, Princeton University, 1972, pp.6, 36–41; and J. Clearfield, 'The Tomb of Cosimo de' Medici in San Lorenzo,' *Rutgers Art Review*, vol. 2, 1981, pp.13–30.

57. In his will of 1297, Aycelin stipulated that his tomb was to lie 'ante pedes maioris altaris Sancte Sabine.' This lost metal relief may have been a precedent for Pecci's bronze floor tomb. On the Aycelin relief and other medieval ecclesiastical floor tombs in front of altars, see Gardner, *The Tomb and the Tiara*, pp.19, 29, 85–8. The tomb of Martin V (†1431) has often been linked to Donatello. Like Aycelin, Martin V asked to be buried before the high altar where his tomb (shipped to Rome only in 1445) was eventually erected. The tomb, currently in the sunken *confessione*, was originally located at pavement level; it is illustrated in Johnson, 'Activating the Effigy,' fig. 14. The spatial inconsistencies of the relief's design are largely resolved when one realizes that it was intended to be viewed by an ecclesiastic positioned above the tomb on the high altar. This viewpoint is discussed and illustrated in Panofsky, *Tomb Sculpture*, p.72, fig. 311. The use of bronze, the relationship between the relief and a viewer standing on the altar, and sixteenth-century texts connecting the project to Donatello's circle suggest that Donatello himself may have been involved in the design, if not necessarily the execution, of the relief in the same quarter century in which he produced the Pecci Tomb. Martin V's tomb and its links to Antonio del Pollaiuolo's late fifteenth-century monument for Sixtus IV (also cast in bronze and placed before an altar) are discussed in greater detail in Johnson, 'In the Eye of the Beholder,' pp.74ff.

58. On the Dati tomb's original location, see J. Wood Brown, *The Dominican Church of Santa Maria Novella at Florence*, Edinburgh: Otto Schulze and Co., 1902, p.121; W. and E. Paatz, *Die Kirchen von Florenz*, Frankfurt: Vittorio Klostermann, 1952, vol. III, pp.702, 785 n.178; Strocchia, 'Burials in Renaissance Florence,' p.366.

59. On S. Croce's old choir, see M. B. Hall, 'The "Tramezzo" in S. Croce, Florence and Domenico Veneziano's Fresco,' *Burlington Magazine*, vol. 112, 1970, pp.797–9; idem, 'The "Tramezzo" in S. Croce, Florence Reconstructed,' *The Art Bulletin*, vol. 56, 1974, pp.325–41. On Sansoni and his tomb, see Pines, 'The Tomb Slabs of Santa Croce,' pp.49–50; Poggetto et al. (as in n.9), p.344; S. B. McHam, *The Chapel of St Anthony at the Santo and the Development of Venetian Renaissance Sculpture*, Cambridge: Cambridge University Press, 1994, pp.20–22.

60. See Ugurgieri, *Le Pompe Sanesi*, vol. I, pp.144, 149, 182, on Sienese bishops buried near high altars.

61. On Siena Cathedral's old choir, see n.4 above.

62. '[S]epultura[m] sui corporis elegit in Ecl[es]ia cathed[r]ali Senarum in loco honorato ut vide[bi]tur et placebit i[n]fr[ascript]is h[e]r[e]d[i] et fideicomissaris suis qui certo tenet q[uo]d facie[n]t ip[s]am sepultura[m] suam honorata[m].' SAA, Dipl. VII, test. no. 7. On Pecci's will, see n.5 above. I would like to thank Ursula Gustorf Johnson for her suggestions regarding this translation.

63. See Jungmann (as in n.48), p.165; S. K. Cohn, Jr., 'Plagues, Consciousness and High Culture in the Early Renaissance,' *Harvard University Center for European Studies: Working Paper Series*, 1985, pp.8–9; idem, *The Cult of Remembrance*, p.272.

64. The number of Sienese wills specifying a particular burial location more than doubled in the first half of the fifteenth century, that is, at the very time that Pecci was writing his own testament. See Cohn, *Death and Property in Siena*, pp.60–61, 65–6, 114.

65. On the use of epitaphs and similar commemorative strategies from the late Trecento onward, see K. Cohen, *Metamorphosis of a Death Symbol: The Transi Tomb in the Late Middle Ages and the Renaissance*, Berkeley: University of California Press, 1973, p.63; Ariès, *The Hour of Our Death*, pp.218–21; E. A. R. Brown, 'Burying and Unburying the Kings of France,' in R. Trexler, ed., *Persons in Groups: Social Behavior as Identity Formation in Medieval and Renaissance Europe*, Binghamton, NY: Medieval & Renaissance Texts & Studies, 1985, pp.243–4; Cohn, *Death and Property in Siena*, p.61; idem, *The Cult of Remembrance*, pp.159–61.

66. 'Je veux et ordonne qu'on construise pour mes restes un tombeau d'albâtre honorable et ... qu'on y place ma statue, mes armes et d'autres ornements nécessaires, afin que mes parents et amis et ceux que j'aurai connus, en passant par là, se souviennent de moi et aient soin d'implorer, pour mon âme, le Très Haut': Mollat, 'Contribution,' p.591.

67. This suggested orientation is supported indirectly by the Quattrocento inventories of Siena Cathedral, which describe the church from the point of view of a beholder standing on the high altar looking westward into the nave, that is, toward Pecci's tomb in the choir. This orientation, as detailed in a 1420 inventory, is discussed by Aronow, 'A Description of the Altars,' pp.230ff.

68. In S. Croce, Florence, for example, twelve of the thirteen figurative floor tombs in the crossing are oriented toward the high altar or to the altar of the nearest chapel. Four additional relief effigies (including Francesco Sansoni's discussed above) in the pavement of the central nave are also turned toward the high altar. On the orientation of the floor tombs in S. Croce, see also Pines, 'The Tomb Slabs of Santa Croce,' pp.22–3.

69. Durandus writes that corpses should be buried with their heads at the west end of the grave so as to be ready to leap up on the Day of Judgment. See Rowell, *The Liturgy of Christian Burial*, p.66.

70. See n.58 above.

71. On the censing and asperging rituals performed by priests oriented toward the choir and congregation, and the distribution of the Host to communicants kneeling at the altar, see A. Fortescue and J. B. O'Connell, *The Ceremonies of the Roman Rite Described*, London: Burns, Oates, and Washbourne Ltd., 1958, pp.96–101, 135–6; J. A. Jungmann, *The Mass of the Roman Rite: Its Origins and Development (Missarum Sollemnia)*, translated by F. A. Brunner, London: Burns and Oates, 1959, pp.347–9.

72. On reenacting the absolution rituals performed at funerals, see Rowell, *The Liturgy of Christian Burial*, p.69.

73. The central scene below the *Coronation* would have been the *Dormition* according to Stubblebine (as in n.13), pp.46–7, and the *Assumption* according to White (as in n.13), pp.86–8. The central panel of the *Maestà* and the *Dormition* are illustrated in Johnson, 'Activating the Effigy,' figs 16, 17.

74. Several tombs in Siena, Florence, and Prato demonstrate the direct formal influence of the Pecci relief. The one closest to the Pecci Tomb, a marble relief for a Franciscan friar, is now in the Bardini Museum, Florence. On this group of tombs, see V. Martinelli, 'Donatello e Michelozzo a Roma (II),' *Commentari*, vol. 9, 1958, pp.15–16; Del Bravo (as in n.3), p.84; Munman, *Optical Corrections*, pp.34, 48 n.134; idem, *Sienese Renaissance Tomb Monuments*, pp.34–63; Pines, 'The Tomb Slabs of Santa Croce,' pp.43–5; Lusanna (as in n.45), fig. 27; A. Natali, 'Per due lastre tombali in San Francesco a Prato,' pp.244–6, and A. Rosenauer, 'Bemerkungen zur Grabplatte des Pietro Cacciafuochi in San Francesco in Prato,' pp.250–52, both in M. Cämmerer, ed., *Donatello-Studien*, Munich: Bruckman, 1989; Rosenauer, 'Donatellos römische Grabmäler,' pp.426–7; Bagnoli (as in n.3), pp.164–9. The use of bronze in the Pecci Tomb also may have influenced other fifteenth-century works, such as the Martin V tomb and Pollaiuolo's Sixtus IV monument (see n.57 above), and the bronze effigies of Mariano Sozzino the Elder (†1467) and Cardinal Pietro Foscari (†1485), which have both been linked to Sienese sculptors. On the last two tombs, see M. Kühlenthal, 'Das Grabmal Pietro Foscaris in S. Maria del Popolo in Rom: Ein Werk des Giovanni di Stefano,' *Mitteilungen des Kunsthistorischen Institutes in Florenz*, vol. 26, 1982, pp.47–62; L. Bellosi, ed., *Francesco di Giorgio e il Rinascimento a Siena, 1450–1500*, Milan: Electa, 1993, pp.198–9, 390–91; and Munman, *Sienese Renaissance Tomb Monuments*, pp.89–106, 118–19, 130–31. Like the Pecci relief, an illusionistic tomb by Antonio Rossellino in S. Croce, Florence, which depicts Leonardo Tedaldi and his wife as if lying in a bed, is intelligible only to a viewer standing at its foot. See J. Beck, 'An Effigy Tomb Slab by Antonio Rossellino,' *Gazette des Beaux-Arts*, vol. 95, 1980, pp.213–17. I would like to thank Rona Roisman for this reference. See also Pines, 'The Tomb Slabs of Santa Croce,' pp.47–50, 523–30.

75. G. Fiocco, 'Michele da Firenze,' *Dedalo*, vol. 12, 1932, p.554, and L. Bruhns, 'Das Motiv der ewigen Anbetung in der römischen Grabplastik des 16., 17. und 18. Jahrhunderts,' *Römisches Jahrbuch für Kunstgeschichte*, vol. 4, 1940, p.264, incorrectly call the donor Giovanni. O. Pellegrini, 'Su di un particolare delle terrecotte di S. Anastasia in Verona,' *Studi storici veronesi*, vol. 2, 1949–50, pp.209–10, makes it clear that the effigy represents Andrea Pellegrini.

76. Masses of St Gregory in particular were often requested as intercessory masses for the dead. See Ariès, *The Hour of Our Death*, pp.158, 174–5.

77. '[C]omando chel mio corpo sia sepellido ne la giesa de Santa nastasia ... nel luogo dove esepelido mio padre ... comando che dapo la morte mia ... mezo tri ani continii sia fatto dir

. . . la messa de Santo grigolo per lanima mia . . . voio esserge scolpito . . . in essa capella . . . in zenochioni orando . . . vogio esser fatta e compida in termene de tri ani da po la morte mia.' Pellegrini (as in n.75), p.211. The will, dated 9 March 1429, the day of Andrea's death, first states that the project should be carried out in S. Maria La Scala but, if this proves to be difficult, that it should be executed in the family chapel in S. Anastasia.

78. It is the solution put forward in the Pellegrini chapel, that of having an actively praying effigy or bust oriented toward an altar, which is seen most often in later European tomb sculpture, especially in the Baroque. On this phenomenon, see Bruhns (as in n.75), pp.253ff., and Johnson, 'In the Eye of the Beholder,' pp.84–96.

4.1   Donatello, floor tomb of Bishop Giovanni Pecci
      (seen from above), Siena Cathedral, after 1427

4.2   Donatello, floor tomb of Bishop Giovanni Pecci (seen from its foot), Siena Cathedral, after 1427

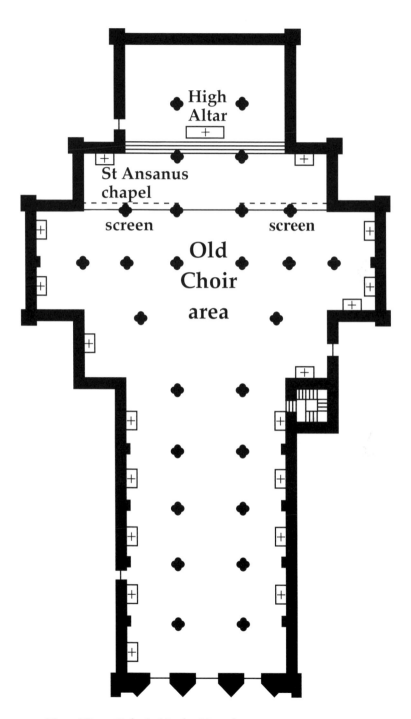

High
Altar

St Ansanus
chapel

screen   screen

Old
Choir
area

4.3   Plan of Siena Cathedral in the fifteenth century

4.4   Floor tomb of Pope Lucius III, Verona Cathedral,
early thirteenth century

4.5   Arnolfo di Cambio (attributed), frieze from Annibaldi tomb, Rome, S. Giovanni in Laterano, later thirteenth century

4.6   Wall tomb of Prior Pietro da Imola, Florence, S. Jacopo in Campo Corbolini, third or fourth decade of the fourteenth century

4.7   Floor tomb of Francesco Sansoni (in front of the high altar), Florence, S. Croce, c.1499

4.8　Michele da Firenze, kneeling effigy of Andrea Pellegrini, Verona, S. Anastasia, c.1435–6

5

Commemorating a real bastard: the chapel of Alvaro de Luna

Patrick Lenaghan

In April 1453, King John II of Castile ordered the execution of his first minister, Alvaro de Luna, for treason. This event marked the spectacular fall of a man whose rise had been equally extraordinary. As the Constable of Castile, he had been the virtual ruler of the kingdom since 1428; yet his tight hold on power had made him controversial: vilified as a usurper of royal prerogative and lionized as the mainstay of the monarchy. His tomb and funerary chapel provided him and his family an opportunity to answer the charges raised against him, and his monument can be interpreted as their effort to redeem his memory by casting him as a Christian knight and member of an illustrious Castilian family (Figs 5.1–5.4).

This image of Alvaro de Luna, which the monument represents, took into account both the visual conventions of fifteenth-century funerary art and the polemic concerning the man. The most effective way to assess the relation between the monument and the polemic is to read the tomb in its physical setting and then examine it in the context of the controversy surrounding the man. When this is done, the artistic innovations of the tomb design can be interpreted as a departure from tradition dictated by the goal of immortalizing the Constable as a moral paragon. The tomb of Alvaro de Luna thus offers an opportunity to study in detail how artistic forms were directed to create a favorable image of the deceased.

*   *   *

As it exists, Alvaro de Luna's funeral chapel represents almost seventy years of his and his family's efforts to stake out their position. In 1430, at the height of his power, the Constable had acquired a prominent space in the most important church in the realm, the Cathedral of Toledo, seat of the Primate of Castile and burial site of several kings of Castile. In an ostentatious gesture,

Luna purchased three chapels off the presbytery and then consolidated them into one large space.[1] There he erected an elaborate bronze tomb for himself and his wife. Reportedly, the tomb contained a mechanical device so the figures could be raised into a kneeling position, thus, creating the illusion that they were attending mass performed at the chapel's altar.[2] During a revolt against the Constable in 1441, however, rebels destroyed the tomb, and the project remained unfinished at the time of his execution. As penalty for treason, John II seized many of Luna's estates but, despite his enemies' wishes, the chapel was neither confiscated nor destroyed. Still, the project languished for three decades because the family's income was now severely reduced. Only in 1489 was the Constable's daughter Maria, the Duchess of El Infantado, who had married into the wealthy and powerful Mendoza family, able to commission new tombs from the sculptor Sebastián de Almonacid.[3] These, with the chapel's altarpiece and accompanying monuments of his relatives, represent the family's final artistic projects to rehabilitate the reputation of Alvaro de Luna. The chapel today is a combination of the architecture which Luna erected and the decoration which his family, principally his daughter, commissioned. Even after such vicissitudes, it is, nonetheless, remarkable that the ensemble presents a coherent and forceful message to the viewer with no hint of the turbulence of John II's reign.

On these tombs, the effigies lie with clasped hands atop rectangular biers: the Constable, depicted as a nobleman wearing a cloak over his armor, and his wife, Juana Pimentel, Countess of Montalbán, clothed like a nun (Figs 5.1, 5.2). Pages sit at their feet, while the bases are decorated with reliefs of Virtues, Apostles, and angels holding coats of arms. Knights of the Order of Santiago, a Spanish crusading order, dedicated to fighting the Moors, kneel at each corner of the Constable's bier while friars have gathered at that of the Countess, who died in 1484.

When viewed from the presbytery – as most people would see them – the monuments are distant and partially hidden by the grate closing off the chapel; the details of the bases are barely visible. Instead, the relation of the kneeling figures to the effigies shapes the perception of the ensemble: the knights and friars frame the bases at each corner, but their heads do not rise above the ledge on which the Constable's and his wife's bodies lie (Fig. 5.3). As their kneeling poses and the tilt of their heads direct attention in and up to the effigies, the figures not only set off the biers but also place the effigies at the apex of a pyramidal composition. Because of their size, the knights and friars take on visual prominence as they gather around the tomb. Genuflecting on one knee while they support the bier with their hands, these figures play the role of pall bearers and mourners. As such, they recreate the funeral ceremonies held for the Constable and his wife and, with their reverential poses, they enhance the solemnity of the event. Moreover, the sculptor has distinguished each statue in its face, clothing, and gesture; this variety of characterization enhances the illusion of a funeral in progress.

These stately individuals, who animate the space and shape the experience of the tomb, represent the sculptor's most significant innovation. As large, free-standing statues grouped around the bier, they recreate the act of mourning and the funeral rites more vividly than any tomb previously constructed in Spain. Earlier monuments, such as that for the Bishop d'Escales (carved by Antoni Canet in Barcelona Cathedral, 1409–12), had included mourners, but generally these were carved in relief or on a smaller scale: here as a series of single figures on the base (Fig. 5.5).[4] By relegating them to this location and separating them from the effigy and each other, the architecture reduces them to emblematic attributes. Consequently, these figures cannot interact directly with the Bishop: they suggest the funeral rites, but as an event distinct from the effigy above them.

Mourners also appear on secular tombs, such as that of John II, carved by Gil de Siloe in the Cartuja de Miraflores, Burgos, in 1489–93 (Fig. 5.6). The King and his wife are shown lying on their bier. Apostles, seated at lecterns and reading books, have gathered around the effigies as if attending the funeral. The difference in scale between these statues and the King's, however, prevents them from engaging as directly with the effigies, which, in turn, undermines the illusion that such ceremonies are actually being reenacted. Similarly, the figures on the base – namely, the Virgin Mary, Virtues, Old Testament Patriarchs, and Carthusians – are enclosed so forcefully within the architecture that they appear more as emblems than as participants in a ritual (Fig. 5.7).

These comparisons suggest how exceptional the Luna chapel is among Spanish funerary monuments for its depiction of a living moment in time. Only in other works by the same sculptor, Sebastián de Almonacid, do comparable tableaux appear. For example, in the tomb of *El Doncel* (Sigüenza Cathedral, 1493–7), he recreates a particular instant: the young man, Martín Vázquez de Arce, perches himself on one arm while he lies calmly reading a book of prayers; a page sits at his feet; and on the base, two squires hold his coat of arms (Fig. 5.8). The sculptor renders these figures with attention to gesture and surfaces so that they enact this scene before the viewer. The Doncel appears engrossed in his reading; the page supports his master's shoe; and the two squires grapple with the shield. Sebastián de Almonacid exploits this immediacy for its expressive possibilities in commemorating the deceased. By making the Doncel seem so alive as he concentrates on his reading, the sculptor underscores the tragedy of his untimely death. The squires, the page and coats of arms vividly evoke the young man's world and his place in it, and although they are not mourners at a funeral, their loss of a master is no less tangible.

The tomb of *El Doncel* confirms the artistry which Sebastián de Almonacid displays in the Luna chapel. It also suggests a sculptor particularly attuned to the possibilities of funerary monuments depicting an actual moment. When he received the commission for Alvaro de Luna's tomb, he made effective use of this talent as well: he recreates the funerary liturgy more vividly by enlarging the mourning figures and representing them three-dimensionally around the bier. In this gesture, the Knights of Santiago honor the Constable because he was the Master of their order; by recognizing their obligation to him, they suggest both his distinguished social position and his piety as their leader. On the other side, friars, presumably from a monastery which the Countess supported, kneel around her body, attesting to her faith and gener-osity.[5] Therefore, even as they evoke the funeral rites, the friars and knights establish both the Constable's and his wife's virtue and social position. More-over, as these statues reenact the ceremony, the monument evokes a sense of loss at the couple's deaths, for the knights and friars represent the dependents and clients left without their protectors. As they evoke this network of social relations, they describe the world that the Constable and his wife lived in, and the rupture that their deaths have created in it. Although this idea ap-pears whenever mourners or retainers are depicted, their physical promin-ence here emphasizes the point.

When viewed as part of the liturgy celebrated in the chapel, the tombs reinforce the image of the couple as devout Christians. Lying in state on their biers with their hands clasped, Alvaro de Luna and his wife would also appear to be attending the masses said at the chapel's altar, as if praying at the very rites they had instituted for their salvation.[6] The predella of the chapel's altarpiece itself underscores this point by depicting the Constable and his wife kneeling and beseeching Christ's intercession. Five years before the tombs were commissioned in 1489, the Countess had already endowed three chaplains, each to say three masses weekly, and on Saturday, one of them to celebrate a sung mass dedicated to the Virgin.[7] Furthermore, anyone witnessing the performance of these prayers would see the connection be-tween monument and liturgy; the Countess had stipulated that at the end of each mass the celebrant should say a response over their burials.[8]

Although the effigies of Luna and his wife surrounded by the knights and friars dominate the viewer's perception of the monument, the iconography of the bases should not be overlooked. Because this decoration was visible solely to those inside the chapel, its message had a more limited audience: the chaplains celebrating the liturgy, the family and any visitors the family admitted. To such viewers, however, the message of these elements would have special meaning, describing as it did their venerable patrons and ances-tors. On the Constable's tomb, figures of Justice and Temperance sit on one side and Fortitude and Prudence on the other (Fig. 5.4); between the personifications of the virtues, angels hold shields bearing the coat of arms of the Order of Santiago which, as master of the order, the Constable was entitled to use. On the short sides, angels hold the Luna coat of arms.[9] Along the sides of the Countess's tomb, apostles flank angels who hold her family coat of arms. The iconography of the bases, therefore, establishes three issues which further validate the couple's commemoration: their family lineage, established in the coats of arms; their moral character, attested to by the virtues and saints; and Alvaro de Luna's distinguished social position as head of the Order of Santiago, proclaimed in the use of the Order's insignia. With regard to the Constable, these three concepts combine to represent him as that exemplar, the Christian knight: a man of noble birth who exercised his military obligations in defense of his faith.

The remaining decoration of the chapel enhances these points. The other monuments, located in the niches along the side walls, reinforce the luster of the Constable's lineage: they represent his ancestors and descendants who had held important posts. The Constable's uncle, Pedro de Luna, and his half-brother, Juan de Cerezuela, had both been archbishops of Toledo, while his son, Juan de Luna, was Count of San Esteban de Gormaz.[10] The family's prestige is emphasized further in the prominent display of its escutcheon on the base of each monument, the architectural decoration, and the altarpiece.

*   *   *

Such an emphatic statement of virtue and power becomes more striking in light of the controversy surrounding Alvaro de Luna. The Constable was attacked on many grounds, but above all for his lineage, moral character and his conduct in office.[11] Several factors made his ancestry dubious. As a foreigner from neighboring Aragón, who was not of the highest nobility, he seemed unfit for the important posts he held. Most seriously, he was an illegitimate son whose father, some alleged, had doubted his paternity and only acknowledged the boy on his deathbed.[12] Luna's enemies also defamed his character, accusing him of insatiable greed, cowardice, deceitfulness, impiety and tyranny. They maintained that he had ingratiated himself into the King's favor with flattery and then abused John II's trust by exercising power unjustly. In effect, he had usurped the King's position. For them, the Constable's conviction and execution for treason provided the ultimate proof of his vices: it was only justice long delayed. His supporters saw things differently, even as they agreed on the issues that framed the debate. Although they glossed over his illegitimacy, they countered that several members of his family were important prelates. Moreover, they claimed the Constable was a paragon of morality: a loyal knight who performed valiant deeds and had willingly put his life in jeopardy for his King.

A similar message, the Constable as a noble Castilian and a Christian knight, appears in his chapel, but the ensemble takes several liberties with the historical record. Although the tomb evokes a stately funeral, the actual event was markedly different. After his execution for treason in Valladolid, Alvaro de Luna's body was interred by a confraternity dedicated to charitable deeds. His head was displayed for nine days on the scaffold where he had died before it was buried with his body. Approximately two months later, when the King entered the city, the Constable's body was reinterred. No matter how sources favorable to him would describe these events, the message was unmistakable: he had been executed for treason.[13] The present tomb asserts its own history: he had been commemorated with an official state ceremony as if he had never been convicted. The work, therefore, offered a striking visual rebuttal to his enemies as his family, and particularly his daughter, the Duchess of El Infantado, who had commissioned the tomb, strove to rehabilitate his memory. The immediacy with which the funeral rites are reenacted strengthened the family's position; impressed by such a vivid monument, the uninformed viewer could not have imagined the deceased had been executed for treason.

The chapel also employs this strategy of denial regarding the Constable's lineage. The ensemble proclaims the glory of the Lunas and Alvaro's distinguished place among them. Yet he was an illegitimate son with a tenuous claim to minor nobility. Because Alvaro de Luna's enemies could invoke the concept that bastards are morally deficient, the tomb's denial of the charge was vital to the rehabilitation of his character. The issue does not rest here. By including tombs of the Constable's relatives who had all held distinguished Castilian titles, the chapel answered the accusation that the Constable was an ignoble Aragonese. Among the illustrious Castilians buried there is Juan de Cerezuela, Archbishop of Toledo, and Alvaro's half-brother. Because Juan and Alvaro were related by their mother, not by their father, the Archbishop was not a Luna at all; nonetheless, the tomb presents him as one more distinguished prelate of the family. When the Duchess of Infantado commissioned the Cerezuela tomb, probably immediately after those of her parents, she was manipulating the details of his lineage. Still, his inclusion invites a discussion of Alvaro de Luna's illegitimacy. The depiction of the Archbishop as a Luna, however, blurs all distinctions of lineage and leads the viewer to consider both brothers as completely legitimate family members. This obfuscation is only possible because the tombs of Alvaro de Luna's parents are not included in the chapel. Their absence may appear particularly striking when so many other relatives are buried here. Nonetheless, the reason for this is obvious enough. The Constable's mother came from humble stock, and his father, although noble, was not of the highest rank. Their presence would inevitably raise the question of Luna's illegitimacy and so suggest that his critics had been right all along. The Duchess was probably only too happy not to erect tombs for her grandparents.

*   *   *

The chapel must also be studied with regard to the chronology and shifts in the polemic surrounding the Constable, particularly because this debate was not static but evolved, with opinions running favorably at some points and unfavorably at others.[14] Since the tomb of Alvaro de Luna represented the Duchess's answer to her father's enemies, the timing of her project should be considered: only thirty-six years after his execution. In addition, her plans should be interpreted in light of the previous design for the ensemble, as it was intended to replace the bronze tomb destroyed in a revolt almost fifty years earlier. When the controversy surrounding the Constable and the history of the chapel are examined together, it emerges that the monument in Toledo Cathedral had become a significant statement in the propaganda concerning Luna's regime, whose meaning depended on the viewer and the politics of the period. The project represented the memory which the Constable and his family wished to perpetuate, while their enemies opposed these undertakings because they were equally determined to establish their own version of the man.

The debate began in the Constable's lifetime and would continue well after his death. During Luna's life, Alvar García de Santa María (1349?–1460) included one of the strongest apologies for him in the Chronicle of John II: 'the King loved the Constable greatly for his virtues and for the great services he rendered him.'[15] This author continues, saying that the King could depend on Alvaro de Luna's total loyalty: 'the Constable . . . was always with him and ready for whatever peril that should occur without having made any agreements with anyone except those that the King had made or ordered to be made.'[16] Finally, Alvaro de Luna's virtues led him to serve the King as a moral paragon: 'he governed the estate and affairs of the King with discretion and courageously and cleanly without the greed that those who are ministers of the King sometimes use.'[17] As a telling sign of Alvaro's integrity, the chronicler points out that although John II had delegated all authority to Luna, the Constable had still insisted that matters involving justice or the King's estate pass through the royal councils.[18]

Not surprisingly, those alienated by Alvaro de Luna's severe regime saw things differently. In 1440, when a league of nobles led by the *Infantes*, cousins of King John II, rebelled in an effort to separate the King from Luna, they issued a charter outlining their grievances. The document begins by describing the good king, whom it contrasts with the tyrant, but the real problem appears at the end: Alvaro de Luna, who has 'forgotten who he was, tempted by an excess of vainglory, pride, and disordered greed.'[19] According to the rebels, the Constable has disrupted the natural order in the realm by drawing all power and wealth to himself and reducing the influence of the great houses; he has done this because he knew that an unnatural and illegal regime like his could only sustain itself by destroying the established order. To support this claim, they cite the long list of the victims of his illegitimate rule. Finally, they point to the moral decline of alarming dimensions that the Constable has visited on the realm:

> Moreover, most powerful lord, he has brought to your very noble and clean court the things most vile and most abhorrent to God and nature, that which is spoken of among all the vices ... which for its ugliness cannot be named or declared by the present [document], but concerning it, it can only be said that the great noblemen of your realms are afraid to send their sons and daughters to be brought up in the royal court and palace.[20]

Although their effort to oust Luna failed, the rebels' criticism continued to dog him. The hatred which he had inspired can be measured tangibly as it bears on his plans for his commemoration. In 1441, during the revolt, the *Infante* Henry ordered the destruction of the tomb which the Constable had raised in Toledo Cathedral. Everything about the chapel would have enraged his enemies. The space itself was an irritating symbol of his arrogance; it had been built on the site of three smaller chapels which he had purchased at the height of his power, only to destroy them to make way for his own monument. The cost and workmanship of the tomb, consisting of figures of the Constable and his wife, were conspicuous emblems of his power. Writing a century later, Pedro Alcocer describes the exceptional monument the rebels destroyed as 'made of gilt brass [bronze] of rich and subtle craftsmanship, constructed in such a way that they [the figures] could be raised and placed kneeling each time that was desired.'[21] When made to kneel and rise, the images would have created the illusion that Alvaro de Luna and his wife were themselves present praying piously, but the elaborate display of virtue would also have suggested – to his detractors – the man's outrageous ego. Most serious, his enemies claimed that this tomb, located in the primatial see of Spain, surpassed the monuments of the kings buried nearby; yet even if it only competed with them, it was still a presumptuous gesture.

If the rebels could not touch the man in 1441, they compensated by laying hands on his image. Their destruction of his tomb shows how they, like many other insurgents in history, took their revenge on monuments when they could not reach their real target; such actions suggest the effectiveness of these images as statements of power and as a means to define memory.[22] But as the Constable taunted his adversaries, it was not his tomb which had fought and defeated them.[23] Nonetheless, he knew only too well that the King could remove him, and this happened in 1453, when John II ordered

Luna's execution. The event was carefully arranged as a demonstration of absolute royal power, but the Constable did not make exactly the spectacle the King had wanted: despite the humiliation, Luna did not lose his composure and died a Christian death without making any admission of his guilt.[24]

After the Constable's death, the chapel and the project for a tomb again became important in the battle to shape his memory. As reported by the fifteenth-century author, Rodrigo Sánchez de Arévalo (1404–70), John II's actions are significant:

Moreover, while Alvaro was alive, he had ordered the marvelous construction of a chapel and remarkable tomb in the most holy church of Toledo. This tomb was then destroyed by the *Infante* Henry son of Peter [sic], but King John trusting to humanity and piety, allowed it to be restored, although many argued strongly against this, lest so imposing a statue stand out in the church in which the Kings of Spain are buried humbly. They added that it seemed improper that one who had been decapitated should enjoy so exalted a tomb in the midst of those crowned with the royal diadem, especially because the inscription of the tomb displayed pride for the greatest achievements. John said to these people, 'Be they true or false, the things which Alvaro ordered written about himself, let them remain untouched, because we think it proper that the dead, since they can do nothing else, write what they wish about themselves. Add that I wish the memory of him who was so readily loved by me not to be destroyed and that all recognize that the clever and powerful Alvaro was able to be killed by me. Let him then be to posterity an outstanding example that a man so very dear to the king was killed by him on account of his arrogance.[25]

John II probably never said this because no tomb stood in the chapel at the time: the first tomb had been destroyed more than ten years previously, and the present monuments with their inscriptions were only commissioned well after the deaths of Luna (1453), the King (1454), and the historian (1470). In all likelihood, Sánchez de Arévalo invented this speech on the basis of the knowledge that John II had shown mercy toward Luna and not seized the chapel. As he describes the event, however, the historian transforms the King's actions and words to resemble those of the Roman Emperor, Severus, whose example he cites.[26]

Although fictitious, Sánchez de Arévalo includes this speech to show John II's moderation and clemency in his confiscation of Luna's estate, and the culminating gesture of this is his decision to leave the Constable's funerary chapel unaltered. The historian doubtless thought that this section was required to explain how Luna, who had been condemned for treason, could be buried with such honor in so prominent a chapel: only because the King's generosity had allowed it. It is significant that Sánchez de Arévalo thought this paradox might bother his readers. Moreover, his efforts to explain it demonstrate the power, which all acknowledged, that ostentatious monuments had to define the memory of a person and consequently the importance of controlling the statement these works made. This account thus shows how an author, writing within twenty years of the events, had interpreted the struggle between the King, the Constable, and his enemies to fashion an image for posterity. Luna's opponents interpreted the ensemble – which dwarfed the royal monuments nearby – as emblems of the same arrogance that had led him to usurp the King's authority and, further, to refuse to acknowledge any guilt on his death. John II took a more sophisticated approach: royal prerogative was all the more absolute if it had toppled someone who could construct such a chapel. The resulting message established the King's prestige. However, it was a dangerous approach because it depended on the memory that the Constable had been justly executed for treason.

At the time, it seemed no one could ever forget the event. Only after Alvaro de Luna's death did his enemies feel confident enough to commit their interpretations to writing, and their version entered the official royal histories.[27] Those who had supported the Constable during his lifetime were now silent because the King had refrained from punishing them. Although he did not write it as part of an official royal chronicle, Fernán Pérez de Guzmán (1376?–1460?) penned one of the most devastating attacks on the Constable. The biography begins 'Alvaro de Luna, Master of Santiago and Constable of Castile, was the bastard son of Alvaro de Luna, a noble and good knight,' before continuing:

> the Constable was small of body and slight of face but he was well composed in his limbs and strong. He was a very good horseman, as expert in arms as in the games of them; he was well-versed in the ways of the palace, very gracious and well reasoned, although he hesitated somewhat in his speech. He was very discreet, a great dissimulator, who feigned and took precautions. He delighted greatly in the use of such arts and stratagems so that it seemed he had them from nature. He was considered a bold man although he never had a great occasion to show this in armed combat. In the struggles and debates of the palace that are a second measure of boldness of spirit, he showed himself very much a man. He prized his lineage greatly, not remembering the humble and lowly part of his mother. He had such a heart and daring as to accept and use the great power which he had attained that he acted more as a king than as a knight; he did so either because he had persisted in this power so long that it had converted his nature or because his arrogance and presumption were so great . . . He was greedy to a large extreme for vassals and treasures; like those who are already bloated but never lose their thirst, he never lost the desire to acquire and have and thus his insatiable greed was never satisfied.[28]

As Pérez de Guzmán evaluates Luna, he implies that the ideal knight is nobly born and characterized by good appearance, physical prowess, bravery, loyalty, temperance and intellect, but the Constable is deficient in every way, appearing as a deceitful, even treacherous, usurper of royal prerogatives. This account is more devastating since it appears impartial, setting forth

Luna's merits only to undermine them in the next breath. Although conceding the Constable's skill at arms, Pérez de Guzmán suggests that the reputation was not backed up with experience on the battlefield. Still, the Constable was, he admits, an undisputed expert at another, but less glorious, form of combat: palace intrigue. Moreover, he abused this 'skill' to obtain the riches for which he had an insatiable appetite and thereby revealed his lack of temperance. He acquired so much wealth and power that he was able to act more like the king than a knight or subject. This behavior, in turn, suggests how he usurped the King's prerogative and authority, which, as treason, was considered his most serious crime and would ultimately cause his downfall. For Pérez de Guzmán, the last outrage is Luna's self-delusion as he forgot his illegitimacy and boasted of his lineage.

Although fifteenth-century authors differ in their assessments of the Constable, whether as a felon guilty of treason or as the flower of nobility, they agree on the criteria. These are, moreover, the very concepts emphasized in the ensemble that his daughter was to construct; to interpret the monument as a statement of the Constable's lineage, virtues, and status, therefore, places it firmly in the debate concerning his memory. The tomb can now be read as a visual statement in this polemic, where, like the texts of his apologists, it presents Alvaro de Luna as a virtuous knight. The ensemble's emphasis on the Luna family's prestige directly answers the insults of the Constable's detractors, such as Pérez de Guzmán, concerning his illegitimacy. Moreover, the ceremony which the kneeling knights of Santiago perform around his bier attests to the Constable's exemplary moral character, his social status, and his position as Christian warrior, all of which his enemies had vigorously assailed. Like the destroyed monument, this work commemorates his piety, but it also makes further claims. The personifications of the virtues on the base can be read not simply as personal attributes but as a description of his regime that answers his enemies' charges: he administered the King's law with Justice; he practiced Temperance when he refrained from enriching himself; and he carried out his policies with Prudence and Fortitude. Finally, the striking immediacy of the ensemble can be interpreted as a visual response to the mordant rhetoric of his opponents.

The monument can be examined further in this context: when the Duchess of El Infantado commissioned the tombs in 1489, the image of the Constable was undergoing a transformation.[29] Several authors, principally poets, had begun to spread a romanticized view; they acknowledged Alvaro de Luna's faults but drew on his noble conduct at the scaffold to present him as a tragic figure and a victim of Fortune.[30] At the end of the fifteenth century, one of Alvaro de Luna's trusted subordinates, Gonzalo de Chacón, wrote a persuasive – if disingenuous – chronicle of the Constable. Although the first edition was not printed until 1546 in Milan, the copies of it which doubtless circulated among the Constable's descendants could have inspired and supported sympathetic treatments of the man.[31] Perhaps this shift in opinion convinced the Duchess that the time was right to order her parents' monument. After reading such texts or hearing the stories of his death, people might well accept the monument's claim that the Constable was the perfect Christian knight. In this case, the historical inaccuracies of the iconography regarding the Constable's lineage and funeral would have been less conspicuous.

Moreover, the tomb was only the latest effort to restore the chapel to its previous splendor. When Alvaro de Luna died, the chapel being without a tomb, the Constable's body was buried elsewhere, and the family lacked both the resources and the political influence to remedy this situation.[32] Despite petitions to John II and his son, Henry IV, the body was not transferred.[33] But the political climate would change yet again: the Constable's daughter married into the Mendoza family, the greatest allies of the new monarchs, Ferdinand and Isabel. These ties made the resumption of the project and the rehabilitation of her father's memory feasible: her husband's uncle, Cardinal Pedro González de Mendoza, served as the monarchs' most trusted advisor and, since 1482, as the Cardinal-Archbishop of Toledo, the site of Luna's empty chapel. At last, the family was able to secure the royal and ecclesiastical permission required to transfer the Constable's body to his chapel.[34] In 1483, Alvaro de Luna's widow and daughter reopened negotiations with the cathedral chapter regarding the chapel and, in the following year, they made a donation for it. After his widow died in 1484, responsibility for the project passed to his daughter, the Duchess, who commissioned the present altarpiece in 1488 and the tombs in 1489 from the sculptor Sebastián de Almonacid.[35]

The next twist concerning the tomb's relation to the memory of the Constable occurred in 1497, just eight years after the work had been commissioned. The rehabilitation of Alvaro de Luna's reputation had apparently progressed so far that the Duchess made a bid to overturn his conviction. In this year, she filed a suit to reclaim part of her father's estate that had been seized by the crown as the penalty for his treason.[36] Because she based her argument on the contention that the Constable had been unjustly executed and the property taken illegally, the chapel's presentation of him as a moral exemplar took on even more urgency for her: the monument could be interpreted as a visual analogy for the image underlying her suit.

The suit became a cause célèbre with the potential to embarrass Ferdinand and Isabel, who prided themselves on their legal administration. Moreover, Isabel would hardly appreciate aspersions cast on John II's justice; she was his daughter, and her succession – which had been contested – depended on this descent. Not surprisingly, the Queen intervened with an adverse judgment. Although the Duchess lost her case, the momentum to rehabilitate her father did not vanish. A little more than a century later, when Pedro Salazar de Mendoza (1550?–1629) came to write his own account of Luna's character, the revision had progressed so far that the historian could answer the charges raised against the Constable point by point.[37] His biography clearly draws on Pérez de Guzmán's account for details, but Salazar de Mendoza rewrites it to defend the Constable's knightly virtue by presenting him as a loyal vassal, a good soldier, prudent counselor and an affable courtier. Where Pérez de Guzmán accuses Luna of dissimulations, Salazar explains how it was 'with those who were lascivious and talkative, [that] he put on a good face but never gave them a part of his deeds.' In answer to the charge that Alvaro de Luna never experienced the dangers of war firsthand, Salazar writes: 'In war, he was very daring and he ordinarily put himself in great danger. He suffered much in combat and also the discomforts of a soldier.' The most serious allegation, that the Constable had usurped the King's authority, draws the comment that 'he spoke at all times with great reverence and submission of the King, his lord.' The need to answer this point probably explains why Salazar begins his description with the claim that 'Don Alvaro was an agreeable courtier, loved by people of all conditions. In all things he fulfilled his obligations as an honorable knight.'

Salazar de Mendoza's revision of Pérez de Guzmán's account can be explained as history written according to family loyalties. Both authors were related to the Mendozas: Pérez de Guzmán was a member of the family and Salazar de Mendoza a client. Not surprisingly, each man presents sympathetic portraits of the Mendozas and their allies. But the definition of who were these allies could change and with it the corresponding vision of history. With regard to Alvaro de Luna, the Mendozas had good reason to reverse their opinion shortly after his death. Although they had been bitter enemies of the Constable during his lifetime, when his daughter later married into the family, she brought with her several of his titles and estates. Consequently, the Mendozas now had an interest in supporting her program to perpetuate the memory of their former enemy because the monument had become a tribute to their own titles as well. So Pérez de Guzmán's villain became an exemplary knight for Salazar de Mendoza.

Such partisan genealogical interest was common at the time. For instance, when another historian, the Marquis of Mondéjar (1628–1708), wrote an account of his family, he spelled out the didactic or exemplary nature of this genre. In his introduction, he tells his grandson, to whom he dedicates the work, that he writes it as a memorial of the family's glory which he hopes will inspire their descendants to act nobly.[38] Viewed from such a perspective, the monument to Alvaro de Luna becomes a memorial to his character and the splendor of his achievements. That the project should be made possible by descendants of his enemies was an unforeseen irony.

* * *

The tomb and chapel of Alvaro de Luna offer a case study of one family's efforts to reshape the memory of a forebear and rehabilitate his character. The extent and success of this undertaking can only be appreciated when the controversy surrounding the man is understood. The virulent disputes Alvaro de Luna occasioned reveal the principal values used to create and categorize his memory: the virtues of the Christian knight, the faithful vassal, and the loyal courtier. At the heart of the debate is the question whether in his service to the King, Luna had acted ignobly, usurping royal prerogative and disrupting the natural order in Castile. His enemies judged his innate vices as the product of his dubious lineage, and some even insinuated that his illegitimacy prevented him from being a true nobleman.

Their attacks had a crucial impact on the tomb as a commemoration of the Constable. Although all monuments and family chapels are by definition memorials constructed to preserve a specific image of an individual, the controversy surrounding Alvaro de Luna and his chapel permits a detailed examination of the way visual forms can be manipulated for the construction of memory. The visual innovations of the tomb, the life-size mourners who recreate a funeral that never happened, are motivated by this agenda of rehabilitation: such a ceremony would only have been held for a paragon like the one which the ensemble commemorates. Furthermore, these figures evoke this rite vividly, thereby enhancing its impact and strengthening its message. Iconographically, the monument depicts the Constable as a virtuous, Christian knight of unblemished lineage and nobility, in short proclaiming the very qualities that his detractors had questioned.

Interpreted from this perspective, the monument becomes a visual statement made by his family to answer their enemies. As such, it resembles the polemical tracts written about the Constable both in its agenda and rhetoric. Not surprisingly, the monument's program addresses the very issues set by the controversy. Further, the tomb and chapel advance an image that distorts and even contradicts historical facts: no such funeral occurred, the Constable's illegitimacy is ignored, and a half-brother from the wrong side of the family is included. Such a free handling of these issues, combining oversight and misrepresentation, resembles that found in the tracts written about the Constable. Moreover, the ensemble, like the chronicles, presents a coherent and effective image that obscures the attacks on Luna even as it answers their charges.

In the end, the family's efforts to rehabilitate the Constable did not succeed completely, and scholars continue to debate the man's political achievements.[39] On the other hand, art historians have been kinder to the tomb, admiring its impact. The same polemical agenda that lay behind the family's revisionist history also guided Sebastián de Almonacid's chisel: the visual evidence suggests nothing but a Christian knight of the noblest birth. The monument describes this concept so effectively that the viewer would never guess that it marks the burial of an illegitimate son convicted for treason. The success of this visual stratagem represents the ultimate victory for his family, particularly his daughter, in their efforts to refashion the memory of Alvaro de Luna.

Frequently cited sources

Azcárate, J. M., ed., *Colección de documentos para la historia del arte en España*, Madrid: Real Academia de San Fernando, and Zaragoza: Museo e Instituto de Humanidades 'Camón Aznar,' 1982.

García de Santa María, A., *Crónica de Juan II*, Colección de documentos inéditos para la historia de España, 100, Madrid: Rafael Marco y Viñas, 1891.

González Palencia, C., 'La capilla de Don Alvaro de Luna en la catedral de Toledo,' *Archivo Español de Arte*, vol. 5, 1929, pp.109–22.

Round, N., *The Greatest Man Uncrowned: A Study of the Fall of Don Alvaro de Luna*, London: Tamesis Books, 1986.

Sánchez de Arévalo, R., *Historiae Hispanicae Partes Quatuor* in Andreas Schottus, ed., *Hispaniae Illustratae seu Rerum Urbiumque Hispaniae, Lusitaniae, Aethiopiae et Indiae Scriptores varii*, part 1, Frankfurt, 1603.

Notes

1. González Palencia, 'La capilla de Don Alvaro de Luna,' pp.109–22.

2. B. Gilman Proske, *Castilian Sculpture: Gothic to Renaissance*, New York: The Hispanic Society of America, 1951, p.181. This exceptional monument reportedly consisted of an image constructed so that it could bow before the altar. Pedro de Alcocer, *Hystoria o descripcion de la imperial cibdad de Toledo*, Toledo: Iuan Ferrer, 1554, folio 79v. See also below note 21.

3. For the documents see González Palencia, 'La capilla de Don Alvaro de Luna,' pp.118–21; see also Azcárate, ed., *Colección de documentos*, pp.242–4. Although the contract for the other monuments, those of the Constable's uncle, half-brother, and son, does not survive, they must also date from this period on stylistic grounds.

4. For earlier examples of monuments with mourners, see the articles by Elizabeth Valdez del Alamo, Anne Morganstern, and Rocío Sánchez Ameijeiras in this volume.

5. I have found no evidence that the Countess endowed any monastery or made such a gift. Further, the contract simply calls for 'four holy friars of the order that her ladyship shall order.' Azcárate, ed., *Colección de documentos*, p.244. Nonetheless, because religious orders expected some gift before appearing in such a funeral, the tomb calls on the viewer to imagine that such compensation has been provided.

6. The history of the endowment of the chapel before 1483 is unknown, but to judge by the power of attorney the Constable's widow and daughter issued, the chapel had none.

7. Sección Osuna, legajo 1847, no. 3, formerly Archivo Histórico Nacional (Madrid), now Archivo Nobiliario in the Fundación Tavera (Toledo).

8. ibid. The text says simply 'at the end of said mass [the sung mass on Saturday], they [the celebrant, the other two priests, and the sacristan] shall leave with a response sung over the burial of the said Master, my lord, on said day of Saturday, and on the other days it shall be chanted. In this way, each of the said chaplains shall leave with a response chanted over the burial on each day that he shall say mass.' The particular prayers are not listed.

9. This escutcheon, a crescent moon, is a pun on his name, *luna*, which in Spanish means moon.

10. Among these distinguished forebears were two other prelates also named Pedro de Luna, the anti-pope Benedict XIII and the Archbishop of Zaragoza. In addition, other family members had served in the retinue of Henry III of Castile and the *infante* Ferdinand of Antequera. Because the

young Alvaro de Luna had grown up in his uncle's household after his father's death, the inclusion of this tomb may owe something to filial loyalty in addition to the desire to commemorate a distinguished lineage.

11. Given the partisan nature of most primary sources regarding Alvaro de Luna, modern historians have had great difficulty coming to an evaluation of the Constable. The most reasonable interpretation can be found in Round, *The Greatest Man Uncrowned*.

12. The story must be interpreted with caution as it is found in a source less than flattering to the Constable: A. de Palencia, *Crónica de Enrique IV*, edited by A. Paz y Meliá, Biblioteca de Autores Españoles, 257, Madrid: Ediciones Atlas, 1973, p.43.

13. G. de Chacón, *Crónica de Alvaro de Luna*, edited by J. de Mata Carriazo, Colección de Crónicas Españolas, 2, Madrid: Espasa Calpe, 1940, p.435, describes the second funeral as occurring in the presence of many 'illustrious and notable prelates and noblemen.'

14. Round, *The Greatest Man Uncrowned*, pp.211–20.

15. García de Santa María, *Crónica de Juan II*, p.304.

16. ibid.

17. ibid., p.308.

18. ibid., p.209.

19. P. Carillo de Huete *Crónica del Halconero de Juan II*, edited by J. Mata Carriazo, Colección de Crónicas Españolas, 8, Madrid: Espasa Calpe, 1946, p.324.

20. ibid., p.331.

21. Alcocer (as in n.2), fol. 79v. Although Alcocer reports that the destruction of the tomb occurred in 1449 during another revolt against the Constable, two earlier sources independently – and more convincingly – describe the event as happening in 1441 at the orders of *infante* Henry: Sánchez de Arévalo, *Historiae Hispanicae Partes Quatuor*, p.236, which reprints his account of *c.*1470; Hernán Núñez de Toledo's gloss on Juan de Mena's *Las Trescientas*, Seville, 1499, fol. 177.

22. Other examples can be found in Antiquity and, later, throughout Europe. They include the ceremony in Avila in 1465 when King Henry IV, represented by a wooden statue, was deposed; the destruction of Michelangelo's bronze statue of Julius II in Bologna (1511); and the decapitation of crowned statues in the French Revolution.

23. H. Núñez de Toledo's gloss on Juan de Mena's *Las Trescientas*, Seville, 1499, fol. 177, reports the following poem Alvaro de Luna directed to Henry on the event:

> Si flota vos combatio,
> en verdad senor infante
> mi bulto no vos prendio,
> quando fuistes mareante,
> por que hiciessedes nada
> a un senblante figura
> que estaua en mi sepultura
> para mi fin ordenada.

24. Round, *The Greatest Man Uncrowned*, pp.211–14.

25. Sánchez de Arévalo, *Historiae Hispanicae Partes Quatuor*, p.236. Translation assistance from Professor Lydia Lenaghan, Barnard College, New York.

26. In fact, he draws attention to the parallel by citing it as a model for John II: paraphrasing his Latin source, the *Historia Augusta*, Sánchez de Arévalo recounts how the Roman had refused to destroy the epitaph which his predecessor had written, saying: 'If Pescennius was such a man, let all know what a man we have often defeated; if he was not such, let all think that we have conquered such a man.' The memory of John II which the historian records seems a retelling of events reconfigured to conform to classical models. Sánchez de Arévalo, *Historiae Hispanicae Partes Quatuor*, p.236. The comparable passage in the Latin text can be found in Aelius Spartianus, *Historia Augusta*, Life of Pescennius Niger XII:4–7 LCL, 1, London, 1960.

27. Palencia (as in n.12).

28. F. Pérez de Guzmán, *Generaciones y semblanzas*, edited by R. B. Tate, London: Tamesis Books, 1965, p.45.

29. Round, *The Greatest Man Uncrowned*, pp.216–20.

30. Among the Spanish poets, the marquis of Santillana and Jorge Manrique commented on the Constable's death: the marquis described the event venomously while Manrique simply pointed to the enormity of his fall within the topos of *ubi sunt*. On the other hand, an admiring Juan de Mena had uttered cautionary words on Fortune during his lifetime. Round, *The Greatest Man Uncrowned*, p.213, quotes Pedro de Escavia's description of the Constable's death: 'He died with a good countenance and good courage, as a knight and a faithful Christian should. May God forgive him, for he handled many great matters in the days when he enjoyed the King's favor.' This passage suggests how the memory of Alvaro de Luna's death was able to change the interpretation of the man.

31. Round, *The Greatest Man Uncrowned*, p.217.

32. According to the *Espasa gran enciclopedia ilustrada*, San Andrés, the site where Alvaro de Luna was first interred, was a burial ground for criminals.

33. Chacón (as in n.13), p.437.

34. On their accession, the Catholic monarchs had intended to be buried in a Franciscan monastery which they had founded in Toledo, San Juan de los Reyes. Because this project would have dwarfed the Constable's chapel, they would have had little reason to feel demeaned by Luna's tomb and deny his daughter's request. Furthermore, at the same time that the Duchess was commissioning her father's monument, Isabel was building an even more lavish work for her father, King John II in the Cartuja de Miraflores. Consequently when Luna's daughter was completing the chapel all comparisons between the project in Toledo Cathedral and the royal tombs would have become more favorable to royal prestige. Finally, with the conquest of Granada, Ferdinand and Isabel decided to commemorate the event by establishing the royal pantheon for the kings of Castile there.

35. For the documents see González Palencia, 'La capilla de Don Alvaro de Luna,' pp.118–21; and Azcárate, ed., *Colección de documentos*, pp.242–4. Although the contract for the other monuments, those of the Constable's uncle, half-brother, and son, does not survive, on stylistic grounds they must also date from this period.

36. L. de Corral, *Don Alvaro de Luna según testimonios inéditos de la época*, Valladolid: Sociedad de Estudios Históricos Castellanos, 1915, pp.15–17.

37. P. de Salazar de Mendoza, *Crónica de la vida de el gran cardenal de España Don Pedro González de Mendoza arzobispo de España*, Toledo, 1625, pp.72–3.

38. The idea was apparently important to him because he repeats it later in the work: 'The greatest happiness of great men, as well as the most certain way to preserve the splendor that they acquired with their merits for their house and families consists always that the children they leave as successors to their house should imitate them in the virtues and glorious actions with which they earned it [splendor].' ('La mayor felicidad de los varones grandes assi como el mas seguro medio de conservar el esplendidor que adquireron en sus merescimientos para sus casa y familias consiste siempre en que los hijos que dexan por successores en ellas les imiten en las virtudes y gloriosas acciones con que le grangearon en cuya circunstancia tan preciable y necessaria para mantenterle continuado, no cede la Mondejar a ninguna de las mas sobresalientes de nuestros Reynos por la copia grande de sus sugetos señalados que ha producido en todas profesiones'). G. Ibáñez de Segovia, Marquis of Mondejar, *Historia de la casa de Mondejar*, Biblioteca Nacional de Madrid MS 3315, fol. 166v.

39. It is significant that this debate continued. As subsequent authors in the sixteenth and seventeenth centuries responded to these accounts, they did not alter the rhetoric of the discussion, and in doing so, they tacitly acknowledged the primacy of the values previously used to define the Constable. When they, in turn, employed this rhetoric in their writings, they transmitted these beliefs to succeeding generations. While this raises difficulties for scholars interpreting the period, it shows how charged the accusations leveled at the Constable were.

5.1   Sebastián de Almonacid, tomb of Alvaro de Luna, Capilla de Santiago, Toledo
Cathedral, 1489

5.2   Sebastián de Almonacid, tomb of Juana de Pimentel, wife of Alvaro de Luna, Capilla de Santiago, Toledo Cathedral, 1489

5.3 Sebastián de Almonacid, detail of kneeling Knight of Santiago from tomb of
Alvaro de Luna

5.4   Sebastián de Almonacid, relief of Temperance from tomb of Alvaro de Luna

5.5   Antoni Canet, tomb of Bishop d'Escales, Barcelona Cathedral, 1409–12

5.6 Gil de Siloe, tomb of John II and Isabel of Portugal, Cartuja de Miraflores,
Burgos, 1489–93

5.7 Gil de Siloe, detail of praying Carthusian from tomb of John II and Isabel of Portugal

5.8 Sebastián de Almonacid, tomb of Martín Vázquez de Arce, Capilla de los Arce, Sigüenza Cathedral, 1493–7

II

Shaping communal memory

6

The font is a kind of grave: remembrance in the Via Latina catacombs

Dorothy Hoogland Verkerk

This essay is dedicated to the memory of Ms Sylvia TenBroek

The early Church, in the process of defining and distinguishing itself, perceived the Christian life as an exodus from the exiled state of sin and flesh to the Promised Land of salvation and spirit. The Christian exodus arrived at its two most significant moments during baptismal and burial rituals conceptualized as progressions, or passages, from exile to homeland. Thus, baptism and entombment were conceived of as mutually referential, creating a seamless, yet multivalent dialogue of inversion where life is death and death is life. The exodus theme, evolving from the Jewish history of exile in Egypt, is woven throughout the entire fabric of Christian ritual.

The Christian conception of death, as a sleep from which one awakens in paradise, required fresh strategies to celebrate the dead, since the Church no longer sanctioned the public displays of sorrow which were characteristic of pagan ceremonies. One means of achieving this idealized approach to death was to recast it in terms of the baptismal rites with its overtones of death and rebirth. Another means was to invoke the heroic biblical dead, the men and women of faith who had passed through their exilic experience and been reborn. The exemplars invoked by the heroes of faith and the prior experience of baptism were mechanisms to structure ideologically the passage between death and life.

The textual and ritual dialogue between baptism and burial, generated by scripture readings, prayers and antiphons, also produced a visual component that addressed the exodus theme. Pictures that illustrated Psalms and stories sung or spoken during those key moments of passage could be fashioned to suit the needs of initiation or interment rituals. Images were the visual techniques that prompted the memory to associate past spoken word and action with present performance. Two series of pictures, one from the fourth century and one from the late sixth century, demonstrate how memory, activated by images and reinforced by ritual action, could bind the past with the present, the dead with the living.

The Via Latina catacomb paintings, specifically Cubiculum C, and the illuminated Ashburnham Pentateuch are studied here together since they provide a case study for analyzing how the story of Exodus was 'retold' visually.[1] Although the sixth-century Ashburnham Pentateuch is the more recent of the two picture series, its illuminations of Exodus address the earlier moment of Christian exodus, baptism, while the older, fourth-century catacomb paintings address the later moment when the passage into the Promised Land is realized. Examining together the two picture series and their ritual contexts allows an insight into the nuances of the exodus theme and, due to the longevity of its 'retellings,' its continued significance.[2] Although the textual sources are clear in showing how baptism and death were intertwined in the minds of Early Christians, the visual techniques in which this was achieved are not fully discussed. Illustrations of the same stories can achieve, through minor changes and associations, commemorative monuments that address the specific needs of their constituents.

Discovered in 1956, the paintings on the walls of Cubiculum C in the Via Latina catacombs, Rome, introduced fresh and more comprehensive Exodus scenes into fourth-century funerary art.[3] One such scene is found in the southeastern niche of the chamber: a robed figure kneels and raises his hands toward a cloud while below a large man leads a crowd toward a tabernacle (Fig. 6.1). Above and behind the tabernacle, an architectural column is shown. Although this curious combination has received various interpretations, I interpret the images as Moses seeing God on Mount Sinai and Christ, the new Moses and Shepherd, guiding his flock to the Heavenly Jerusalem. My interpretation is rooted in the centrality of the exodus theme in early church rituals.

Separated by over two hundred years, the late sixth-century Ashburnham Pentateuch (Paris, Bibliothèque Nationale, MS nouv. acq. lat. 2334) also addressed the theme of exodus for contemporary Christians, showing the significance of the biblical Exodus story for baptismal rites.[4] These two series of pictures attest to how visual narratives, based on the same stories from Exodus, were appropriated and transformed to create a historical continuity between past actions and present rituals. The catacomb murals include a greater array of subjects, yet they reiterate the overarching theme of exodus. Thus, I refer to both the specific events from Jewish history, as laid down in the Book of Exodus, and to their allegorical meaning in the rites of the early church.

The Ashburnham Pentateuch's Exodus illustrations transform the actions of past history through pictorial references to contemporary events, specifically the rituals surrounding baptism – the Christian's first rite of passage. The tomb paintings call to mind the words spoken in the ceremonies of dying and burial, the Christian's final rite of passage.[5] The catechisms and sermons the Christian received at baptism and the Psalms sung during the funerary ceremonies are the matrices from which the paintings derive their meaning, creating an association between the heroic dead of the past and the present dead.[6] The tomb paintings, within the contextual frame of baptismal and death rites, are multivalent by means of association and memory.[7]

André Grabar was the first scholar to link the paintings in Cubiculum C to the Ashburnham Pentateuch (Fig. 6.2).[8] He observed that the two cycles share Moses on Mount Sinai talking to God in the cloud and a tabernacle. In the manuscript, Moses on Sinai is found at the top left of folio 76r and in the tomb it is the figure reaching toward a cloud; the tabernacles are below in each tableau.

The wall painting and manuscript share several other scenes as well: the Pillar of Cloud and Fire that led the Israelites during their exodus and a sacrifice. In the catacomb the Pillar is adjacent to Abraham's Sacrifice of Isaac (Fig. 6.3); in the codex, it is adjacent to Moses offering sacrifices surrounded by Israelites, immediately above and to the right of the tabernacle.[9] The key difference is that the tomb shows the Pillar as an architectural column, while the manuscript depicts the Pillar as a hand-held candle.[10]

The tomb and the manuscript also share the inclusion of a Crossing of the Red Sea scene. The Crossing is found in the northwestern niche of Cubiculum C, opposite Moses on Mount Sinai and the crowd led to the tabernacle (Fig. 6.4). In the Ashburnham Pentateuch the Crossing of the Red Sea is found on the lower half of folio 68r (Fig. 6.5). In each picture, the Israelites precede the larger figure of Moses. Chariots and drowning Egyptians fill the waters of the Red Sea in both the mural and the illustration. The only essential iconographic difference, yet an important one, between the two depictions is the absence of a Pillar in the tomb's Crossing. The hand-held candle in the Ashburnham Pentateuch was an additional motif inserted by the manuscript's maker, indicating a deliberate choice.

The candle is a visual prompt to the Christian audience that this Crossing of the Red Sea is more than a narrative from Jewish history: it is the primary type for Christian baptism.[11] The Church reiterated Exodus stories, especially the Crossing of the Red Sea, during baptismal rituals to prefigure the Christian's ritual experience of 'crossing' the waters of the baptismal font. The large candle refers to the paschal candle, used during the Easter vigil to symbolize both the Pillar and Christ, the Light of the World, leading the new Israelites out of bondage to sin and into the Promised Land of eternal life.[12] The Easter vigil, which took place on Holy Saturday before Easter Sunday, was the primary service in the Christian liturgical year for the baptism of

catechumens, or initiates, into the Church. During the Easter vigil, the dea-
con held a large candle in his hands when he led the baptismal candidates to
the baptistery while Psalm 41(42), the *Quemadmodum*, was sung: 'As a hind
longs for the running streams, so do I long for thee, O God.'[13] The scriptural
lessons read during the Easter vigil always included the story of the Crossing of the Red Sea (Exod. 14).[14] In this way, the story of Exodus and the rite
of baptism were inextricably linked in the minds of Early Christians.[15] The
Crossing of the Red Sea as a type for the Christian baptism is derived from St
Paul in his letter to the Corinthians: 'You should understand, my brothers,
that our ancestors were all under the pillar of cloud and all of them passed
through the Red Sea; and so they all received baptism into the fellowship of
Moses in cloud and sea' (1 Cor. 10.1–2). For any fourth-century Christian, the
story of the Jewish Exodus would be the story of their baptism.[16]

The early Church also invoked the Exodus story to understand Christian
death as a passage from earthly existence into life eternal. The Crossing of
the Red Sea in the Via Latina tomb is a typological reference to baptism to
remind the Christians visiting the tomb that they have already passed from
spiritual death into a spiritual rebirth. Exodus conceptually linked baptism
and death.

St Paul interweaves baptism and physical death in his letter to the
Romans, chapter 6:

> Have you forgotten that when we were baptized into union with Christ Jesus we
> were baptized into his death? By baptism we were buried with him, and lay dead,
> in order that, as Christ was raised from the dead in the splendor of the Father, so
> also we might set our feet upon the new path of life. (Rom. 6.3–4)

St Paul was, no doubt, the primary source for the depiction of baptism in
the catacombs and on sarcophagi.[17] Ambrose, the fourth-century Bishop of
Milan, reiterates this theme in his discussion of the baptismal rite: 'it is
not earth which washes, but water. So it is that the font is a kind of grave.'[18]
Ambrose is speaking to the newly baptized members of his congregation
about the Easter vigil, the service that they had experienced for the first time.

The ideological relationship between baptism and death is important to
our understanding of the funerary practices that took place in the Via Latina
tomb. Fourth-century liturgical books of death rites do not survive. Fourth-
century baptismal liturgies, on the other hand, are well documented. The
most important source of fourth-century Roman baptismal rites is Ambrose's
sermon, *De sacramentis*, which explains to the recently initiated Christians the
meaning of their baptism and their first partaking of the Eucharist.[19]

Considering the Christian concept of baptism as spiritual death and physical death as rebirth, it is not surprising to find Ambrose quoting the same
Psalms that are found in later Roman liturgical books. It seems clear that

the Church used the Psalms and lessons heard at baptism for funerary rites. Readings from the Book of Job, Psalm 22 (*Dominus reget me*), Psalm 41 (*Quemadmodum*), and Psalms 113–15 (*In exitu Israhel de Aegypto; Dilexi quoniam exaudiet; Credidi propter*) were the most important biblical texts for funerary processions and were incorporated into the fifth- and sixth-century death rites with accompanying prayers and antiphons.[20] It is at the intersection of biblical texts cited by Ambrose and found in the Roman death rite that I believe the meaning of the tomb paintings can be reconstructed.

Roman funerary practices encouraged the singing of Psalms to demonstrate the joyous nature of death for a Christian and to lighten the hearts of the mourners. At the moment of his mother's death, for example, Augustine's friends began to sing Psalm 100 to quiet the tears of his son.[21] Death rituals also included a *viaticum* that was the deathbed reception of the Eucharist.[22] This sacrament was repeated if death were delayed because it was vital that the body of Christ be in the mouth at the moment of death. The last partaking of the Eucharist was so important to Christians that two early councils condemned the abuse of the *viaticum* because it was being administered to corpses. Christ himself closely linked the partaking of bread with the resurrection in John 6.54: 'Whoever eats my flesh and drinks my blood possesses eternal life, and I will raise him up on the last day.' In the tomb, the Christian's last partaking of the Eucharist is alluded to in the scene of Abraham sacrificing Isaac, the preeminent type for Christ's sacrifice and heard in the Roman canon of the Mass.[23] The Ashburnham Pentateuch refers to the Christian's first partaking of the Eucharist in the illustration of Exodus 24 where Moses reads the covenant and sacrifices holocausts. In the manuscript, chalices and loaves of bread are substituted for the animal sacrifices and are a visual sign that this is not an Old Testament altar but a New Testament altar.[24] After passing through the waters of the font, the Christian partakes of the Eucharistic bread and wine for the first time. The *viaticum*, the last Eucharist, sustains the Christian through the passage into the grave.

Since baptism was sometimes delayed – for example, the deathbed baptism of Constantine, and the adult baptisms of Augustine and Ambrose – emergency baptism was frequently given so the *viaticum* could be received.[25] The idea that the sacraments of baptism and the Eucharist could guarantee an individual's salvation was so strongly held that St Paul felt compelled to warn Christians not to baptize those who were already dead.[26] The tomb visually links baptism with the *viaticum* by juxtaposing the Crossing with Moses Striking the Rock (Fig. 6.6). This juxtaposition reflects the words of the funerary Psalm 113 (114): 'When Israel came out of Egypt . . . the sea looked and ran away . . .' The Psalm ends with a reference to Moses Striking the Rock: 'Dance, O earth, at the presence of the Lord . . . who turned the rock into a pool of water, the granite cliff into a fountain.'[27]

Ambrose also refers to the Crossing and Moses Striking the Rock to explain that the Christian who passes through the water of the font does not die but rises again.[28] Ambrose refers three times to Moses Striking the Rock as a type not only for baptism but also for the water and wine of the Eucharist.[29] Thus, the tomb paintings illustrate the Old Testament stories that the Church used to teach its catechumens.[30] Through the sacraments of baptism and the Eucharist the Christian, like the Israelites, will come out of Egypt into the Promised Land of eternal paradise.

In the lower half of folio 76r in the Ashburnham Pentateuch the visual cues of the hand-held candle and a Christian altar transform the Old Testament tabernacle into a New Testament church (Fig. 6.2).[31] The candle, found just above and to the right of the white tent that flanks the tabernacle on the right, is substituted for the more typical architectural column. The altar, found in the center of the tabernacle, is substituted for the Ark of the Covenant. The altar is covered by a white cloth with red markings and carries a reliquary niche on the front side. Moses and Aaron on either side of the tabernacle pull back the curtains and gesture invitingly because through the sacraments of baptism and the Eucharist – prefigured in the previous scenes of the Crossing and Moses Sacrificing – the Christian for the first time freely enters the Church, the House of God.[32]

In light of its funerary context, the tabernacle depicted in the Via Latina catacomb is properly identified as the heavenly House of God referred to in the funerary Psalms. The House of God, or heavenly tabernacle, is accessible to the Christian dead through baptism and the *viaticum*.[33] These significant rites are visually alluded to in the tomb paintings whose subjects were understood as prefigurations of baptism and the Eucharist. The last partaking of the Eucharist and the singing of Psalms over the corpse are explicitly depicted in the contemporary catacomb of S. Sebastiano, demonstrating that these were accepted themes for tomb decoration.[34]

Of all the funerary psalms, Psalm 22(23) is especially important since it speaks so directly to the death experience; it was sung as part of the funeral ceremonies, and it was recited as part of Ambrose's baptismal instruction:

The Lord is my shepherd; I shall want nothing. He makes me lie down in green pastures, and leads me beside the waters of peace; he renews life within me, and for his name's sake guides me in the right path. Even though I walk through a valley dark with death I fear no evil, for thou art with me, thy staff and thy crook are my comfort. Thou spreadest a table for me in the sight of my enemies; thou hast richly bathed my head with oil, and my cup runs over. Goodness and love unfailing, these will follow me all the days of my life, and I shall dwell in the house of the Lord my whole life long.

Ambrose explains the true meaning of the Psalm to his newly baptized catechumens: the table prepared in the wilderness and the overflowing cup are the Eucharist, and Christ is the Shepherd. If read from a fourth-century Christian point of view, Psalm 22 (23) links the Eucharist (*viaticum*), baptism, death and the heavenly house of God. Thus, I would argue that in the tomb the man carrying a rod and leading a crowd of people toward a temple structure is not Joshua leading the Israelites into the promised land as Tronzo suggested (Fig. 6.1).[35] Rather, I believe the scene should be interpreted as Christ, the Shepherd, leading his people through the valley of death to dwell in the house of the Lord.

Contemporary funerary rites support this identification. The fourth-century Bishop Serapion of Thmuis († after 360), in the earliest surviving prayer over the deceased, entreats Christ to refresh her soul in green pastures, a direct quotation from Psalm 22 (23).[36] Clement of Rome in 96 AD also invokes Psalm 22 (23) when speaking of the coming resurrection.[37] Christ leading the Christian into the Lord's tabernacle is repeated in Psalm 115 (116) and twice in Psalm 41(42): 'I call to mind how I marched in the ranks of the great to the house of God . . . Send forth thy light and thy truth to be my guide and lead me to thy holy hill, to thy tabernacle.' Augustine, in his catechetical instructions, states clearly that David was prophesying Christ when he wrote his Psalms.[38] As Moses led his people through the waters of the Red Sea, the priest leads the catechumens through the waters of baptism, and Christ leads the deceased through the valley of the shadow of death into eternal life. The Crossing and the Heavenly Tabernacle, on opposite walls of Cubiculum C, are pendants, both theologically and pictorially. Fortified by the *viaticum* the deceased Christian is shepherded by Christ to the heavenly home promised at baptism. The exile is over.

As Frederick Paxton has convincingly argued, the early Roman death rites were built around the concept that resurrection, the cessation of the exilic state, is seeing God in the flesh. The theme of a Christian soul in a heavenly court with God as defense counsel is reiterated not only in the Book of Job, but also in Psalms 41(42) and 115(116), those key funerary Psalms.[39] The journey to see God is the organizing theme in the Roman death rite.[40] The epitaph for Pope Celestine (†432) makes explicit the Roman conception of resurrection: 'The earth now covers the earthly part of him, but the soul, that knows not death, lives and in full consciousness enjoys the vision of Christ.'[41]

The scenes of Moses talking to God in the cloud in both the tomb and the manuscript illustrate typologically the Christian's ability to see God (Figs 6.1, 6.2). This peculiar scene is not Moses receiving the Law because there is no scroll or tablet exchanged between God and Moses in either representation.[42] Ambrose explains that at baptism the Christian sees clearly what was once a mystery. At death, the Christian sees God face to face. According to the Exodus text, on Mount Sinai Moses has already passed through the Red Sea, received the covenant, and sacrificed his offering, or his Eucharist; only then was he allowed to climb the mountain where he sees God.[43] Quoting St Paul, Paulinus of Nola, in his *consolatio* to grieving parents, states emphatically that whereas Moses was under the ancient veil, Christians see God's face.[44]

In his first encounter with God, Moses turns his face away from the Burning Bush, which is depicted on the opposite wall next to the Crossing of the Red Sea (Fig. 6.7). St Luke transforms the Old Testament narrative into an assurance of resurrection: 'That the dead are raised to life again is shown by Moses himself in the story of the burning bush, when he calls the Lord, the God of Abraham, Isaac, and Jacob. God is not God of the dead but of the living.'[45] Psalm 115 (116), one of the standard funerary psalms, reiterates this theme: 'I will walk in the presence of the Lord in the land of the living.'

The exodus to God also informs the choice of depicting Job on a dunghill in the funerary context of the tomb (Fig. 6.8).[46] On the left side of the tomb, Job sits on his dunghill, shown as a pile of rocks, while his wife, Sitis, offers him bread.[47] Besides the Psalms previously cited, readings from Job were customary during the burial ceremonies. The contest between Satan and God for Job's soul revolves around the question whether Job will curse and turn his face from God.[48] On his dunghill, Job clings to the hope that he will be vindicated, one of the most quoted passages in early and even modern death rites: 'But in my heart I know that my vindicator lives and that he will rise last to speak in court; and I shall discern my witness standing at my side and see my defending counsel, even God himself, whom I shall see with my own eyes.' As early as 96 AD, Clement of Rome frequently turns to Job's example to assure Christians who had lost family to martyrdom, that they will see God in their perfected flesh.[49]

The arcosolium walls include two events from the Book of Jonah. On the left wall, Jonah emerges from the sea monster's mouth (Fig. 6.9). On the right wall, Jonah lies under the gourd vine (Fig. 6.10). Jonah's story also reiterates the themes of resurrection and of seeing God. Jonah's refusal to prophesy is described four times as fleeing from the face of God. While in the belly of the sea monster, he prays: 'I thought I was banished from thy sight and should never see thy holy temple again.' The textual and thematic similarity between Jonah's prayer and Psalm 41 (42), the *Quemadmodum*, is generally overlooked.[50] In both the hymns, the supplicant cries out for God's mercy from watery depths that threaten to overwhelm. Both Jonah and the psalmist view their salvation as dwelling in the House of God. The connection between Jonah's hymn and the funereal *Quemadmodum* gives a richer meaning to the myriad depictions of Jonah found in Early Christian funerary art. Jonah's story of rebirth is found repeatedly in other catacomb paintings as an assurance of resurrection. Unlike other Roman tomb paintings, however, Jonah does not gaze downward but upward to see the Good Shepherd with his own eyes.[51] The painting of the Good Shepherd is placed in the arch of the arcosolium, which covers the spot where the sarcophagus would be placed (Fig. 6.11).

Images of Christ on the ceiling of the tomb speak to the two themes illustrated in the Old Testament scenes below: the Good Shepherd and the Advocate (Fig. 6.11). Placed in the arch of the arcosolium, the Good Shepherd, like Moses, leads his flock through the waters of baptism and the valley of death into the House of the Lord. In the vault of the cubiculum proper, the badly damaged Christ is almost illegible.[52] What remains can be deciphered as the philosopher Christ seated with a book and capsa full of scrolls. In keeping with the theme of the tomb, he can be interpreted as the defense counsel who will advocate for the Christian soul when it sees God face to face.[53]

The temptation of Adam and Eve in the arcosolium is the visual reminder of human frailty, the loss of paradise, and the need of redemption (Fig. 6.11).[54] The words of St Paul were often invoked: 'As in Adam all men die, so in Christ all will be brought to life.'[55] Here is the point of departure for the Christian's exodus through sin, death, and rebirth. Ambrose explains that through sin comes death, but death puts an end to sin; therefore, death necessitates the resurrection. Ambrose, of course, drew upon the Genesis text, 'Dust you are, to dust you shall return.'[56] The antiphon, *De terra formasti me*, followed by a Psalm, was said over the body after it was washed and placed on a bier.[57] In the arcosolium, Adam and Eve in paradise are a reminder of the frailty of human flesh, a theme repeated in the Psalms, the New Testament, and in Roman funerary imagery and liturgical rites.[58]

The concerted effort of the early Church fathers to conceive of death as a festive occasion caused the day the Christian died to be celebrated as the Christian's true birthday, the *dies natalis*.[59] Paulinus of Nola describes the anniversary of St Felix's death as the festival of the saint's birthday: 'the day on which he died physically on earth and was born for Christ in heaven above.'[60] Paulinus's birthday poem was written in 403, a near contemporary of the Via Latina tomb. Paulinus conceives of St Felix's church as the saint's tomb, which was decorated with Old Testament paintings. His poem is a literary description of what perhaps the tomb meant for the mourners in the Via Latina tomb. He hoped the paintings would encourage the pious to sing psalms while they sat at vigil on the anniversary of St Felix's death, or rather, his birthday:

See how they now in great numbers keep vigil and prolong their joy throughout the night, dispelling sleep with joy and darkness with torchlight . . . the congregation shows a higher devotion in its lusty rendering of holy hymns with voices undefiled, and in its sober sacrifice of sung praise to the Lord.[61]

At the end of the poem Paulinus prays on his own behalf:

Let me not continue as an earthly Adam, but be born of the virgin earth, fashioned as a new form after putting off the old man . . . May I hasten to the honeyed streams of the promised land . . . May I be offered like the young Isaac as a living victim to God . . . The final day approaches, the Lord is now nigh; it is already time to rise from sleep, ready and awake for the Lord's knocking. May I obtain a safe departure from Egypt, and journey under the guidance of the Law through the divided waters of my storm-tossed heart; so I may escape the Red Sea's billows and, when Pharaoh is drowned, sing of the Lord's triumph.[62]

Paulinus gives a moving eyewitness account of how images of the heroic dead of the past were experienced by a person looking to his own death. It is not a mere recalling of the stories, but a self-identification with the dead whose 'storm-tossed hearts' had found the Promised Land.

As we have seen, these Old Testament types figured not only in the funerary Psalms, but also in the sermons heard after baptism as well as in the paintings which served to recall to memory the lessons of the spoken word. Peter Cramer offers a noteworthy insight into the technique of memory that Ambrose used in his sermons directed at the recently baptized: 'By making the neophytes *remember* what has been said, done, felt over Lent and Easter, Ambrose is able to make them imagine all the better the *sense* of their experience.'[63] Paulinus articulated in personal terms how the tomb and its imagery functioned in the minds of Early Christians. More than merely illustrating Old Testament stories, the pictures provided a visual linking of past and present. They also assured a heavenly reward, since the tomb acted as a dynamic and experiential memorial to the resurrection promised to the Christian at baptism, the first passage from death into life. For the bereaved family singing Psalms to lighten the sad vigil in the tomb, the funerary space created a memorial to the exodus experience of the deceased as well as a promise to those living whose exodus was not yet complete.

Frequently cited sources

Translations of the Bible are from the *New English Bible* (NEB).

Ferrua, A., *The Unknown Catacomb: A Unique Discovery of Early Christian Art*, introduction by B. Nardini, translated by I. Inglis, New Lanark, Scotland: Geddes & Grosset, 1991.

Paxton, F., *Christianizing Death: The Creation of a Ritual Process in Early Medieval Europe*, Ithaca, NY: Cornell University Press, 1990.

Rush, A., *Death and Burial in Christian Antiquity*, Washington, DC: The Catholic University of America Press, 1941.

Tronzo, W., *The Via Latina Catacombs: Imitation and Discontinuity in Fourth-century Roman Painting*, University Park, PA: Pennsylvania State University Press, 1986.

Tyrer, J. W., *Historical Survey of Holy Week, Its Services and Ceremonial*, London: Alcuin Club, 1932.

Notes

1. The Via Latina catacombs are assumed to be older because they were closed at an early date. For the history of the catacombs, see A. Bosio, *Roma sotterranea*, Rome, 1632; R. W. Gaston, 'British Travellers and Scholars in the Roman Catacombs, 1450–1900,' *Journal of the Warburg and*

Courtauld Institutes, vol. 46, 1983, pp.144–65; J. Osborne, 'The Roman Catacombs in the Middle Ages,' *Papers of the British School at Rome*, vol. 53, 1985, pp.278–328. The dating of the Ashburnham Pentateuch is discussed by D. Wright, 'The Canon Tables of the Codex Beneventanus and Related Documents,' *Dumbarton Oaks Papers*, vol. 33, 1979, pp.137–55. The origin of the manuscript is debated; most recently I have argued for Rome in 'Roman Book Illumination 400–700 AD and the Ashburnham Pentateuch,' in J. Williams, ed., *Imaging the Early Medieval Bible*, University Park, PA: Pennsylvania State University Press, 1999, pp.97–120.

2.   The exodus theme is recurrent through Christian art and literature: see, for example, H. Kessler, 'Passover in St Peter's,' *Journal of Jewish Art*, vols 12–13, 1986/1987, pp.169–78; J. Freccero, *Dante: the Poetics of Conversion*, edited by R. Jacoff, Cambridge, MA: Harvard University Press, 1986; J. Bunyan, *A Pilgrim's Progress from this World to that which is to Come*, 1678.

3.   H. Marrou, 'Une catacombe pagano-chrétienne récemment découverte à Rome,' *Bulletin de la Société Nationale des Antiquaires de France*, 1956, pp.77–81; A. Ferrua, *Le pitture della nuova catacomba di Via latina*, Vatican City: Pontificio Istituto di Archeologia Cristiana, 1960; idem, *The Unknown Catacomb*; J. Fink, 'Die römische Katakombe an der Via Latina,' *Antike Welt*, vol. 7, 1969, pp.3–14; L. Kötzsche-Breitenbruch, *Die neue Katakombe an der Via Latina in Rom: Untersuchungen zur Ikonographie der Alttestamentlichen Wandmalereien*, Münster/Westfalen: Aschendorffsche Verlagsbuchhandlung, 1976; Tronzo, *The Via Latina Catacombs*, p.198.

4.   O. von Gebhardt, *The Miniatures of the Ashburnham Pentateuch*, London: Asher & Co., 1883; R. Sörries, *Christlich-antike Buchmalerei im Überblick*, Wiesbaden: Dr. Ludwig Reichert Verlag, 1993; B. Narkiss, 'Reconstruction of Some of the Original Quires of the Ashburnham Pentateuch,' *Cahiers archéologiques*, vol. 22, 1972, pp.19–38; F. Rickert, 'Zu den Stadt- und Architekturdarstellungen des Ashburnham Pentateuch (Paris, Bibl. NAT. NAL 2334),' in *Actes du XIe congrès international d'archéologie chrétienne*, 1986, Studi di antichità cristiana, vol. 41, Rome: Ecole Française de Rome, Pontificio Istituto di Archeologia Cristiana, 1989, pp.1341–54; H. J. van Ginhoven, 'Le miniaturiste du Pentateuque de Tours ou Pentateuque d'Ashburnham et sa méthode de travail (Paris, Bibliothèque nationale, Nouv. acq. lat. 2334),' *Cahiers archéologiques*, vol. 42, 1994, pp.65–74.

5.   A. van Gennep, *The Rites of Passage*, 1910, reprint, translated by G. L. Caffee, Chicago: University of Chicago Press, 1960; I. Morris, *Death-Ritual and Social Structure in Classical Antiquity*, Key Themes in Ancient History, vol. II, Cambridge: Cambridge University Press, 1992, especially pp.8–15.

6.   The association with the heroic dead is an important first step toward venerating saints, the 'Very Special Dead': see P. Brown, *The Cult of the Saints: Its Rise and Function in Latin Christianity*, Chicago: University of Chicago Press, 1981; idem, *Society and the Holy in Late Antiquity*, Berkeley/Los Angeles: University of California Press, 1982, pp.177–9, 226–8.

7.   Traditionally, scholars sought one interpretive principle for all the catacomb paintings: see T. Buser, 'Early Catacomb Iconography and Apocalypticism,' *Studies in Iconography*, vol. 6, 1980, pp.3–15; F. P. Bargebuhr, *The Paintings of the 'New' Catacomb of the Via Latina and the Struggle Against Paganism*, Heidelberg: Carl Winter – Universitätsverlag, 1991; P. C. Finney's comprehensive bibliography, in *The Invisible God: The Earliest Christians on Art*, New York/Oxford: Oxford University Press, 1994, pp.3–14; T. Klauser, 'Studien zur Entstehungsgeschichte der christlichen Kunst IV,' *Jahrbuch für Antike und Christentum*, vol. 4, 1961, pp.136–45; idem, 'Erwägungen zur Entstehung der altchristliche Kunst,' *Zeitschrift für Kirchengeschichte*, vol. 76, 1965, pp.1–11. The relationship to Jewish art is discussed by G. Stemberger, 'Die Patriarchenbilder der Katakombe in der Via Latina im Lichte der jüdische Tradition,' *Kairos*, vol. 16, 1974, pp.19–78; K. Weitzmann and H. L. Kessler, *The Frescoes of the Dura Synagogue and Christian Art*, Washington, DC: Dumbarton Oaks, 1990; K. Schubert, 'Jewish Pictorial Traditions in Early Christian Art,' *Jewish Historiography and Iconography in Early and Medieval Christianity*, Compendia Rerum Iudaicarum ad Novem Testamentum, 2, P. J. Tomson and P. A. Cathey, eds, Assen/Maastricht: Van Gorcum; Minneapolis, MN: Fortress Press, 1992, pp.141–260. A crucial counter-argument is made by L. V. Rutgers, 'The Jewish Catacombs of Rome Reconsidered,' *Proceedings of the World Congress of Jewish Studies*, vol. 10, 1989, pp.29–36.

8.   Included in E. Josi, 'Découverte d'une série de peintures dans l'hypogée de la voie Latine,' *Comptes-rendus des séances de l'Académie des Inscriptions et Belles-Lettres*, 4th series, vol. 83, Paris: Auguste Durand Libraire, 1956, pp.275–7.

9.   Fol. 76r, illustrating Exod. 24.

10.   An architectural column is the standard portrayal of the Pillar in the Latin West: see J. Wilpert, *I sarcophagi cristiani antichi*, Vatican City: Pontificio Istituto di Archeologia Cristiana, 1932, vol. I, plate LXXXVII(4); vol. II, plates CCIX (3), CCX (1,2), CCXI (1,2), CCXVI (8); G. Jeremias, *Die Holztür der Basilika S. Sabina in Rom*, Tübingen: E. Wasmuth, 1980, plates 26, 28; Tronzo, *The Via*

Latina Catacombs, fig. 5. This combination of Moses on Mount Sinai, a tabernacle, a sacrifice, and a Pillar survives only in these two pictorial cycles. The iconographic connection argues for an origin in Rome for the Ashburnham Pentateuch, which I develop more fully in 'Roman Book Illumination 400–700 AD and the Ashburnham Pentateuch' (as in n.1). The hand-held candle is easily identified as the Pillar because it is the same candle that appears in the Crossing of the Red Sea where it leads the Israelites in the lower right-hand corner of fol. 68r and is labeled *columna nubis*.

11. M. Haykin, ' "In the Cloud and in the Sea": Basil of Caesarea and the Exegesis of 1 Cor. 10:2,' *Vigiliae Christianae*, vol. 40, 1986, pp.134–44; J. P. Lewis, 'Baptismal Practices of the Second and Third Century Church,' *Restoration Quarterly*, vol. 26, 1983, pp.1–17; L. de Bruyne, 'L'initiation chrétienne et ses reflets dans l'art paléochrétien,' *Revue des Sciences Religieuses*, vol. 36, 1962, pp.27–85; J. Daniélou, *The Bible and the Liturgy*, Notre Dame, IN: University of Notre Dame Press, 1960, pp.86–98; P. Lundberg, *La typologie baptismale dans l'ancienne église*, Leipzig: A. Lorentz, 1942; F. J. Dölger, 'Der Durchzug durch das Rote Meer als Sinnbild der christlichen Taufe,' *Antike und Christentum*, vol. 2, 1930, pp.63–9.

12. D. H. Verkerk, 'Exodus and Easter Vigil in the Ashburnham Pentateuch,' *The Art Bulletin*, vol. 77, 1995, pp.94–105; T. M. Finn, *Early Christian Baptism and the Catechumenate: West and East Syria*, Collegeville, MN: The Liturgical Press, 1992; A. Wharton, 'Ritual and Reconstructed Meaning: The Neonian Baptistery in Ravenna,' *The Art Bulletin*, vol. 69, 1987, pp.358–75. The term *Pasch* is derived from the Hebrew *Pesach*, or Passover: see G. Dix, *The Shape of the Liturgy*, 2nd edition, London: Dacre Press, 1964, pp.338–440.

13. Tyrer, *Historical Survey of Holy Week*, p.158; P. Underwood, 'The Fountain of Life in Manuscripts of the Gospels,' *Dumbarton Oaks Papers*, vol. 5, 1950, pp.41–138.

14. Tyrer, *Historical Survey of Holy Week*, pp.156–60.

15. The continuity of the Exodus typology is witnessed in the Procession to the Font depicted as a Crossing of the Red Sea in the eleventh-century Bari Benedictional (Bari, Archivo della Cattedrale); M. Avery, *The Exultet Rolls of South Italy*, Princeton: Princeton University Press / London: Oxford University Press, 1936, plate XIII; H. Belting, 'Byzantine Art Among Greeks and Latins in Southern Italy,' *Dumbarton Oaks Papers*, vol. 28, 1974, pp.3–29, especially p.19; G. Cavallo et al., *Exultet, Rotoli liturgici del medioevo meridionale*, Rome: Istituto Poligrafico e Zecca dello Stato Libreria dello Stato, 1994, p.148; especially valuable is T. F. Kelly, *The Exultet in Southern Italy*, New York / Oxford: Oxford University Press, 1996.

16. Augustine's highly influential *De catechizandis rudibus*, 2.34, states this explicitly. Dölger (as in n.11), pp.63–9; H. M. Riley, *Christian Initiation: A Comparative Study of the Interpretation of the Baptismal Liturgy in the Mystagogical Writings of Cyril of Jerusalem, John Chrysostom, Theodore of Mopsuestia, and Ambrose of Milan*, Washington, DC: Catholic University of America Press, 1974.

17. E. Sauser, 'Das Paschamysterium in den sogenannten frühchristlichen Passionssarkophagen,' in P. Granfield and J. A. Jungmann, eds, *Kyriakon: Festschrift Johannes Quasten*, vol. II, Münster / Westfalen: Aschendorff, 1970, pp.654–62; A. M. Fausone, *Die Taufe in der frühchristlichen Sepulkralkunst*, Vatican City: Pontificio Istituto di Archeologia Cristiana, 1982; L. Kötzsche-Breitenbruch, 'Das Elfenbeinrelief mit Taufszene aus der Sammlung Maskell im British Museum,' *Jahrbuch für Antike und Christentum*, vol. 22, 1979, pp.195–208; T. Velmans, 'Quelques versions rares du thème de la fontaine de vie dans l'art paléochrétien,' *Cahiers archéologiques*, vol. 19, 1969, pp.29–43.

18. *De sacramentis* 19, in E. Yarnold, trans., *The Awe-Inspiring Rites of Initiation: Baptismal Homilies of the Fourth Century*, Slough: St Paul Publications, 1972, p.117.

19. The validity of using the Milanese rite to understand the Roman rite is accepted among liturgical scholars since, as Ambrose himself states, 'we take [the Roman Church] as our prototype, and follow her rite in everything,' *De sacramentis* 3.5.

20. Paxton, *Christianizing Death*, pp.19–46; J. Quasten, *Music & Worship in Pagan & Christian Antiquity*, translated by B. Ramsey, Washington, DC: National Association of Pastoral Musicians, 1983, pp.160–68; D. Sicard, *La liturgie de la mort dans l'église latine des origines à la réforme carolingienne*, Münster / Westfalen: Aschendorff, 1978; R. Rutherford, 'Psalm 113 (114–15) and Christian Burial,' *Studia Patristica*, vol. 13, 1975, pp.391–5; J. M. C. Toynbee, *Death and Burial in the Roman World*, Ithaca, NY: Cornell University Press, 1971; Rush, *Death and Burial*, pp.170–73.

21. *Confessiones* 9.12.

22. Paxton, *Christianizing Death*, pp.32–4; A. Rush, 'The Eucharist: The Sacrament of the Dying in Christian Antiquity,' *Jurist*, vol. 34, 1974, pp.10–35; G. Grabka, 'Christian Viaticum: A Study of Its Cultural Background,' *Traditio*, vol. 9, 1953, pp.1–43; P. Browe, 'Die Sterbekommunion im Altertum und Mittelalter,' *Zeitschrift für Katholische Theologie*, vol. 60, 1936, pp.1–54, 210–40.

23. Ambrose, *De sacramentis* 4.27; G. G. Willis, *A History of Early Roman Liturgy to the Death of Pope Gregory the Great*, Rochester, NY: The Boydell Press, 1994, pp.23–32; K. Stevenson, *Eucharist and Offering*, New York: Pueblo Publishing, 1986, pp.74–98; R. P. C. Hanson, *Eucharistic Offering in the Early Church*, Nottingham: Grove, 1979.

24. cf. Cambridge, Corpus Christi College MS 286, fol. 125; see F. Wormald, *The Miniatures in the Gospels of St Augustine* (Corpus Christi College MS. 286), Cambridge: Cambridge University Press, 1954, plate 1.

25. Rush, *Death and Burial*, pp.92–101.

26. 1 Cor. 15.29: 'Again, there are those who receive baptism on behalf of the dead. Why should they do this? If the dead are not raised to life at all, what do they mean by being baptized on their behalf?' See R. E. DeMarris, 'Corinthian Religion and Baptism for the Dead (1 Cor. 15.29): Insights from Archaeology and Anthropology,' *Journal of Biblical Literature*, vol. 114, 1995, pp.661–82.

27. Rutherford (as in n.20), pp.391–2.

28. *De sacramentis* 2.12.

29. ibid., 2.12; 4.18; 5.3.

30. A. G. Martimort, 'L'iconographie des catacombes et la catéchèse antique,' *Rivista di archeologia cristiana*, vol. 25, 1949, pp.105–14. For the catechumenate, see W. Harmless, *Augustine and the Catechumenate*, Collegeville, MN: The Liturgical Press, 1995; L. D. Folkemer, 'The Study of the Catechumenate,' in *Conversion, Catechumenate, and Baptism in the Early Church: Studies in Early Christianity*, vol. XI, E. Ferguson, D. M. Scholer and P. C. Finney, eds, New York/London: Garland Press, 1993, pp.244–65; M. Dujarier, *A History of the Catechumenate: The First Six Centuries*, New York: Sadlier, 1979; R. M. Grant, 'Development of the Christian Catechumenate,' in *Made, Not Born: New Perspectives on Christian Initiation and the Catechumenate, from the Murphy Center for Liturgical Research*, Notre Dame, IN: University of Notre Dame Press, 1976, pp.32–49.

31. Heb. 9.1–12; Acts 7.44–50; Rev. 15.5–6.

32. Verkerk (as in n.12), p.103.

33. B. Kühnel, 'Jewish Symbolism of the Temple and the Tabernacle and Christian Symbolism of the Holy Sepulchre and the Heavenly Tabernacle,' *Journal of Jewish Art*, vols 12–13, 1986/1987, pp.147–68; idem, *From the Earthly to the Heavenly Jerusalem: Representations of the Holy City in Christian Art of the First Millennium*, Freiberg im Breisgau: Herder, 1987. The notion of the afterlife spent in a dwelling, or house, is an ancient one: see F. Cumont, *After Life in Roman Paganism*, New Haven, CT: Yale University Press, 1923, pp.48–57.

34. A. Ferrua, *La basilica e la catacomba di S. Sebastiano. Catacombe di Roma e d'Italia*, vol. III, Vatican City: Pontificia Commissione di Archeologia Sacra, 1990, figs 26, 27.

35. Tronzo, *The Via Latina Catacomb*, pp.51–65, argues for a programmatic theme of salvation, identifying these scenes as Moses receiving the Law and Joshua leading the Israelites into the Promised Land. See also M. Cagiano de Azevedo, 'Una singolare iconografia veterotestamentaria nell'ipogeo della via Latina,' *Atti della Pontificia Accademia Romana di Archeologia, Rendiconti*, vol. 34, 1961–2, pp.111–18, who argues that the figure is Moses; U. Schubert, *Spätantikes Judentum und frühchristliche Kunst*, Vienna: Verlag Herold, 1974, pp.30–31; K. Schubert and U. Schubert, 'Marginalien zur "Sinai-Szene" in der Katacombe der Via Latina in Rom,' *Kairos*, vol. 17, 1975, pp.300–302. Compare the scene to Cubiculum O where the figure of Lazarus is prominent; see: Ferrua, 1991, fig. 137, and also J. Fink, 'Lazarus an der Via Latina,' *Römische Quartalschrift für christliche Altertumskunde und Kirchengeschichte*, vol. 64, 1969, pp.209–17.

36. *Sacramentum Serapionis* 30, in F. X. Funks, ed., *Didascalia et Constitutiones Apostolorum*, vol. II, 1905, reprint, Turin: Bottega d'Erasmo, 1979, pp.193–4.

37. *Epistula ad Corinthios* 26.2, in J. B. Lightfoot and J. R. Harmer, trans., *The Apostolic Fathers*, 2nd edition, revised by M. W. Holmes, Grand Rapids, MI: Baker Book House, 1989, p.43; see also John Chrysostom, *Homilia* 4 in *Hebraeos* 5.

38. *De catechizandis rudibus* 2.38, in *St Augustine: The First Catechetical Instruction [De Catechizandis Rudibus]*, translated by J. P. Christopher, Ancient Christian Writers, vol. II, Westminster, MD: Newman Press, 1946, p.69.

39. Job 19.25–7; Psalm 41: 'I will praise him continually, my deliverer, my God. Plead my cause and give me judgement against an impious race'; Psalm 115: 'For he has given me a hearing whenever I have cried to him.'

40. Rush, *Death and Burial*, pp.44–71.

41.   J. Janssens, *Vita e morte del Cristiano negli epitaffi di Roma anteriori al sec. VII*, Analecta Gregoriana Series Facultatis Theologiae. Sectio B., n.73, Rome: Università Gregoriana Editrice, 1981, p.27.

42.   Compare this to the similar scene in Cubiculum O, where the Law is clearly represented: Ferrua, *The Unknown Catacomb*, fig. 137.

43.   The early Church conceived of the Offering as a Eucharist: Hanson (as in n.23); Stevenson (as in n.23). See also G. Feeley-Harnik, *The Lord's Table: Eucharist and Passover in Early Christianity*, Philadelphia: University of Pennsylvania Press, 1981; P.-A. Février, 'A propos du repas funéraire: culte et sociabilité *Christo Deo. pax et concordia sit convivio nostro*,' *Cahiers archéologiques*, vol. 26, 1977, pp.29–45.

44.   *Carmina* 31.347–8; Paulinus quotes 2 Cor. 3.18. Within the context of the tomb imagery, I interpret Paulinus and St Paul quite literally as the Christian being in proximity to God, as the shepherd gathers his sheep around him, since the visual arts cannot depict 'inner seeing' or 'knowing' as argued by Finney (as in n.7), pp.277–80.

45.   Luke 20.37.

46.   The depiction of Job on a dunghill in funerary art I develop more fully in 'Job and Sitis: Curious Figures in Early Christian Funerary Art,' *Mitteilungen zur Christlichen Archäologie*, vol. 3, 1997, pp.20–29. See also S. Terrien, *The Iconography Of Job through the Centuries: Artists as Biblical Interpreters*, University Park, PA: Pennsylvania State University Press, 1996, pp.17–29.

47.   An English translation of the folktale about Job and his wife Sitis is provided by R. A. Kraft, H. Attridge, R. Spittler, and J. Timbie, *The Testament of Job According to the SV Text*, Missoula, MT: Society of Biblical Literature & Scholars' Press, 1974; L. L. Besserman, *The Legend of Job in the Middle Ages*, Cambridge, MA: Harvard University Press, 1979. On Sitis, also see P. W. van der Horst, 'Images of Women in the Testament of Job,' in M. A. Knibb and P. van der Horst, eds, *Studies on the Testament of Job*, Society for New Testament Studies, 66, Cambridge: Cambridge University Press, 1989, pp.93–116.

48.   Job 3.3.

49.   *Epistula ad Corinthios* 26.3.

50.   A general survey of the literary sources is provided by Y.-M. Duval, *Le livre de Jonas dans la littérature chrétienne greque et latine*, Paris: Etudes Augustiniennes, 1973.

51.   cf. Ferrua, *The Unknown Catacomb*, fig. 71.

52.   cf. Tronzo, *The Via Latina Catacomb*, p.78.

53.   On the *viaticum* as defender and advocate for the deceased, see Paxton, *Christianizing Death*, p.39.

54.   A useful survey of images of Adam and Eve in tombs is offered by R. Valabrega, 'L'iconografia catacombale di Adamo ed Eva,' *Rivista di Storia e Letteratura Religiosa*, vol. 22, 1986, pp.24–55. See also D. Korol, 'Zum Bild der Vertreibung Adams und Evas in der neuen Katakombe an die via Latina und zur anthropomorphischen Darstellung Gottvaters,' *Jahrbuch für Antike und Christentum*, vol. 22, 1979, pp.175–90.

55.   1 Cor. 15.22; see also Rom. 5.12: 'It was through one man [Adam] that sin entered the world, and through sin death, and thus death pervaded the whole human race.'

56.   Gen. 3.19; see also Job 10.9: 'Remember that thou didst knead me like clay; and wouldst thou turn me back into dust?'; Job 34.15: 'All that lives would perish on the instant, and man return again to dust.'

57.   Based on the work of Sicard (as in n.20), Paxton, *Christianizing Death*, pp.38–9, provides the basic structure of the old Roman *ordo defunctorum* rubric and psalmody which survives in manuscript form only as early as the eighth century. He argues that this structure emerged from fourth- and fifth-century Roman burial practices.

58.   Ps. 102(103).14: 'For he knows how we were made, he knows full well that we are dust'; Ps. 103(104).29: 'Then thou hidest thy face, and they are restless and troubled; when thou takest away their breath they fail and they return to the dust from which they came.' The links between the robes of paradise and baptism are discussed by S. Brock, 'Clothing Metaphors as a Means of Theological Expression in Syriac Tradition,' in M. Schmidt, ed., *Typus, Symbol, Allegorie bei den östlichen Vätern und ihren Parallelen im Mittelalter*, Eichstätter Beiträge, 4, Regensburg: Pustet, 1982, pp.11–38; B. Murdoch, 'The Garments of Paradise: A Note on the "Wiener Genesis" and the "Anegenge",' *Euphorion Zeitschrift für Literaturgeschichte*, vol. 61, 1967, pp.375–82. For a similar, though later, discussion see P. H. Jolly, *Made in God's Image? Eve and Adam in the Genesis Mosaics at San Marco, Venice*, Berkeley/Los Angeles/London: University of California Press, 1997.

59. Rush, *Death and Burial*, pp.72–87.

60. Paulinus of Nola, *The Poems of St Paulinus of Nola*, translated by P. Walsh, Ancient Christian Writers, 40, New York/Paramus, NJ: Newman Press, 1975, Poem 21, p.178.

61. *Carmina* 27.542–67; Paulinus of Nola (as in n.60), pp.290–91.

62. *Carmina* 27.607–635; Paulinus of Nola (as in n.60), pp.292–3.

63. P. Cramer, *Baptism and Change in the Early Middle Ages, c.200–c.1150*, Cambridge: Cambridge University Press, 1993, p.66.

6.1   Exodus Scenes, Cubiculum C, Via Latina, Rome, *c.*315–25

6.2   Exodus Scenes, Ashburnham Pentateuch, fol. 76r, late sixth century

6.3   Abraham's Sacrifice, Cubiculum C, Via Latina

6.4   Crossing the Red Sea, Cubiculum C, Via Latina

6.5   Crossing the Red Sea, Ashburnham Pentateuch, fol. 68r

6.6   Moses Striking the Rock, Cubiculum C, Via Latina

6.7   Moses at the Burning Bush, Cubiculum C, Via Latina

6.8   Job and Sitis, Cubiculum C, Via Latina

6.9   Jonah Spewed from the Sea Monster, Cubiculum C, Via Latina

6.10   Jonah under the Gourd Vine, Cubiculum C, Via Latina

6.11 Adam and Eve, the Good Shepherd, Peacock, Orant, Jonah, Cubiculum C, Via Latina

7

Memory and the social landscape in eleventh-century Upplandic commemorative practice

Kyle R. Crocker

This chapter is a curious contribution to the collection. It does not address the sepulchral arts as they are generally understood, nor the liturgy connected with them, nor any pictorial or narrative system meant to prompt memory of the dead, sainted or ordinary. Rather it discusses aspects of a commemorative practice represented in a well-known, but underutilized class of memorials – the *runstenar* or 'rune-stones,' and related carvings of Late Viking Age Scandinavia. More specifically, it suggests how, during the conversion period in the early Swedish kingdom, this practice memorialized relations between the living and the dead, grafting them onto the land; and how, through such, the same practice helped to construct a veritable social landscape containing all relationships within the community. After offering some general theoretical hypotheses on this commemorative practice, the chapter focuses on some prominent memorial groups in the region around Lake Vallentuna in east central Uppland as a case study of the weaving of 'social memory' into a particular landscape.

Between the late tenth and early twelfth centuries, following the royal precedent of Harald Blatand at Jelling, the custom of raising stones with runic inscriptions (or alternatively, carving such inscriptions on exposed rock surfaces) spread throughout most of Scandinavia. The practice was most popular in eastern Scandinavia, particularly in Uppland and surrounding provinces where nearly two thousand examples, some fragmentary, have been recorded.[1] The inscriptions are highly formulaic, terse, and clear. Generally, they simply name a person or persons sponsoring the memorial and the deceased in whose memory it stands, usually with a term or terms of kinship qualifying the relationship. For example: 'Signiut and Avith had this stone raised to Ofæig, their father . . .' Not uncommonly, there are additions to the core formula: reference to some notable accomplishment, an unusual circumstance of death, 'good works' such as road clearing or bridge building undertaken as part of the commemoration, or a short prayer for the deceased. In Uppland especially, the carver would often attach his name in a signature formula.[2] The artistic elaboration of the carving is more variable. Very rarely are figurative elements introduced, but the band-animal that usually carries the runic text is increasingly developed as a quasi-autonomous pattern, often supplemented by other zoomorphic elements, the whole design becoming a cunning ornament in its own right. More frequently than prayers in the texts, cross forms are integrated into these designs. In total, the Upplandic corpus represents a rich source for the study of social history and the artistic idiom of the Late Viking Age.

Still, the precise function of the memorials and the causes of the virtual explosion of this commemorative practice in Uppland pose intertwined and very expansive questions, with more complex answers than might first seem apparent. Clearly this commemorative practice, contained within the protracted mission period, is bound with the process of Christianization. Yet the runic memorials are more than pious remembrances of the dead or even witnesses to the new-found piety of the living. The practice may have been encouraged by the missionary church, yet it was not exactly imported; its roots are indigenous and pagan. Nor are the memorials directly associated with early churches and church burial, although some were moved to church ground in the twelfth century and later, at times even incorporated in the fabric of stone churches. Nearly all memorials were originally raised in the countryside, near farmsteads and along thoroughfares, hence the connection with commemorative road and bridge building.[3] Certainly, as long recognized, the *runstenar* and related carvings served the living as much as the dead. Prestige monuments, they celebrated family pride and confirmed the status of landowners. Most importantly perhaps, they recorded or legitimized rights of inheritance. The massive statistical research and deft analysis by Birgit Sawyer convincingly demonstrates the role of the memorials in asserting rights to landed property.[4] Yet the practice constitutes more, I think, than the simple equivalent of posting a certificate of title.

Many have suspected what Sawyer has recently articulated. This complex of commemorative actions and objects should be viewed as, to use her term, a 'crisis symptom,' a complicated reflex to the deep paradigmatic, almost convulsive, changes overtaking Swedish society through the period.[5] In a time of radical transition, enormous tensions were generated. Along with the essential, if gradual, change of religious world-view came the conflict between the traditional burial with grave goods in the family cemetery and newly-prescribed burial, ungifted, in church ground. The new Church vied with the elite class not only for authority, but also for land and other property. The uneven expansion of contested royal power eroded customary local political structures, or in some areas introduced a new element into their operations. Pressures mounted for the consolidation of landed property, with more coming under the control of strong farmers and magnates.[6] The memorials can be seen as both mediating these tensions, and manipulating their outcomes. Through them, networks of social identity, structures of economic and political dominance and dependency, the fabric of social life and social memory were woven and rewoven upon what mattered most – the land itself.

Let me expand on this. As Patrick Geary has argued, inheritance of property was the fundamental exchange between the dead and the living in Early Medieval Europe.[7] In reciprocation for the dead's gift of life and land (and everything coefficient with these) the living return memory, memorialization through prayer or monument or, as in our context, both. This dual exchange defined the fluid boundaries of the kingroup and relations within it. In other words, relations with the dead, enacted through commemoration, structured living social relationships. In early Upplandic society, as elsewhere in Early Medieval Scandinavia, the kingroup so defined was the hub of further, also fluid, structures of exchanges: economic ties between owner and tenant, hierarchies of political support and dependency, including coresponsibilities in feud and other legal contests.[8] Rivalry, too, between elite families was enacted in a landscape resonant with memory, embodied most conspicuously in runic memorials. It also should be noted that this society was not yet 'bookish' in the ways of Latin Christendom, did not yet have priests who so fully interceded in the exchanges of living and dead as in the examples cited by Geary.[9] But the society was at least semi-literate; in my surmise, most people of consequence, and many lower ranking freemen, could puzzle through an inscription. *Runstenar*, both in text and ornament, combined with the particular forms of the social landscape and vital memory, commingling and reenforcing one another. The memorial inscription is not a simple 'aid' to memory. Bound to the land that binds all social relationships, the stones and the wider commemorative practices they represent become the dynamic structures of memory.

It is necessary at this point, I think, to show how all this works in a specific, extended example or 'case study,' even if space allows just the barest sketch. At the same time, the role of artistic form within the whole dynamic can be brought forward. The region of our interest lies in east-central Uppland, surrounding Lake Vallentuna, roughly twenty kilometres north of modern Stockholm, and about the same distance to the southeast of the crucially important Late Viking Age royal town of Sigtuna (Fig. 7.1). Gently rolling countryside, broken by forests and bogs, it was well settled in the Iron Age, particularly prosperous in the eleventh century. Its scores of memorials include several key historical texts and many distinguished designs by the most prominent carvers of the Upplandic tradition. (Genealogical charts useful in the following discussion can be found in Appendix A; transliterated and normalized inscriptions in Appendix B.)

The regional tradition was initiated by Ulf of Barista when he had a simple, unornamented stone (U336) set up for his paternal uncle Onæm somewhere on their estate. Ulf was probably an important man in the area, and certainly a widely traveled one. The famous memorial group at Yttergärde (U343–4) raised sometime later by his sons records that he 'took three gelds in England.' The last of these army payments was evidently that paid by Knut the Great in 1018, giving us a rare fixed date, but it is still difficult to judge when Ulf might have died.[10] In any case, well before his death, Ulf participated in one of the greatest early commemorative projects in the wider region (Figs 7.2, 7.3). He is named as sponsor in one of a pair of memorials (U161) honoring his kinsman, probably affinal cousin, Ulf of Skulhambr, raised on the home estate to the west of the lake near the modern farm of Risbyle. The other stone (U160) names the Skulhambr heirs and includes a prayer: 'God and God's mother help his spirit and soul, grant him light and paradise.' Inscribed on tall, narrow stones that break the horizontal silhouette of the low sloping shore, the designs are confident versions of the primitive zoomorphic style popular in the early stage of this tradition.

A more impressive and politically significant monument was built by the Skulhambr people, again led by the eldest son Ulfkell, across the lake at the site of Bällsta (Figs 7.4, 7.5). Here, among settings of smaller stones that once defined a special precinct, a pair of inscribed slabs (U225–6) assert that 'they made here the *thingstad*' (assembly place) and continuing in verse:

Never will a memorial	better be made
than the one Ulf's sons	built after him,
hale young men	after their father.
They raised the stones	and the staff set up,
and all the mighty	emblems of honor.
Also does Gyrid	grieve for her husband;
in a song of sorrow	shall he be remembered.

The implications of this remarkable verse merit some elaboration. Not simply a prideful assertion of superiority, its references to a *staf* (staff or post) and *inn mikla jartekum* (the great tokens or signs) evoke a connection to pre-Christian cenotaphs of chieftains, as Gyrid's song recalls the funerary laments made for heroes. Together with the scale of the monument and the strategic location of the site, this aristocratic elegy strongly suggests that the family was one of old wealth and prestige. The connection with the northern area of the region is worth stressing. The widow Gyrid was almost undoubtedly old Onæm's daughter; she is the link between Barista and Skulhambr. About the same time as the death of Ulf of Skulhambr, she and her sister Gudlaug had a stone (U328) raised in Onæm's memory upcountry on the farm at Lundby, which they probably had inherited from him. Its ornament is closely related to Ulf's memorials, and it is tempting to attribute this work to one of the carvers of the Risbyle-Bällsta complex.[11] At all events, it is clear that in the first wave of 'crisis', that is, the first phase of the explosion of commemorative practice, the landscape around Lake Vallentuna was being 'mapped' by an illustrious local extended family into social memory, potentially as part of an economic and political consolidation. The particular places so marked were themselves the result of interactions of the natural and the human, the communal and the familial: principal farmsteads such as Skulhambr, the nodal points of economic networks, and probably the customary (pagan) cemeteries on them as at Yttergärde, thoroughfares including the lake itself, and the assembly place at Bällsta.[12] To travel through the region would have been much more than simply to traverse a countryside; one would move through a web of relationships, reminded at crucial points of those persons and lineages forming the warp of the social fabric of one's own experience.

Both *runstenar* art and social dynamics in the region, however, continued to change. Some years after the commemorations by the Skulhambr family, but probably before the death of Ulf of Barista, the more humble stone u137 was raised south of the lake at Broby in memory of a certain Gag (?) by his parents Ostæin and Estrid (Fig. 7.6). Modest as it is, it begins one of the longest, most complex, and well studied of family series in the Upplandic corpus.[13] Shortly after Gag's memorial, the so-called Täby (or Jarlebanke) family undertook a far more ambitious project at the same site (Fig. 7.6, u135–6). It honored Ostæin himself who, the text of u136 informs us, 'sought Jerusalem and met his end in Greece.' In addition to the inscribed stones, the surviving sons and widow built a bridge and raised a *haug* or mound. This religiously retrospective cenotaph strikes one as reflecting the same medial or transitional spirit as the staff and 'mighty emblems' at Bällsta. The Täby family was probably well established around the southern shores of the lake by this time, and in the next generation their influence seems to have expanded further to the south. The eldest brother Ingefast, together with a son Hæming, had a carving made for his wife Ragnfrid along a road he cleared towards a channel to the sea at Edsviken (u148), and upon his own death was memorialized by a number of stones or carvings along the same track (u101, 143, and 147). Within their typologically developed patterns (Fig. 7.6) these texts establish connections with yet another family to the northwest at Harg into which the matriarch, Estrid, had married after Ostæin's death. The elegant carvings (u309–10) at a bridge-site near Harg belong to roughly the same phase of artistic development.

It was later in this third generation, however, that the Täby family reached the height of its power, at least as expressed through commemorative practice.

Although the textual evidence is not fully explicit, it is likely that upon Hæming's (premature?) death his younger half-brother Jarlebanke became head of the kindred. The first memorials sponsored mainly by this man, notable mostly for their conservatism, are confined to the family's home area (U140 and 150). One lost text (U149) stated that he cleared the road and raised the stone for his own sake. This immodest gesture is nothing, however, compared to the campaign of self-aggrandizement that followed it. Just north of Täby, on the road to Bällsta, Jarlebanke had a large bridge or causeway constructed, marking it with four large rune-stones, in addition to many smaller uncarved *bautil-stenar* (Fig. 7.7). Their inscriptions repeat nearly the same formula: 'Jarlebanke had these stones raised to himself while living, and made this bridge for his soul's sake.' Still more unusual is the added assertion: '(He) alone owned all Täby.' Nor was this project the end of Jarlebanke's ambitions in remapping local memory. In a very careful multidisciplinary study of 1988, Helmar Gustavson and Klas Selinge concluded that one of the bridge-stones (U212) was moved and carved on the reverse side with a further inscription reading: 'Jarlebanke had (the) stone raised to himself while living, and established the thing-place, and alone held all this hundred.'[14] They identify this *thingstad* as a site near Gullbro to the *north* of the lake.

Further conclusions could be drawn from this. Jarlebanke's claim to the *hundari* (a large administrative district) was probably more of overlordship, of public supremacy, than outright ownership. We cannot know Jarlebanke's relation to the Svear king, but his assertion may exemplify the political and economic consolidations referred to earlier, its very assertiveness indicating the level of social disruption incurred. By any reckoning, the design of these memorials is archaistic. I would suggest this was a deliberate referencing not only to the earliest memorials of the Täby family, but also to those raised two generations earlier by the Skulhambr family. Even as Jarlebanke replaced their thingplace, extending his influence into the heart of an area where they had formerly held sway, he echoed their prominence, interlaced his status with theirs, and layered the way he was to be perceived with the ways they were remembered. We might think of the families as old rivals, but their membership in a common Christian community complicated the rules by which the old games of rivalry were played. Like the landscape itself, social memory cannot be erased. Still, as the social dynamics of the landscape changed, the memory inscribed on it necessarily needed to be augmented, rearranged, and selectively adjusted to the changing circumstances of local power. It is significant that on Jarlebanke's own death, his heirs raised a single memorial (U142) in their old home territory, but on the road to Skulhambr.[15]

However complex this example seems, I have sketched here only a partial skeleton of a once vital social body whose collective memory was anchored in the physical landscape by runic memorials and associated monuments. Among the Skulhambr and Täby kindreds were other prominent families in the Vallentuna district who responded similarly to the crisis of radical change in the eleventh century through a commemorative practice that fulfilled multiple functions. A dynamic community mobilized its memory of its dead as it sought both to stabilize and to redefine its fluid living relationships, the social and political patterns inherited – like the land itself – from these same dead. Memory, in its structuring through commemoration within the social landscape, was integral to the society's reinvention of itself. The implications of all this for rural communities beyond Uppland, I leave to others' consideration. Yet in conclusion I would add that the ways memorial arts functioned in the vital exchange between living and dead, their efficacy at all junctures in the construction of the social fabric, is far more diverse and richly textured than we have previously supposed.

Appendix A

The Barista / Skulhambr family

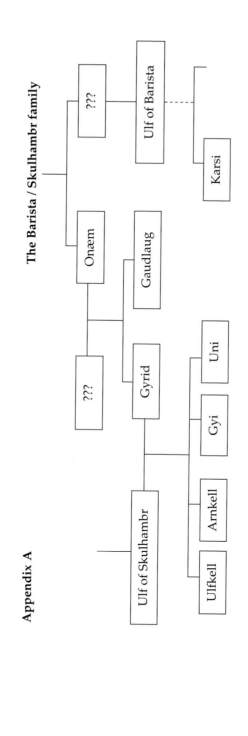

The Täby family

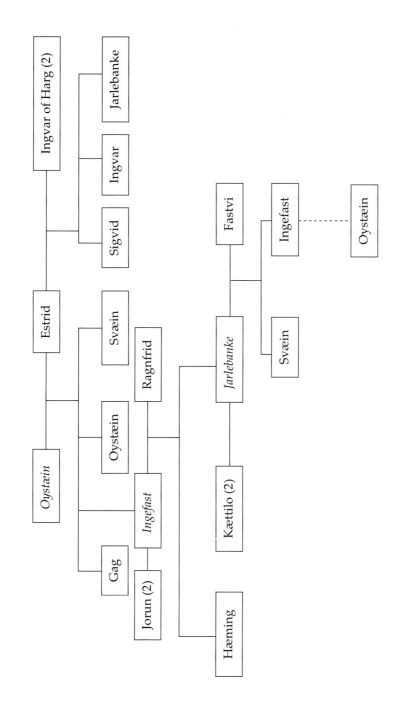

U336 (Orkesta kyrka): Ulfr let ræisa stæin þenna æftir Onæm, faðurs broður sinn. Þæir byggu baðir in Baristam.

U343-4 (Yttergarde): Karsi ok ... þæir letu ræisa stæin þenna æftir Ulf, faður sinn. Guð hialpi hans ... ok Guðs moðir. // En Ulfr hafir [a] Ænglandi þry giald takit. Þet vas fyrsta þet's Tosti galt. Þa [galt] Þorkætill. Þa galt Knutr.

U160-61 (Risbyle) Ulfkætill ok Gyi ok Uni þæir letu ræisa stæin þenna æftir Ulf, faður sinn goðan. Hann byggi i Skulhambri. Guð hialpi hans and ok salu ok Guðs moðir, le hanum lius ok paradis. // Ulf hiogg i Bar[i]stam æftir Ulf i Skulhambri, mag sinn goðan. Ulfkell let haggva.

U225-6 (Ballsta): [Ulfkell?] ok Arnkell ok Gyi þæir gærðu hiar þinstað ... Munu æigi mærki / mæiri verða, // þan Ulfs synir / æftir gær[ðu], // [sniall]ir svæinar, / at sinn faður. [226] Ræistu stæina / ok staf unnu // ok inn mikla / at iarteknum. // Ok Gyriði / gats at veri. // þy man i grati / getit lata. [detached line] Gunnarr hiogg stæin.

U328 (Lundby): Gyrið ok Guðlaug þar letu ræisa stæin þenna æftir Onæf, faður sinn, ok æftir Ansur, bonda sinn. Rað þessa!

U137 (Broby): Oystæinn ok Æstriðr ræistu stæina æftir Gag [?], sun sinn.

U135-6 (Broby): Ingifastr ok Oystæin ok Svæin letu ræisa stæina þessa at Oystæinn, faður sinn, ok bro þessa gærðu ok haug þenna. // Æstriðr let ræisa stæina þessa at Oystæinn, bonda sinn, es sotti Iorsalir ok ændaðis i Grikkium.

U148 (Hagby, Sparingsberg): Ingifastr let rista runar þessar æftir Ragnfriði, kvinnu sina, ok [Hæ]m[i]ngr æftir moður sina.

U101 (S. Satra): Hæmingr ok Jarlabanki þæir letu brant ryðia
ok broar giæra æftir faður sinn ok Æstriðr æftir syni sina
Ingifast ok Invar. Guð hialpi and þæira.

U143 (Hagby): Jorun let gærva broar æftir boanda senn ok
Hæmingr ok Jarlebanki æftir Ingifast, Æstrið æftir Ingvar,
algoðan dræng.

U147 (Hagby, Sparingsberg): Jorun ... þar letu haggva stæina
[æf]ti[r] Ingifast ok Ingvar.

U150 (Karby): Jarlabanki ok Fastvi letu ræisa stæina æftir
Svæin, sun sinn.

U140 (Broby): [Jar]laba[nki] ... Hann ændaðis i Grikkium.

U149 (Hagby): Jarlabanki let ... [s]tæin at sialfan sik ok braut
ryðia.

U127 (Danderyds kyrka): Jarlabanki let ræisa stæina þessa at
sik kvikvan, ok bro þessa gærði fyr and sina, ok æinn atti
Tæby allan.

U164 (Taby ta): Jarlabanki let ræisa stæin[a] þessa at sik
kvikvan, ok bro þessa gærði fyr and sina, ok æinn atti Tæby
allan. Guð hialpi and hans.

U165 (Taby ta): Jarlabanki le[t ræi]sa stæina þessa at sik
kvikvan, ok bro þessa gærði fyr and si[na ...] atti allan Tæby.

U212 (Vallentuna kyrka): [A] Jarlabanki let ræisa stæin þenna
a[t sik kvi]kvan. Hann atti æinn Tæby allan. [Guð hialpi]
and hans. [B] Jarlabanki let ræisa stæin þenna at sik kvikvan,
ok þingstað þenna gærði, ok æinn atti alt hundari þetta.

U261 (Fresta kyrka): Jarlabanki let ræisa stæina þessa at sik
kvikvan, ok bro þessa gærði fyr and sina, ok æinn atti allan
Tæby.

U142 (Fallbro): Ingifastr let ræisa stæin ok bro gæra æftir
Jarlabanka, faður sinn ok sun Jorunar, ok Kætilöy let at
bonda sinn. Öpir risti.

Frequently cited sources

Geary, P., *Living with the Dead in the Middle Ages*, Ithaca, NY: Cornell University Press, 1994.
Gräslund, A.-S., 'Runstenar, bygd och gravar,' *Tor*, vol. 21, 1987, pp.241–62.
— 'Some Aspects of Christianisation in Central Sweden,' in R. Samson, ed., *Social Approaches to Viking Studies*, Glasgow: Cruithne Press, 1991, pp.45–52.
Gurevich, A., *Historical Anthropology of the Middle Ages*, Chicago: University of Chicago Press, 1992.
Gustavson, H., and K.-G. Selinge, 'Jarlebanke och hundaret: Ett arkeologiskt/runologiskt bidrag till lösningen av ett historiskt tolkningsproblem,' *Namn och Bygd*, vol. 76, 1988, pp.19–83.
Herschend, F., *The Recasting of a Symbolic Value: Three Case Studies on Rune-Stones*, Uppsala: Societas Archaeologica Upsaliensis, 1994.
Lindqvist, S., 'Jarlebanke-släktens minnesmärken,' in G. Hallström, ed., *Nordiska arkeologmötet i Stockholm: Berättelse över mötet och dess förhandlingar*, Stockholm: Kungliga Vitterhets historie och antikvitets akademien, 1923.
Miller, I. M., *Bloodtaking and Peacemaking: Feud, Law, and Society in Saga Iceland*, Chicago: University of Chicago Press, 1990.
Sawyer, B., *Property and Inheritance in Viking Scandinavia: The Runic Evidence*, Alingsås: Viktoria Bokförlag, 1988.
— 'Viking-Age Rune-Stones as a Crisis Symptom,' *Norwegian Archaeological Review*, vol. 24, 1991, pp.97–112.
— and P. Sawyer, *Medieval Scandinavia: From Conversion to Reformation, circa 800–1500*, Minneapolis, MN: University of Minnesota Press, 1993.
Sveriges runinskrifter, Stockholm: Almqvist and Wiksell, 1935–.
Thompson, C. W., *Studies in Upplandic Runography*, Austin, TX: University of Texas Press, 1975.

Notes

1. Most Swedish inscriptions are published in the *Sveriges runinskrifter*, and are referenced by province (U = Uppland) and article numbers. Finds subsequent to these volumes are published in *Fornvännen: Tidskrift for svensk antikvarisk forskning*, Stockholm: Kungliga Vitterhets historie och antikvitets akademien.

2. On core formulae and types of additions, see C. W. Thompson, *Studies in Upplandic Runography*, pp.11–21. Other scholars have argued that particular adjectives applied to proper names or kinds of additions are not random phenomena, but indicative of particular regional or local historical circumstances: see F. Herschend, *The Recasting of a Symbolic Value: Three Case Studies on Rune-Stones*.

3. On the original setting of memorials, see A.-S. Gräslund, 'Runstenar, bygd och gravar'; and idem, 'Some Aspects of Christianisation in Central Sweden.'

4. B. Sawyer, *Property and Inheritance in Viking Scandinavia: The Runic Evidence*. For wider considerations of inheritance in Early Medieval Scandinavia, see relevant discussions in A. Gurevich, *Historical Anthropology of the Middle Ages*.

5. B. Sawyer, 'Viking-Age Rune-stones as a Crisis Symptom.'

6. On the difficult and interrelated questions of the expansion of the early Swedish monarchy and consolidation of landed property, see B. and P. Sawyer, *Medieval Scandinavia: From Conversion to Reformation, circa 800–1500*, pp.80–99, 129–43, and the more detailed studies cited there.

7. Among the various important works by Geary on this topic, see 'Exchange and Interaction between the Living and the Dead in Early Medieval Society,' in idem, *Living with the Dead in the Middle Ages*, pp.77–92.

8. For one of the most thorough studies of kinship and politics, albeit in a distinct cultural zone, see I. M. Miller, *Bloodtaking and Peacemaking: Feud, Law, and Society in Saga Iceland*.

9. Geary, *Living with the Dead*, pp.85–6.

10. The dating of the Yttergärde memorials (and fixed chronology in general) is a long vexed issue in runographic studies, especially since these carvings are firmly attributable to the important rune-master Asmund Karesun. For a summary of the several problems, see Thompson, *Studies*, pp.152–61.

11. Several interesting questions of attribution or relations between identifiable carvers, their 'schools,' and circles of patronage cannot be taken up here, even though they may be central to the wider issues involved. Wessén and Jansson claimed the work at Lundby to be by Ulf of

Barista, *Upplands runinskrifter*, vol. II, part 1, pp.56–7. A claim might also be made for the Gunnar who named himself as the carver of the Bällsta stones. There is probably not enough runographic evidence, however, to prove either case.

12. The frozen surface of Lake Vallentuna formed part of a great 'winterway' running north–south through the wider region and used into Early Modern times.

13. In addition to the article on U142 in *Sveriges runinskrifter*, vol. VI, part 1, pp.208–17, see S. Lindqvist's classic 'Jarlebanke-släktens minnesmärken,' and the recent treatment by H. Gustavson and K.-G. Selinge, 'Jarlebanke och hundaret: Ett arkeologiskt/runologiskt bidrag till lösningen av ett historiskt tolkningsproblem.'

14. It has long been understood that several stones were moved from the original bridge site to churches in the region: U127 to Danderyd, U212 to Vallentuna, and U261 to Fresta. According to Gustavson and Selinge, 'Jarlebanke och hundaret,' the Vallentuna stone was moved and recarved during Jarlebanke's lifetime, replaced at the bridge site by the smaller U165 which has a simpler design than U164, the only member of the original group still extant on the site.

15. The memorial raised at Fällbro is 'signed' by the prolific carver Öpir, whose seemingly progressive style (contrasting with the Jarlebanke self-commemorations) was very much in favor in the region by this time. See M. Åhlén, *Runristaren Öpir: En monografi*, Runrön 12, Uppsala: Institutionen för Nordiska Språk, 1997.

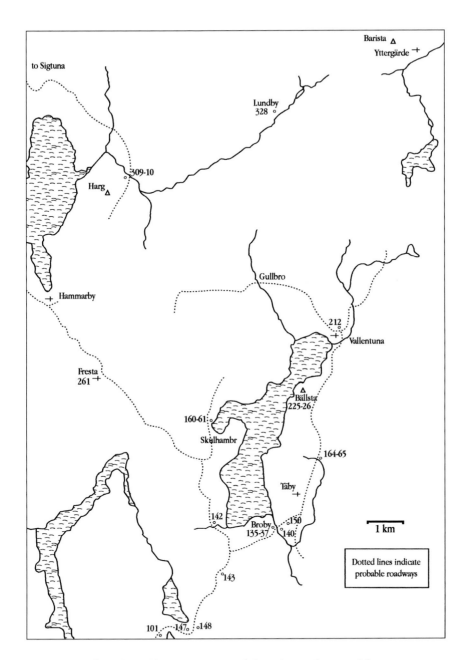

7.1   Map of the Lake Vallentuna region with key sites and memorials

7.2   The Risbyle memorial U160

7.3   The Risbyle memorial U161

7.4   The Bällsta 'thingplace', after a woodcut by J. Peringskiöld

7.5   The Bällsta memorial u226

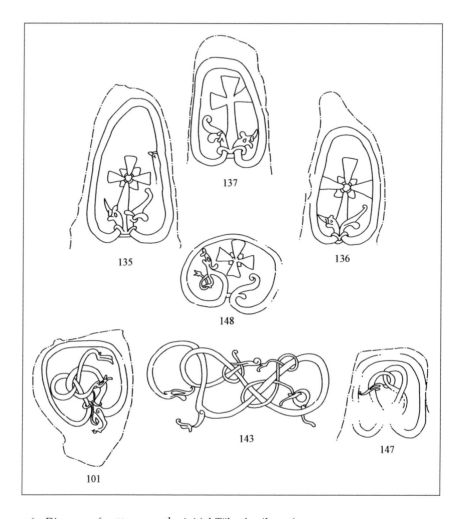

7.6 Diagram of patterns on the initial Täby family series

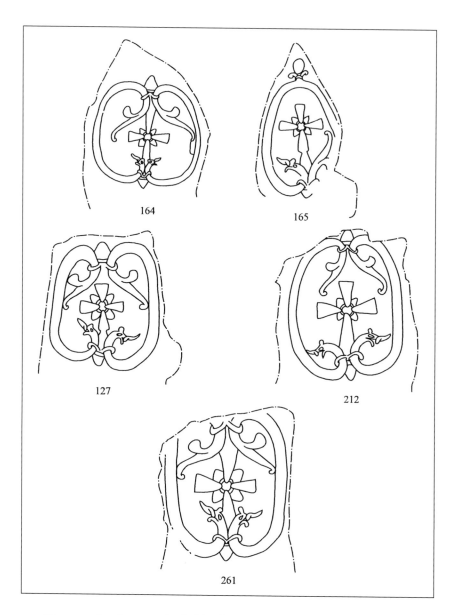

164

165

127

212

261

7.7   Diagram of patterns on the Jarlebanke bridge-stones

8

Stolen property: St Mark's first Venetian tomb and the politics of communal memory

Thomas E. A. Dale

The saint's tomb was a nexus of political and ecclesiastical power in the medieval city. Beyond perpetuating his *praesentia* or physical presence as a focus of communal intercession, the tomb could evoke a sacred past to legitimize current civic institutions.[1] Just as the communal memory of the saint was constantly revised or reinvented in texts, so pictorial images could serve to adapt the *memoria* of the saint to the changing exigencies of the cult over time.[2]

St Mark's first Venetian tomb is an instructive case study in the evolving politics of communal memory. Lacking the venerable Roman origins boasted by other powerful Italian cities, the fledgling Venetian state stole the Evangelist's relics from Alexandria in 828 and orchestrated their first resting place in Venice as tangible evidence for a newly invented sacred past appropriated from the local church on the *terra firma*.[3] By the end of the eighth century, Aquileia, the inland capital of the Roman province of Venetia and Histria, had sustained its claim to ecclesiastical primacy in the region by tracing her apostolic succession back to St Mark. Venice now claimed Aquileia's mantle by virtue of possessing the founding apostle's relics. Venetian apologists justified the theft on the grounds that Mark had preached his gospel on the Venetian *terra firma* prior to his career in Alexandria. The relics were thus 'returning home.'[4] From the early eleventh century on, the city's chroniclers further argued that Mark's episcopacy had been transferred from Aquileia to the Venetian protectorate of Grado at the time of the Lombard invasion in 568. It was to this island that the Aquileians had fled, and Venetian sources invented a letter from Pope Pelagius II to confirm the *de facto* transfer of authority to Grado in 579. By the end of the eleventh century, Venice also explicitly bound its temporal power to Mark. The Doge was invested with the *vexillum* of St Mark at the high altar of S. Marco, immediately above the Evangelist's relics.

At the time of the translation in 828, the Venetians entombed Mark's body in a corner of the Doge's palace, but the relics were moved at least twice, first to the new ducal basilica dedicated to Mark in the 830s, and then to the crypt of the present church in 1094. Realizing the ideological significance of Mark's initial resting place on their own soil, the Venetians assiduously orchestrated the memory of the original site some two centuries after the relics had been removed. The 'invention' or rediscovery of the relics, following the completion of the new church of S. Marco in 1094, was a conventional rite of passage which renewed the saint's presence amongst his community.[5] By the thirteenth century, however, Venetian writers had transformed the 'invention' of relics into a state miracle known as the *Apparitio*.[6]

The reappearance of the Evangelist's relics at his original tomb site is recounted in three nearly contemporary texts: Martino da Canal's *Estoires de Venise*, Jacobus de Voragine's *Legenda aurea* and the *Annales venetici breves*.[7] According to these sources, Mark's relics were hidden in the first ducal chapel of S. Marco, and their location was known only to a few Venetians who died without divulging their secret. Thus, by the time the church was rebuilt in the eleventh century, the Venetians no longer knew where their patron saint was buried. Seeking divine intervention, the Patriarch and Doge led the citizens in fasting and prayer for three days and a penitential procession around the city. Finally, as the Patriarch celebrated mass on the third day, St Mark himself intervened. The saint caused marble revetment to fall, thus revealing his relics within the hollow southwest leg of the southeast tetrapilon supporting the central dome (Fig. 8.1: no. 8). Later chronicles further identified this site with the corner of the old ducal palace where Mark's relics were first deposited in 828–9.[8]

Michelangelo Muraro has astutely characterized the *pilastro del miracolo* as 'fulcrum' of the basilica and symbolic 'omphalos' of the Venetian state.[9] Placed on the principal ducal axis of the basilica, the pier marks the processional route traveled by the Doge between the *porta media* communicating with the palace to the south and the ducal seat in the Cappella S. Clemente. The reliquary pier also stands behind the great porphyry pulpit where the Doge was acclaimed from the thirteenth century on.[10] Both iconic and narrative images signal its importance. A twelfth- or thirteenth-century encaustic painting of Archangel Michael, dressed in the Byzantine imperial *loros*, serves as appropriate guardian on its east side (Fig. 8.2) and an elaborate *opus sectile* mosaic inscribed with a cross appears on the adjacent south face.[11] Muraro also found an allusion to the miraculous splitting of the stone facing of the reliquary pier in the prophecy of Daniel inscribed in a mosaic on the opposite side of the transept: 'this is the stone cut out of the mountain without hands' (Dan. 2.45). Finally, the miracle itself is depicted in a mid-thirteenth-century mosaic cycle on the west wall of the south transept (Figs 8.7–8.8).

Developing Muraro's thesis further, I will explore how the pictorial and ritual memory of Mark's first Venetian tomb were adapted over time to amplify its role as *locus* of spiritual and temporal authority. My discussion will focus on three narrative mosaics executed around the site in the twelfth and thirteenth centuries: the Reception of Mark's Relics, the Deposition of Christ, and the *Apparitio*.

The Reception of Mark's Relics: a portrait of the Venetian commune

The mid-twelfth-century mosaic of the Reception of Mark's Relics culminates a detailed account of Venice's claim on Mark in the two choir chapels (Figs 8.1: no. 3, no. 6; 8.3; 8.4).[12] The Cappella S. Pietro mosaics outline the foundation of the Church of Aquileia by Mark, his subsequent career and martyrdom in Egypt. Here too, the transfer of the Aquileian See to the Venetian patriarchs of Grado is documented in the forged letter of Pope Pelagius.[13] The mosaics of the Cappella S. Clemente are devoted to the theft of Mark's relics from Alexandria and the return voyage to Venice. The two-part composition of the Reception of Relics spans the northwest corner of the chapel. On the north wall (Fig. 8.3), the relic ship has arrived at port, sails furled as the merchants prepare to disembark. The procession of Venetian dignitaries ashore is carefully positioned on the adjacent west vault (Fig. 8.4) to coincide with the site of Mark's tomb below. What is more, the designer of the mosaic emphasized this juxtaposition by depicting an isolated column at the far left (southwest corner) of the mosaic.[14]

The narrative action of the procession has been transformed into an official, hieratic portrait of the Venetian Commune. Executed on a distinctly larger scale than the relic ship, it balances the symbolic image of the city at right with a frontal array of figures embodying the constituencies listed in the titulus above: 'With happy hearts, the pontiffs, clergy, people, and the Serene Doge receive (the relics of Mark) with praises and melodious songs.'[15] This contrasts sharply with an earlier twelfth-century version on the Pala d'Oro (Fig. 8.5). The enamel focuses on the movement of the relics: three merchants, accompanied by Venetian soldiers, carry the casket to a domed church, where they are met by a procession of clergy, headed by Bishop Ursus. The mosaic conforms instead to the hieratic mode of the politically charged, twelfth-century frescoes of popes confronting emperors in the Lateran Palace.[16] What is more, the Venetian mosaic incorporates significant changes in personnel. In conformity with the new configuration of the Venetian Commune, Bishop Ursus, who receives the relics of Mark in the Pala d'Oro panel, is replaced in the mosaic by the Patriarch of Grado and seven other bishops. The Patriarch's elevated dignity is indicated both by costume and by gesture. He is attired in a gold embroidered dalmatic and chasuble with a t-shaped pallium indicating his metropolitan status. Two of his suffragans show their deference by supporting his outstretched arms.[17] Six of the other seven bishops represent the episcopates of the Venetian lagoon under the Patriarch's authority. A seventh bishop may represent Zara, the metropolitan seat of Dalmatia. Pope Hadrian IV subjected Zara to the Venetian Patriarchate in 1154 so that it would exercise the supra-metropolitan authority implied by the patriarchal title.[18]

The mosaic further departs from the Pala d'Oro by prominently featuring secular authority in the person of the Doge, his sword-bearer and five patricians. The Doge's entourage, as Hanns Hubach has recently proposed, is probably the *consilium sapientium*.[19] This elected body of patricians, representing the Venetian *populus* included in the inscription, shared power with the Doge from the 1140s on.[20] The joint appearance of Doge and Patriarch also has a contemporary resonance. This pontiff first established permanent residence in Venice during the twelfth century, and had no official status in the ducal chapel. Locked in a jurisdictional dispute during the 1140s, patriarch and doge only reached a lasting concord in 1149 under Doge Domenico Morisini.[21]

The narrative of the Reception of Relics is thus modified to unite contemporary Venetian institutions under Mark's patronage. Substituting the patriarch and hierarchy of Venetian bishops for the historical figure of Ursus, the mosaic uses the site of Mark's first Venetian tomb to validate the transfer of authority from the see the Evangelist established at Aquileia to the Venetian Patriarchate of Grado. At the same time, Venetian custody of Mark's relics justifies the Doge's temporal authority.

This pictorial affirmation of the sacred roots of ducal authority at Mark's tomb site would have been all the more poignant for the medieval beholder in light of contemporaneous ritual. From the reign of Domenico Selvo in the 1070s, the new basilica of S. Marco replaced the Cathedral of Castello as the venue for ducal elections and investiture. During these ceremonies Mark himself was invoked to invest the Doge with his *vexillum*.[22]

Mark's tomb and the sepulchre of Christ

A second narrative mosaic, the Deposition of Christ, relates to the tomb site in a less obvious way (Figs 8.1: no. 7; 8.6). Two fragments from the upper left corner of this composition were recovered in 1954 on the northeast leg of the tetrapilon, immediately beneath the government portrait just described: one depicts angels above the transverse arm of the Cross, the other, four grieving women.[23] The latter fragment is duplicated so closely in the fresco of the Deposition at nearby Aquileia that it is possible to reconstruct the Venetian composition in its entirety. I have argued more fully elsewhere that this image was set apart from the Passion cycle to provide a backdrop for the liturgical *Depositio* on Good Friday.[24] A sixteenth-century Venetian Book of Ceremonies suggests that a temporary *sepulcrum* was once set up at the base of the pier to enclose the eucharistic relics of Christ from Good Friday to Easter.

The choice of this awkward site between the legs of the pier may be explained by the desire to juxtapose the tombs of Christ and Mark. Both tombs were placed under the personal custody of the Doge in his official role as *Verus Gubernator et Patronus* of the Basilica.[25] Just as the Doge oversaw the deposition of the relics of Mark, initially in his palace and then in his ducal chapel, so on Good Friday he served as custodian of the tomb of Christ, providing his signet ring to seal it shut.[26] These sacral bonds uniting the Doge with Christ and Mark were further emphasized by the design on the seal: as early as the reign of Pietro Polani (1130–48), it depicted the Evangelist investing the Doge with his *vexillum*.[27]

From tomb to miraculous reliquary column

The mid-thirteenth-century *Apparitio* mosaics on the west wall of the south transept, immediately opposite the reliquary column, renew the role of Mark's tomb site as a focus of civic authority (Figs 8.7, 8.8).[28] In this pictorial appendix to the previous narrative of Mark's translation to Venice in the choir mosaics, the saint's tomb is once again the focus of group portraits of the Venetian church and state under the leadership of the Doge.

The titulus inscribed above the two-panel composition summarizes three phases of the miraculous reappearance of the relics of St Mark: 'For three days the people fast and pray to the Lord; the stone pillar opens up; then they take up the saint and lay him out.'[29] In keeping with the function of the *Apparitio* miracle to proclaim St Mark's continuing presence in Venice, these images project a self-conscious realism. The generalized stage props used in the twelfth-century mosaic of the Reception of the Relics (Fig. 8.4) give way to a recognizable cross-section of the basilica, complete with its arcades, galleries, and five domes, as well as the two pulpits recently purloined from Constantinople. Instead of hovering over a gold ground, figures now occupy a fictive space within the architectural setting.

In the *Preghiera* at left (Fig. 8.7), the Patriarch of Grado stands at the high altar to lead the city in a supplicatory prayer for the recovery of the relics. Behind him in the sanctuary, the clergy and acolytes prostrate themselves, while the Doge and a group of counsellors stand with heads bowed in the Gospel pulpit. Clusters of patrician men and women stand or kneel behind them with arms outstretched in prayer. Here, as in the adjacent panel, the Doge alone is inscribed (DUX) to indicate his elevated status as patron of the church and custodian of Mark's relics.

The setting of the right-hand panel, depicting the miracle itself (Fig. 8.8), has appropriately been shifted to show a north–south section of the basilica across the transept. The reliquary column, though simplified in architectural detail, is accurately positioned at far right in the south transept adjacent the ducal pergola, and immediately opposite the actual site. The Patriarch of Grado and the clergy again lead the Venetians as witnesses to the opening of the reliquary column of St Mark. Then follow the Doge with four counsellors and the patrician families who seem to flood into the transept from the narthex as if at the tail end of the penitential procession. A more universal recognition of the state miracle is suggested by the presence of a foreign prince at the far left, identified by Demus as Philippe de Courtenay, son of Baldwin I.[30] The Venetians held the Latin Emperor's son as surety for a loan between 1248 and 1261.

A third scene, the *Collocatio* or entombment of the relics, appears on the eastern spandrel of the southwest arch in the tribune of the adjacent crossing pier (Fig. 8.9). On the opposite side of the same arch Constantine and Helena flank the True Cross (Fig. 8.10). Both mosaics date from the mid-seventeenth century, but they probably replaced medieval images of the same subjects. Leaving aside stylistic modifications, the iconography of both compositions is essentially medieval, and the *Collocatio* is actually alluded to in the inscription over the main panel of the *Apparitio*.[31] Thus, these mosaics would appear to conform to edicts issued by the Procuratoria of S. Marco beginning in 1566, mandating the preservation of the original iconography and inscriptions of any mosaics replaced within the basilica.[32]

If accepted as iconographically authentic, the mosaic of Constantine and Helena with the Cross sheds light on the political meaning of the *Apparitio* miracle for thirteenth-century Venice. First, the display of the Cross adjacent the *Apparitio* evokes the Invention of the Cross to authenticate the miraculous invention of Mark's relics by the Doge. This parallel would have been particularly poignant at a time when the Doge was simultaneously promoting a new festival of the *Apparitio* and the miraculous survival of two important relics of the True Cross, the Blood of Christ, and the Head of John the Baptist, from the treasury fire of 1231.[33] Debra Pincus has demonstrated that Doge Ranieri Zen vaunted this second state miracle in a relief set within the treasury wall; moreover, he wrote his ambassadors in Rome in 1265 to persuade the Pope that the miracle should be officially propagated throughout Christendom. Recording the advent of the relics of the Cross and Blood to Venice after the Fourth Crusade, the Doge claims that their preservation from the fire confirms Christ's own desire that these relics be brought from Constantinople to reside with those of Mark in Venice.[34]

Besides justifying the theft of spiritual properties to Venice from the East, these juxtaposed images of the *Apparitio* and the vision of the Holy Cross

between Constantine and Helena would have bolstered Venetian pretensions to Byzantine temporal authority. Just as the theft of Mark's relics helped
Venice establish its autonomy from Byzantium in the ninth century, so the
Passion relics, acquired from Constantinople in the aftermath of the Fourth
Crusade in 1204, provided spiritual sanction for Venetian rule over Byzantine territory – 'one quarter and a half of the Roman Empire,' as ducal titles
boasted. In a general way, the Doge's ostentatious collection of Passion relics
in his palace chapel, like Saint Louis's trove in the Sainte-Chapelle, followed
the example of the Byzantine Emperor's Bucoleon Palace chapel.[35] In the case
of the True Cross, however, the Doge's power as custodian of the state relics
could be compared more specifically to the sacrosanct model of the first
Christian Emperor.

According to early Byzantine chronicles, Constantine, repeating his experience at the Milvian Bridge, conquered Byzantion after witnessing as many as
three apparitions of the True Cross.[36] Thereafter he made it the talisman for
the city he rededicated as Constantinople in 330.[37] Similarly, the thirteenth-
century chronicler, Martino da Canal, confirms that St Mark's relics, after
their rediscovery in 1094, became a talisman for the Doge, insuring Venetian
victories over Byzantium itself in 1204, and later, other Italian city states like
Genoa and Pisa.[38] Moreover, in celebrating the '*Columna apparitionis sancti
marci*' the Venetians seem consciously to have emulated the column which
Constantine set up in the Forum on the site of one of his visions of the
Cross.[39] Today, only the charred porphyry shaft of Constantine's column
survives, but medieval texts claim that the monument sheltered numerous
relics in a chapel at its base, including part of the wood of the Cross which
Helena discovered in Jerusalem.[40] Significantly, both the vision and relics of
the True Cross were represented by a sculptural group, set up opposite the
column perhaps by the end of the fourth century: it depicted Constantine,
Helena, and two angels flanking the Cross, the very image placed opposite
Mark's column in S. Marco (Fig. 8.10).[41]

Intimately connected with the fate of its respective city, each column played
a central role in civic ritual. Constantine's column was a station for processions on the anniversary of the city's dedication, the beginning of the Byzantine New Year, religious feasts, and imperial triumphs.[42] Venice's reliquary
column was likewise the site of the city's rededication to Mark and the focus
of an annual triumphal procession which passed from the church out into
Piazza S. Marco.[43] After recounting Doge Ranieri Zen's naval victory over
Genoa, Martino da Canal observes that 'the Venetians have no other festival
for the victories which the Lord has given them, apart from a procession to
Saint Mark . . . And on the feast of Saint Mark . . . in June, the mass is sung
after the procession in front of the church of the Evangelist. And the Venetians
hold that festival in honor of a beautiful miracle.'[44]

After 1204, the Venetians could also claim that the power invested in Constantine's talisman had passed to them with the relics of the Cross. The chronicler Marco, writing in 1290, found prophetic sanction for this idea. When Constantine set up his column, Marco affirms, he inscribed a Latin text on its base, foretelling the city's fall to the Latins when the cross fell from its summit.[45] The Venetians fulfilled this promise when they helped conquer Constantinople in 1204.

That St Mark's reliquary-column exercised the Venetian imagination so long after its contents had been removed in 1094 testifies to the ideological significance of the tomb. As the angel proclaims to Mark in the thirteenth-century *Praedestinatio* legend, the city and its church were destined to be built around Mark's transplanted tomb.[46] Emptied of Mark's remains, the site itself became a relic and thence a focal point for miracles, images, and rituals which periodically reinvented the memory of Mark's advent to Venice as guarantor of the city's present institutions and its future prosperity.

Frequently cited sources

Cameron, A., and J. Herrin, *Constantinople in the Early Eighth Century*, Leiden: E. J. Brill, 1984.
Dale, T., 'Inventing a Sacred Past: Pictorial Narratives of Saint Mark the Evangelist in Aquileia and Venice, c.1000–1300,' *Dumbarton Oaks Papers*, vol. 48, 1994, pp.53–104.
Demus, O., *The Church of San Marco in Venice: History–Architecture–Sculpture*, Dumbarton Oaks Studies, 6, Washington, DC: Dumbarton Oaks, 1960.
— *The Mosaics of San Marco in Venice*, 2 vols, Chicago: University of Chicago Press, 1984.
Martino da Canal, *Estoires de Venise*, edited by A. Limentani, Civiltà veneziana (Fonti e Testi, 12), Florence: L. S. Olschki, 1972.
Muraro, M., 'Il pilastro del miracolo e il secondo programma dei mosaici marciani,' *Arte Veneta*, vol. 29, 1975, pp.60–65.
Polacco, R., *San Marco: La basilica d'oro*, Milan: Berenice, 1991.
Sinding-Larsen, S., *Christ in the Council Hall: Studies in the Iconography of the Venetian Republic*, Acta ad archaeologiam et artium historiam pertinentia, 5, Rome: L'Erma di Bretschneider, 1974.

Notes

1. On *praesentia*, see P. Brown, *The Cult of the Saints*, Chicago: University of Chicago Press, 1982, pp.86–105. On the evocation of a sacred past, see Dale, 'Inventing a Sacred Past'; the useful overviews in B. Abou-El-Haj, *The Medieval Cult of Saints*, Cambridge: Cambridge University Press, 1994, pp.7–32; and J. Fontaine, 'Hagiographie et politique, de Sulpice Sévère à Venance Fortunat,' *Revue d'histoire de l'église de France*, vol. 62, 1976, pp.113–40.

2. On the interpretive aspect of medieval memory (invention and composition), see M. Carruthers, *The Book of Memory*, Cambridge: Cambridge University Press, 1990, pp.189–220, 259: 'Adaptation, the essential conduct of *memoria ad res* lies at the very basis of medieval literary activity.' More recently, in her discussion of the reliquaries in the treasury of Sainte-Foy at Conques, Amy Remensnyder has felicitously described this process as 'imaginative memory.' See her article, 'Legendary Treasure at Conques: Reliquaries and Imaginative Memory,' *Speculum*, vol. 71, 1996, pp.884–906, especially pp.884–6.

3. For Venice's perpetual search to forge links with Antiquity, see P. Fortini Brown, *Venice and Antiquity*, New Haven, CT: Yale University Press, 1996. For the theft of the relics, see Dale, 'Inventing a Sacred Past,' pp.55–9, and Demus, *The Church of San Marco*, pp.19–44.

4. Quoting Peter Damian, Jacobus de Voragine affirms that Mark's body 'was returned to Italy, so that the land where it had been given him to write his gospel won the privilege of possessing his sacred remains.' Jacobus de Voragine, *The Golden Legend*, vol. I, Princeton, NJ: Princeton University Press, 1993, p.243.

5. On the meaning of *inventio* (invention) in the context of the cult of relics see *Thesaurus Linguae Latinae*, Leipzig: G. B. Taubner, 1956–70, vol. VII, part 2, pp.152–3; and M. Heinzelmann, *Translationsberichte und andere Quellen des Reliquienkultes*, Turnhout: Brepols, 1979, pp.77–80.

6. See M. Muraro, 'Il pilastro del miracolo.'

7. Martino da Canal, *Estoires de Venise*, part II, chapter 60, p.219; Jacobus de Voragine, *The Golden Legend*, 1993, vol. I, pp.245–6; H. Simonsfeld, ed., *Annales venetici breves*, MGH, Scriptores, vol. XIV, p.70. For later versions of the legend, see G. Monticolo, 'L'apparitio ed i suoi manoscritti,' *Nuovo Archivio Veneto*, series 2, vol. 5, 1895, pp.111–77. The recovery of the relics is first recorded without miraculous connotations in an early twelfth-century text: see R. Cessi, 'L'apparitio Sancti Marci dal 1094,' *Nuovo Archivio Veneto*, series 5, vol. 65, 1964, pp.113–15.

8. See Demus, *The Mosaics of San Marco*, vol. II, p.28.

9. Muraro, 'Il pilastro del miracolo,' p.60: 'Quello che per qualche tempo era stato il suo reliquiario, il Pilastro del miracolo, divenne il fulcro della basilica, quasi l'"omphalos" dello Stato veneziano.'

10. For the ducal axis, see Sinding-Larsen, *Christ in the Council Hall*, pp.199–203; idem, 'Chiesa di stato e iconografia musiva,' in B. Bertoli, ed., *La basilica di San Marco: arte e simbologia*, Venice: Edizioni Studium Cattolico Veneziano, 1993, pp.25–45, especially pp.38–42. For the ducal pergola, see Martino da Canal, *Estoires de Venise*, part II, chapter 87, p.248.

11. See Demus, *Mosaics of San Marco*, vol. I, p.29 and fig. 24; and Polacco, *San Marco*, p.241 and color plate on p.16. In the thirteenth-century renovation of the Pala d'Oro, which surmounts the altar over Mark's eleventh-century tomb, Michael once again assumes the role of guardian, prominently occupying the central axis of the upper zone. See H. R. Hahnloser and R. Polacco, eds, *La Pala d'Oro*, Venice: Canal & Stamperia Editrice, 1994, p.39, plate XLII. Immediately opposite the reliquary pier, a mosaic pavement depicting two adossed arcades may also allude to the palace chapel, the site where the relics were originally deposited, and which Venetians conflated with the site of the eleventh-century miracle. See X. Barral i Altet, *Les mosaïques de pavement médiévales de Venise, Murano et Torcello*, Paris: Picard, 1985, p.85.

12. See Dale, 'Inventing a Sacred Past,' pp.67–78; Demus, *Mosaics of San Marco*, vol. I, pp.57–72, plates 38–77.

13. Demus, *Mosaics of San Marco*, vol. I, p.56, plate 57.

14. This part of the mosaic was restored in the fifteenth century but it seems to reproduce a medieval detail. Compare Demus, *Mosaics of San Marco*, vol. I, plates 63 and 78.

15. The complete inscription reads: PONTIFICES CLERUS P(O)P(U)L(U)S DUX M(E)NTE SERENUS LAUDIBUS ATQUE CHORIS EXCIPIUNT (CORPUS SANCTI MARCI) DULCE CANORIS.

16. See C. Walter, 'Political Imagery in the Medieval Lateran Palace,' *Cahiers archéologiques*, vol. 21, 1971, pp.109–36, especially pp.119–23; G. Ladner, 'I mosaici e gli affreschi ecclesiastico-politici nell'antico Palazzo Lateranense,' *Rivista di archeologia cristiana*, vol. 12, 1935, pp.265–92, fig. 5; and M. Stroll, *Symbols as Power: The Papacy Following the Investiture Contest*, Leiden: E. J. Brill, 1991, pp.16–35, plates 8–10.

17. This gesture conforms to a long-standing tradition of representing priestly authority, which Schapiro has traced back to the episode of Aaron and Hur supporting the arms of Moses at the Battle of the Amelekites. See M. Schapiro, *Words and Pictures: On the Literal and the Symbolic in the Illustration of a Text*, The Hague: Mouton, 1973, reprinted in *Words, Script, and Pictures: Semiotics of Visual Language*, New York: George Braziller, 1996, pp.25–45.

18. Dale, 'Inventing a Sacred Past,' pp.74–6.

19. H. Hubach, 'Pontifices, clerus–Populus, dux. Osservazioni sul significato e sullo sfondo storico della più antica autorappresentazione della società veneziana,' in A. Niero, ed., *San Marco: aspetti storici ed agiografici*, Venice: Marsilio, 1996, pp.370–97.

20. Demus, *The Church of San Marco*, pp.50–51; G. Rösch, *Der venezianische Adel bis zur Schliessung des Grossen Rats*, Sigmaringen: J. Thorbecke, 1989, pp.81–8.

21. Demus, *The Church of San Marco*, pp.42–3; P. Kehr, 'Rom und Venedig bis ins XII. Jahrhundert,' *Quellen und Forschungen aus italienischen Archiven und Bibliotheken*, vol. 19, 1927, pp.1–180, especially pp.129–35.

22. Sinding-Larsen, *Christ in the Council House*, pp.159–66; A. Pertusi, 'Quedam regalia insignia: ricerche sulle insegne del potere ducale a Venezia durante il medioevo,' *Studi veneziani*, vol. 7, 1965, pp.71ff.; R. Cessi, 'L'investitura ducale,' *Atti dell'Istituto Veneto di Scienze Lettere ed Arti, Classe di Scienze morali e Lettere*, vol. 126, 1967/8, pp.284–6.

23. Polacco, *San Marco*, pp.13–17; Demus, *Mosaics of San Marco*, vol. I, pp.209–12; G. Galassi, 'I nuovi mosaici scoperti in San Marco a Venezia,' *Arte veneta*, vol. 9, 1955, pp.243–8.

24. T. Dale, 'Easter, Saint Mark and the Doge: The Deposition Mosaic in the Choir of San Marco in Venice,' *Thesaurismata*, vol. 25, 1995, pp.21–33.

25. See Demus, *The Church of San Marco*, pp.44–5.

26. For the texts, see Dale, 'Easter, Saint Mark and the Doge,' appendices; Sinding-Larsen, *Christ in the Council Hall*, p.215 n.5; and G. Cattin, *Musica e liturgia a San Marco*, Venice: Edizioni Fondazione Levi, 1990–92, vol. II, pp.46–7.

27. N. Papadopoli Aldobrandini, *Le monete di Venezia*, reprinted Bologna: Forni, 1967, vol. I, pp.79, 83, 88; G. Majer, 'La bolla del Doge Domenico Morosini, 1148–56,' *Archivio Veneto*, series 5, vol. 100, 1959, pp.1–10.

28. Dale, 'Inventing a Sacred Past,' pp.85–8; Polacco, *San Marco*, pp.241–3; Demus, *Mosaics of San Marco*, vol. II, pp.27–32; Muraro, 'Il pilastro del miracolo,' pp.63–4.

29. P(ER) TRIDUT (= TRIDUUM) PLEBS IEIUNAT D(OMI)N(U)MQ(UE) PRECANTUR PETRA PATET S(AN)C(TU)M MOX COLLIGIT E(T) COLLOCAN(TUR).

30. Demus, *Mosaics of San Marco*, vol. II, pp.30–31.

31. For similar medieval burial scenes in S. Marco – without the Baroque angels – see Demus, *Mosaics of San Marco*, vol. I, plates 43, 357, 358. For Constantine and Helena with the Cross, see A. Frolow, *Les reliquaires de la vraie Croix*, Paris: Institut d'Etudes byzantines, 1965, pp.217–25.

32. Demus, *Mosaics of San Marco*, vol. I, pp.10–11.

33. See Demus, *Mosaics of San Marco*, vol. II, p.66; and D. Pincus, 'Christian Relics and the Body Politic: A Thirteenth-Century Relief Plaque in the Church of San Marco,' in D. Rosand, ed., *Interpretazioni veneziane*, Venice: Arsenale, 1984, pp.39–57.

34. 'Ecce Vestrae prudentiae duximus presentibus declarandum: quoddam miraculum noviter in festo Beatae Ascensionis Domini sacrae Reliquiae cum ligno Crucis sanctae, ampulla de vero Sanguine Christi et verticem Beati Joannis Baptistae more solito ostensae fuissent dictae per fratres Praedicatores, quos ad hoc clamari fecimus qualiter dictae Sanctae Reliquiae de Hierusalem, per operam Sanctae Helenae in Constantinopolim fuerunt deportatae, et qualiter Dominus Noster Jesus Christus ipsas in Civitate Venetiarum cum Corpore Beati Marci, Evangelistae sui voluit collocari, nec non ingenti miraculo quod ostendere voluit per ipsas Reliquias cum ab igne, et vastitate intactae per ordinem relato, dictum fratrem postmodum per fratres, et alios quod vere miraculum erat quod Dux, et homines Venetiarum clausis oculis sic transibant quod hoc tam grande, et gloriosum miraculum, quod ad tantam roborationem fidei noscebatur. Summo Pontifici Ecclesie Romanae minime revelabant, ad hoc ut veritate cognita, et per mundi partes solemniter et diligenter divulgato in multarum animarum edificatione indulgentia praeberetur.' B. Cecchetti, *Documenti per la storia dell'Augusta ducale basilica di San Marco*, Venice: Ferdinando Ongania, 1886, no. 97. Cf. Pincus (as in n.33), p.57.

35. Both the denomination, '*sancta capella*,' and the collection of sacred relics of Christ's Passion in the French monarch's palace chapel seem to have been inspired by the Byzantine example of the Bucoleon Palace chapel in Constantinople. See H. Belting, *The Image and Its Public*, New Rochelle: A. D. Caratzas, 1990, pp.203–21, especially p.206. Similarly, with the splendid collection of holy relics and precious objects from Byzantium gathered in the treasury of S. Marco, the ducal basilica became a new '*sancta capella*' projecting Venetian 'imperial' pretensions.

36. The eighth-century '*Parastaseis Symtomoi Chronikai*' mentions three apparitions of the Cross to Constantine in different locations in Constantinople. See A. Cameron and J. Herrin, *Constantinople in the Early Eighth Century*, pp.79–81, 129, 135, 192–3.

37. On the role of the Cross in the Christianization of the new capital, see G. Dagron, *Constantinople imaginaire*, Paris: Presses universitaires de France, 1984, pp.87–90; idem, *Naissance d'une capitale*, Paris: Presses universitaires de France, 1974, p.408.

38. For example, Martino da Canal records that the Venetians celebrated the feast of the *Apparitio* after the battle of Trapani against the Genoese. See *Estoires de Venise*, part II, chapters 59–60, pp.216–18; Demus, *Mosaics of San Marco*, vol. II, p.29.

39. Here I part company with Muraro who finds for the reliquary column not a Byzantine model but a Roman one: the *lapis niger*. See Muraro, 'Il pilastro del miracolo,' p.60.

40. On the Column of Constantine and its chapel, see M. Karamouzi, 'Das Forum und die Säule Constantini in Konstantinopel,' *Balkan Studies*, vol. 27, 1986, pp.219–36; W. Müller-Wiener, *Bildlexikon zur Topographie Istanbuls*, Tübingen: Wasmuth, 1977, pp.255–7; C. Mango,

'Constantinopolitana,' *Jahrbuch des deutschen Archäologischen Instituts,* vol. 80, 1965, pp.306–13. For the relics within the column, see Cameron and Herrin, *Constantinople in the Early Eighth Century,* pp.85, 219; A. Frolow, 'La dédicace de Constantinople dans la tradition byzantine,' *Revue de l'histoire des religions,* vol. 127, 1944, pp.76–7 nn.1, 2; and G. Majeska, *Russian Travellers to Constantinople in the Fourteenth and Fifteenth Centuries,* Washington, DC: Dumbarton Oaks, 1984, pp.260–63.

41. Cameron and Herrin, *Constantinople in the Early Eighth Century,* pp.79–81, 192–3; Dagron (as in n.37), pp.88–9.

42. Constantine Porphyrogenitus records three feasts in the tenth century: *De cerimoniis,* book I, chapters 1, 10, 39, 41, edited by A. Vogt, Paris: Société d'Edition 'Les Belles Lettres,' 1935, vol. I, 22–4 (Nativity of the Virgin), 67–8 (Monday after Easter), 153–64 (Annunciation); vol. II, Commentaire, pp.74–5. The same author refers to triumphal processions to the column in *De cerimoniis,* book II, chapter 19, edited by J. Reisk, *Corpus Scriptorum Historiae Byzantinae,* Bonn: E. Weber, 1829, vol. I, pp.607–12. Two later chroniclers mention the column of Constantine in connection with New Year's celebrations: Pseudo-Kodinos, *Traité des offices,* edited by J. Verpeaux, Editions du Centre National de la Recherche Scientifique, 1966, p.242; Nicephorus Gregoras, *Byzantina historia,* book VIII, chapter 5, edited by L. Schopen, Corpus Scriptorum Historiae Byzantinae, 6, vol. I, Bonn: E. Weber, 1829, p.385. Cf. Majeska (as in n.40), p.263.

43. For the earliest extant text of the *Apparitio* liturgy – an early Trecento addition to the thirteenth-century Antiphonary – see Cattin (as in n.26), vol. I, p.231, vol. II, pp.98–9, vol. III, pp.263–6. The sixteenth-century compilation of the liturgy, 'De inventione corporis sancti marci,' records the procession and censing of the *columna*: *Ritum ecclesiasthicorum cerimoniale iuxta ducalis ecclesie sancti marci venetiam consuetudinem,* Venice, Biblioteca Nazionale Marciana, cod. lat.III.CLXXII (= 2276), fols 28r–28v.

44. Martino da Canal, *Estoires de Venise,* part II, chapter 59, pp.217–19.

45. Venice, Biblioteca Nazionale Marciana, cod. It. XI.24 (= 6802) fols 78r–79v, transcribed by A. Pertusi in 'Le profezie sulla presa di Costantinopli (1204) nel cronista veneziano Marco (*c.* 1292) e le loro fonti bizantine,' *Studi veneziani,* new series, vol. 3, 1979, pp.13–46.

46. Demus, *Mosaics of San Marco,* vol. II, pp.186–7.

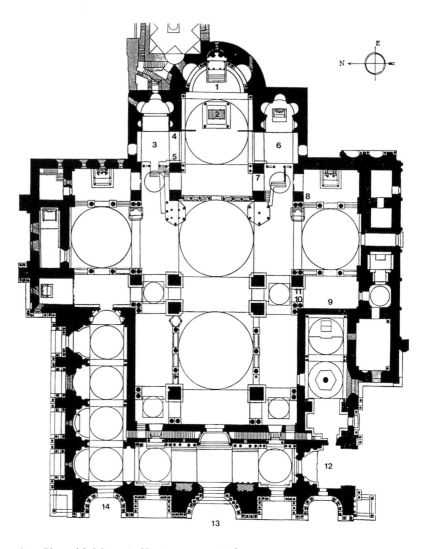

8.1   Plan of S. Marco in Venice, consecrated 1094

8.2 Pilastro del Miracolo, marble pier with encaustic panel of the Archangel Michael, S. Marco in Venice, twelfth century

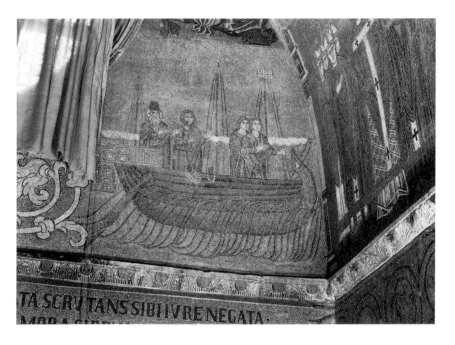

8.3   Arrival of the relics of St Mark in Venice, mosaic, Cappella S. Clemente,
      S. Marco in Venice, c.1155

8.4 Reception of Mark's Relics in Venice, Cappella S. Clemente, S. Marco in Venice, *c.*1155

8.5   Reception of Mark's Relics in Venice, enamel plaque from Pala d'Oro, S. Marco
in Venice, 1105

8.6   Reconstruction of Deposition of Christ, mosaic, S. Marco in
      Venice, *c.*1100–1150

8.7   *Preghiera,* mosaic, south transept, S. Marco in Venice, *c.*1260–65

8.8   *Apparitio*, mosaic, south transept, S. Marco in Venice, *c.*1260–65

8.9   *Collocatio*, mosaic, southwest tribune of central dome, S. Marco in Venice,
c.1260–65, restored c.1650

8.10 Constantine and Helena with the True Cross, mosaic, southwest tribune of central dome, S. Marco in Venice, *c*.1260–65, restored *c*.1650

9

Dream images, *memoria*, and the Heribert Shrine

Carolyn M. Carty

Works of medieval art can astound not only by their beauty but also by their complexity. Multi-layered in meaning through their imagery and often in their structure, these objects provide insight into the richness and inventiveness of medieval thought, which for ecclesiastical objects had edification as its goal. Such is the case with the Heribert Shrine where the image of the dream intersects with the concretization of the memorial process, creating a dynamic interaction between object and viewer.

As the writings of most cultures attest, the nocturnal activity of dreaming has fascinated mankind throughout the centuries, and its causes have been attributed variously to God, the devil, indigestion, or our psychological state.[1] In seeking to assess the merits of dreaming, the medieval period already had important commentaries on which to draw – from Plato, Aristotle and Macrobius to Church Fathers such as Augustine and Gregory the Great.[2] Despite frequent skepticism about the validity of the dream experience, as well as admonitions for ordinary people to be wary of false dreams and the practices of divination, the dream's biblical and hagiographic heritage made it a powerful tool for furthering specific ends. As a phenomenon experienced by all, it had an immediacy and commonality not shared by the miraculous and thus an inherent believability; however, it was the dream's ability to bridge the gap between heaven and earth that was its most significant attribute.[3] In this light, hagiographic and monastic dreams existed in the social consciousness as markers of divine intervention in the lives of those whom God had privileged.

While most dreams were transitory and not remembered, those whose purpose was to further the divine plan were so important that they had to be remembered, first by the dreamer himself and then by others, to be acted upon and learned from. Thus these dreams had to be rendered tangible, preserved for memory through the media of texts, both oral and written, and of images. For example, as I have demonstrated elsewhere, dreams often served as authorization for building campaigns, and the memory of these structures' divine beginnings was not only spiritually but also economically and politically vital.[4] When one views the well-known image of the dream regarding the building of Cluny III, one is not merely viewing an amusing or naive hagiographical anecdote but a visual justification for the building enterprise, the success of which first hinges upon the monk Gunzo's memory for the structure's actualization, and then upon the viewer's remembrance of the saints' command to the ailing monk for that structure's justification.[5] The mass of ropes which SS Peter, Paul, and Stephen unfurl above the dreaming Gunzo becomes a visible depiction of their command that he commit to memory the specific dimensions for the new church and relate them to Abbot Hugh. The amount of space the ropes occupy in the tiny miniature becomes a visual analogue to the enormous size of Cluny III as opposed to the more modest dimensions imposed by the Farfa Customary; these ropes thus function as an aid for viewers, not only those contemporary with the event but also those who would come long after, to remember that the size of the building enterprise is directly related not to an overweening abbot but to a divine command. Thus the dream remembered served as authorization both for the present and in the future.

Just as the dream itself was the means of penetration into the spiritual realm, the dream image, especially when positioned at the beginning of a hagiographic narrative sequence as it is on the Charlemagne Shrine at Aachen, the Hadelin Shrine at Visé, and the Heribert Shrine at Deutz, became the viewer's entry into the dreamer's realm and the memorial mediator between past and present and between heaven and earth.[6] The dream, serving as predictor of succeeding events, facilitated the recollection of the saint's *vita* by providing a point of entry while simultaneously providing a rich, extra-narrative memorial thread between the saint and others who had also experienced heaven-sent dreams.[7] As the divine entered the life of the saint, propelling him to fulfill his saintly mission on earth, the viewer, too, was invited to share in the journey as witness to the events that followed and to remember the illustrious life. This memorial function was particularly compelling when, as the decoration of a reliquary shrine, it was conjoined with the physical remains of the saint himself, relics left as efficacious instruments to cause heaven once again to interact miraculously with earth. In particular, on the twelfth-century shrine of St Heribert of Deutz, an eleventh-century Archbishop of Cologne and Chancellor to Emperor Otto III, two dream scenes, each positioned as the first in a series of six enamel roundels that decorate each side of the shrine's roof, exemplify the dream's memorial function (Fig. 9.1).[8] These dreams attest to Heribert's dual role: first as leader in the worldly and political sphere and then as leader in the spiritual sphere.

The upper semicircle of the first roundel (Fig. 9.2) with its accompanying inscription, 'A vision of the sun splendidly marks the birth of the offspring,' pictorializes the event as it is recounted in Rupert of Deutz's twelfth-century *Vita Heriberti*, an elaboration of an eleventh-century life by Lambert of Deutz, from which the creator of the Heribert Shrine also drew.[9] As Heribert's father, Count Hugo, and a visiting Jew, here identified as Aaron, sleep, each sees in a dream the extraordinary light that fills the room in which Heribert is born.[10] A fragmentary sun, positioned at the top center of the semicircle, emits five shafts of light which enter the Count's towered and turreted palace and branch off to their intended recipients, three entering through a large central opening to the room of the birth and one each penetrating the lateral arches under which sleep the Count and the Jew. Both lie with their heads facing outward to the edge of the semicircle, a clear indication that they do not witness the scene with their corporeal eyes but rather with visionary eyes provided with sight through the efficacy of the heavenly beam which ends at their respective heads. In the central trilobed arch where the birth has occurred, a maidservant takes the newborn Heribert from his mother as the central beam of light shines directly on his head. For the viewer, this birth scene recalls representations of the Nativity of Christ in which beams of heavenly light announce his birth.[11] However, the visual borrowing in the case of the Heribert Shrine is more than fortuitous since Rupert in his *Vita* explicitly compares the birth of Heribert to the birth of Christ.[12] Furthermore, the artist, in placing the father and the Jew in separate fields and thereby requiring that a separate ray of light descend to each, reinforces the Christological parallel, for the two separated men thus become symbolic of the announcement of Christ's birth to both believers and non-believers, an apostolic mission which the saints still carry out in time.[13]

The event continues in the lower semicircle with the arrival of the awed and trembling servant who announces the auspicious birth to the men who, as Rupert tells us, converse at once about the meaning of their mutual phenomenon.[14] The accompanying inscription, 'His father and the Jew foresaw this thus,' confirms the dream's validity.[15] Visually the scene in this half of the roundel is actually more striking than the one above it. Now awake and dressed in noble attire, the father sits majestically in state beneath a curtain draped from the rod that separates the upper and lower scenes, his iconic image intensified by his size and frontality as well as by the word PATER that appears below his feet. Like Christ, Heribert has sprung from a noble lineage and will illuminate all who come into contact with him. The light of the saint has even penetrated the spiritually blind Jew who not only witnesses the event but also, as Rupert recounts, predicts Heribert's future renown.[16]

At the same time as this dream invokes the memory of Heribert's auspicious beginnings, it also invokes for the viewer the memories of those other saints whose births were announced through the appearance in a dream of a shining light. When before his birth the mother of Saint Daniel Stylites saw two great lights in her dream, her husband said it was proof that the child would outshine the stars.[17] Similar dreams foreshadowed the births of Saint Eutyche, Patriarch of Constantinople in the sixth century, Saint Loup of Sens in the seventh century, Saint Ariald of Milan in the eleventh century and Saint Franche in the twelfth century.[18]

These dreams, in turn, find biblical precedent in one of the more frequently depicted dreams in the Early Medieval period, the New Testament first dream of Joseph, in which the angel revealed to him the purpose of Christ's earthly mission.[19] By analogy, the hagiographic dream allowed the saint to follow in the footsteps of Christ by continuing that mission. And just as Joseph learned through the vehicle of the dream Christ's future role in the salvation of mankind, so the dreamer – in this instance both Heribert's father and Aaron the Jew (and vicariously the viewer) – becomes privy to the role of the future saint in the continuation of that salvific process. Thus, here compressed in a single roundel are prompts for recollecting the circumstances of Heribert's birth and future renown, the fact that his birth follows a venerable hagiographic tradition, and the paradigmatic association with Christ himself.

For the viewer, the dream also provides the point of entry to the events of the succeeding roundels on this side of the shrine where Heribert's life will confirm the validity of the dream.[20] The beams of light in the first roundel have not only indicated Heribert's sanctity but also seemingly effected it, for in the very next scene the young schoolboy Heribert has a halo. The remaining five roundels on this first side of the shrine emphasize Heribert's role as recipient: his education at the cathedral school of Worms and the monastic school of Gorze, his ordination and his appointment as Chancellor to Otto III, his investiture with the archiepiscopal insignia and then with the pallium in Rome, his return across the Alps and his humble entry barefoot into the city of Cologne, and finally his examination and his consecration as Archbishop of that city, thereby fulfilling his renown foretold in the dream.

As the creator of the shrine's iconography initiated Heribert's rise to power with a dream on the first side of the shrine, on the second side of the shrine he postponed the depiction of an earlier event in the *Vita* so that again a dream could inaugurate Heribert's spiritual and miraculous acts (Fig. 9.3).[21] Here, impelled by his own dream, Heribert will become the agent, initiating his public deeds of building, pastoral care, healing, and political reconciliation, until in the last roundel he finally comes full circle to his death, a scene which, on the shrine, is back to back with his birth and one in which light again appears.

While in the dream on the first side of the shrine Heribert's mother is cast in the role of Mary, in this second dream Mary herself – whose enthroned image on the end of the shrine intersects the narrative series of roof roundels – comes to the Archbishop in order to convey to him, as the inscription indicates, the form and location of the abbey that he and Emperor Otto III had vowed to build in her honor (Fig. 9.3).[22] Once again, Heribert's dream evokes *memoria*, prompting the viewer to remember a time-honored, religiously authenticated topos, for the dream as motivation for ecclesiastical construction had a long-standing textual tradition since the fifth century, ultimately finding its roots in the Old Testament dream of Jacob.[23]

In this roundel the artist has again combined two events – here the dream and its fulfillment. In the lower half of the roundel, the nimbed and tonsured Heribert sleeps turned away from the Virgin in the central medallion. As she looks down on him with her hand raised to convey her message, he raises his right hand in her direction to indicate his awareness of and compliance with her command. In the upper half of the roundel, the dream's fulfillment is already in progress as two workmen busily construct the abbey church in which Heribert himself will be subsequently interred.[24]

In this scene, the presence of Heribert's successor, Pilgrim (identified in the roundel by the inscription *Pilegim[us]*), is enigmatic, for the *Vita Heriberti* makes no mention of Pilgrim as part of this event.[25] In fact, the *Vita Heriberti* statement that Heribert's successor was not someone the monks of Deutz expected to succeed Heribert seems to make Pilgrim's actual physical presence at this event unlikely.[26] Because Mary faces the sleeping Heribert to whom she clearly gestures, there is no conclusive indication that Pilgrim actually participates in the dream. However, once again the artist's use of light might provide a clue. As Mary, described by the inscription as the 'glorious mother of light,' imparts her message to Heribert, flames of light emanate from the lower half of the medallion enframing her.[27] While Heribert's receptive hand intersects this light, Pilgrim, passively sleeping with his hand covering his mouth, is not touched by it.[28] Instead, a candlestick, its flame inclined in Heribert's direction, seems to stand as intermediary. Earlier in the *Vita*, in commenting on the significance of the light at Heribert's birth, Rupert describes Heribert as a great candlestick that will exalt the light of the Lord when Heribert accedes to the episcopal seat of Cologne, for in Rupert's view the mission of the consecrated bishop is to be the bearer of Christ's light to the world.[29] If then, through Heribert, Pilgrim receives the light, Pilgrim serves as confirming witness to the miraculous event, as did Aaron the Jew in the shrine's first roundel. Furthermore, as Heribert's successor, he represents the continuation of that confirmation even beyond Heribert's death, a perpetuator of the memory of the dream. Pilgrim's very position in the roundel can be likened to a marginal gloss to the narrative, a visual extension of the *Vita* in time.[30] Pilgrim thus becomes an analogue of the viewer likewise enjoined through seeing the vision to remember its content and its meaning.

The power of its individual elements notwithstanding, the Heribert Shrine, along with other similarly constructed reliquaries, may have a more intriguing connection with *memoria*, for the entire Heribert Shrine itself can be viewed as an analogue of memory. Medieval writers referred to memory as a compartmented treasure chest in which the discrete pieces of information would be appropriately sorted and stored for future retrieval.[31] Two of the chest metaphors used to describe memory, *scrinium* and *arca*, are also used in medieval sources to designate reliquary shrines.[32] If one views the Heribert Shrine in this light, one sees that the decorative elements of the shrine, like the sensory phantasms of memory, have been systematically arranged into discrete compartments, each assigned its appropriate place in the shrine's comprehensive program.

The ends of the shrine are reserved for the major personages, Mary, protectress of the abbey, enthroned and holding the Christ Child (Fig. 9.4), and Heribert, flanked by Charity and Humility, enthroned beneath Christ as judge of mankind (Fig. 9.5). The lower portions of the shrine emphasize Heribert's forebears (Figs 9.1, 9.6). Prophets, silently prophesying on their scrolls, are positioned on flat enamel strips, not only recalling strapwork on a treasure chest but also, together with the pilasters above them, preserving the memory of the earlier iron-banded wooden chest that contained Heribert's remains and that was encased within the reliquary shrine at its completion.[33] Apostles, speaking through their open books the tenets of the Apostles' Creed, are placed on seats (*sedes*) in cell-like spaces (*cellae*), both terms metaphors for memory.[34] The pilasters dividing the roof into discrete compartments are themselves segmented into small enamel squares highlighting the struggle between the virtues and the vices, emblem of the fight the faithful must wage to achieve the heavenly realm, here personified by angels in semicircles at the pilasters' ends (Figs 9.1, 9.3). Embossed on the roof's gilded background, itself teeming with life (an allusion to Heribert's having vanquished famine and drought?), in the compartments between pilasters, small medallions of the saints remind the viewer of the company Heribert now shares and of his intercessory role (Fig. 9.2). Finally, here amidst this backdrop, the key events of Heribert's *vita* have been distilled *summatim* to roundels of images circumscribed by summary text, their form allowing them to be seen simultaneously as coins of the treasure chest whose riches are to be mined and as miniature oculi – windows (*fenestellae*) to the life of the saint who lies within.[35] Functioning as *picturae*, pictures serving as markers in the meditational journey (*ductus*) to be followed in viewing the shrine, the roundels present Heribert's life in condensed form (*brevitas*), offering the viewer the opportunity for ruminative amplification as he moves both inwardly and sequentially, either pausing to isolate a roundel or passing on to meditate on its relationship to those which surround it.[36] Often the roundels themselves are compartmentalized by columns and arcades (*intercolumnia*), archi-tectural mnemonic devices for establishing sites (*loci*) for the various images (*imagines*) within each *pictura* that need to be remembered.[37] In sum, the reliquary shrine viewed as a treasure chest or *arca* paradoxically has its outer casing stripped away, everting memory as it were, making its contents open for all to see so that the viewer can store them in his own memory where the images will be distilled and ruminated upon. These elements of *memoria* are presented to the viewer for *meditatio*, so that in the memorial process he may through reflection and spiritual application provide his own gloss to this text. Akin to Aaron the Jew and to Pilgrim, the viewer must become a wit-ness and carry the meaning forward in time. And if, as Mary Carruthers has argued, the gathering of commentary is crucial in establishing an *auctor*, then the *vita* of a saint is never finished until the end of time.[38] Thus the thoughts and prayers added by those who visited the memorial tomb site continued to provide the 'gloss' to the pictorial *vita* and thereby perpetually authorized that saint's life, continuing even till now over eight hundred years hence.

The images on the Heribert Shrine provide the testimony that authenti-cates the sanctity of the relics within it by bearing witness to that sanctity. The dream providing entrance to the *vita* corroborates that sanctity by show-ing the saint in direct communication with the divine. In addition, it reminds the viewer that that contact is now perpetual, the saint functioning as an intercessor for those not yet in that privileged state. And the images in the roundels of the shrine clearly demonstrate that Heribert, a man whose life had been marked by divine intervention, was a saint to be remembered in times of need. In the spiritual sphere, he could cast out devils, restoring the soul to God; in the physical and social spheres, he could avert famine and drought; and in the political sphere, he could bring even an emperor to his knees.[39] The images on the reliquary shrine form a visual analogue of the saint within the shrine, the embodiment of his life in visual as opposed to textual form. Each worthy of contemplation in itself, when put together all the images reconstruct the saint's life, re-member and resurrect, as it were, the body within the shrine from birth to death, culminating in a secured place in heaven, where Heribert, now flanked by Charity and Humility, sits as intercessor among his forebears, the Prophets and Apostles, in the sight of God.

The end is in the beginning. The dream which opened the *vita* with a glorious light foreshadowed eternal light, the reward for a life of charity and humility now offered to the viewer for emulation. Heribert, at birth flanked by his mother and her maidservant (Fig. 9.2), now in eternity is flanked by Charity and Humility, and now himself enthroned, he is watched over not by his earthly father but by his heavenly father appearing in a medallion above him (Fig. 9.5). However, remembering the saint's life was not an end in itself but a means to salvation.[40] The viewer too must see the light, become through the gloss he provided to the *vita* an author of his own *vita*. Therefore viewing the shrine was an opportunity not only to witness and remember but also to participate. Recollection must lead to action if the viewer hoped to share eternity with the saint within.

The creators of the Heribert Shrine were clearly aware of the power of its very materials to initiate that process. The gems and crystals that adorn the shrine, its gleaming gold fabric and its brilliantly colored enamels not only allude on this church-shaped *arca* to the Heavenly Jerusalem but also serve as sensory stimuli to entice the viewer to contemplation.[41] Then once hooked, the viewer is to 'read' the shrine's images – not merely to store them but to enter into a conversation with them and to ruminate upon them, collecting the 'coins' for his *arca* or treasure chest. Through the process of *translatio*, he is to move them to his own *loci*, the cells (*cellae*) and arcades (*intercolumnia*) of his memory spaces. Just as the young Heribert at the cathedral school of Worms in the shrine's education roundel labors under the discipline of his teacher to copy on his tablet the exemplars of the letters of the alphabet that will enable him to read and write, so too the viewer, who needs to be edu-cated by the shrine's message, must discipline his life by copying onto the wax tablet of his own memory the exemplar of the life he sees before him, so that through the process of *inventio*, he can compose the story of his own life.[42] As the author of his own *vita*, the viewer must enclose and clothe (*venustare*) the matter (*res*) of that *vita* just as the shrine encloses and, in its re-membering function, clothes the saint within. Like Heribert, the viewer must put on the garments of Charity and Humility so that his soul will be beautiful in the sight of God.[43]

Finally, in this process of shaping his own *vita*, his *arca*, from the indi-vidual components of the Heribert Shrine, the viewer becomes the *architectus*, the master builder, of that *vita*, and since the Heribert Shrine as *arca* takes the form of a church, the viewer is analogously constructing his own *arca* in the form of a church, the very symbol of the route to his salvation, building it, as it were, on the shoulders of Heribert, who stands on the Apostles, who, in turn, are supported by the Prophets, who ultimately find their foundation in Christ. In the process of the viewer's edification, the images on the shrine serve as *machinae*, tools, for hoisting up the walls of the life the viewer con-structs through the process of emulation.[44]

In sum, as the viewer contemplates the images on the Heribert Shrine, like Heribert he must strive through an exemplary life for contact with the divine, finding his vocation in the Christian schema, serving God and his fellow man through the Church, casting out his own demons, reconciling with his enemies, winning his struggles over the vices that confront him, so that finally at his own death, having clothed himself with the virtues of

Charity and Humility, he may greet his Judge so as to take his place with those exemplars who have gone before him: the Prophets, Apostles, Heribert, and Christ himself. Thus, as heaven had come down to the saint through the medium of the dream, the viewer through reflection on the shrine's images was to reverse the journey, ascending heavenward through prayer, recollection and action, eventually to join the saint in eternity through the aid of his intercessory powers.

Frequently cited sources

Carruthers, M., *The Book of Memory: A Study of Memory in Medieval Culture*, Cambridge: Cambridge University Press, 1992.
— *The Craft of Thought: Meditation, Rhetoric, and the Making of Images, 400–1200*, Cambridge: Cambridge University Press, 1998.
Carty, C. M., 'Dreams in Early Medieval art,' unpublished PhD thesis, University of Michigan, 1991.
— 'The Role of Gunzo's Dream in the Building of Cluny III,' *Gesta*, vol. 27, 1988, pp.113–23.
— 'The Role of Medieval Dream Images in Authenticating Ecclesiastical Construction,' *Zeitschrift für Kunstgeschichte*, vol. 62, 1999, pp.45–90.
Dinter, P., *Rupert von Deutz*, Vita Heriberti: *Kritische Edition mit Kommentar und Untersuchungen*, Bonn: Ludwig Röhrscheid, 1976.
Kaiserin Theophanu: Begegnung des Ostens und Westens um die Wende des ersten Jahrtausends, Gedenkschrift des Kölner Schnütgen-Museums zum 1000. Todesjahr der Kaiserin, 2 vols, A. von Euw and P. Schreiner, eds, Cologne: Schnütgen Museum, 1991.
Lambert of Deutz, *Vita Heriberti*, MGH, Scriptores, vol. IV, Hanover, 1841, pp.739–53.
Müller, H., *Heribert, Kanzler Ottos III. und Erzbischof von Köln*, Cologne: H. Wamper, 1977.
— 'Heribert, Kanzler Ottos III. und Erzbischof von Köln,' *Rheinische Vierteljahrsblätter*, vol. 60, 1996, pp.16–64.
Ornamenta Ecclesiae: Kunst und Künstler der Romanik, 3 vols, edited by A. Legner, Exhibition Catalog, Schnütgen Museum, Josef-Haubrich-Kunsthalle, Köln; Cologne: Schnütgen Museum, 1985.
Schnitzler, H., *Rheinische Schatzkammer: Die Romanik*, Düsseldorf: L. Schwann, 1959, plate volume.
— *Der Schrein des Heiligen Heribert*, Mönchengladbach: B. Kühlen, 1962.

Notes

This paper was first presented in the session 'Between the Living and the Dead: Commemoration and the Sepulchral Arts' organized by Elizabeth Valdez del Alamo and Carol Pendergast at the International Congress on Medieval Studies in Kalamazoo, 1995. A version entitled 'Dream Images and the Heribert Shrine: The Art of Memory' was also presented at the Midwest Art History Society Conference, 18–20 March 1999, Detroit Institute of Arts, Detroit, Michigan. I would like to thank Thomas H. Haug for his astute criticism and editorial assistance at the various stages of this paper.

1. For a brief overview of the anthropological aspect of dreaming, see F. X. Newman, 'Somnium: medieval theories of dreaming and the form of vision poetry,' unpublished PhD thesis, Princeton University, 1962, pp.1–5. See also W. Wolff, *The Dream – Mirror of Conscience: A History of Dream Interpretation from 2000 B.C. and a New Theory of Dream Synthesis*, Westport, CT: Greenwood Press, 1952; S. Freud and D. E. Oppenheim, *Dreams in Folklore*, edited by J. Strachey, translated by A. O. M. Richards, New York: International Universities Press, 1958; P. Burke, 'L'histoire sociale des rêves,' *Annales: Economies, Sociétés, Civilisations*, vol. 28, 1973, pp.329–42; B. Tedlock, ed., *Dreaming: Anthropological and Psychological Interpretations*, Cambridge: Cambridge University Press, 1987; S. Parman, *Dream and Culture: An Anthropological Study of the Western Intellectual Tradition*, New York: Praeger, 1991.

2. For a brief discussion of the validity of dreams for the medieval period, see Carty, 'Role of Gunzo's Dream,' pp.113–16. The literature on dreams is enormous, even when one does not take into account works that have as their primary focus the psychological or anthropological aspects of the dream experience. The scope narrows when one considers those works which relate to the medieval period. For a discussion of the secondary literature on dreams that has a bearing on the study of dream images through the twelfth and early thirteenth centuries, see Carty, 'Dreams in Early Medieval art,' pp.3–5. To this should be added the following recent works: M. E.

Wittmer-Butsch, *Zur Bedeutung von Schlaf und Traum im Mittelalter*, Krems: Medium Aevum Quotidianum, 1990; M. Lieb, *The Visionary Mode: Biblical Prophecy, Hermeneutics, and Cultural Change*, Ithaca, NY/London: Cornell University Press, 1991; S. M. Oberhelman, *The Oneirocriticon of Achmet: A Medieval Greek and Arabic Treatise on the Interpretation of Dreams*, Lubbock: Texas Tech University Press, 1991; L. M. Bitel, 'In Visu Noctis: Dreams in European Hagiography and Histories, 450–900,' *History of Religions*, vol. 31, 1991, pp.39–59; S. F. Kruger, *Dreaming in the Middle Ages*, Cambridge: Cambridge University Press, 1992; C. Manhes-Deremble, *Les vitraux narratifs de la cathédrale de Chartres: Etude iconographique*, Paris: Le Léopard d'Or, 1993; R. Hiestand, ed., *Traum und Träumen: Inhalt, Darstellung, Funktionen einer Lebenserfahrung in Mittelalter und Renaissance*, Düsseldorf: Droste, 1994; P. C. Miller, *Dreams in Late Antiquity: Studies in the Imagination of a Culture*, Princeton, NJ: Princeton University Press, 1994; P. Dutton, *The Politics of Dreaming in the Carolingian Empire*, Lincoln, NE: University of Nebraska Press, 1994; R. K. Gnuse, *Dreams and Dream Reports in the Writings of Josephus: A Traditio-Historical Analysis*, Leiden, New York and Cologne: E. J. Brill, 1996; T. Ricklin, *Der Traum der Philosophie im 12. Jahrhundert: Traumtheorien zwischen Constantinus Africanus und Aristoteles*, Leiden, Boston and Cologne: E. J. Brill, 1998; S. Bogen, 'Denkformen in Bildergeschichten: Traumbilder in der christlichen Erzählkunst bis 1300,' unpublished PhD thesis, Philipps-Universität (Marburg), 1998; Carty, 'Role of Medieval Dream Images.'

3. Celestial communication is, of course, characteristic of waking visionary experiences as well. However, during the Middle Ages, in artistic representations there was not always an unequivocal distinction between dream and vision. In some depictions of textual dreams, the dreamer's eyes are open, as are St Joseph's in the depiction of his second dream (the angel's admonition to flee into Egypt) on the porch relief at Moissac or on the *Arca Santa* in the Cámara Santa in Oviedo Cathedral. For an illustration of the former, see M. Schapiro and D. Finn, *The Romanesque Sculpture of Moissac*, New York: George Braziller, 1985, p.108, fig. 120, and p.77, detail of fig. 120; for an illustration of the latter, see P. de Palol and M. Hirmer, *Early Medieval Art in Spain*, New York: H. N. Abrams, 1967, plate 75. Conversely, in some depictions of textual waking visions, the visionary is shown asleep with his eyes closed, that is, as a dreamer, as, for example, is St John the Evangelist in the Gerona *Beatus* of 975 (fol. 107) in his vision before the opening of the Seventh Seal or Ezekiel in the Winchester Bible (I [2], fol. 172) in his vision of the four winged beasts. For an illustration of the Gerona *Beatus* folio, see ibid., plate 47; for the Winchester Bible folio, see W. Oakeshott, *The Artists of the Winchester Bible*, London: Faber and Faber, 1945, plate XXXIV.

4. Carty, 'Role of Gunzo's Dream' and 'Role of Medieval Dream Images.'

5. Paris, Bibliothèque Nationale, MS lat. 17716, fol. 43. For an illustration of this miniature, see Carty, 'Role of Gunzo's Dream,' figs 1, 2. Carruthers discusses Gunzo's dream in light of Ezekiel's temple vision within the context of the trope of the 'place of the Tabernacle.' See *Craft of Thought*, pp.226–8, a slightly expanded version of her discussion of this dream in 'The Poet as Master Builder: Composition and Locational Memory in the Middle Ages,' *New Literary History*, vol. 24, 1993, pp.899–900. C. Rudolph relates the Gunzo story to the biblical story of the Tabernacle of Moses. See his 'Building-Miracles as Artistic Justification in the Early and Mid-Twelfth Century,' in *Radical Art History: Internationale Anthologie – Subject: O. K. Werckmeister*, edited by W. Kersten, Zurich: Zurich InterPublishers, 1997, p.401.

6. The literature on the early thirteenth-century Charlemagne Shrine is considerable. See R. Lejeune and J. Stiennon, *The Legend of Roland in the Middle Ages*, 2 vols, London and New York: Phaidon, 1971, vol. I, pp.169–77, which includes important earlier bibliography. See also H. Schnitzler, *Rheinische Schatzkammer*, pp.19–21; U. Nilgen, 'Amtsgenealogie und Amtsheiligkeit: Königs- und Bischofsreihen in der Kunstpropaganda des Hochmittelalters,' in K. Bierbrauer, P. Klein, and W. Sauerländer, eds, *Studien zur mittelalterlichen Kunst, 800–1250*, Festschrift für Florentine Mütherich zum 70. Geburtstag, Munich: Prestel, 1985, pp.217–34; H. P. Hilger, 'Zum Karlsschrein in Aachen,' *Jahrbuch der rheinischen Denkmalpflege*, vols 30–31, 1985, pp.55–74. For a discussion of the dream scene on this shrine, see Carty, 'Role of Medieval Dream Images,' pp.65–8, 71–3.
   On the late eleventh-, early twelfth-century Hadelin Shrine, see P. Bruyère, *L'église Saint-Martin de Visé: Guide du visiteur*, Visé: Wagelmans, 1987, pp.43–51, and A. Chevalier, *La châsse de saint Hadelin à Visé*, Gembloux: J. Duculot, 1973, which gives earlier relevant bibliography. See also *Rhein und Maas: Kunst und Kultur, 800–1400*, 2 vols, Cologne: Schnütgen Museum, 1972/3, vol. I, p.242, and S. Collon-Gevaert, J. Lejeune, and J. Stiennon, *A Treasury of Romanesque Art: Metalwork, Illuminations and Sculpture from the Valley of the Meuse*, translated by S. Waterston, London and New York: Phaidon, 1972, pp.85, 212. For a discussion of the dream scene on this shrine, see Carty, 'Dreams in Early Medieval art,' pp.46–8.
   On the twelfth-century Heribert Shrine, see M. Seidler, 'Schrein des hl. Heribert,' in *Ornamenta Ecclesiae*, vol. II, pp.314–23, which cites the relevant bibliography. Unfortunately Seidler's dissertation, 'Studien zum Reliquienschrein des heiligen Heribert in Deutz (Stadt Köln):

Rekonstruktion einer Entstehung,' unpublished PhD thesis, University of Bonn, 1992, is not yet available. Other than articles, to date H. Schnitzler's small monograph *Der Schrein des Heiligen Heribert* remains the only single work available that is devoted entirely to the shrine. For a discussion of this shrine's foundation dream in the context of the dream as a motivation for ecclesiastical construction, see Carty, 'Role of Medieval Dream Images,' pp.48, 51–3.

7. The dream as initiator of the narrative sequence is akin to a *Bildeinsatz*, a name given by the Austrian scholar O. Schissel von Fleschenberg to a rhetorical device used at the beginning of a work, the purpose of which was to present proleptically and allegorically the theme or plot that followed. See E. Keuls, 'Rhetoric and Visual Aids in Greece and Rome' in E. A. Havelock and J. P. Hershbell, eds, *Communication Arts in the Ancient World*, New York: Hastings House, 1978, pp.121–2.

8. On the historical Heribert, see H. Müller, *Heribert* and 'Heribert.' See also C. A. Lückerath, 'Die Kölner Erzbischöfe von Bruno I. bis Hermann II. in Annalen und Chroniken,' in *Kaiserin Theophanu*, vol. I, pp.68–9.

9. MAGNIFICE PROLIS NOTAT ORTVM VISIO SOLIS. For Rupert's *Vita*, see Dinter, *Rupert von Deutz* and for Lambert's, see Lambert of Deutz, *Vita Heriberti*. See also H. Müller, 'Die *Vita sancti Heriberti* des Lantbert von Lüttich,' in *Kaiserin Theophanu*, vol. I, pp.47–58.

10. Dinter, *Rupert von Deutz*, p.35. While Rupert mentions the presence of the Jew, he does not mention his name. While Lambert of Deutz also mentions the light, he makes no mention of the Jew: *Vita Heriberti*, p.741. Therefore the name Aaron that appears on the enamel either comes from yet another source or is the invention of the artist.

11. Examples of such Nativity scenes nearly contemporary with the Heribert Shrine appear on an enamel panel from the portable altar of Eilbertus of Cologne and an enamel panel (probably from an altar antependium) now in the Hildesheim Cathedral treasury. For illustrations of these panels see P. M. de Winter, *The Sacral Treasure of the Guelphs*, Cleveland, OH: Cleveland Museum of Art/Indiana University Press, 1985, p.66, fig. 74, for the former and p.71, fig. 81, for the latter.

12. Dinter, *Rupert von Deutz*, p.35.

13. For a discussion of the Jews in Worms and Cologne-Deutz during Heribert's lifetime and the period of the creation of the shrine, see J. Van Engen, *Rupert of Deutz*, Berkeley/Los Angeles/London: University of California Press, 1983, pp.241–8; Dinter, *Rupert von Deutz*, pp.92–4, 125–6; K. Schilling, ed., *Monumenta Judaica: 2000 Jahre Geschichte und Kultur der Juden am Rhein: Handbuch*, Cologne: J. P. Bachem, 1963, pp.49–55; H. Müller, *Heribert*, pp.49–50, 229–31. According to Müller, p.230, it was probably in Heribert's episcopacy that the Jews established their first synagogue in Cologne. See also idem, 'Heribert,' pp.42–3.

14. 'Et evigilantes continuo loquebantur ad alterutrum, quasi proprium singuli narraturi sompnium, quippe qui nescirent commune fuisse vel unum': Dinter, *Rupert von Deutz*, p.34.

15. HOC PREVIDIT ITA PATER EIVS ET ISRAHELITA.

16. 'Judeus quoque presagium future claritatis eius acceperit, qui et patri eius dixit: "Certissime noveris, quia, quod nascitur tibi, teipsum iocundidate replebit suosque natales magno sui nominis splendore illustrabit"': Dinter, *Rupert von Deutz*, p.35.

17. P. Saintyves, *En marge de la légende dorée: Songes, miracles et survivances*, Paris: Emile Nourry, 1930, pp.57–8.

18. ibid., p.58. For these and other instances, also see F. Lanzoni, 'Il sogno presago della madre incinta nella letteratura medievale e antica,' *Analecta Bollandiana*, vol. 45, 1927, pp.225–61.

19. For a list of representations of this dream and the sources which illustrate them, see Carty, 'Dreams in Early Medieval art,' Appendix I, Joseph, St: doubts about Mary dispelled, pp.160–63.

20. For illustrations of the roundels of the Heribert Shrine, see Schnitzler, *Der Schrein des Heiligen Heribert*, pp.27–38, or his more accessible *Rheinische Schatzkammer*, figs 90–95. All but three roundels, those depicting Heribert's birth, his consecration as Archbishop and his death, appear in *Ornamenta Ecclesiae*, vol. II, pp.318–22.

21. In Rupert's *Vita Heriberti*, as well as in Lambert's, the miracle of the rain (depicted in the third roundel on this side of the shrine) precedes the dream regarding the founding of Deutz (depicted in the first roundel on this side of the shrine): Dinter, *Rupert von Deutz*, pp.49–52, 54–5; Lambert of Deutz, *Vita Heriberti*, p.746.

22. Otto III's participation is mentioned by both Lambert, ibid., and Rupert, in Dinter, *Rupert von Deutz*, p.52. Otto died at the age of twenty-one in 1002, and the construction of the first abbey church took place from 1002 until 1003. See U. Krings, 'Kirchenbauten der Romanik in Köln,' in *Ornamenta Ecclesiae*, vol. II, pp.102–3, which gives a brief history of the church, and G. Binding,

'Ottonische Baukunst in Köln,' in *Kaiserin Theophanu*, vol. I, pp.293, 296–7. Both Lambert and Rupert recount that the first church fell down and was immediately rebuilt with the help, according to Lambert, of more experienced out-of-town builders ('peritiores architectos ab externis finibus'): Lambert, *Vita Heriberti*, pp.746–7, and Rupert, in Dinter, *Rupert von Deutz*, pp.55–6. This second church was constructed according to the centralized plan, similar to that of Aachen and St Gereon: Krings, p.102. B. Singleton sees it also as 'partly inspired by the Pantheon' and 'an important monument of Otto III's political policy of "Renovatio Imperii Romanorum".' See his 'Köln-Deutz and Romanesque Architecture,' *Journal of the British Archaeological Association*, vol. 143, 1990, p.49. In the shrine's roundel, the image of the church with its centralized plan must be seen as a reference to this second church which Heribert dedicated in 1019–20. On the site on which Heribert constructed this church, see M. Gechter, 'Das Kastell Deutz im Mittelalter,' *Kölner Jahrbuch für Vor- und Frühgeschichte*, vol. 22, 1989, pp.373–416. Gechter reproduces a twelfth-century seal from the abbey that depicts a conception of the church similar to that on the shrine's roundel: p.391, fig. 9.

23. See Carty, 'Role of Medieval Dream Images.'

24. Heribert died on 16 March 1021. Sometime during Archbishop Anno's episcopacy (1056–75), an altar was erected over Heribert's burial site. On 30 August 1147 Archbishop Arnold I of Cologne solemnly raised Heribert's remains. See Müller, *Heribert*, pp.306–15, and Schnitzler, *Schrein des Heiligen Heribert*, p.6.

25. Neither Rupert's *Vita* nor Lambert's mentions Pilgrim (Archbishop of Cologne from 1021–36) in connection with this event. Dinter notes that in regard to this scene 'Pilgrim is an addition of the enamel painters': *Rupert von Deutz*, p.96. In the chronology of the archbishops of Cologne, there are no other archbishops of Cologne named Pilgrim up to the time the Heribert Shrine was made in about 1170. See W. Neuss and F. W. Oediger, eds, *Das Bistum Köln von den Anfängen bis zum Ende des 12. Jahrhunderts*, Geschichte des Erzbistums Köln, 1, Cologne: J. P. Bachem, 1964, Table of Contents, Part Two, for a list of the archbishops from 787 to 1191. On Archbishop Pilgrim see ibid., pp.180–83, as well as H. Müller, 'Die Kölner Erzbischöfe von Bruno I. bis Hermann II. (953–1056),' in *Kaiserin Theophanu*, vol. I, pp.28–9, and C. A. Lückerath (as in n.8), pp.69–70.

26. 'Et quia de successore mentionem fecerat, altius in planctum excitati velut pupilli iam deserti percunctabantur et queritabant, quisnam tanto presule viduatam recepturus esset matrem ipsorum ecclesiam. "Ille" aiebant "vir vite venerabilis est, et ille alius utcumque idoneus est," atque ita diversorum qualitates perpendendo sollicitudinem suam invicem anhelando conferebant. At ille prophetico, ut iam supra dictum est, predoctus spiritu: "Neque illum" inquit "neque hunc, quem putatis, sed peregrinum episcopum habebitis, et hic in hac ecclesia pontificatus officium brevi tempore amministrabit"': Dinter, *Rupert von Deutz*, p.79. Migne's version of Rupert's *Vita* reads: 'sed Pillegrinum habebitis episcopum': PL, vol. CLXX, col. 422. In Lambert's *Vita*, p.753, in response to the monks' concerns, Heribert directly names Pilgrim as his successor 'Piligrimus Coloniae post me non in longum praesidere habet.'

27. LVMINIS INCLITA MAT[ER].

28. The gesture of the hand covering the mouth in sleep is exceedingly rare in dream representations from the ninth to the thirteenth century. While there are at least two other depictions showing the dreamer with his hand over his mouth, only one of these seems specifically to call attention to itself as in the shrine roundel. In the Winchester Bible representation of Ezekiel's vision of the four winged beasts, Ezekiel's coverlet, between his right hand and his face, only partially covers his right eye, his nose, and his mouth. For an illustration, see Oakeshott (as in n.3), plate XXXIV. However, in the representation of the dream of the Magi in the Bruchsal Evangeliary, a late twelfth-, early thirteenth-century Rhenish manuscript, one sleeping Magus, his hand enclosed in his sleeve, deliberately covers both his nose and his mouth. For an illustration, see A. Boeckler, *Deutsche Buchmalerei vorgotischer Zeit*, Königstein im Taunus: K. R. Langewiesche, 1953, p.58, or G. Schiller, *Iconography of Christian Art*, 2 vols, translated by J. Seligman, Greenwich, CT: New York Graphic Society, 1971–2, vol. I, plate 272. This gesture and that in the shrine roundel perhaps relate to the mythic belief that the soul during sleep could escape from the body via these orifices. See J. G. Frazer, *The Golden Bough: A Study in Magic and Religion*, 3rd edition, New York: Macmillan, 1935, vol. III, p.33. For a discussion of the physical characteristics of dreamers, see Carty, 'Dreams in Early Medieval art,' pp.21–4.

29. 'Cum ergo tante sedi preese deberet et super tale tantumque candelabrum exaltanda esset hec lucerna Domini, habendo tot facultates, habendo etiam nomen et ius eximium apud fastigium terreni imperii, sicut sequens narratio declarabit, non indigneri videri debet, quod Iudeus quoque presagium future claritatis eius acceperit . . . Lux fulgebit hodie super nos, consecratus est pontifex veri luminis baiulus, eorumque sortitus est ministerium, quibus dictum est: Vos estis lux mundi et cetera. Quis dubitet hoc evenisse per providentiam sive ordinationem Domini

eadem cura vel gratia, qua memoratum signum eo nascente premisit? Verum de hac re suo loco plenius dicendum erit; nunc ad inceptum revertamur': Dinter, *Rupert von Deutz*, p.35. Rupert also refers to this metaphor three more times in his *Vita*, pp.37, 46–7, 62.

30. On the relationship between glossed texts and memory, see Carruthers, *Book of Memory*, pp.213–18, where she writes: 'Truly it is commentary and imitation which make a text an "auctor" – not the activities of its writer but of its readers': p.214.

31. See ibid., pp.39–41, 42–5, where Carruthers discusses the terms *scrinium* and *arca* as models for memory and provides the medieval sources.

32. J. Braun, *Die Reliquiare: Des christlichen Kultes und ihre Entwicklung*, Freiburg im Breisgau: Herder and Co., 1940, pp.31–2 (*arca*), 34–6 (*scrinium*).

33. For an illustration of this wooden chest, see J. Braun, 'Der Heribertusschrein zu Deutz, seine Datierung und seine Herkunft,' *Münchner Jahrbuch der bildenden Kunst*, new series, vol. 6, no. 2, 1929, p.111, fig. 2. This inner shrine was on view in Sankt Heribert in Deutz in 1988 while the outer shrine was undergoing restoration. In 1147 Heribert's remains were solemnly removed from their burial place in the abbey church, and the present shrine was commissioned for them; see *Thioderici aeditui Tuitensis opuscula*, MGH, Scriptores, vol. XIV, Hanover, 1883, pp.570–71. No document exists to give a firm basis for dating the shrine; however, nearly all scholars date it for stylistic reasons to the 1160s. One dissenter, P. Lasko, does not accept the argument *ex silentio*. He dates the shrine to the 1150s, believing that its style exhibits 'a formative, immature stage' of the styles found on the shrines of the 1160s and that furthermore it is unlikely Heribert's remains would have been 'kept in an undecorated wooden sarcophagus for more than twenty years without even a start being made to provide more appropriate housing for his relics.' See P. Lasko, *Ars Sacra, 800–1200*, 2nd edition, New Haven, CT/London: Yale University Press, 1994, pp.202–4.

34. The disposition of the Apostles on the shrine is reminiscent of a passage in Bishop Bruno's *Vita quinque fratrum*. Bruno tells us that Saint Romuald admonished his monks to sit in their cells as if in paradise and put to the back of their memory everything worldly so that they would be focused on spiritual things ('Sede in cella quasi in paradiso: proice post tergum de memoria totum mundum, cautus ad cogitationes'): *Vita quinque fratrum*, paragraph 32, Monumenta Poloniae Historica, 6, Krakow, 1893, reprint 1961, p.427. For a discussion of the rhetorical use of the metaphor *cella*, see Carruthers, *Book of Memory*, pp.35–8.

35. In his *Didascalicon*, Hugh of Saint Victor uses the trope of the striking of a coin to explain how images are imprinted on the mind: 'When a coiner imprints a figure upon metal, the metal, which itself is one thing, begins to represent a different thing, not just on the outside, but from its own power and its natural aptitude to do so. It is in this way that the mind, imprinted with the likenesses of all things, is said to be all things and to receive its composition from all things and to contain them not as actual components, or formally, but virtually and potentially': *The Didascalicon of Hugh of St Victor: A Medieval Guide to the Arts*, translated by J. Taylor, New York: Columbia University Press, 1991, p.47. For the Latin, see *Hugonis de Sancto Victore*, Didascalicon: De Studio Legendi: A Critical Text, The Catholic University of America Studies in Medieval and Renaissance Latin, 10, Washington, DC: The Catholic University of America Press, 1939, book I, chapter 1, pp.5–6. Hugh elaborates on this metaphor in his *De Tribus Maximis Circumstantiis Gestorum*: 'You see how a money-changer who has unsorted coins, divides his one pouch into several compartments . . . Then, having sorted the coins and separated out each type of money in turn, he puts them all in their proper places, since the differentiation of his compartments preserves the separation and distinction of the items, and thus keeps them unmixed': Carruthers, *Book of Memory*, p.261. For the Latin see W. M. Green, 'Hugo of St Victor: *De tribus maximis circumstantiis gestorum*,' *Speculum*, vol. 18, 1943, p.488.

36. For a discussion of *pictura* in general, see Carruthers, *Book of Memory*, pp.221–3, and for its relation to *ductus*, see eadem, *Craft of Thought*, p.204. On the concept of *ductus*, ibid., pp.77–81. On the relationship of *brevitas* to memory, ibid., pp.63–5, 274–5. Just as memory is associative, so too the shrine can have many associative meanings, leading the viewer on his mental journey in many meditative directions according to the mental stores he has created in his own memory.

37. Carruthers sees the arcade motif as possibly deriving from the use of architectural features as *loci* for memory, specifically in this case to *intercolumnia* or the spaces between columns, the only architectural motif that had an 'unbroken history.' See *Book of Memory*, pp.93, 139. See also eadem, *Craft of Thought*, pp.270–71, where she discusses the associative value of the word *arca* in terms of its meaning both arch and ark or chest. M. T. Clanchy cites a specific instance in *From Memory to Written Record: England, 1066–1307*, 2nd edition, Oxford and Cambridge, MA: Blackwell, 1993, pp.163–4. For the relationship between *imagines* and *pictura*, see Carruthers, *Craft of Thought*, p.204.

38.   See note 30 above.

39.   For casting out devils: Dinter, *Rupert of Deutz*, pp.59–60; for its depiction on the shrine, see Schnitzler, *Rheinische Schatzkammer*, fig. 94, bottom, or *Ornamenta Ecclesiae*, vol. II, p.321, fig. 10. For famine and drought: Dinter, pp.49–52; for its depiction on the shrine, Schnitzler, fig. 94, top, or *Ornamenta Ecclesiae*, vol. II, p.320, fig. 9. For the political sphere: Dinter, pp.72–4; for its depiction on the shrine, Schnitzler, fig. 95, top, and *Ornamenta Ecclesiae*, vol. II, p.321, fig. 11. On the relationship between Heribert and Henry II, see Müller, *Heribert*, pp.160–94, and idem, 'Heribert,' pp.33–8.

40.   As Carruthers notes, 'memorial' in the medieval sense means 'making present the voices of what is past, not to entomb either the past or the present, but to give them life together in a place common to both in memory': *Book of Memory*, p.260. However, the memorial process also looked to the future, for, in engaging in that process, one incorporated the past into the present for the purpose of movement forward into a time that had yet to come, a movement toward eternity when, according to Christian theology, the earthly distinction of past, present, and future would become the unity of the eternal present.

41.   In describing the new Jerusalem, John says: 'The building of the wall thereof was of jasper stone: but the city itself pure gold, like to pure glass. And the foundations of the wall of the city were adorned with all manner of precious stones. The first foundation was jasper: the second, sapphire: the third, a chalcedony: the fourth, an emerald: the fifth, sardonyx: the sixth, sardius: the seventh, chrysolite: the eighth, beryl: the ninth, a topaz: the tenth, a chrysoprasus: the eleventh, a jacinth: the twelfth, an amethyst. And the twelve gates are twelve pearls, one to each': Apoc. 21.18–21.

42.   For an illustration of the education roundel see Schnitzler, *Rheinische Schatzkammer*, fig. 90, top half of the lower roundel, or *Ornamenta Ecclesiae*, vol. II, p.318, fig. 2, upper half. For a discussion of the use of wax tablets during the twelfth century, see Clanchy (as in n.37), pp.118–19. The use of the wax tablet as a metaphor for memory can be found in Cicero's *Ad Herennium*, book III, chapter 17: 'Those who know the letters of the alphabet can thereby write out what is dictated to them and read aloud what they have written. Likewise, those who have learned mnemonics can set in backgrounds what they have heard, and from these backgrounds deliver it by memory. For the backgrounds are very much like wax tablets [*loci cerae*],' in *Ad C. Herennium de Ratione Dicendi (Rhetorica ad Herennium)*, translated by H. Caplan, Cambridge, MA: Harvard University Press, 1954, reprint 1964, pp.208–9. Martianus Capella uses nearly the identical metaphor in his *De Nuptiis Philologiae et Mercurii*: 'As what is written is fixed by the letters on the wax, so what is consigned to memory is impressed on the places, as on wax or on a page; and the remembrance of things is held by the images, as though they were letters,' as quoted in F. Yates, *The Art of Memory*, Chicago: University of Chicago Press, 1966, p.51.

43.   On the rhetorical use of the metaphor of clothing an object (*venustas*) to give it eloquence and grace, see Carruthers, *Craft of Thought*, pp.127, 230.

44.   For a discussion of building metaphors, see ibid., pp.16–24.

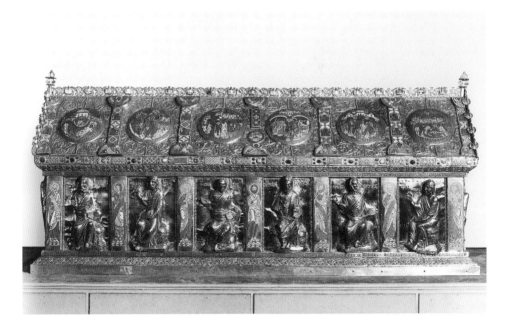

9.1   Heribert Shrine, Paul side, *c.*1160–70, Cologne-Deutz, Sankt Heribert

9.2 Birth of Heribert, enamel plaque of the Heribert Shrine, Peter side, *c*.1160–1170, Cologne-Deutz, Sankt Heribert

9.3   Dream of Heribert, enamel plaque of the Heribert Shrine, Paul side, *c.*1160–1170, Cologne-Deutz, Sankt Heribert

9.4   Mary enthroned, Marian end of Heribert Shrine, *c.*1160–70, Cologne-Deutz, Sankt Heribert

9.5   Heribert enthroned, Heribert end of Shrine, c.1160–70, Cologne-Deutz, Sankt
Heribert

9.6 The Prophet Naum, the Apostle Simon, and the Prophet Joel, Heribert Shrine, Paul side, *c.*1160–70, Cologne-Deutz, Sankt Heribert

10

The Queen's body and institutional memory: the tomb of Adelaide of Maurienne

Kathleen Nolan

This essay is dedicated to the memory of Stephen Gardner, whose vision of the cultural and political life of twelfth-century Paris has been the inspiration for my work on monuments linked with twelfth-century women.

The tomb slab of Adelaide of Maurienne, the first surviving effigy of a French queen and one of the very earliest examples of figural sepulchral sculpture from twelfth-century Paris, is still located in the church of Saint-Pierre-de-Montmartre, in Paris (Fig. 10.1).[1] It is in fragmentary condition, but it must have closely resembled the nearly contemporary cenotaph made for the remains of the Merovingian Queen Fredegonde (Fig. 10.2).[2] Adelaide, who was the wife of Louis VI, was among the most active of all Capetian queens in governance; she bore seven royal sons, and was of the most distinguished Carolingian descent. In spite of all this, upon her death in 1154 she did not join her husband, Louis VI, in the royal necropolis at Saint-Denis. Instead she was buried in the abbey church at Montmartre, a venerable foundation that Louis and Adelaide had rebuilt and converted to a Benedictine women's monastery (Fig. 10.3).

   This essay addresses three issues. First, the site of Adelaide's burial, at Montmartre rather than Saint-Denis, the locus of Capetian burial since Hugh Capet, where both her lineage and her extraordinary political activism would seem to have destined her. The second issue is the historicism implicit in Adelaide's tomb, the evocation of the venerated past through artistic forms, that marked the revival of monumental art and architecture in twelfth-century Paris. The final issue is the impetus behind this remarkable, little-studied funerary monument. Adelaide's burial formulated communal memory within the monastery at Montmartre. It also suggests that French queens maintained dynastic memory through their burials in a manner significantly different from that of kings. The case of Adelaide of Maurienne is especially valuable in understanding Capetian practice, since we know more about her tomb and its architectural surround than we do for any other French queen of the eleventh, twelfth, or early thirteenth centuries.[3]

Adelaide of Maurienne stood at the apogee of what Marion Facinger described as the partnership between king and queen early in the Capetian dynasty.[4] Adelaide's name appears forty-five times in charters signifying her participation in the decision-making process.[5] Facinger noted that Adelaide was not excluded from any aspect of the continually expanding royal authority, from granting protection to monasteries and churches to granting communal status to towns.[6] As a symbol of her partnership role, the Queen's regnal year appears, for the first time, along with the King's own, in royal acts.[7] Adelaide was also enmeshed in the political intrigues of the Parisian court in the 1120s and 1130s, most notably having machinated the temporary fall from grace of Louis's seneschal, Stephen of Garlande.[8]

Adelaide's dynastic associations, both in terms of lineage and progeny, were also formidable. Adelaide was of Carolingian descent, an issue of increasing concern to the Capetian dynasty in the twelfth century.[9] Adelaide, moreover, fulfilled the primary responsibility of a medieval queen, to produce a living male heir, with spectacular success. She and Louis had at least eight sons, seven of whom survived past infancy, as well as one daughter.[10] Adelaide's first born son, Philip, was consecrated as King during his father's lifetime, at the age of thirteen. When he died two years later, in 1131, after being thrown from his horse, he was buried at Saint-Denis with full royal honors.[11]

At the time of Adelaide's death in 1154, Saint-Denis had been the primary locus of Capetian burial since Hugh Capet was buried there in 996.[12] The only exception was Louis VI's father, Philip I, who chose instead to be buried at Saint-Benoît-sur-Loire when he died in 1109. Suger wrote that in so doing, he had acted against what was 'quasi jus naturalis.'[13] The tradition was not, of course, as firmly fixed as the monks of Saint-Denis would have liked, and Louis VII followed his grandfather's example in electing to be buried elsewhere.[14]

The presence of Capetian queens at Saint-Denis was by no means as inevitable. In the eleventh century, only Constance of Arles, second wife of Robert the Pious, was buried there, and in the twelfth century, only Constance of Castile, the second wife of Louis VII, who preceded her husband in death by two decades.[15] Apparently the dynastic numen that was so important to Suger and other abbots of Saint-Denis did not reside in the female royal body, or at least its absence was not regarded by them as being almost against natural law. At Saint-Germain-des-Prés in Paris, on the other hand, the remains of Merovingian queens as well as kings were part of the project to reinstall the royal tombs in the choir in time for the 1163 consecration, so that they might serve as a conspicuous reminder of early royal patronage at Saint-Germain.[16]

In 1975 Alain Erlande-Brandenburg published his magisterial study of the tombs and burial rituals of the French monarchy in the Middle Ages. In his book, significantly entitled *Le roi est mort*, whenever a king was buried somewhere other than Saint-Denis, Erlande-Brandenburg assumed a political motivation for the choice of a non-Dionysian site.[17] In the case of a queen buried somewhere else, however, Erlande-Brandenburg assumed that the option of burial at Saint-Denis had been denied her, and spoke of the queens who were buried there as having been thus 'privileged.'[18]

Even in Adelaide's case, Erlande-Brandenburg assumed that she had been excluded from Saint-Denis because of her remarriage after the death of Louis VI. Adelaide did remarry in 1139, but to Matthew of Montmorency, the Constable of France, who was closely connected with the royal house.[19] She herself managed her dower lands after her remarriage, and under the title of *Regina Francorum*, administered a portion of the royal domain.[20]

I believe that the queens not buried at Saint-Denis were not so much excluded against their will from the dynastic burial site, as following a separate, reginal burial tradition, as indeed, John Carmi Parsons has persuasively argued for certain English queens.[21] The Capetian queens not at Saint-Denis were buried on the premises of some other religious institution, generally in a monastic house with which they had established a direct, financial relationship, since for the laity the privilege of burial within the church was limited, at least in principle, to a founder of the institution.[22] The practice of queens founding or endowing religious houses was a strong tradition for the Capetians, beginning with Hugh Capet's wife, another Queen Adelaide of Carolingian descent, who restored the venerable monastery of Argenteuil, which had fallen into ruins by the late tenth century.[23] Several subsequent Capetian queens were buried at institutions that they had either founded or significantly benefitted. Sometimes they had directly acted in the interests of the institution in question. For example, Suzanne, repudiated first wife of Robert the Pious, was a significant benefactor of the abbey of Blandigny, where she was buried.[24] Others in this category include Adelaide herself, buried at her foundation at Saint-Pierre-de-Montmartre; the unfortunate Ingeborg, at a commandery near Corbeil that she had founded on her dower lands; and Blanche of Castile, wife and widow of Louis VIII and mother of Louis IX, at the Cistercian abbey of Maubisson, of which she was the founder.[25] The list may also include Anne of Russia, the widow of Henry I, who remarried after her husband's death. While her place of burial is not clear, there is a strong possibility that she was buried at Saint-Vincent at Senlis, of which she was the founder.[26] In other cases the relationship was more indirect, as in the case of Bertrade of Montfort, who was buried in the priory of Haute-

Bruyère, a dependency of Fontevrault, which had been founded on her dower lands.[27]

My argument here is that Capetian queens were in a sense freed, whether voluntarily or not, from the dynastic obligation to be buried at Saint-Denis. They were able instead to be interred in institutions with which they had been closely associated during their lifetimes, and so, by their place of burial, were able to continue those ties, at once spiritual and financial, that medieval society saw as bridging the gap between the living and the dead.[28]

The case of Adelaide of Maurienne is a valuable example of how this exchange functioned for Capetian queens. The church of Saint-Pierre-de-Montmartre occupies the presumed martyrdom site of St Dennis, where a sanctuary had stood since the early Middle Ages (Fig. 10.3).[29] An extensive Merovingian necropolis, which came to light in 1875 during the construction of the nearby Sacré Coeur, revealed the traces of a Merovingian cult structure around which the burials were clustered.[30] In 1096 the priory on the site became the property of Saint-Martin-des-Champs.[31]

In 1133 King Louis VI and Adelaide of Maurienne decided to found a women's monastery on the site, and were given the church at Montmartre and its dependencies in exchange for other properties in Paris.[32] The following year, the foundation charter of the new monastery stated that Louis had acted according to the prayers and urging of his wife Adelaide.[33] Adelaide's critical role in the founding of this abbey demonstrates her activism in the tradition of reginal philanthropy toward religious institutions. Her gift to Saint-Vincent-de-Senlis, founded by Anne of Russia, the widow of Henry I, who may well have been buried there, also suggests her awareness of this tradition.[34] In addition to this and other gifts to male institutions, there is also evidence of her special interest in women's houses. Adelaide is described as the sole founder of another abbey for women, Saint-Jean-de-Cuise, which she continued to endow, and gifts to other female monasteries are also recorded.[35]

In the church at Montmartre that Louis VI and Adelaide built for the nuns, the choir, the space reserved for the nuns, was dedicated to the Virgin and to St Dennis, while the altar of the nave, which served a parish function, was dedicated to St Peter. The choir, transept, and first bay of the nave were apparently complete at the time of the papal consecration in 1147.[36] Together with the nearby chapel of Saint-Martyr, the new church served as the sixth station of the octave of St Dennis (9–16 October).[37] Thus, the church was part of the liturgical procession that originated in the early twelfth century linking the abbey of Saint-Denis with sites associated with St Dennis in and around Paris.[38] Only the main church survived the Revolution, and in recent times has been known exclusively as Saint-Pierre.[39]

The hallowed history of the site seems to have been clearly in the minds of the builders of Louis and Adelaide's new church (Fig. 10.4). At Saint-Pierre-de-Montmartre, both actual *spolia*, in the form of reused Merovingian capitals atop antique marble columns, and historicizing twelfth-century forms evoked the church's connection with the earliest days of Parisian Christianity (Fig. 10.5). The late Stephen Gardner noted that the use of Merovingian elements and allusions reflected the newly-awakened consciousness throughout Paris of the venerable local past.[40] Most recently William Clark has observed that in their original location in Saint-Pierre, Merovingian columns and capitals would have bracketed the nuns' space and served as a constant reminder of the time-honored history of their monastery.[41]

Within the historically resonant space of Saint-Pierre-de-Montmartre, Adelaide's tomb similarly evoked and manipulated visual forms from the past. Adelaide's tomb slab is of incised limestone that was originally set with multicolored stone, like a large-scale mosaic (Fig. 10.1).[42] The holes in the stone suggest there must also have been an overlay of metal ornament.[43] The extremely rare technique used for Adelaide's tomb was also used in a contemporary effigy made for the Merovingian Queen Fredegonde for her revamped tomb at Saint-Germain-des-Prés, completed by 1163 (Fig. 10.2).[44] The royal status of both queens is emphasized by their crowns, as well as their long, unbound hair and gesture of affirmation, which appear to allude to the coronation ritual.[45]

Erwin Panofsky, who discussed Fredegonde's tomb, but did not know Adelaide's, assumed that there was a continuity of practice in the production of mosaic tomb slabs from the Merovingian period into the twelfth century. He thus believed that the Fredegonde effigy was simply a 'modern' twelfth-century replica of the Merovingian original.[46] In fact, there is no evidence that the Merovingians used mosaic-type tombs, and only very isolated examples of the technique survive from earlier in the twelfth century.[47] The Fredegonde tomb, like the now lost tomb of her husband Chilperic, was instead an effigy created from scratch, *ex novum*, in the early 1160s for Saint-Germain-des-Prés as part of the calculated campaign to exploit the Parisian abbey's venerable royal relics and to counter the claims of Saint-Denis to being the exclusive locus of royal burial.[48] The choice of the mosaic-like technique for this purpose is also significant. It doubtless called to mind the now lost mosaic from the Saint-Denis west portal in the late 1130s, and thus may have reenforced the Parisian abbey's reference to its own ancient history.[49]

The circumstances behind the creation of Fredegonde's effigy give us insight into the impetus behind Adelaide's tomb. In 1153 Adelaide parted from her second husband and entered the community at Saint-Pierre-de-Montmartre. She apparently took holy orders and died at the monastery the following year.[50] Adelaide was presumably buried in the choir before the main altar, as befitted a royal founder.[51] No documents survive to tell us who

commissioned her remarkable funerary monument nor what its date is relative to the Fredegonde effigy.[52] The monastics at Saint-Pierre could, like their
counterparts at Saint-Germain, have elected to commemorate their royal
founder in an elaborate and historicizing tomb.[53] The likeliest sponsor of the
tomb, however, is Queen Adelaide herself, given her exceptional independ-
ence and her vigorous patronage of women's institutions.[54] Adelaide must
have known of her right as foundress to be buried within the church itself.
She must also have known of the long history of Montmartre as a burial site,
since the existence of the Merovingian necropolis was doubtless revealed
during the construction of Adelaide's church after 1134.[55] Her sense of her
own Carolingian heritage may have inspired her, or the artisans working at
her direction, to use the historically potent form that her effigy took.[56]

Once enshrined in a conspicuous tomb before the main altar, the remains
of the royal founder may have allowed the community at Montmartre to
exploit its venerable past in a way that helped to ensure the future of the
monastery. Adelaide's body enabled the nuns of Montmartre, like the monks
of Saint-Germain-des-Prés, to be linked with Saint-Denis as a locus of royal
burial, an association that, for Saint-Pierre, was strengthened by shared rituals of the cult of St Dennis.[57] The presence of the remains of the royal founder
interred in front of the main altar doubtless served as a talisman to the nuns,
a visible reminder both of the monastery's revered history as the site of the
martyrdom of St Dennis, first Bishop of Paris, and of its more recent and
royal foundation as a women's abbey. The Queen's body thus added to the
prestige already derived from the Merovingian necropolis of Saint-Pierre-de-
Montmartre as a site of Christian burial.

This valuable recent and ancient past was of great strategic importance to
the nuns of Montmartre, given the lesser financial means of female institutions and their vulnerability in an age of active strict enclosure.[58] The visible
presence of the royal founder may have helped the nuns at Saint-Pierre
withstand the forces that undid the women's houses of Argenteuil, in 1129,
of Saint-Eloi, Paris, in 1107, and of Notre-Dame et Saint-Jean in Laon, in
1128, and also threatened the distinguished abbey at Chelles in 1133.[59] The
potency of the royal relic was strengthened by its distinctive style, which
reenforced the claim, in an uncertain present, to a distinguished past.[60]

The tomb of Queen Adelaide at Saint-Pierre-de-Montmartre was thus united
to the institution's memory in multiple ways. It participated in the self-
conscious historicism of the mid-twelfth century and in the skillful exploita-
tion of relics of all kinds in that period, as well as in the competition between
monasteries to possess the tangible remains of royal dynasties. And for the
women's house that possessed Adelaide's body, it also evoked the presence
of a powerful founder against possible threats to the monastery's autonomy.

It is clear that at Saint-Pierre the tomb of Queen Adelaide experienced a powerful afterlife, perpetuating the ties that had existed between Adelaide and her foundation during her lifetime and linking the relics of the founder to the abbey's most ancient roots. Adelaide's tomb, ironically enough, thus possessed a potent and individualized imagery absent from her husband's tomb at Saint-Denis, which was marked only by an inscription until the abbey's spectacular reinstallation of its own royal relics in the late thirteenth century.[61] Thus it was the tomb of a queen, whose burial tradition was more individualized, in a sense more personal than that of a king, with his dynastic obligations, that produced the first full surviving effigy of a contemporary ruler in France.[62]

Frequently cited sources

Brown, E. A. R., 'Burying and Unburying the Kings of France,' in R. C. Trexler, ed., *Persons in Groups: Social Behavior as Identity Formation in Medieval and Renaissance Europe*, Papers of the Sixteenth Annual Conference of the Center for Medieval and Early Renaissance Studies, Binghamton, NY: Medieval and Renaissance Studies and Texts, 1985, pp.243–66.

Deshoulières, F., 'L'église Saint-Pierre-de-Montmartre,' *Bulletin monumental*, vol. 77, 1913, pp.5–13.

Dumolin, M., 'Notes sur l'abbaye de Montmartre,' *Bulletin de la Société de l'histoire de Paris et de l'Ile-de-France*, vol. 58, 1931, pp.145–238, 244–325.

Erlande-Brandenburg, A., *Le roi est mort: étude sur les funérailles, les sépultures, et les tombeaux des rois de France jusqu'à la fin du XIIe siècle*, Geneva: Droz, 1975.

Facinger, M. F., 'A Study of Medieval Queenship: Capetian France, 987–1237,' in W. M. Bowsky, ed., *Studies in Medieval and Renaissance History*, vol. V, Lincoln: University of Nebraska Press, 1968, pp.3–47.

Gerson, P. L., ed., *Abbot Suger and Saint-Denis: A Symposium*, New York: The Metropolitan Museum of Art, 1986.

Lewis, A. W., *Royal Succession in Capetian France: Studies on Familial Order and the State*, Cambridge, MA: Harvard University Press, 1981.

Luchaire, A., *Etudes sur les actes de Louis VII*, Paris: Alphonse Picard, 1885; reprinted, Brussels: Culture et Civilisation, 1964.

— *Histoire des institutions monarchiques de la France sous les premiers Capétiens*, Paris: Alphonse Picard, 1888.

— *Louis VI le Gros. Annales de sa vie et de son règne*, Paris: Alphonse Picard, 1890; reprinted, Brussels: Culture et Civilisation, 1964.

Parsons, J. C., ed., *Medieval Queenship*, New York: St Martin's Press, 1993.

— ' "Never was a body buried in England with such solemnity and honor": The Burials and Posthumous Commemorations of English Queens to 1500,' in Anne Duggan, ed., *Queens and Queenship in Medieval Europe*, London: Boydell & Brewer, 1997, pp.317–37.

Périn, P., P. Velay, and L. Renou, 'Eglise Saint-Denis, devenue Saint-Pierre-de-Montmartre,' *Collections Mérovingiennes du Musée Carnavalet*, exhibition catalogue, Paris: Le Musée Carnavalet, 1985, pp.94–113.

Wright, G. S., 'A Royal Tomb Program in the Reign of St Louis,' *The Art Bulletin*, vol. 56, 1974, pp.224–43.

Notes

This essay originated in a paper presented in the session, 'Between the Living and the Dead: Commemoration and the Sepulchral Arts,' organized by Elizabeth Valdez del Alamo and Carol Pendergast for the May 1995 meeting of the International Congress on Medieval Studies. I am grateful to both session organizers for their warm encouragement and insightful suggestions. I should also especially acknowledge the assistance of John Carmi Parsons, whose work on English queens has greatly enriched my work on their French counterparts. I am particularly grateful to him for sending me, when my essay was in its final stages, the manuscript of his stimulating article, ' "Never was a body buried in England with such solemnity and honor": The Burials and Posthumous Commemorations of English Queens to 1500.' I am also indebted to William Clark for sharing with me the rich results of his ongoing work, to which I will refer below, on the architecture of the church of Saint-Pierre-de-Montmartre.

1. The tomb slab of Adelaide of Maurienne has not been widely discussed in the literature on twelfth-century sculpture nor the sepulchral arts, no doubt at least in part because of its fragmentary condition. It is true, however, that French queens and their monuments have not, in general, been as systematically discussed as their English counterparts. See below, n.3, for important sources for French and English queens. The principal discussion of Adelaide's tomb appears in Erlande-Brandenburg, *Le roi est mort*, pp.89–90, 160–61. Accounts of the discovery of the tomb slab appeared in the 1901 edition of the *Commission du vieux Paris, procès verbaux*: L. Sauvageot, 'Découverte d'une pierre tumulaire du XIIe siècle à l'église Saint-Pierre-de-Montmartre,' pp.108–9, and C. Sellier, 'Communication de M. Charles Sellier relative au tombeau de la reine Adélaïde de Savoie et aux sépultures conventuelles et paroissiales de Montmartre,' pp.109–18. Brief references to the tomb slab appear in E. A. R. Brown, 'Burying and Unburying.'

2. Every author who has discussed the Adelaide effigy has noted its resemblance to Fredegonde's monument: see, for example, Sauvageot (as in n.1), p.108; Erlande-Brandenburg, *Le roi est mort*, pp.160–61; Brown, 'Burying and Unburying,' p.243. The most recent discussion of the effigies of Adelaide and Fredegonde, that of W. Clark, argued for a date in the mid-1150s for the Saint-Germain tombs: 'Defining National Historical Memory,' forthcoming.

3. The comprehensive catalog of tombs in Erlande-Brandenburg's *Le roi est mort* is an invaluable resource, supplying all of the surviving evidence concerning the burials of the French kings and queens. As noted below, the burial place of Adelaide of Poitou, wife of Hugh Capet, is unrecorded. The tombs of the two queens who were buried at Saint-Denis, Constance of Arles, †1032, and Constance of Castile, †1160, were without sculpture or ornament until the great tomb project at Saint-Denis during the reign of Louis IX. For these two queens, see *Le roi est mort*, pp.158, 162. For the funerary monuments erected at Saint-Denis in the thirteenth century, see G. Wright, 'A Royal Tomb Program,' and E. Brown, 'Burying and Unburying.' Of the queens not at Saint-Denis, in the years before Adelaide, Anne of Russia may have been buried at Saint-Vincent-de-Senlis, but no solid information survives: *Le roi est mort*, pp.88–9, 159. We are more knowledgeable about the tomb of Bertrade of Montfort, †1128, who was buried at Haute-Bruyère under a copper plate that survived until the Revolution, but of which no description survives: Erlande-Brandenburg, *Le roi est mort*, pp.89, 160.

4. Still the best source for Capetian queenship is Facinger, 'A Study of Medieval Queenship,' pp.2–48 (pp.27–35 for the career of Adelaide). Adelaide also figures in the rather general study of French queenship by F. Barry, *La reine de France*, Paris: Les Editions du Scorpion, 1964, pp.80–81; in the informative study by B. B. Rezak, 'Women, Seals, and Power in Medieval France, 1150–1350,' in M. Erler and M. Kowaleski, eds, *Women and Power in the Middle Ages*, Athens, GA: University of Georgia Press, 1988, pp.61–82 (pp.63–4 for Adelaide's use of seals); and most recently in A. Poulet, 'Capetian Women and the Regency: The Genesis of a Vocation,' in Parsons, ed., *Medieval Queenship*, pp.93–116 (pp.107–8 for Adelaide, which concentrates on the limits placed upon queens' political power). Other discussions of Adelaide appear in studies devoted chiefly to male monarchs, such as A. Luchaire, *Histoire des institutions monarchiques*, pp.147–8, 150–51, 179–80; idem, *Louis VI*, pp.xlvi–l, and the relevant charters discussed below; idem, *Etudes sur les actes de Louis VII*, pp.12–14, 45–6; M. Pacaut, *Louis VII et son royaume*, Paris: S.E.V.P.E.N., 1964, pp.36–7, 40–41, 95–6; A. W. Lewis, *Royal Succession*, pp.54–6, 61–2, 107; and M. J. Dufour, *Recueil des actes de Louis VI. Roi de France (1108–1137)*, Paris: Diffusion du Boccard, 1993, vol. III, pp.119–221.

Until recently, few studies had focused on the ritual and political life of French queens, valuable exceptions, for the fourteenth century, being the work of C. R. Sherman, 'The Queen in Charles V's "Coronation Book": Jeanne de Bourbon and the "Ordo ad reginam benedicendam",' *Viator*, vol. 8, 1977, pp.255–309, and 'Taking a Second Look: Observations on the Iconography of a French Queen, Jeanne de Bourbon (1338–1378),' in N. Broude and M. D. Garrard, eds, *Feminism and Art History: Questioning the Litany*, New York: Harper & Row, 1982, pp.100–117. Scholarship in the 1990s has devoted more attention to queens in general in their own right. In the forefront of this effort is John Carmi Parsons, editor of *Medieval Queenship*, with his many contributions to English reginal history. See, among his numerous studies, 'Ritual and Symbol in the English Queenship to 1550,' in L. O. Fradenburg, ed., *Women and Sovereignty*, Cosmos, 7, Edinburgh: Edinburgh University Press, 1992, pp.60–77; 'Mothers, Daughters, Marriage, Power: Some Plantagenet Evidence, 1150–1500,' in Parsons, ed., *Medieval Queenship*, pp.63–78; and *Eleanor of Castile: Queens and Society in Thirteenth-Century England*, New York: St Martin's Press, 1995.

Scholarship on French queens continues to lag behind that of their English counterparts. While much valuable information on the funerary practice and sepulchral art of French queens is included in Erlande-Brandenburg's *Le roi est mort*, these aspects of French queenship have not yet received the consideration that Parsons has given to female English monarchs in his wide-ranging essay, 'The Burials and Posthumous Commemorations.' An important exception is the work of E. McCartney, 'The King's Mother and Royal Prerogative in Early Sixteenth-Century France,' in Parsons, ed., *Medieval Queenship*, pp.117–41, and 'Ceremonies and Privileges of Office: Queenship in Late Medieval France,' in J. Carpenter and S.-B. MacLean, eds, *Power of the Weak: Studies on Medieval Women*, Urbana and Chicago: University of Illinois Press, 1995, pp.178–219.

5. Facinger, 'Medieval Queenship,' pp.33–4.

6. ibid., p.29. For charters involving protection of monasteries and churches see Luchaire, *Louis VI*, nos 310, 569, 570, 585. Charters granting communal privileges are nos 419 and 435. Adelaide's consent is mentioned along with that of her eldest son, Philip, or after his death in 1131, that of the future Louis VII.

7. Facinger, 'Medieval Queenship,' p.28. The first mention of Adelaide's regnal year on a charter appeared in 1115, the year of her marriage.

8. Luchaire, *Histoire des institutions monarchiques*, pp.179–80, and *Louis VI*, pp.xlv–xlvi, and nos 399, 426. In 1127, at Adelaide's urging, Louis VI stripped Stephen of the offices of seneschal and chancellor (no. 399). In 1128, while Stephen was in disgrace, Adelaide ordered the rasing of his luxurious houses in Paris (no. 426). For a further discussion of the career of Stephen of Garlande, see R.-H. Bautier, 'Paris au temps d'Abélard,' *Abélard en son temps. Actes du Colloque International organisé à l'occasion du 9e centenaire de la naissance de Pierre Abélard (14–19 mai 1979)*, Paris: Belles lettres, 1981, pp.21–77 (pp.58–69, for Stephen).

9. Lewis, *Royal Succession*, pp.106–7, discussed the growing importance of Carolingian connections for Capetians in the late eleventh and twelfth centuries. Adelaide was also related to the Countess of Flanders: Luchaire, *Louis VI*, no. 187, and Lewis, *Royal Succession*, p.247 n.43; and to Pope Calixtus II: Lewis, p.268 n.16.

10. For the evidence for Adelaide's sons and daughter, Constance, see Lewis, *Royal Succession*, pp.57–8, 248–9 n.61.

11. ibid., p.56. Suger stated that he was buried according to royal custom at Saint-Denis, in the tomb of the kings on the left side of the altar of the Holy Trinity: *The Deeds of Louis the Fat*, translated by R. Cusimano and J. Morrhead, Washington, DC: Catholic University of America Press, 1991, p.150. See also Erlande-Brandenburg, *Le roi est mort*, p.76.

12. For Saint-Denis as the Capetian necropolis, see G. Wright, 'A Royal Tomb Program,' pp.224–43; G. M. Spiegel, 'The Cult of St Denis and the Capetian Kings,' *Journal of Medieval History*, vol. 1, 1975, pp.43–70; Erlande-Brandenburg, *Le roi est mort*, pp.68–86; E. M. Hallam, 'Royal Burial and the Cult of Kingship in France and England, 1060–1330,' *Journal of Medieval History*, vol. 8, 1982, pp.359–80; and E. Brown, 'Burying and Unburying,' pp.241–4.

13. For Suger's response to the choice of burial of Philip I, see Wright, 'A Royal Tomb Program,' pp.226–7 (citing the description of Philip's death and burial in *Vita gloriosissimi Ludovici*: 'dicebant siquidem qui ab eo audierant quod a sepultura patrum suorum regum, quae in ecclesia beati Dionysii quasi jure naturali habetur,' as found in A. Lecoy de la Marche, *Oeuvres complètes de Suger*, Société de l'Histoire de France, 139, Paris: J. Renouard, 1867, pp.47–8); and Brown, 'Burying and Unburying,' p.242.

14. Erlande-Brandenburg, *Le roi est mort*, p.76; Brown, 'Burying and Unburying,' pp.243–4.

15. Erlande-Brandenburg, *Le roi est mort*, p.75, for Constance of Arles, and p.77, for Constance of Castile.

16. W. W. Clark, 'Spatial Innovations in the Chevet of Saint-Germain-des-Prés,' *Journal of the Society of Architectural Historians*, vol. 38, 1979, p.360 n.36; and Brown, 'Burying and Unburying,' pp.242–3.

17. For example, he reasoned that Philip I had chosen to be buried at Saint-Benoît-sur-Loire as a reflection of the expansion of the royal domain along the Loire: pp.75–6.

18. Erlande-Brandenburg, *Le roi est mort*, p.8. He acknowledged that the question of why a queen was not buried with her husband at Saint-Denis is not easily resolved, and alluded to what he charmingly described as the 'vie matrimoniale agitée' of the early Capetians as a probable explanation: p.75. Several of the queens not buried at Saint-Denis were repudiated by their husbands and thus probably did not have the option of being buried at Saint-Denis, although only in the case of Ingeborg, Philip Augustus's rejected second wife, do we know of a repudiated Queen who requested and was denied burial at Saint-Denis. See p.75 for the earlier repudiated queens, Suzanne, first wife of Robert I, and Bertha, wife of Philip I; and pp.77, 90, for Ingeborg.

19. Facinger, 'Medieval Queenship,' pp.44–5, citing Luchaire, *Louis VI*, p.lxiv, noted that the constable was one of the king's four chief officers, who would be closely allied with the king. Luchaire, *Histoire des Institutions Monarchiques*, pp.167–8, discussed the evolution of the office of *constabularius*.

20. Facinger, 'Medieval Queenship,' pp.44–5. After the death of Louis VI, Adelaide still appears as the consenter to or petitioner of numerous royal acts, even after her retirement from court; Luchaire, *Etudes sur les actes de Louis VII*, nos 90, 110, 118, 172, 182, 258. It was also during her dowager years that Adelaide began sealing in her own right: Rezak (as in n.4), pp.63–4.

21. Parsons, 'The Burials and Posthumous Commemorations,' pp.325–31.

22. The restrictions on the burial of the laity within churches are articulated, closest to our period, in the writings of the thirteenth-century liturgist, Durandus of Mende, in his *Rationale divinorum officiorum*, Naples: J. Dura, 1859, p.37: 'Nullum ergo corpus debet in Ecclesia, aut prope altare, ubi corpus Domini et sanguinis conficitur, sepeliri, et nisi corpora sanctorum Patrum, qui dicuntur patroni, idest defensores, qui meritis suis totam defendunt patriam, et Episcopi, Abbates, et digni Presbyteri, et laici summa sanctitatis.' The text is discussed by P. Ariès, *The Hour of Our Death*, translated by H. Weaver, New York: Oxford University Press, 1981, pp.46–7. The example of one Capetian Queen demonstrates the force of the prohibition on burial of lay persons in the church. Adele of Champagne, second wife of Louis VII, asked permission to be buried with her husband, who had died many years earlier, in the Cistercian abbey of Barbeau, which he had founded. The monks denied permission to the dowager Queen, on the basis that she herself was not a founder: Erlande-Brandenburg, *Le roi est mort*, p.90. For the evolution of the Christian desire to be buried in churches, initially for the protection of the saints buried therein, see Peter Brown, *The Cult of the Saints*, Chicago: University of Chicago Press, 1981; and Ariès, *The Hour of Our Death*, pp.46–51, 71–3, who noted that by the twelfth century, the attraction was proximity to the altar and the celebration of the Mass.

23. For Early Medieval queens as the founders of monastic houses, see P. Stafford, *Queens, Concubines, and Dowagers: The King's Wife in the Early Middle Ages*, Athens, GA: University of Georgia Press, 1983, pp.178–89. For the restoration of Notre-Dame at Argenteuil by Adelaide of Poitou, see A. Lesort, 'Argenteuil,' in *Dictionnaire d'histoire et de géographie ecclésiastiques*, Paris: Letouzey et Ane, 1930, vol. IV, p.23. For the lack of information concerning the site of this Adelaide's burial, see Erlande-Brandenburg, *Le roi est mort*, pp.75, 88. Excavations at Argenteuil in recent years, under the direction of Jean-Louis Bernard, have revealed the foundations of the Romanesque abbey church.

24. Suzanne was repudiated by Robert the Pious and at her death was buried beside her first husband at Blandigny: Erlande-Brandenburg, *Le roi est mort*, p.88.

25. For Ingeborg, Erlande-Brandenburg, *Le roi est mort*, p.91, and for Blanche of Castile, pp.91, 165.

26. Erlande-Brandenburg, *Le roi est mort*, pp.88–9.

27. Bertrade joined a Fontevriste house after her husband's death in 1108. In 1112, Louis VI helped to found the priory of Haute-Bruyère on land that had been given to Bertrade as part of her dower, and in 1128 Bertrade was buried there. Erlande-Brandenburg, *Le roi est mort*, pp.89, 160.

28. For the sense of interconnectedness between the living and dead that so distinguishes the medieval attitude toward death from our own, see, in addition to Brown (as in n.22), the brilliant essays by Patrick Geary in two recent books, *Phantoms of Remembrance: Memory and Oblivion at the End of the First Millennium*, Princeton, NJ: Princeton University Press, 1994, and especially *Living with the Dead in the Middle Ages*, Ithaca, NY: Cornell University Press, 1994. For a revealing study of a case close in time to Adelaide, see Clark Maines, 'Good Works, Social Ties, and the Hope for Salvation: Abbot Suger and Saint-Denis,' in P. L. Gerson, ed., *Abbot Suger and Saint-Denis*, pp.76–94.

29. The chief published studies for Saint-Pierre-de-Montmartre are: E. de Barthélémy, ed., *Recueil des chartes de l'abbaye royale de Montmartre*, Paris: H. Champion, 1883; Deshoulières, 'L'église Saint-Pierre de Montmartre'; Dumolin, 'Notes sur l'abbaye de Montmartre'; as well as two brief notices: Denis Fossard, 'L'église Saint-Pierre, anciennement Saint-Denis,' in 'Les anciennes églises suburbaines de Paris (IVe-Xe siècles),' *Paris et Ile-de-France. Mémoires de la Fédération des Sociétés Historiques et Archéologiques de Paris et de l'Ile-de-France*, vol. 11, 1960, pp.208–25; and A. Erlande-Brandenburg, 'Eglise Saint-Pierre-de-Montmartre,' in *Dictionnaire des Eglises de France*, IVc, Paris: Robert Laffont, 1968, pp.103–4. For the history of the abbey during the Merovingian period, see the excellent short essay by P. Périn et al., 'Eglise Saint-Denis, devenue Saint-Pierre de Montmartre.'

30. Périn, 'Eglise Saint-Denis,' p.98.

31. Dumolin, 'Notes,' pp.147–8.

32. Dumolin, 'Notes,' pp.149–50.

33. '(E)t prece et consilio karissime uxoris nostre Adelaidis regine,' Barthélémy (as in n.29), pp.60–61; Dumolin, 'Notes,' pp.149–52; Luchaire, *Louis VI*, no. 536. The original foundation charter does not survive, but is reproduced in four thirteenth-century copies in the Archives Nationales as well as several later copies.

34. Luchaire, *Etudes sur les actes de Louis VII*, no. 172, for the 1146 confirmation by Louis VII of Adelaide's gift to the abbey. It is not always this obvious that the twelfth-century Capetians were aware of their predecessors' acts and practices. A. Lewis, for example, suggested that Louis VI would not have been aware of the high status awarded Hugh Capet's Queen Adelaide, but maintained that Adelaide's Carolingian ancestry would have been known: *Royal Succession*, pp.55, 106–7. In this instance, however, the charter of 1129 in which Louis VI confirmed the foundation and privileges of Saint-Vincent demonstrates that Louis and Adelaide, a consenter to the document, were aware that Anne of Russia had founded the abbey: Luchaire, *Louis VI*, no. 446. Thus, in the mid-twelfth century there is at least some evidence for the sense of queenly group identity like that persuasively described by Parsons for English queens in a later period: 'The Burials and Posthumous Commemorations,' pp.328–31.

35. Two acts of Louis VII that post-date Adelaide's death make clear her relationship with Saint-Jean-de-Cuise. A document from 1155 noted Adelaide's foundation of the monastery, and one from 1170 confirmed a donation by Louis's late mother to the institution: Luchaire, *Etudes sur les actes de Louis VII*, pp.347, 592. Adelaide's gift to the nuns of Saint-Rémi-les-Senlis is known through an 1157 confirmation of her donation: Luchaire, *Etudes sur les actes de Louis VII*, p.399.

36. Erlande-Brandenburg (as in n.29), p.104; Deshoulières, 'L'église,' pp.8–9. The document that Barthélémy published as the dedication account, which mentions SS Dennis, Rusticus, and Eleutherius, is apparently the record of a ceremony that the Pope celebrated in the Martyrs' Chapel in the same year: see Deshoulières, p.9 n.1.

37. For the Martyrium chapel, see Dumolin, 'Notes,' pp.148–9.

38. For octave celebrations in general, see H. LeClercq, DACL, vol. XII part 2, cols 1883–6; and F. Cabrol, 'Octave,' *The Catholic Encyclopedia*, New York: Encyclopedia Press, 1911, vol. XI, pp.204–5. For the liturgy of the Octave of St Dennis, see M. Huglo, 'Le chants de la Missa Graeca de Saint-Denis,' in J. Westrup, ed., *Essays Presented to Egon Wellesz*, Oxford: Oxford University Press, 1966, pp.74–83; and N. K. Rasmussen, 'The Liturgy at Saint-Denis: A Preliminary Study,' in P. L. Gerson, ed., *Abbot Suger and Saint-Denis*, pp.41–7 (pp.41, 44, for the octave liturgy). The implications of the octave procession for the seven churches that comprised its circuit is discussed only in the unfinished book by S. Gardner, 'A consciousness of place: Paris and Parisian architecture, 1120–1155.' Gardner's brilliant study linked the rebuilding or restoration of at least five of the seven stational churches to the growing cult in the twelfth century of St Dennis as national and monarchical patron saint (chapter 2, pp.21–4; chapter 4, p.6). The manuscript of Gardner's book will be available for scholars' consultation in the library of The Cloisters, New York.

39. Deshoulières, 'L'église,' p.10.

40. S. Gardner, 'The Influence of Castle Building on Ecclesiastical Architecture in the Paris Region, 1130–1150,' in K. Reyerson and F. Power, eds, *The Medieval Castle: Romance and Reality*, Medieval Studies at Minnesota, Dubuque, Iowa: Kendall/Hunt, 1984, pp.97–123. Much of Gardner's work on twelfth-century Paris is contained in an unpublished book (see n.38 above). The discussion of Saint-Pierre as a structure that uses architectural language to describe and affirm its own history appears in chapter 4, pp.11–12.

41. William Clark is preparing a major study of twelfth-century Parisian architecture and the forces shaping it: *Continuity and Contextuality: Capetian Kings and Merovingian Revival in Paris, 1130–1160*. Related publications to date include 'Merovingian Revival Acanthus Capitals at Saint-Denis,' in *L'acanthe dans la sculpture monumentale de l'antiquité à la renaissance*, Paris: Editions du Comité des Travaux Historiques et Scientifiques, 1993, pp.345–56; and ' "The Recollection of the Past is the Promise of the Future." Continuity and Contextuality: Saint-Denis, Merovingians, Capetians, and Paris,' in V. C. Raguin, K. Brush, and P. Draper, eds, *Artistic Integration in Gothic Buildings*, Toronto: University of Toronto Press, 1995, pp.92–113. I am particularly grateful to Professor Clark for sending me the text of his essay, 'Defining National Historical Memory in Parisian Architecture, 1130–1160,' in N. Gauthier and H. Galinie, eds, *Grégoire de Tours et l'espace gaulois. Actes du Congrès international, Tours, 3–5 November, 1994*, Tours: Revue archéologique du Centre de la France, 1997, while the collection was still in press, as well as for his many generous suggestions about my project.

42. Erlande-Brandenburg, *Le roi est mort*, pp.160–61; for the discovery of the tomb slab and its appearance at the time, see the report by the architect charged with the restoration of Saint-Pierre, Louis Sauvageot (as in n.1), p.108.

43. I am grateful to Marion Roberts for her suggestion concerning the function of the holes in the tomb slab.

44. Erlande-Brandenburg, *Le roi est mort*, pp.139–40; K. Bauch, *Das mittelalterliche Grabbild. Figürliche Grabmäler des 11. bis 15. Jahrhunderts in Europa*, Berlin: de Gruyter, 1976, p.42. As Erlande-Brandenburg noted, the Fredegonde effigy contains very thin pieces of porphyry, serpentine, and marble set in mortar, with fine strands of copper outlining the drapery and forming rosettes on the border of the slab. The effigies of the two queens are not quite identical in technique. Fredegonde's face, hands, and feet are of reserved stone, apparently originally painted, as the illustration by Du Tillet would suggest, while Adelaide's face was presumably inlaid: Erlande-Brandenburg, *Le roi est mort*, p.139, and fig. 48.

45. The work of C. R. Sherman (as in n.4) is a useful source for the coronations of French queens. Sherman discusses the stipulation that the queen's hair be unbound, presumably because of the anointment that was part of the queen's consecration, in 'The Queen in Charles V's "Coronation Book",' pp.271–2. The *ordo* that she cites as making this stipulation is of uncertain date, but apparently at least as old as the early twelfth century: n.63.

46. E. Panofsky, *Tomb Sculpture: Four Lectures on Its Changing Aspects from Ancient Egypt to Bernini*, New York: Abrams, 1964, pp.49–50.

47. For example, the mosaic effigy of William, Count of Flanders (†1109), from the church of Saint-Bertin in Saint-Omer: Panofsky (as in n.46), p.50, fig. 191. The Merovingians generally used plaster or stone sarcophagi without figural imagery, such as those unearthed near the church of Saint-Pierre-de-Montmartre: see Périn, 'Eglise Saint-Denis,' pp.100–107, figs 19–34. Exceptions do exist, as Elizabeth Valdez del Alamo has reminded me, such as the figural sarcophagus of Agilbert, at Jouarre, but these, too, are very different from the mosaic tombs that Panofsky envisioned.

48. W. Clark (as in n.16), p.360 n.36. See also the discussion of Saint-Germain in Elizabeth Brown, 'Burying and Unburying,' p.243.

49. For a persuasive reconstruction of the iconography of the lost mosaic, see P. Z. Blum, 'The Lateral Portals of the West Façade of the Abbey Church of Saint-Denis: Archaeological and Iconographical Considerations,' in Gerson, ed., *Abbot Suger and Saint-Denis*, pp.209–14. As Suger told us about his mosaic, the technique was 'contrary to modern custom'; in Suger's hands it represented an obvious evocation of the Early Christian past by one of the most skillful manipulators of imagery and fact of his era. The monks of Saint-Germain may have been attempting, in a sense, to out-Suger the (by now deceased) Suger. Suger, 'De Administratione,' in E. Panofsky, ed. and trans., in *Abbot Suger on the Abbey Church of St-Denis and Its Art Treasures*, Princeton, NJ: Princeton University Press, 1979, pp.46–7. For Suger as an adroit user of the past, see T. G. Waldman, 'Abbot Suger and the Nuns of Argenteuil,' *Traditio*, vol. 41, 1985, pp.239–72.

50. Dumolin, 'Notes,' p.156.

51. While it is reasonable to assume that Adelaide's tomb held pride of place and lay before the main altar, we cannot be absolutely sure of this. Erlande-Brandenburg cited a late-seventeenth-century source that stated that the tomb was positioned before the main altar until 1643, when it was transferred to the nuns' choir: *Le roi est mort*, p.160, citing M. Felibien, *Histoire de l'abbaye royale de Saint-Denys en France*, Paris, 1706, reprinted Paris, 1973, vol. I, p.160. Dumolin was of the same opinion: 'Notes,' p.156. At the time of the discovery of the slab in 1901, it lay face down among the debris in front of the main altar, which included funerary slabs from much later abbesses: see Sellier (as in n.1), p.109. The advantages of proximity to the locus of the celebration of the mass are discussed above and by the authors cited in n.16.

52. The Fredegonde effigy must have been complete by the 1163 consecration of the choir. Based on the Gaignières's drawing of the lost effigy of Fredegonde's husband, Chilperic, Erlande-Brandenburg linked Chilperic's tomb with the St Anne portal of the Cathedral of Paris, usually dated *c.*1160: *Le roi est mort*, p.139, fig. 47. Most recently Clark (as in n.2) has suggested a dating of the mid-1150s for the Saint-Germain effigies. If indeed Adelaide commissioned her tomb before her death, it seems likely that the effigies made for the Merovingian founders of Saint-Germäin-des-Prés were made subsequent to and in emulation of the innovative and historically evocative tomb erected for the still prominent and powerful dowager Queen.

53. Elizabeth Brown assumed that Louis VII was involved in the commissioning of his mother's remarkable tomb. She apparently based her assumption on Louis's desire to have an elaborate tomb himself and thus to be buried at his new monastery at Barbeau, rather than at Saint-Denis,

where the tradition was of simple, unadorned tombs: 'Burying and Unburying,' pp.243–4. His interest in effigies appears not to have extended to his female relations, however, for when Louis's wife Constance of Castile died in 1160, she was buried at Saint-Denis, where, inevitably, her tomb was unadorned: Erlande-Brandenburg, *Le roi est mort*, p.162. However strongly Adelaide's tomb seems linked to the nuns of Montmartre and their founder, we should always remember that the question of what it means to be a patron was a complicated one in the medieval period, as Madeline H. Caviness so brilliantly demonstrated in 'Anchoress, Abbess, and Queen: Donors and Patrons or Intercessors and Matrons,' in J. H. McCash, ed., *The Cultural Patronage of Medieval Women*, Athens, GA: University of Georgia Press, 1996, pp.105–54.

54. See above, n.26, for Adelaide's patronage of women's houses.

55. For the Merovingian necropolis, see Périn, 'Eglise Saint-Denis,' pp.98–9.

56. For Adelaide's widely-known Carolingian heritage, see Lewis, *Royal Succession*, p.107. There are a handful of earlier examples of retrospective funerary monuments that commemorate the Early Medieval rulers of France, but most have not survived intact. Circa 1140, enthroned stone figures carved in the round, representing the Carolingian kings Louis IV and Lothair, were made for their burial church, Saint-Rémi, in Reims: Willibald Sauerländer, *Gothic Sculpture in France, 1140–1270*, translated by J. Sondheimer, New York: Abrams, 1973, p.395, plate 28, illustration 15; and Erlande-Brandenburg, *Le roi est mort*, pp.119–20, 155–6. Assumed to be close in date were the wood effigies of Merovingian kings at Saint-Médard in Soissons and the seated effigy of the Merovingian King Dagobert, apparently the only effigy at Saint-Denis before the massive tomb program of the thirteenth century; for Saint-Médard, see Erlande-Brandenburg, *Le roi est mort*, pp.119–20; for Dagobert, see Wright, 'A Royal Tomb Program,' pp.229–39, figs 4, 5; and Erlande-Brandenburg, ibid. There is also one funerary portrait of a contemporary monarch which apparently pre-dated that of Adelaide of Maurienne: see below, n.62, for the effigy of Queen Bertrade of Montfort.

57. See above, n.38.

58. For the question of the enclosure of nuns, see R. Gazeau, 'La clôture des moniales au XIIe siècle en France,' *Revue Mabillon*, vol. 58, 1974, pp.289–308; J. T. Schulenburg, 'Strict Active Enclosure and Its Effects on the Female Monastic Experience (*c*.500–1100),' in J. A. Nichols and L. T. Shank, eds, *Distant Echoes: Medieval Religious Women*, vol. I, Kalamazoo: Cistercian Publications, 1984, pp.51–86; as well as the discussion in P. D. Johnson, *Equal in Monastic Profession: Religious Women in Medieval France*, Chicago: University of Chicago Press, 1991, pp.157–63.

59. The monastic reforms of the late eleventh and early twelfth centuries affected women's religious houses in France both by restricting their rights to govern their own affairs, as noted above in n.58, and occasionally 'reforming' them for suspected infringements of monastic discipline. These reforms generally consisted of expelling nuns and replacing them with monks or regular canons. A convenient source for the expulsions, and near expulsions, of nuns from monasteries in the early twelfth century is Bautier (as in n.8), p.42 for Saint-Eloi, and pp.70–71 for the other monasteries. For Suger's acquisition of Argenteuil for Saint-Denis, see the excellent discussion by Waldman (as in n.49), pp.239–72; as well as the brief discussion in G. Constable, 'Suger's Monastic Administration,' in Gerson, ed., *Abbot Suger and Saint-Denis*, pp.20–21.

60. Willibald Sauerländer noted that sculptural style, as well as architectural features, in the mid-twelfth century could be deliberately retrospective, evoking the past through its formal vocabulary as well as specific imagery. He made this argument, tellingly enough, for the Dagobert effigy, apparently produced around the middle of the twelfth century for the tomb of that Merovingian ruler at Saint-Denis: paper presented at the Sewanee Medieval Colloquium, The University of the South, April 1982. For the Dagobert effigy, see Wright, 'A Royal Tomb Program,' pp.229–39, figs 4, 5.

61. For the reluctance to include figural imagery in tombs at Saint-Denis until the thirteenth century, see Brown, 'Burying and Unburying,' pp.242–4; for the elaborate program of royal tombs under Louis IX, Wright's excellent article remains the best source, 'A Royal Tomb Program,' passim.

62. One effigy of a contemporary royal figure may pre-date our Queen's. Bertrade of Montfort, who had joined the order of Fontevrault after the death of Philip, was buried in 1128 in the priory of Haute-Bruyère, which had been founded on her dower lands. She was buried in the choir, under a copper plaque, which survived until the Revolution (see above, n.3). Erlande-Brandenburg indicated that there must have been some sort of representation of the Queen on the plaque, although no description of it survives: Erlande-Brandenburg, *Le roi est mort*, p.89. Bertrade's tomb may thus provide a precedent, perhaps known to Adelaide and the nuns at Montmartre, of a queen who joined a women's monastery of which she had been a patron, and was buried in the place of honor in the choir, with her tomb, exceptionally, bearing the image of the founder Queen.

10.1   Paris, Saint-Pierre-de-Montmartre, tomb slab of Adelaide of Maurienne,
mid-twelfth century

10.2 Saint-Denis (formerly Saint
Germain-des-Prés), tomb slab of
Fredegonde, mid-twelfth
century

10.3   Monastery of Saint-Pierre-de-Montmartre in 1625

10.4   Saint-Pierre-de-Montmartre, interior from west, consecrated in 1147

10.5   Saint-Pierre-de-Montmartre, capitals, north side of apse

11

Monumenta et memoriae: the thirteenth-century episcopal pantheon of León Cathedral

Rocío Sánchez Ameijeiras

'Monumenta itaque et memoriae pro mentis admonitione dictae.'
Isidore of Seville, Etymologiarum (XV, 11, 1)

When referring to the different terms used to designate burials, Isidore of Seville explains the etymology of *monumentum* by its commemorative function: 'monuments, therefore, are what serve to awaken memories [of the deceased] in the mind.' Communal remembrance and celebration of the deceased found expression in several types of observances during the Middle Ages; the importance given these rituals is reflected in medieval tomb imagery. At the same time, sepulchral art was also conceived as a means of pastoral propaganda.

The thirteenth-century episcopal pantheon in León is an example of the combination of commemoration and propaganda, with the intention of manipulating the collective memory of the city in order to articulate episcopal authority. The pantheon's arrangement presents the bishops as the building blocks from which the church itself was constructed, a visual metaphor for episcopal dignity and continuity with the past. Further, the highly individualized iconography of the tombs makes it clear that several Leonese bishops played an active role in the design of their monuments. In this paper, I will examine a number of devices employed in the Leonese episcopal pantheon that were intended to recall variously the bishops' individual accomplishments, personal devotion, traditional rituals, sacramental dogmas or the very history of the See.

Despite the restorations carried out in León's Cathedral during the nineteenth century, seven surviving thirteenth-century monuments can be seen in the transept and the chevet of the church (Fig. 11.1).[1] These are the tombs of the bishops Alvito (†1063); Manrique de Lara (†1205); Rodrigo Alvarez (†1232); Arnaldo (†1235); Martín Arias (†1242); Nuño Alvarez (†1252), and Martín Fernández (†1289). Although all the monuments were erected in the thirteenth century, most of them were originally conceived for the former

Romanesque church, and were later renovated and embedded in the walls of the new Gothic building. There can be no doubt that the construction of a series of retrospective episcopal monuments was a carefully considered enterprise carried out in the second half of the thirteenth century. An analysis of the earlier states of the sepulchres allows us to understand both the background of this undertaking and the reasons behind the choice of only certain prelates' monuments for reconstruction.

The tomb of Bishop Rodrigo Alvarez: commemorative rituals and pastoral propaganda

The earliest surviving richly decorated monument of a bishop in León Cathedral, or in any church of Castile and León, is that of Rodrigo Alvarez, who ruled the diocese between 1208 and 1232 (Fig. 11.2).[2] This seminal monument was decorated by local sculptors who must have been familiar with artistic ideas from the late twelfth- and early thirteenth-century Ile-de-France. Its design reflects French *enfeu* prototypes in which the lower registers of the monuments are decorated with earthly scenes, whereas the tympanum and the archivolts display heavenly images.[3] Nevertheless, the imagery of the monument differs from French examples. Whereas in French monuments the tympana show the deceased kneeling before the enthroned Virgin, an elaborate Crucifixion was sculptured in the Leonese tympanum. In addition, the decorative motifs on the front of the French sarcophagi were replaced with a representation of acts of charity in León. The complex iconographical content of the Leonese monument must not have been conceived by the sculptors, but rather by the Bishop himself, or some learned associate of his. This phenomenon has to be understood in light of the historical circumstances of the Leonese Church during the first third of the thirteenth century, circumstances which would result in the conception of the episcopal tomb as an element of pastoral propaganda and as an image of the bishop's exemplary authority.

The only scene common to all the French examples and to Rodrigo's monument is that of the absolution of the deceased Bishop. The lost monument of Pierre de Châtereleault, once at Fontevraud Abbey, showed a similar scene.[4] In both cases the officiating priest is assisted by a large number of acolytes carrying crosses, candlesticks and censors. On the Leonese tomb there are clerics surrounding the effigy of the deceased prelate. Also present at the ceremony are laymen desperately tearing their hair out and rending their garments in order to express their grief at the death of Bishop Rodrigo. The expressive Leonese citizens are practising an ancient tradition of mourning and lamentation well documented in the Iberian Peninsula. Diatribes against the excessive expression of emotion with dramatic and exaggerated gestures, by laymen as well as the clergy, appear repeatedly in medieval Hispanic religious literature.[5] From the eleventh century on, these diatribes appear almost exclusively in ecclesiastical literature, whereas secular chronicles, although written by monks, describe in great detail all types of excess on the occasion of the death of a loved one. For example, the anonymous author of the *Primera crónica de Sahagún* depicts the citizens of Sahagún lamenting the death of Alfonso VI in 1109 by 'tearing out their hair and ripping their clothes.'[6] A century later the *Crónica latina de los reyes de Castilla* records the mourning Castilians after the death of Alfonso VIII in 1214: 'All the women began to wail and the men threw ashes on their heads and wore sackcloth.'[7] The ritual lamentation for the death of a queen is represented on the sarcophagus lid of Queen Blanca in Santa María La Real in Nájera, who died in 1156.[8] There, one can make out several attitudes among the mourners corresponding to their different social status. The King, don Sancho, faints and Blanca's sister doña Sancha collapses, while the lamenting women follow the ancient classical formulae of tearing out their hair and ripping their clothes. Yet another modality for mourning is an attitude of containment, the dignified acceptance of death promoted by the Church.[9] This modal distinction can be seen again in Bishop Rodrigo Alvarez's tomb in León. Only laymen are represented with the expressive gesticulation of the 'llanto.' The difference between containment of grief and expressivity in tomb sculpture should be understood as a reflection of the different attitudes of the laymen and the clergy toward death. The mourning laymen make up a dynamic group. The ritual movement is evoked by their progressive bowing down before the deceased, while the clerics stand, even if one of them tears his hair out and another one rends his garments.

The insertion of the grieving laymen on Rodrigo's tomb represents the introduction of a lamentation scene, usually reserved for the tombs of high civil authorities, into the tomb of a bishop. The story of Bishop Rodrigo's life enables us to understand the status of civil patron which he earned and which appears on his tomb. As Peter Linehan has pointed out, during periods in which the authority of the monarch was weakened, bishops usually filled the vacuum of power and became the only civil authority of the city, even in, as with this case, a *civitas regia*. Rodrigo lived through the continual confrontations between the Leonese and Castilian monarchs which took place during the first three decades of the century. As Lucas de Túy, his fellow citizen and historian, wrote, Rodrigo played a decisive role in the pacification and subsequent unification of the kingdom carried out by King Fernando III, for whom he defended the city of León.[10] As his epitaph reminds us: 'He was the pinnacle of peace and piety, an exemplar of honesty.'[11] It was Bishop Rodrigo's status as a civil authority that made it possible to introduce into his tomb the lamentation heretofore reserved for high-ranking laymen.

With the inclusion of the group of laymen, the sense of the absolution scene shifts from a merely commemorative description of a liturgical ceremony – as in French tombs – to an active appeal to the intended audience for the monument: the lay citizens of León. The invocation of the audience parallels the rhetorical device used in the epitaph, which reads as follows: 'For this you will have to lament, León, for you have lost a patron who will never be equalled by anyone as yet unborn.' An appeal is also made to the audience by the reliefs on the front of the sarcophagus, decorated with a scene of charity (Fig. 11.3). Two servants emerging from the episcopal palace carry a barrel of wine on a staff, while two other servants hand out bread to a crowd of beggars. The image alludes to the charitable nature of the deceased, another of the virtues with which he is credited in his epitaph: 'here was the food and the drink; here, the beggars' clothes; here was one who provided everything for everybody.' Indeed, the sculptors suggested that his virtue rose to the level of sainthood by utilizing a hagiographical model, the charity of Saint Anthony, as it appears in a stained-glass window at Chartres Cathedral.[12]

By the thirteenth century, the representation of a cleric's charity had a long literary and pictorial tradition, which gradually evolved from allegorical images into narrative scenes.[13] The scene of charity on the Leonese tomb, however, is not a generic one.[14] The funerary context of the charitable acts, and the absence of Rodrigo, presumably deceased, allows us to witness a specific and, in medieval Spain, well documented ceremony, the anniversary alms – *pitança de aniversarios*. Although the Bishop's will has unfortunately been lost, that this is the event depicted can be supported by the large number of twelfth- and thirteenth-century documents describing the custom. An anniversary meal with bequests to feed the poor was a practice often begun during one's lifetime, then maintained by the family or religious community after one's death. For example, the Cluniac monks from San Zoilo of Carrión de los Condes instituted 'the feeding of the monks and twelve poor people' for the soul of Bishop Raimundo of Palencia on the anniversary of his death. Prior Humbertus of the same congregation ordered for his anniversary 'the care of all the old men giving them food, bread and wine in abundance and the feeding of twelve poor people.'[15] The choices made in these bequests are conditioned by eucharistic references: the number twelve, as the number of Apostles, is not fortuitous, nor are the specifications of bread and wine, as at the Last Supper. In León one can also find bequests determined by Christological parameters: to feed the poor on the third day after one's death, as with Christ's Resurrection; after forty days, as with his Ascension to Heaven; and *'ad capud anni,'* on the anniversary.[16]

This ceremony, as with the ritual lamentation, seems to be a Christian assimilation of ancient rites that ecclesiastical authorities had tried to eradi-

cate much earlier.[17] But while the lamentation of the citizens of León sculptured on the tomb of Rodrigo reminds the spectators of a ceremony that
took place at the moment of the prelate's death, the relief of the *pitança de
aniversarios*, or anniversary alms, illustrates a ritual that was to be performed
every year. As such, it would have functioned as a mnemonic device, destined to imprint the last wishes of the deceased on the memory of the living.
This method achieved the desired results: thirteen years after the death
of Rodrigo, the archdeacon, Petrus Ioannis left in his will a contribution of
two hundred and twenty *moropitinos* for the anniversary of the deceased
prelate.[18]

The scene of charity, with its bread and wine finds a doctrinal counterpart
in the Crucifixion on the tomb's tympanum (Fig. 11.2). The inclusion of
the Crucifixion reflects a renewed interest in the Eucharist evident in many
funerary monuments from Burgos, slightly earlier than the Leonese ones,
and on which one of the smaller sides of a sarcophagus was usually reserved
for the Agnus Dei.[19] For the choice of the Crucifixion there is an important
local precedent in the painted decoration of the Leonese royal pantheon in
the monastery of San Isidoro.[20] Once again, the introduction of this scene
and its particular formulation reflects Leonese, and specifically the Bishop's,
concerns.

The traditional Crucifixion with the two thieves, executioners, the sun, the
moon, censing angels, and John and Mary at the foot of the Cross, is modified on the Bishop's tomb. An opposition is established between the Virgin
Mary collecting the blood of Christ in a chalice and her counterpart, an
executioner collecting the blood of the thief Gestas, a contrast which confers
a marked sacramental tone to the scene (Fig. 11.4).[21] In fact, in thirteenth-
century Castilian missals, the Virgin often appears collecting Christ's blood
at the foot of Calvary.[22] With the Eucharistic chalice of everlasting salvation
in Mary's hand, she becomes an allegory of Ecclesia. In contrast, the executioner's cup corresponds to the chalice of 'abomination and filthiness' that
John describes in the hands of the Whore of Babylon (Apoc. 17.4–5; 18.2–3).
An image of the Whore with her cup traditionally illustrates a detailed ex-
cursus on heresies that forms part of Beatus's commentaries on the Apocalypse. In fact, a long literary tradition associates poison, bile, or bad wine,
with heretics.[23] As a counterpart to Ecclesia, the executioner is converted into
an image of heresy by means of his cup. Thus, the marked eucharistic accent
of the prelate's tomb is coupled with an explicit admonition against heresy.
All these allusions take on special resonance when considered within the
domain of the biography of Bishop Rodrigo and contemporary events in his
city. Lucas of Túy, in *De altera vita fideique controversiis adversus Albigensium
errores*, tells of the efforts of this prelate to eradicate the poison of Albigen-
sian heresy when it first appeared in León.[24] The heretics, apart from preaching

rigid discipline, denied, among other things, eucharistic transubstantiation and priestly authority to administer communion.

Most likely for the same reasons, an unusual formula was employed for the *elevatio animae* in the monument: a classical apotheosis – the soul standing on an eagle and being sustained by two angels – which gave an emphatic and triumphal tone to the scene of the elevation of the soul (Fig. 11.5). The Leonese heretics denied that the souls of the just went to heaven, 'ad solatium animarum.'[25] The eagle also suggests a sacramental allegory found in contemporary sermons: the eagle, like the soul, is called by the prospect of eating broken flesh at the altar of God. The passage appears in Matt. 24.28 and Luke 17.37, 'Wheresoever the body shall be, there shall the eagles also be gathered together,' and is explained by Saint Martín of León with these words: 'Because the remembrance of Christ's Passion has to be celebrated, and the bread and the wine will be converted into the body and the blood of Our Lord by the mystery of holy prayer, eagles will fly to be fed in Heaven so they will reach life through His death.'[26] When the monument was restored in the second half of the century, a scroll inhabited with eagles picking clusters of grapes was added between the right paired colonnettes, stressing the monument's allusion to this sacramental allegory.

The tomb of Rodrigo assumes, apart from its commemorative and didactic functions, a singularly apologetic tone. The complex layout of the Leonese tomb complies with the aesthetic ideas of Lucas of Túy.[27] As Serafín Moralejo has recently pointed out, for the Leonese historian there were four functions that figurative decoration within the church would have to carry out: defend the faithful, transmit learning, inspire good behavior and adorn the place of worship with appropriate images. But there was more to it than this. Lucas of Túy also showed an acute perception of the functional value that a tomb could exercise as a generative element of worship and a propagator of ideas. In *De altera vita*, written in the mid-twelve-thirties, he relates how, after the death of Bishop Rodrigo, the tomb of the heretic ringleader, Arnaldo (†1216), began to be venerated. Lucas, with the consent of the civil authorities, destroyed the *fanum* constructed over the monument and, after desecrating the remains of the heretic, threw the latter onto a heap of manure.[28] Perhaps Lucas of Túy himself had something to do with Bishop Rodrigo's monument design.

Along with these mnemonic and apologetic functions of the tomb, another important aspect of its imagery must be taken into account: the inclusion of all the social classes that form the monument's audience. Not only the canons of the Cathedral, who had to fulfill the last wishes of the prelate, but also the laymen of León and paupers could identify themselves in Bishop Rodrigo's monument. Even the heretics, personified in Gestas, are invited there to learn Catholic doctrine on the Eucharist.

The tomb of Bishop Martín Arias: the stability of episcopal dignity

The sepulchral monument of Bishop Rodrigo was a seminal work in the development of Castilian-Leonese tomb design. It was to become the proto-type for a long line of episcopal monuments.[29] The tomb of Bishop Martín Arias (†1242), which betrays its influence, was carved around 1242 by a workshop led by a skilled sculptor trained in the best French ateliers (Fig. 11.6).[30] There is every reason to believe that the tomb is substantially com-plete. Its sculpture has often been related to the Master of the *Virgen Blanca* who participated in the carving of the west portal of the Leonese Cathedral in the third quarter of the century, but stylistic elements of the tomb suggest that it was carved by a workshop of the previous generation, trained in the atelier of Reims.[31] On the grounds of style, the episcopal *gisant* garbed in full pontifical vestments is clearly associated with the statue of Pope Calixtus on the right portal of the western façade in Reims.

For the 'modern' sculptors, up-to-date on the latest French monuments, the design of Rodrigo's tomb may have seemed somewhat antiquated, for although it was used as a model, significant changes were introduced into the design. Once again the will of the person commissioning the work may have determined the choice of the model and some of the alterations that the master sculptor introduced. He omitted the doctrinal references in the Cruci-fixion scene, for heresy had been eradicated in León. But other novelties in the display of the imagery show that the sculptor could not transcend his training. He subjected the plan of Rodrigo's tomb to a strict scholastic order-ing – clerics and layman have their own separate positions in the structure of the tomb (Figs 11.2, 11.6). He also remained faithful to French formulae in the heavenly scenes: 'the Mass of the Dead performed in Heaven,' as Erwin Panofsky described the scene, welcomes the soul of the Bishop carried by angels in a cloth. He also updated the scene of the *pitança*, or almsgiving, by including diversified types of poor people, widows, and the motif of a father with a baby on his shoulders (Fig. 11.7). These types appear in the hagio-graphical models that he might have known, for example the scene of the death of Saint Firmin in Amiens.[32]

Despite the differences, the complex relationship between imagery and audience that characterized Rodrigo's monument can also be recognized in the tomb of Bishop Martín. The nature of the potential audience had changed, however. Some of the beggars on Martín's monument bear the characteristic attributes of pilgrims on the way to Santiago de Compostela – a pilgrim's staff and a scrip with a scallop shell (Fig. 11.7). The presence of the pilgrims going to Santiago and the choice of a composition from hagiographical sources clearly associate Bishop Martín with certain saints well-known for their char-ity and their protection of pilgrims. Examples are Saint John of Ortega or

Saint Dominic of La Calzada, whose funerary monuments had been reconstructed some decades earlier.[33] The choices may reflect the efforts of the See of León to attract pilgrims to the Cathedral and away from its more famous rival, the royal monastery of San Isidoro.

Despite the similarities between the monuments of Bishops Rodrigo and Martín, these two iconographically related tombs did not form a visually unified ensemble. Nonetheless, their standardized type stresses the role of the episcopal tomb itself as a format to express the stability of episcopal dignity. With the bishop-elect officiating at the absolution of his predecessor on the left of the recessed relief, the episcopal tombs visualize continuity. For the Leonese bishops, reality was quite different, rather more a play of accidents of fate. The cathedral canons had openly and continually confronted the bishops during the first half of the century, with the result that before and after the prelacy of Bishop Martín Arias, several episodes of short prelacies with vacant sees follow one another.

The tomb of Bishop Martín Fernández and the new episcopal pantheon

Bishop Martín Fernández acceded to the episcopal seat in 1254. His close relations with the monarchy allowed him to promote the construction of the new Cathedral, and his long tenure was characterized by the strengthening of episcopal power, successfully opposing the recalcitrant canons. He made use of, among other things, the dictates of successive synodal constitutions which reflected the intention of establishing the provisions of the Fourth Lateran Council in León. A year before his death, he ordered in his will that he be buried in his tomb set in the choir of the Cathedral (Figs 11.1, 11.8).[34] Both the documentary evidence and the style of the tomb niches carved for some of the older sarcophagi suggest that it was he who gave the episcopal pantheon its new, unified form. The unity he imposed on the bishops' tombs expressed in visual terms not only the centralization of power he was able to achieve, but also the apostolic notion of episcopal dignity, and last, but not least, an ideologically shaped history of the See itself.

A significant shift in Leonese tomb design and imagery is inaugurated by Bishop Martín Fernández's monument, which still remains in its original location.[35] The triple-bayed structure of the mural tomb emerges as the result of adapting the tomb to the decorative design of the wall in such a way that it gives the effect of a 'diaphanous wall,' thus allowing the contemplation of the absolution of the body of the deceased prelate and the traditional scenes of popular grief. A number of iconographical innovations are to be found in the reliefs of the recessed tympana, which show a prospective design focused on saintly intercession.

The scene of the charity of St Martin represented in the right tympanum sustains multiple layers of meaning. First, it serves as a metaphor for the deceased Bishop's charity, a tradition which can be traced back to the beginning of the century in Castilian funerary art. In poetry, Gonzalo de Berceo utilized the charity of St Martin as both a metaphor and simile when referring to the charity of St Dominic, Abbot of Silos: 'Lord Saint Dominic, greatly honored confessor / ought to be compared with Saint Martin / he who saw Our Lord Christ covered with his cloak / is he who gave his cloak to a miserable beggar.'[36] On the cenotaph of St John of Ortega in the church of San Juan de Ortega, near Burgos, the same device is applied by the sculptor to describe that Castilian saint's charity. It is precisely St Martin's vision of Christ with the cloak, a vision he had in the last moment of his life, that justifies the custom of representing Martin in funerary contexts; another example is carved on the tomb lid of a prince in nearby Las Huelgas.[37] In the vision, Christ addressed Martin with the same words that Matthew attributed to him in his description of the Last Judgment (Matt. 25.40): 'Whatever you may have done to the least of my brethren you also did to me.'[38] Thus, St Martin's vision was associated with charity and the good deeds of the deceased that will be weighed at the Last Judgment; and in the Leonese episcopal monument the charity of St Martin demonstrates the increased importance given to the patron saint as intercessor at the time of death.

The Passion of Christ occupies the two remaining tympana of Bishop Martín Fernández's monument. Once again, the occupant of the tomb appears to have played an active role in formulating a design that reflects his own private devotion as well as a number of contemporary factors. The diagrammatic presentation of the Crucifixion and the serene containment of Christ in the earlier tombs is now replaced by a dramatic narrative in two separate scenes, the Flagellation and the Crucifixion, in which Christ's suffering appears to be concentrated in the uncomfortable position of his crossed feet. The *mise en scène* betrays the influence of mendicant spirituality, tending to dramatize and humanize episodes from the Gospels. The favorable attitude of Martín Fernández toward the friars is well known.[39] In addition, the proliferation of Crucifixions in funerary sculpture of the thirteenth century probably reflects the incorporation of the *Dies irae* into the Mass for the Dead. In the Leonese case, the amount of pathos in the representation of divine suffering might suggest the prayer's supplication by the fearful resurrected souls before the judge of frightful majesty: 'why on thy cross such pangs sustain, if now those sufferings must be in vain.'[40] The imagery of the tomb of Martín Fernández stresses, then, a new concern for saintly intercession and private devotion, undoubtedly fed by the increasing spread of the doctrine of Purgatory and remission of sin.

But the prelate did not forget the efficacy of sepulchral art as a vehicle of pastoral expression. Certain provisions dictated in the synodal constitutions allow us to attribute the idea of building an episcopal pantheon in León to Martín Fernández. In 1267 he issued an order forbidding burials inside the churches of his bishopric, even when the church had two or three aisles, as formerly allowed.[41] The order, stricter than the civil law provisions on this matter, must have had immediate consequences; the only thirteenth-century tombs set inside the Cathedral are episcopal tombs, while the cloister was reserved for the canons and their families. The prohibition was repeated in the synodal constitutions of 1288, a little before the prelate wrote his will, in which he refers to his own tomb.

The same workshops of sculptors who were already active in the church, and who introduced the French *rayonnant* style to León, participated in the carving of the cathedral portals. They also worked on the Martín Fernández monument, and on the modifications that six of the seven episcopal tombs underwent in their final installation. The eleventh-century sarcophagus of Alvito was set on supports in the main chapel of the new Gothic building, although it was removed from there in the sixteenth century (Fig. 11.1). The *enfeu* of Bishop Rodrigo was reconstructed and restored (Fig. 11.2). The paired colonnettes which support the archivolts, the inhabited scrolls carved in the intercolumniation, and the outer archivolt were made by a sculptor who worked on the western portal (Fig. 11.12).[42] The same style can be seen in a frieze with absolving clerics now installed in the cloister. The frieze was produced to decorate a new niche embellished with archivolts adorned with censing angels, made for the originally free-standing sarcophagus of Bishop Manrique de Lara (†1205) (Fig. 11.9). Although the continuous refurbishment of the Leonese Cathedral in subsequent centuries resulted in further alterations to the tomb, the lid of the sarcophagus can still be seen fixed to the wall.[43] The sarcophagi of Bishop Arnaldo (†1235, Fig. 11.10) and Bishop Nuño (†1252), were embedded into the wall in the same way. Arnaldo's, originally decorated solely with a processional cross over the cover and etched with an epitaph, was now flanked by two free-standing censing angels, and a relief with the *elevatio animae* of the deceased was carved at the end of the recess.[44] The humblest sepulchral monument of the series, that of Bishop Nuño, also shows the characteristic mitred arch with censing angels in the archivolts.[45]

There can be no doubt that the unusual feature of these mitred arches framing the renovated monuments must have resulted from adapting the old free-standing sarcophagi to the decorative design of the new cathedral walls. This was probably the work of the artists who produced the south façade portal, dedicated to St Froilán, and the same decoration may be seen in the archivolts of the west façade. On the grounds of stylistic analysis, all the alterations and reconstructions of the old tombs can be dated to the third quarter of the century, making it clear that they were carried out under the prelacy of Bishop Martín Fernández.

The figured history and foundations of the Leonese Church

The erection of a series of episcopal monuments against the interior walls of a cathedral is an artistic undertaking that had already been carried out in other western European churches, for example twelfth-century Trier and thirteenth-century Wells.[46] At St-Denis, the tombs of several abbots of the twelfth and thirteenth centuries were reinstalled and embellished around 1259, at the same time that the royal monastery commissioned new effigy tombs to commemorate, retrospectively, the former kings and queens of France.[47]

Such adaptations, which served to absorb the past into contemporary discourse, occurred as well in the representation of an episcopal pantheon in a Castilian sculpture. On the end of the sarcophagus of the Bishop-Saint Peter of El Burgo de Osma, a posthumous miracle carried out by the deceased prelates of the See is represented (Fig. 11.11). As 'the living rock of the church,' the dead prelates arose from their tombs in order to cast out a simoniac bishop who intended to be buried near them.[48] The sequence of pointed arches over their sarcophagi is similar to the effect of the new Leonese *enfeu* tombs. It bears witness to the extent that the idea of the episcopal pantheon as a functional entity inside the church was an integral part of Hispanic clerical mentality in the mid-thirteenth century.

The constitution of an episcopal pantheon inside the church must have been, then, a conscious choice of Bishop Martín Fernández. Undoubtedly it could serve as a visual metaphor for continuity with the past, but perhaps it was also an image of discontinuity. The selection of the prelates who deserved to be so commemorated was not random. Only two prelates prior to the thirteenth century, Froilán and Alvito, earned the right to have their monuments inside the church. They had played an important role in the history of the See, and both had merited the crown of sainthood. Froilán was a reformer saint, believed to have established a canonical rule in the tenth-century Cathedral. The eastern portal of the south façade of the new Gothic building was dedicated to him, and his reliquary was placed near the main altar. The *Historia Silense* attributed to Alvito the invention of the relics of St Isidore in eleventh-century Seville, but his premature death in obscure circumstances determined that the beneficiary of the discovery was to be the neighbouring monastery of San Isidoro, instead of the Cathedral. The subsequent history of the See went unrecorded until the episcopate of Manrique, under whose prelacy the Cathedral became the protector of the city while its powerful rival San Isidoro began to decline. Lucas of Túy attributes to

Manrique the intention of rebuilding the Cathedral and, although he could not achieve his aim, a new chapter house with a rich sculptural program conceived to exalt the See was carried out. It was he who recovered the memory and the relics of St Froilán, and ordered a new sarcophagus for Alvito. Under his prelacy, the canons of St Isidore had to transfer ecclesiastical juridical power to the Cathedral.[49] The extant monuments correspond to thirteenth-century prelates, and the absence of three thirteenth-century bishops – Pedro Muñiz, Pelayo Pérez and Martín Alfonso – can be justified by their short prelacies.[50]

The building of the episcopal pantheon in León was one of the works undertaken by Bishop Martín Fernández, with the aim of reinforcing the authority of the bishop as opposed to the power of the canons, the problematic situation that he inherited from his predecessors in 1254.[51] Some motifs represented on the church portals, therefore, have the intention of reaffirming and legitimizing episcopal authority, which emanated directly from the Pope, and ultimately from God. On the lintel of the central portal of the west façade, St Peter at the Heavenly gates receives the Pope and a bishop who head the procession of the blessed (Fig. 11.13). All levels of the ecclesiastical hierarchy are represented on the external archivolt of the left portal, from the subdeacon, in the lower spandrel, to the Pope, in the upper (Fig. 11.12). The group crowned by Christ in the keystone, at the same time the head (*caput*) and the highest stone (*lapis in summo*), is a metaphor of the divine origin of episcopal power.[52]

The installation of the old tombs, embedded within the tomb niches in the walls of the new church, and the construction of the tomb of Martín Fernández, promotor of the enterprise, following the guidelines laid down by the structure of the church wall, was not, then, an arbitrary decision. As H. A. Tummers has pointed out, from the thirteenth century onwards, at the same time as sepulchral typology was enriched, there was a close correspondence between tomb types and social groups.[53] The preference of the *enfeu* type for ecclesiastical tombs in the interior of the cathedrals fulfills the notion of episcopal dignity. Old Testament aedilic metaphors reworked by Paul in Eph. 2.19–22, identify the apostles and the prophets with the foundations of the spiritual church: 'You are the fellow citizens of the saints, and the domestics of God, built upon the foundation of the Apostles and Prophets, Jesus Christ himself being the chief cornerstone: In whom all the building, being framed together, groweth up into an holy temple in the Lord. In whom you are also built together into an habitation of God in spirit.'

These familiar metaphors, transmitted, commented on, transformed in exegetic literature and incorporated into liturgical formulae of the dedication of churches throughout the Middle Ages, must have exercised their influence as much on the constitution of episcopal pantheons in the interior of the churches as on the structure of the individual episcopal funerary monuments.[54] The incorporation of the bodies of the bishops into the fabric of the cathedral walls made visible Paul's words. Thus, as representatives of the mission of St Peter in León, the deceased prelates, immured in their tombs, became figuratively and literally the foundations of the Leonese church.[55]

Frequently cited sources

Bauch, K., *Das mittelalterliche Grabbild: Figürliche Grabmäler des 11. bis 15. Jahrhunderts in Europa*, New York: Walter de Gruyter, 1976.

Berceo, Gonzalo de, *La vida de Santo Domingo de Silos*, edited by T. Labarta de Chaves, Madrid: Castalia, 1987.

Franco Mata, A., *Escultura gótica en León*, León: Instituto 'Fray Bernardino de Sahagún' de la Excelentísima Diputación Provincial de León, 1976.

Linehan, P. 'La iglesia de León a mediados del siglo XIII,' in *León y su historia: miscelánea histórica*, vol. III, León: Centro de Estudios e Investigación 'San Isidoro,' 1975, pp.1–30.

— *Spanish Church and Society, 1150–1300*, London: Variorum Reprints, 1983.

— *The Spanish Church and the Papacy in the Thirteenth Century*, Cambridge: Cambridge University Press, 1971.

Lucas of Tuy, *De altera vita fideique controversiis adversus Albigensium errores*, in *Bibliotheca maxima veterum patrum*, vol. XXV, Lyon, 1677.

Panofsky, E., *Tomb Sculpture: Its Changing Aspects from Ancient Egypt to Bernini*, London: Thames and Hudson, 1964.

Risco, M., *España sagrada*, vol. XXXV: *Memorias de la Santa Iglesia esenta de León de los siglos XI, XII y XIII fundadas en las escrituras y documentos originales, desconocidos en la mayor parte hasta ahora, y muy útiles para la historia particular de esta ciudad y su iglesia, y para la general del reyno*, Madrid: Antonio Marín, 1784.

Sánchez Ameijeiras, R., 'Dos ejemplos de patronazgo en la iconografía de la escultura funeraria gótica leonesa,' in *Actas del VII Congreso Español de Historia del Arte (Murcia, 1988)*, vol. I, Murcia: Universidad de Murcia, 1992.

— 'Investigaciones iconográficas sobre la escultura funeraria del siglo XIII en Castilla y León,' unpublished PhD thesis, Universidad de Santiago de Compostela, 1993.

Sauerländer, W., *La sculpture gothique en France (1140–1270)*, Paris: Flammarion, 1979.

Notes

I would like to express my gratitude to Serafín Moralejo for his useful suggestions and to Elizabeth Valdez del Alamo for her close reading of the article and generous help with the translation. Translations of the Vulgate are from the Douay Rheims Bible.

1. For the restorations, see I. González-Varas Ibáñez, *Las catedrales de León. Historia y restauración (1859–1901)*, León, Colección Historia y Sociedad, 1, León: Universidad de León, 1989. The general bibliography on the Leonese episcopal tombs includes: V. G. González Dávila, *Teatro eclesiástico de las iglesias metropolitanas y catedrales de los reynos de las dos Castillas*, Madrid: Francisco Martínez, 1651, pp.403–6; M. Risco, *España sagrada*, vol. XXXV, pp.294–302; idem, *Iglesia de León y monasterios antiguos y modernos de la misma ciudad*, Madrid: Blas Román, 1792, pp.71–4; J. M. Quadrado, *España. Sus monumentos y artes. Su naturaleza e historia. Asturias y León*, Barcelona: Daniel Cortezo, 1885, pp.457–70; D. de los Ríos, *La catedral de León*, Madrid, 1895 (facsimile, León: Ambito, 1989), pp.66–7, 90, 95–6; M. Gómez Moreno, *Catálogo monumental de España. Provincia de León*, vol. I, Madrid: Ministerio de Instrucción Pública y Bellas Artes, 1925, pp.238–44; F. B. Deknatel, 'The 13th-Century Gothic Sculpture of the Cathedrals of Burgos and León,' *The Art Bulletin*, vol. 17, 1935, pp.243–389, especially pp.324–5, 377–8; M. D. Berrueta, *La catedral de León*, Madrid: Plus-Ultra, 1951, pp.103–5; J. Ainaud de Lasarte and A. Durán Sampere, *Escultura gótica*, Ars Hispaniae, 7, Madrid: Plus-Ultra, 1954, p.41; Franco Mata, 'Escultura funeraria en León y su provincia,' *Hidalguía*, 1971, pp.407–30; eadem, *Escultura gótica en León*, pp.425–49; J. Yarza Luaces, *La edad media*, Historia del Arte Hispánico, 2, Madrid: Editorial Alhambra, 1978 (1980), p.241; E. Gómez Moreno, *La catedral de León*, León: Editorial Everest, 1984, pp.36, 42–3; J. Yarza Luaces, 'Depesas facen los omnes de muchas guisas en soterrar muertos,' *Fragmentos*, vol. 2, 1984, pp.4–19; J. Azcárate Ristori, *Arte gótico en España*, Madrid: Editorial Cátedra, 1990, pp.180–82; R. Sánchez Ameijeiras, 'Dos ejemplos,' pp.81–6;

Sánchez Ameijeiras, 'Investigaciones,' pp.39–63, 220–43. In a new edition of her book, Franco Mata incorporates some conclusions from this chapter, citing it as forthcoming: *Escultura gótica en León y provincia, 1230–1530*, León: Diputación de León, 1998, pp.381–7.

2. The tomb was restored in the second half of the century, when two animal-headed supports were embedded as corbels for the new outer archivolt, and the right colonettes recarved. For iconographic sources, see Sánchez Ameijeiras, *Investigaciones*, pp.53–7.

3. The relationship between Rodrigo's tomb and French examples was pointed out for the first time by H. Keller, 'Der Bildhauer Arnolfo di Cambio und seine Werkstatt,' *Jahrbuch der preussischen Kunstsammlungen*, vol. 55, 1934, pp.205–28, especially p.215; accepted by J. Gardner, 'The tomb of Cardinal Annibaldi by Arnolfo di Cambio,' *The Burlington Magazine*, vol. 114, 1972, pp.136–41, especially pp.140–41; idem, 'Arnolfo di Cambio and Roman Tomb Design,' *The Burlington Magazine*, vol. 115, 1973, pp.420–31; reviewed by R. Sánchez Ameijeiras, 'Dos ejemplos,' pp.81–3. The model for the Leonese tomb is probably an early one, such as the monument of Archbishop Henri de France (†1170), built around 1180, whose remains today make up the so called *Porte Romane* of Reims Cathedral; see Sauerländer, *La sculpture gothique*, pp.98–9, plates 56–7. For the definition of *enfeu* tombs, see Panofsky, *Tomb Sculpture*, pp.58–61. For the evolution of the type, see Bauch, *Das mittelalterliche Grabbild*, especially 'Das Nichengrab,' pp.45–62.

4. On this now destroyed tomb at Fontevraud, see Bauch, *Das mittelalterliche Grabbild*, pp.45–62, fig. 84. The scene of the absolution of the deceased was also carved in the monument of Henri of France. Four acolytes can still be seen in the lateral walls: ibid., pp.51–4, figs 70–73.

5. Although secular literature and chronicles, even when written by clerics, describe a variety of excessive behavior, the bishops dictated synodal constitutions forbidding these demonstrative manifestations of grief inside the church or during the liturgical ceremonies in the house of the deceased. See A. Arranz Guzmán, 'La reflexión sobre la muerte en el medioevo hispánico,' *España Medieval*, vol. 5, 1986, pp.109–24; M. J. Gómez Bárcena, 'La liturgia de los funerales y su repercusión en la escultura funeraria gótica en Castilla,' in M. Núñez Rodríguez and E. Portela Silva, eds, *La idea y el sentimiento de la muerte en la historia y en el arte de la Edad Media*, Santiago de Compostela: Universidad de Santiago de Compostela, 1988, pp.31–55.

6. 'destrozadas las crines e rotas las bestiduras,' 'Primera crónica de Sahagún,' in A. Ubieto Arteta, *Crónicas anónimas de Sahagún*, Zaragoza: Anubar, 1987, p.20.

7. 'Omnes mulieres sumpssere lamenta viri consperxerunt pulvere capita accinti ciliciis induti saccis,' G. Cirot, 'Une chronique latine inédite des Rois de Castille,' *Bulletin Hispanique*, vol. 14, 1912, pp.30–46, 109–18, 244–74, 353–74 especially 370; vol. 15, 1913, pp.18–37, 170–87, 268–83, 411–27. The text is inspired by the Lamentations of Jeremiah. In the same chronicle the passage which describes the grief of the Queen Leonor for the death of her son Fernando (†1211) is inspired by the *Planctus Beatae Mariae* tradition.

8. For this tomb and the modal distinction of gestures of despair among the various social classes, see R. Sánchez Ameijeiras, 'Ecos de la *Chanson de Roland* en el sepulcro de la reina Doña Blanca (†1156) en Santa María la Real de Nájera,' *Lecturas de Historia del Arte*, vol. 2, 1990, pp.206–15. New arguments for this view, in E. Valdez del Alamo, 'Lament for a Lost Queen: The Sarcophagus of Doña Blanca in Nájera,' *The Art Bulletin*, vol. 78, no. 2, 1996, pp.311–33, republished in this volume.

9. This is exemplified by the mothers who mourn the Massacre of the Innocents on the sarcophagus lid of Doña Blanca as described by Valdez del Alamo (as in n.8).

10. P. Linehan, 'La iglesia de León,' pp.1–30; idem, *Spanish Church and Society*, pp.12–76; idem, *The Spanish Church and the Papacy*, pp.268–75. When Alfonso VII, 'the Emperor,' died in 1157, he divided the kingdom between his sons. This produced constant confrontations between Castile and León until Fernando III of Castile succeeded in unifying the kingdom in 1230: C. Sánchez Albornoz, 'La sucesión al trono de los reinos de León y Castilla,' in J. M. Font Rius, ed., *Instituciones medievales españolas*, Mexico City: Universidad Nacional Autónoma de México, Instituto de Investigaciones Históricas, 1945, pp.59–65; J. González, *Reinado y diplomas de Fernando III*, 3 vols, Córdoba: Monte de Piedad y Caja de Ahorros, 1980–86, especially vol I.

11. The epitaph of Bishop Rodrigo reads as follows: SUB ERA MCCLX PACIS ET PIETATIS APEX: EXEMPLAR HONESTI: HIC RODERICUS ERAT PONTIFICATUS HONOR: HIC CIBUS ET POTUS FUIT: HIC ET VESTIS EGENIS: OMNIBUS HIC UNUS OMNIA FACTUS ERAT: ERGO TUUM LEGIO LUGE CECIDISSE PATRONUM AUT VIX AUT NUMQUAM IAM PARITURA PARENS.

12. See Y. Delaporte and E. Houvet, *Les vitraux de la cathédrale de Chartres*, Paris, n.d., fig. XXXVI.

13. For example, the illustration of the death of Lambert, abbot of Saint-Bertin, includes the ascension of his soul to Heaven accompanied by the allegorical figures of *Patientia* and *Elemosina*,

in a codex at the Municipal Library in Boulogne-sur-Mer, MS 46, fol. 1; Panofsky, *Tomb Sculpture*, p.60, fig. 240; Bauch, *Das mittelalterliche Grabbild*, p.285, fig. 425. In the sepulchral arts, Charity appeared first in the shrines of saints. The virtues were included in the decoration of the *'arca aurea'* of Saint Gilles and on the ciborium of Saint James's shrine at Compostela, according to the descriptions in the *Codex Calixtinus*: A. Shaver-Crandell and P. Gerson, with A. Stones, *The Pilgrim's Guide to Santiago de Compostela: A Gazetteer*, London: Harvey Miller, 1995, pp.76, 93; S. Moralejo, 'Le trésor et le chantier de Compostelle,' *Les cahiers de Saint-Michel de Cuxa*, vol. 11,1980, pp.203–4. In these early cases it is always an allegorical figure of virtue which is represented. See A. Katzenellenbogen, *Allegories of Virtues and Vices in Medieval Art: From Early Christian Times to the XIIIth Century*, London: Warburg Institute, 1939, passim; R. Freyhan, 'The Evolution of the *Caritas* Figure in the 13th and 14th Centuries,' *Journal of the Warburg and Courtauld Institutes*, vol. 2, 1948, pp.68–86.

14. At Chartres, the scenes of charity and distribution of bread are also more than merely generic. J. Welch Williams has demonstrated a documented medieval practice of the offering of bread in churches: *Bread, Wine and Money: The Windows of the Trades at Chartres Cathedral*, Chicago: University of Chicago Press, 1993, pp.38–72. The scene carved on the trumeau socle of the south porch of Chartres is identified by Williams with the offering and distribution of eulogy bread: ibid., pp.48–51, figs 40–43.

15. In this case the anniversary was instituted while he was still alive and continued after death. It is specified that the alms and meals should be made 'VI Kalendas Decembri' until his death, and 'post obitum, ad die anniversario transferatur (after his death, transferred to the day of his anniversary).' For the documents, 'ita reficiat fratres et XII pauperes' and 'festive et plenarie de pane et vino, de generale et pietantia omnes seniores largiter procuret simul et XII pauperes bene reficiat': J. A. Pérez Celada, *Documentación del monasterio de San Zoilo de Carrión (1074–1300)*, Palencia: Junta de Castilla y León, 1986, pp.40–41, 68–71.

16. J. M. Fernández Catón, *Colección documental del archivo de la catedral de León. VI (1188–1230)*, León: Caja de Ahorros y Monte de Piedad, Archivo Histórico Diocesano, 1991, pp.233, 260, 483. In other documents the word *pitancia* is used, as for example in the will of Juan Cibriánez in 1250: 'Al convento de Sant Esidro X morabedís pora pintancia. Al convento de Caruallar X morabedís pora pitancia'; the one of Isidro Pérez 'al monasterio de Cauayar V stopos de pan por pitancia . . . a los frayres descalzos V stopos de pan por pitancia'; and others, see J. M. Ruiz Asencio, *Colección documental del archivo de la catedral de León. VIII (1230–1269)*, León: Caja de Ahorros y Monte de Piedad, Archivo Histórico Diocesano, 1993, pp.168, 171, 383.

17. M. Sánchez, *Vida popular en Castilla y León a través del arte (Edad Media)*, Madrid: Ambito, 1982, p.106. As late as 1541 the Bishop of Mondoñedo, Lugo, had to forbid funerary meals inside the church: S. L. Pérez López, 'Religiosidad popular y superstición en el Sínodo Mindoniense de Fray Antonio de Guevara (1541) y su contexto histórico,' *Estudios Mindonienses*, vol. 1, 1985, pp.269–84, especially p.281. Another ancient ceremony closely related to this was the offering of bread at tombs. The passage that relates the entombment of Licórides in the *Libro de Apolonio* testifies to the continuity of this practice in the Middle Ages: *Libro de Apolonio*, edited by P. Cabanas, Madrid: Castalia, 1969, pp.93, 95.

18. J. M. Ruiz Asencio (as in n.16), vol. VIII, p.133.

19. The Eucharistic symbol of the Agnus Dei within a *clipeus* held by four angels is on the cenotaph of Saint John of Ortega, near Burgos. A simplified version is reproduced on the sarcophagus of a prince who died in 1194, in Las Huelgas (Burgos). For funerary monuments of Burgos see M. Gómez Moreno *El panteón real de Las Huelgas de Burgos*, Madrid: CSIC, 1947, passim; M. J. Gómez Bárcena, *Escultura gótica funeraria en Burgos*, Monografías Burgalesas, Burgos: Excelentísima Diputación Provincial de Burgos, 1988.

20. A. Viñayo González, *Pintura románica. El panteón real de San Isidoro*, León: Isidoriana, 1971, p.41, fig. 27. A related scene, the Descent from the Cross, is carved on the short end of the lid of Doña Blanca's sarcophagus in Nájera, see E. Valdez del Alamo (as in n.8), Fig. 2.3 in this volume.

21. For the thieves at the Crucifixion, see M. B. Merback, *The Thief, the Cross, and the Wheel: Pain and the Spectacle of Punishment in Medieval and Renaissance Europe*, Chicago: University of Chicago Press, 1998; London: Reaktion Press, 1999.

22. J. Yarza Luaces, 'Iconografía de la Crucifixión en la miniatura española. Siglos X al XIII,' *Archivo Español de Arte*, vol. 46, 1973, pp.13–19.

23. For example, the motif is used by Gonzalo de Berceo when referring to Saint Dominic of Silos and his fight against heresy: 'Orava muy afirmes al su Señor divino / a los ereges falsos que semnan mal venino, / que los refiriesse, cerráseles el camino, / que la fe non botasse la fez de su mal vino': *Vida de Santo Domingo de Silos*, p.75.

24. *De altera vita*, book II, chapter 7. A homily written two decades earlier by St Martín of León, the *Sermo XXII in Coena Domini*, corroborates this: 'et quia sanguinem Christi sumunt ut aliud vinum, vertitur in eis fel draconum et venenum aspidum insanabilem' (To those who drink the blood of Christ as if it were wine, may the bile of the dragon and the venom of the asp spill upon them): PL, vol. CCVIII, col. 919. On the presence of heretics in León, see A. Martínez Casado, 'Cátaros en León. Testimonio de Lucas de Túy,' *Archivos Leoneses*, vol. 37, 1983, pp.263ff.

25. Lucas of Túy, *De altera vita*, book I, chapter 1 writes: 'Contra illos qui dicunt Dominum Christum Jesum vel Sanctos eius in hora mortis sanctorum non adesse ad solatium animarum et nullius anima exire de corpore sine gravi dolore'; see also F. J. Fernández Conde, 'Albigenses en León y Castilla a comienzos del siglo XIII,' in *León Medieval. Doce estudios. Ponencias y communicaciones presentadas al coloquio 'El Reino de León en la Edad Media,' congreso de la Asociación Luso-española para el Progreso de las Ciencias*, León: Colegio Universitario, 1978, pp.97–114, especially p.100.

26. 'Quia memoria passionis Christi celebratur, et panis et vinum per mysterium sanctae orationis in corpus et sanguinem ejusdem Domini nostri Jesu Christi transsuntantiatur; advolant aquilae coeli ad escam, ut de morte ejus vitam percipiant': *Sermo XX in Coena Domini*, PL, vol. CCVIII, col. 854. On resurrectional and eucharistic connotations of eagles and hawks, see B. and G. Kühnel, 'An Eagle Physiologus Legend on a Crusader Capital from the Coenaculum,' in *Norms and Variations in Art: Essays in Honour of Moshe Barasch* (special issue of *Hebrew University Studies in Literature and the Arts*), Jerusalem: Magnes Press, 1983, pp.36–48; P. Binski, 'The Angel Choir at Lincoln and the Poetics of the Gothic Smile,' *Art History*, vol. 20, no. 3, 1997, pp.358–61. I know of only one precedent for the eagles so closely related to the deceased in Hispanic funerary sculpture: in the sarcophagus of Queen Doña Sancha now in Jaca the eidolon in a mandorla is flanked by two eagles (Fig. 2.4 in this volume); L. Herrero Romero, 'Notas iconográficas sobre el tránsito del alma en el románico español,' in J. Yarza Luaces, *Estudios de Iconografía Medieval Española*, Barcelona: Universidad Autónoma de Barcelona, 1984, pp.32–6.

27. The text had been already commented upon by M. Schapiro in his classic article 'On the Aesthetic Attitude in Romanesque Art,' reprinted in M. Schapiro, *Romanesque Art*, Selected Papers, vol. I, New York: G. Braziller, 1977, pp.28–101. S. Moralejo, 'D. Lucas de Túy y la "actitud estética" en el arte medieval,' *Euphrosyne. Revista de Filología Clásica*, vol. 22, 1994, pp.241–346, reviewed the interpretation of some passages from *De altera vita* presented by C. Gilbert, in 'A Statement of the Aesthetic Attitude around 1230,' *Hebrew University Studies in Literature and the Arts*, vol. 12, 1985, pp.125–52.

28. Lucas of Túy, *De altera vita*, book III, chapter 9.

29. Besides the tomb of Martín Arias (†1242), the tomb of Rodrigo served as a model for the tombs of some bishops at Avila and León Cathedrals; Franco Mata, *Escultura gótica*, pp.503–4.

30. See note 1 for bibliography. Most authors call the Bishop Martín, without surname: see Franco Mata, *Escultura gótica*, p.429, n.36. Because D. Berrueta called him Martín Rodríguez, the subsequent literature repeated this, even A. Ubieto Arteta, *Listas episcopales medievales*, Zaragoza: Anubar, 1989, vol. I, p.197. Nevertheless, Linehan, in 'La iglesia de León a mediados del siglo XIII,' p.15, cites a document from Vatican registers in which Bishop Martín Arias appears at the head of the Leonese see in 1240: *Les régistres de Grégoire IX (1227–41)*, edited by L. Auvray, Paris, 1890–1955, numbers 920, 3591 and 5231. His epitaph reads: PRIMA ZAMORENSIS MARTINUM PONTIFICAVIT, ET LEGIONENSIS SEDES POSTREMA VOCAVIT. QUOD SIBI TANTA FUIT, DOMINO FACIENTE, POTESTAS, NOBILITAS MERUIT, ET PROBITAS, ET HONESTAS. ERA MCCLXXX ET QOTO XVIII KALENDAS FEBRUARII. For other opinions about this tomb, see L. Morganti, 'La celebrazione degli anniversari e l'affirmazione del concetto di purgatorio nel XIII secolo: il monumento di Martín II Rodríguez nella cattedrale di León e Lucas de Tuy,' *Arte medivale*, II serie, Anno X, no. 2, 1996, pp.99–121.

31. The soft modelling in low relief that characterizes some statues of the French Cathedral appears not only in the Leonese tomb, but also on the Puerta del Sarmental of Burgos Cathedral, carved between 1235 and 1240. Thus, Burgos is probably the intermediate stage between the French activity of this workshop and its work in León: Sánchez Ameijeiras, 'Investigaciones,' pp.58–62. Some local sculptors worked on Bishop Martín Arias's monument under the supervision of the French master; they carved the outer archivolt. For the traditional stylistic relationships, see Franco Mata, *Escultura gótica*, pp.429–35.

32. For the Amiens portal, see W. Sauerländer, *La sculpture gothique*, fig. 134; and S. Murray, *Notre-Dame, Cathedral of Amiens: The Power of Change in Gothic*, Cambridge: Cambridge University Press, 1996, pp.96–121. For the 'Mass of the Dead performed in Heaven,' see Panofsky, *Tomb Sculpture*, pp.60–61.

33. For the tomb of Saint John of Ortega in the parish church of San Juan de Ortega (Burgos), see S. Valdivieso Ausín, *San Juan de Ortega, hito vivo en el camino de Santiago*, Burgos: Santuario de

San Juan de Ortega, 1985, pp.108–10; J. Pérez Carmona, *Arquitectura y escultura románicas de la provincia de Burgos*, 2nd edition, Burgos: Facultad Teológica del Norte de España, 1959, reprinted 1974, pp.263–4; R. Sánchez Ameijeiras, 'Una empresa olvidada del primer gótico hispano: la fachada de la sala capitular de la catedral de León,' *Archivo Español de Arte*, no. 276, 1996, pp.389–406, especially pp.404–6. For the tomb at Santo Domingo de la Calzada, see S. Moralejo, '¿Raimundo de Borgoña (†1107) o Fernando Alfonso (†1214)? Un episodio olvidado en la historia del panteón real compostelano,' in *Actas del coloquio de historia medieval 'Galicia en la Edad Media' (Santiago de Compostela, La Coruña, Pontevedra, Vigo, 13–17 julio, 1987)*, Madrid: Sociedad Española de Estudios Medievales, 1990, p.168, n.27.

34. 'que fagan sepultar nuestro cuerpo en la sepultura que fesimos faser en el Coro de nuestra iglesia': M. Risco, *España sagrada*, vol. XXXVI: *Memorias de la Santa Iglesia de León, concernientes a los cinco últimos siglos, con un copioso apendice de concilios, escrituras, y otros documentos muy útiles para la historia particular de esta ciudad y su iglesia, y para la general de reyno*, Madrid: Blas Román, 1787, appendix CLVIII; Z. García Villada, *Catálogo de los códices y documentos de la catedral de León*, Madrid: Imprenta clásica española, 1919, no. 1101. The word 'coro' does not necessarily mean the architectural choir; it is often used for the transept and presbytery of the church.

35. Today the tomb is quite damaged, and the epitaph is illegible, but M. Gómez Moreno (as in n.1) could still read: 'BEATUS PAUPER . . . EAT FLENTIBUS HIC FLEBAT GAU . . .' An Epiphany is barely visible on the front of the urn.

36. 'Sennor Santo Domingo confessor tan onrado / deve a Santo Martino seer aparejado, / que vido a Don Cristo del manto abrigado / el que dado ovo al mesquino lazrado,' Gonzalo de Berceo, *La vida de Santo Domingo de Silos*, p.111.

37. For the tomb at San Juan de Ortega, see n.33; for the tomb of the prince at Las Huelgas, see Gómez Bárcena (as in n.19), pp.187–8. There are several parallels for the association of the act of charity and the last vision of the life of St Martin in the monumental sculpture of La Rioja at the end of the twelfth century. In a capital of the lateral portal of San Miguel de Irache both scenes are represented together as they are on a capital in the cloister of Tudela Cathedral. See M. Melero Moneo, *Escultura románica y del primer gótico en Tudela*, Tudela: Editorial del Centro Cultural Castel Ruiz, 1997, pp.128–9, figs 53, 54; J. E. Uranga and F. Iñíguez, *Arte Medieval Navarro*, vol. III, Pamplona: Editorial Arantzadi, 1973, pp.10, 150, 169, plates 187b, 268, 315.

38. Compare 'Quam diu non fecistis uni de minoribis his, nec mihi fecistis' from Matt. 24.25, with 'Vere memor Dominus dictorum suorum (qui ante preadixerat: "Quam diu fecistis uni ex minimis istis mihi fecistis") se in paupere professus est fuisse vestitum; et ad confirmandum tam boni operis testimonium in eodem se habitu quem pauper acceperat, est dignatus ostendere': Sulpicio Severo, *De vita Beati Martini*, in PL, vol. XX, col. 162.

39. In his synodal legislation he gave them the opportunity to practice their pastoral skills. Martín Fernández also founded individual chapels in honor of St Francis and St Dominic in the apse of the new church, and it is possible that the inclusion of a mendicant friar (St Francis?) among the elect on the lintel of the Last Judgment portal could have been conditioned by his dictates. On the favorable attitude of this Bishop toward the friars, see Linehan, *Spanish Church and the Papacy*, p.72. On the dedication of the chapels, see Z. García Villada (as in n.34), no. 1101, and E. Lambert, *El arte gótico en España en los siglos XII y XIII*, reprint, Madrid: Cátedra, 1985, p.229. The mendicant friar was identified by Franco Mata, *Escultura gótica*, p.144.

40. 'Redemisti crucem passus, / Tantus labor non sit cassus': *Dies irae*, in *The Treasury of the Sacred Heart: A Complete Prayerbook for Catholics*, Turnhout: Henri Proost, 1956, p.132.

41. 'Que ninguun Clerigo non sea osado de soterrar en la Eglesia dientro algun ome finado, aunque la Eglesia haya dos naves o tres': M. Risco, *España sagrada*, vol. XXXVI: *Memorias de la Santa Iglesia de León, concernientes a los cinco últimos siglos, con un copioso apéndice de concilios, escrituras, y otros documentos muy útiles para la historia particular de esta ciudad y su iglesia, y para la general de reyno*, Madrid: Blas Román, 1787, pp.248, 254; A. García y García, *Synodicon Hispanicum*, vol. III, Madrid: BAC, 1984. pp.233–50.

42. Compare these scrolls with the vegetal decoration on the lintel of the Last Judgment Portal. For additional views of the latter, see Franco Mata, *Escultura gótica*, pp.252–5, plate LXXXVI.

43. The epitaph reads as follows: SUB ERA MLA CC XXXXIII VI KAL MARTII PRAESUL MANRICUS JACET HIC, RATIONIS AMICUS SENSU CONSILIO, MORIBUS, ELOQUIO. PUBLICA MORS PESTIS, SI CEDERE POSSIT HONESTIS CEDERET HUIC MIRO VIS VIOLENTA VIRO. At the beginning of the sixteenth century the monument was reemployed as an altar for St Erasmus and the martyrdom of the saint was painted on the recessed tympanum. It was then that the lid of the sarcophagus was removed and fixed to the wall. A relief representing the absolution of the deceased now in the cloister could have formed part of this monument, for its size and unusual shape conform to the end of the

recess in the wall. The style of the piece allows its attribution to the same sculptors who carved the episcopal pantheon. For the sixteenth-century alterations, see A. de Lobera, *Grandezas de la muy antigua e insigne ciudad e iglesia de León*, Alcalá de Henares, 1595; reprint, León: Lancia, 1987, p.77; G. González Dávila (as in n. 1), p.403.

44.   The epitaph reads: HIC YACET FAMULUS DEI ARNALDUS EPISCOPUS / HUJUS ECCLESIAE QUI OBIIT ERA MCCLXXIII / IN DIE OCTAVO OCTOBRIS ANNO MCCXXV. The original sarcophagus of Arnaldo is of a type usually found in monastic cemeteries; the lid is similar to the one of Victor, the second abbot of St Georges of Boscherville who died in 1210. For this tomb see J. Adhémar, 'Dessins d'archéologie du XVII siècle,' *Gazette des Beaux Arts*, vol. 84, 1974, pp.5–192, especially p.20, no. 57. On the alterations carried out in the chapel where the tomb of Arnaldo lies, see D. de los Ríos, *La catedral de León*, León: Ambito, Diputación de León, 1985, vol. II, p.135.

45.   Don Nuño's tomb is now hidden behind a confessional box which makes it impossible to photograph well.

46.   The origins of episcopal cemeteries can be traced back in episcopal lists, or the portraits of bishops painted on the walls of the church, as in Poitiers or Vercelli: M. Carrasco, 'Spirituality and Historicity in Pictorial Hagiography: Two Miracles of Saint Albinus of Angers,' *Art History*, vol. 12, 1989, pp.1–21, especially pp.2–3. On Vercelli, see J.-Ch. Picard, *Le souvenir des évêques: Sépultures, listes épiscopales et culte des évêques en Italie du Nord des origines au Xe siècle*, Paris: Bibliothèque de l'Ecole Française de Rome, 1990. On Trier, F. J. Ronig, ed., 'Die Ausstattung,' in F. J. Ronig, ed., *Der Trierer Dom*, Rheinische Verein für Denkmalpflege und Landschaftsschutz, Jahrbuch, 1978–9, Neuss: Verlag Gesellschaft für Buchdruckerei, 1980, pp.243–5, figs 68–70; E. Gierlich, *Die Grabstätten der Rheinischen Bischöfe vor 1200*, Mainz, 1990, pp.79–80. For Wells, see P. Binski, *Medieval Death: Ritual and Representation*, Ithaca, NY: Cornell University Press, 1996, p.94.

47.   On Capetian burials at Saint-Denis and elsewhere in Paris, see the article by K. Nolan in this volume; for Saint-Denis, see Bauch, *Das mittelalterliche Grabbild*, pp.32, 73; Adhémar (as in n.44), pp.31–2, nos 124–7. The remains of these monuments are now in the Musée Cluny in Paris.

48.   On the history of the See and the identification of these scenes on the saint's tomb, see J. M. Martínez Frías, *El gótico en Soria. Arquitectura y escultura monumental*, Salamanca: Universidad de Salamanca/Excelentísima Diputación Provincial de Soria, 1980, pp.133–6.

49.   See Sánchez Ameijeiras (as in n.33), pp.400–402.

50.   Don Pedro Muñiz, chosen in June 1205, was promoted to the See of Compostela a year later, and was buried in the Cathedral of Santiago. On his bronze tomb, now destroyed, see J. Carro, 'Sepultura e inscripción del arzobispo Don Pedro Muñiz,' *Cuadernos de Estudios Gallegos*, vol. 6, 1951, p.287; and S. Moralejo (as in n.33), pp.161–79, especially n.24. Pelayo Pérez and Martín Alfonso were only *electi* and died shortly before being promoted. For Leonese episcopal lists, see M. Risco, *España sagrada*, pp.277–82, 299–300; A. Ubieto Arteta (as in n.30), vol. I, pp.195–8.

51.   See Linehan, 'La iglesia de León,' pp.14–33; 'The Spanish Church and the Papacy,' pp.268–75.

52.   Several architectural elements were understood during the Middle Ages as images of the biblical Corner Stone. The key of an arch and the key of a vault fit especially well with the text of Matt. 26.42: 'Lapidem quem reprobaverunt aedificantes. Hic factus est caput anguli'; or the one of Paul, Eph. 2.19: 'summo angulari lapide Christo Iesu.' The Leonese keystone expresses figuratively not only the aedilic metaphor but also Christ's role and His place in the institution of the Church. For the identification of these themes, see Franco Mata, 'La iconografía de las portadas de la catedral de León,' *Revista de la Universidad Complutense*, vol. 22, 1973, pp.55–97; eadem, *Escultura gótica*, pp.93–100, 144–5. For aedilic metaphors, see G. Ladner, 'The Symbolism of the Biblical Corner Stone in the Medieval West,' *Medieval Studies*, vol. 4, 1942, pp.43–60.

53.   See H. A. Tummers, *Early Secular Effigies in England: The Thirteenth Century*, Leiden: E. J. Brill, 1980, pp.7–15.

54.   On the history of aedilic metaphors in Christian exegesis, see the classic studies by J. Sauer, *Symbolik des Kirchengebäudes und seiner Ausstattung in der Auffassung des Mittelalters*, Freiburg im Breisgau, 1924; Ladner (as in n.52); J. Hani, *Le symbolisme du temple chrétien*, Paris: Guy Trèdaniel, 1978, pp.55–68. The tradition of this metaphor is well known by St Martin of León, as can be seen in his *Sermo in dedicatione Ecclesie II*, in PL, vol. CCVIII, col. 249.

55.   Berceo's words for referring to saintly confessors are: 'Our forefathers, those who have laid the foundations of our Holy Church' ('Nuestros antecesores que de Santa Eglesia fueron cimentadores'): Gonzalo de Berceo, *Vida de Santo Domingo de Silos*, p.71.

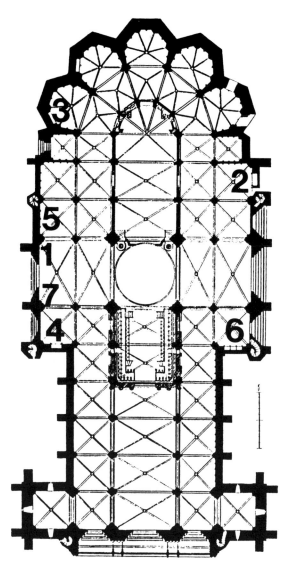

1 Tomb of Manrique de Lara (†1205)
2 Tomb of Rodrigo Alvarez (†1232)
3 Tomb of Arnaldo (†1235)
4 Tomb of Martín Arias (†1242)
5 Tomb of Nuño Alvarez (†1252)
6 Tomb of Martín Fernández (†1289)
7 Tomb of Saint Alvito (†1063)

11.1 León Cathedral, plan with the thirteenth-
       century Leonese episcopal tombs indicated
       (after Dehio/von Bezold)

11.2 Tomb of Bishop Rodrigo Alvarez (†1232), León Cathedral, *c*.1230, reinstalled *c*.1268–89

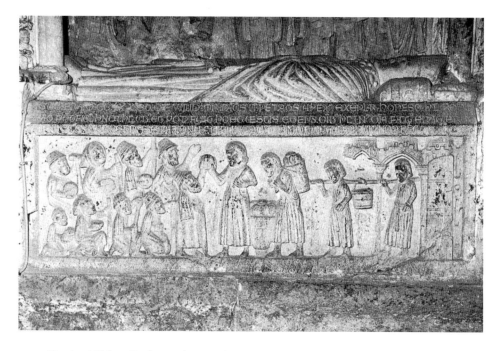

11.3   Tomb of Bishop Rodrigo Alvarez, detail: Anniversary Alms (*Pitança de aniversarios*)

11.4   Tomb of Bishop Rodrigo Alvarez, detail: Executioner with Cup

11.5 Tomb of Bishop Rodrigo Alvarez, detail: *Elevatio Animae*

11.6   Tomb of Bishop Martín Arias (†1242), León Cathedral, c.1240, reinstalled
c.1268–89

11.7   Tomb of Bishop Martín Arias, detail: Anniversary Alms

11.8   Tomb of Bishop Martín Fernández (†1289), León Cathedral, prior to 1289

11.9 Tomb of Bishop Manrique de Lara (†1205), León Cathedral, *c.*1205, reinstalled
*c.*1268–89

11.10   Tomb of Bishop Arnaldo (†1235), León Cathedral, c.1235, reinstalled
c.1268–89

11.11   Tomb of St Peter of El Burgo de Osma, Cathedral of El Burgo de Osma,
        *c.*1258, detail: Miracle of the Deceased Prelates

11.12 León Cathedral, west porch, right portal, detail: The Ecclesiastical Hierarchy, third quarter of the thirteenth century

11.13   León Cathedral, west porch, central portal, detail: Pope and Bishop among
the Elect, third quarter of the thirteenth century

Index

Individuals whose tombs are mentioned in the volume are listed under 'tomb, of individual'.